International law from MUP

The Melland Schill name has a long-established reputation for high standards of scholar-ship. Each volume in the series addresses major international law issues and current developments. Many of the previous volumes, published under the name 'Melland Schill Monographs', have become standard works of reference in the field. Interdisciplinary and accessible, the series is vital reading for students, scholars and practitioners of international law, international relations, politics, economics and development.

MANCHESTER
UNIVERSITY PRESS

Keeping the peace

The United Nations and the maintenance of international peace and security

Second edition

N. D. WHITE

Senior Lecturer in Law
University of Nottingham

Manchester University Press

Manchester and New York

Distributed exclusively in the USA by St. Martin's Press

Published by Manchester University Press
Oxford Road, Manchester M13 9NR, UK
and Room 400, 175 Fifth Avenue, New York, NY 10010, USA

Distributed exclusively in the USA by
St. Martin's Press, Inc., 175 Fifth Avenue, New York,
NY 10010, USA

Distributed exclusively in Canada by
UBC Press, University of British Columbia, 6344 Memorial Road,
Vancouver, BC, Canada V6T 1Z2

British Library Cataloguing-in-Publication Data
A catalogue record for this book is available from the British Library

Library of Congress Cataloging-in-Publication Data applied for

ISBN 0 7190 4854 0 *hardback*
     0 7190 4855 9 *paperback*

First published 1997

01 00 99 98 97   10 9 8 7 6 5 4 3 2 1

Photoset in Times
by Northern Phototypesetting Co. Ltd, Bolton

Printed in Great Britain
by Redwood Books, Trowbridge

CONTENTS

FOREWORD

The time between the two editions of this book covers a remarkably fertile period of United Nations' activity in relation to international peace and security. The idea of 'keeping the peace', in its widest sense, has dominated the 1990s. As such, the second edition of Dr White's substantial analysis of international law and practice was keenly awaited and will be warmly welcomed. The renaissance of the Security Council is considered and analysed in both political and legal terms. Close examination is given to the relationships between the Security Council and the General Assembly and between the Security Council and the International Court of Justice. The massive expansion in the law, practice and ambit of peacekeeping is considered at length. This book remains an indispensable guide to issues of fundamental importance.

Dominic McGoldrick
International and European Law Unit
University of Liverpool

PREFACE

The basis of this second edition can be traced back to the publication of *The United Nations and the Maintenance of International Peace and Security* in 1990. That book was essentially based on the practice of the UN in the field of collective security during the Cold War. As was stated in the 1993 re-working of the original, *Keeping the Peace*, momentous events have occurred since that original work. Instead of paralysis in the Security Council and rhetoric in the General Assembly, the world witnessed an active Council and a less antagonistic Assembly, though the tensions between the two organs remained.

This development has continued apace, necessitating the expansion of the chapters dealing with the Security Council, in particular the introduction of new sections on the creation of international criminal tribunals, the development of the Council's powers and the possibility of judicial review of the use or misuse of those powers, along with the incorporation of vast amounts of practice by the primary body. Chapters eight and nine on UN peacekeeping have had to be completely rewritten not only because of the huge expansion in the number of peacekeeping forces authorised by the UN, but also because of the many forms that those forces have taken, requiring a more conceptual approach to constitutional and legal issues as well as the practice of peacekeeping. It was decided not to continue with a complete catalogue of increasingly brief case histories in chapter nine, although Part Three overall attempts to cover all the forces authorised by the Security Council by analysing them under relevant themes, principles and functions.

Although developments in the activities of the General Assembly have been less, that organ has not been ignored, nor has its impressive amount of practice during the Cold War been forgotten. This past practice is considered alongside new developments such as its increased support for free elections and democratisation. Although the Assembly is relatively dormant at the moment, the development of its powers that occurred during the first forty-five years is still valid and may be re-activated with the next great shift in world order. This is illustrative of the approach taken in this book that although the political climate has changed dramatically at the UN, a development which has primarily affected the Security Council, the legal principles, while being developed and perhaps extended by recent practice, have their origins in the Charter as interpreted by the Council and Assembly during the Cold War and have therefore remained relatively constant. The increased use of the enforcement mechanisms of Chapter VII as well as the further development of the peacekeeping function by the Security Council in the post-Cold War era have added to the body of precedent on the use (and possibly abuse) of those legal powers.

In order to discern the political changes as well as the development of legal powers, this second edition retains the basic division into three parts, on the Security Council, the General Assembly and Peacekeeping, though there is increased coverage throughout of the increasingly significant roles of the International Court and the Secretary General. Peacekeeping is dealt with separately because of the unique nature of the function and also because the 'blue helmets' can be authorised by either organ, although naturally it is dominated by the Security Council. Each of the three Parts contains a chapter on the historical and political context, followed by a chapter on the legal parameters, and finally a chapter on the practice and effectiveness of the UN. Of course these three elements cannot realistically be considered in isolation from one another, and the influences of law on politics and *vice versa* is fully considered, but what the basic division does, or hopes to do, is to increase accessibility for the reader, whether he or she is interested in politics or law or simply wants an account of the workings of the United Nations in the realm of peace and security.

I would like to express my thanks to Robert Cryer who greatly assisted in locating many of the primary and secondary sources that have been incorporated or referred to in this second edition.

This book is dedicated to my wife Gillian, and my sons Daniel and Hugh.

N. D. White
Nottingham

ABBREVIATIONS

ADF	Arab Deterrent Force
A.J.I.L.	*American Journal of International Law*
A/PV	General Assembly Provisional Records
B.Y.B.I.L.	*British Year Book of International Law*
CIS	Commonwealth of Independent States
EC	European Community
ECOMOG	Economic Community of West African States Monitoring Group
ECOWAS	Economic Community of West African States
EPLF	Eritrean People's Liberation Front
EU	European Union
FMLN	Farabundo Marti National Liberation Front
FRELIMO	Liberation Front of Mozambique
GAOR	General Assembly Official Records
H.R.L.J.	*Human Rights Law Journal*
IAEA	International Atomic Energy Agency
ICAO	International Civil Aviation Organisation
ICJ	International Court of Justice
I.C.J. Rep.	International Court of Justice Reports
I.C.L.Q.	*International and Comparative Law Quarterly*
ICTR	International Criminal Tribunal for Rwanda
ICTY	International Criminal Tribunal for the Former Yugoslavia
IFOR	Implementation Force
ILC	International Law Commission
I.L.M.	*International Legal Materials*
Keesing's	*Keesing's Record of World Events*
MINUGUA	United Nations Mission in Guatemala
MINURSO	United Nations Mission for the Referendum in Western Sahara
MPLA	Popular Movement for the Liberation of Angola
NATO	North Atlantic Treaty Organisation
NGO	Non-Governmental Organisation

N.I.L.R.	*Netherlands International Law Review*
NPFL	National Patriotic Front of Liberia
OAS	Organisation of American States
OAU	Organisation of African Unity
OECS	Organisation of Eastern Caribbean States
ONUC	United Nations Operation in the Congo
ONUCA	United Nations Observer Group in Central America
ONUMOZ	United Nations Operation in Mozambique
ONUSAL	United Nations Observer Mission in El Salvador
ONUVEH	United Nations Observer Group for the Verification of Elections in Haiti
ONUVEN	United Nations Mission to Verify the Electoral Process in Nicaragua
OSCE	Organisation on Security and Cooperation in Europe
POLISARIO	Popular Front for the Liberation of the Sanguia el-Harura and the Rio de Oro
RENAMO	Mozambique National Resistance
RPF	Rwandese Patriotic Front
SCOR	Security Council Official Records
SFOR	Stabilisation Force
SNA	Somali National Alliance
S/PRST	Security Council Presidential Statement
S/PV	Security Council Provisional Records
SWAPO	South West African People's Organisation
UDI	Unilateral Declaration of Independence
UNAMIR	United Nations Assistance Mission for Rwanda
UNASOG	United Nations Aouzou Strip Observer Group
UNAVEM	United Nations Angola Verification Mission
UNCIO	United Nations Conference on International Organisations
UNCIVPOL	United Nations Civilian Police
UNCRO	United Nations Confidence Restoration Operation in Croatia
UNDOF	United Nations Disengagement Observer Force
UNEF	United Nations Emergency Force
UNFICYP	United Nations Force in Cyprus
UNGOMAP	United Nations Good Offices Mission in Afghanistan and Pakistan
UNHCR	United Nations High Commissioner for Refugees
UNIFIL	United Nations Interim Force in Lebanon
UNIIMOG	United Nations Iran–Iraq Military Observer Group
UNIKOM	United Nations Iraq–Kuwait Observation Mission
UNIPOM	United Nations India–Pakistan Observation Mission
UNITA	National Union for the Total Independence of Angola
UNITAF	Unified Task Force
UNMIBH	United Nations Mission in Bosnia and Herzegovina

UNMIH	United Nations Mission in Haiti
UNMOGIP	United Nations Military Observer Group in India and Pakistan
UNMOP	United Nations Mission of Observers in Prevlaka
UNMOT	United Nations Mission of Observers in Tajikistan
UNOGIL	United Nations Observer Group in Lebanon
UNOMIG	United Nations Observer Mission in Georgia
UNOMIL	United Nations Observer Mission in Liberia
UNOMUR	United Nations Observer Mission in Uganda–Rwanda
UNOSOM	United Nations Operation in Somalia
UNOVER	United Nations Observer Mission to Verify the Referendum in Eritrea
UNPREDEP	United Nations Preventive Deployment Force
UNPROFOR	United Nations Protection Force
UNSCOB	United Nations Sub-Commission on the Balkans
UNSF	United Nations Security Force
UNSMIH	United Nations Support Mission in Haiti
UNTAC	United Nations Transition Assistance Authority in Cambodia
UNTAES	United Nations Transitional Administration for Eastern Slavonia, Baranja and Western Sirmium
UNTAG	United Nations Transition Assistance Group
UNTEA	United Nations Temporary Executive Authority
UNTS	United Nations Treaty Series
UNTSO	United Nations Truce Supervision Organisation
UNYOM	United Nations Yemen Observation Mission
WEU	Western European Union

PART ONE

The Security Council

INTRODUCTION

The demise of the League and the creation of the UN

The principal function of the United Nations is to maintain international peace and security.[1] Throughout the complex Great Power negotiations which led to the conference at San Francisco in 1945, the emphasis was on a particular body within the United Nations, the Security Council, performing that role. Indeed, this is reflected within the provisions of the UN Charter, which, *inter alia*, gave the Security Council 'primary responsibility' for the maintenance of international peace, accompanied by comprehensive powers to enable it to fulfil that role.[2] The Great Powers did not foresee the General Assembly having any substantive powers, intending merely to have it as a meeting place for the representatives of States. However, the smaller powers at San Francisco managed to secure sufficient provisions in the Charter to enable the Assembly to develop an important subsidiary role in the maintenance of international peace. This development will be examined in Part Two, for the moment our emphasis is on the Security Council.

This introduction is mainly concerned with giving a background to the United Nations viewed in the light of the League experience and the Great Power negotiations which preceded the adoption of the UN Charter. It must be remembered that throughout these negotiations it was the UN Security Council which was intended to embody the principal aim of the United Nations, namely the maintenance of international peace through a system of collective security. It is also essential at this stage to explain in more detail the concept of collective security and its relationship with the more traditional concept of collective defence. The importance of these concepts will become apparent, particularly in the detailed discussion of the Security Council's use of enforcement powers.

The League of Nations had failed to keep world peace primarily because the idea of collective security was far weaker than the individual State's desires to protect their national interests. One of the statesmen behind the creation of the League, President Wilson of the United States, saw the Organisation replacing the previous balance of power system with a centralised body comprising powerful States acting in concert as the trustees of world peace.[3] Paradoxically, it was the United States' refusal to join which could be said to be the first example of a powerful State believing that collective security was not in its best interests.

Although the Covenant of the League of Nations did contain innovative provisions for collective security and provided for the imposition of embargoes and possibly collective military sanctions against offending States,[4] the League was doomed to failure because sovereign States continued to see national interests as paramount over collective interests despite the horror of the First World War, a situation exacerbated by the requirement in Article 5 of the Covenant of unanimity for most substantive decisions of the Council or Assembly of the League. Overriding considerations of national power resulted in the dilution of the League's powers to such an extent that the question of imposition of sanctions under Article 16 became not one for the consideration of the Council or Assembly, but for each individual member, evidenced by the piecemeal and ineffective sanctions imposed against Italy after its invasion of Abyssinia in 1935. The failure to impose any sort of collective measures against aggressors meant the inevitable demise of the League.

The United Nations, in particular the Security Council, represented the world's second attempt at developing a feasible system of collective security.[5] The Organisation had its origins, indirectly, in the 'Declaration by the United Nations' of 1 January 1942[6] which did not refer to any world body, instead it concentrated on spelling out the Allied programme to be pursued against the Axis powers to end the Second World War. Nevertheless, the idea of the United Nations continuing after the war was outlined in the Moscow Declaration of October 1943,[7] in which the Big Four: China, the United Kingdom, the United States and the Soviet Union, recognised 'the necessity of establishing, at the earliest possible date, a general international organisation based on the principle of sovereign equality of all peace loving States, and open to membership by all such States, large and small, for the maintenance of international peace and security'.

The ideal of collective security was behind this statement, though by juxtaposing the notion of a world body with that of State sovereignty, the clash between collective and national interests had not been removed. The major lesson of the League had not been learned. Nevertheless, to give collective interests primacy over national interests would be to have created a world government. In practice, the most that could be done was to give the world body, through the Security Council, greater powers for collective measures which might weigh more heavily on the scales against the counter-balance of national interests.

Comprehensive proposals from the Big Four were discussed by those States at Dumbarton Oaks between August and October 1944, resulting in a far reaching and detailed agreement concerning the Organisation.[8] They agreed that the Security Council should have the function of maintaining international peace through collective measures if necessary. However, they also decided that the Great Powers, the Big Four plus France, should have a special position on the Council consisting of permanent representation with special voting rights which would ensure that no substantive decisions would be taken by the Council without their unanimous concurrence. The right of veto was further refined at the Yalta Conference in February 1945.

Whether the necessity of Great Power unanimity is regarded as an idealistic attempt to continue where the Allies finished after the end of the war, or more cynically, as a recognition by those Powers of each others' and their own national interests being paramount over any collective interests, it is realistic to state that without the power of veto the Organisation would probably not have been born, and even if created, it would not have been able to take enforcement action against the Great Powers, particularly the Soviet Union and the United States, without devastating effects. At San Francisco the right of veto was accepted by the other States with little challenge, possibly because most delegates preferred, at least publicly, to lean towards an idealistic vision of Great Power unity providing future collective security.[9] Furthermore, the voting system on the Security Council, which when adopted required seven votes out of eleven (nine out of fifteen since 1966) 'including the concurring votes of the permanent members',[10] was an improvement on the requirement for unanimity of both permanent and non-permanent members on the League's Council.

Generally the delegates were enthusiastic about collective security but unduly optimistic about permanent member unanimity. President Roosevelt recognised this in a speech made a few months before the conference at San Francisco, in which he said that, 'the nearer we come to vanquishing our enemies the more we inevitably become conscious of the differences among the victors'.[11]

The marriage of convenience which resulted in unanimity during the war was terminated after a brief honeymoon in San Francisco. Within two days of the Council's first meeting the Cold War, in the form of a complaint by Iran of the Soviet Union's presence in its country, was on the Council's agenda, followed two days later by a Soviet complaint of the British presence in Greece. This set the tone which severely restricted the Security Council for over forty years. It was only in the late 1980s when the Soviet Union changed its policy from that of confrontation to that of cooperation with the West that the world began to see the Security Council using its teeth in the form of enforcement action under Chapter VII, a process that seems set to continue with the collapse of the Soviet Union in 1991 and the emergence of Russia as the inheritor of the permanent seat.

The concepts of collective security and collective defence

A collective security system entails the centralisation of a society's coercive mechanisms.[12] As a corollary the members of that society, in this case States, give up a great deal of their individual freedom to indulge in self-help, and are generally restricted to a limited right of self-defence, usually until the central authority takes over their protection. As shall be seen, the UN Charter contains all the rudiments of such a system, whereas the League of Nations did not. It is true to say that the League did contain a somewhat ambiguous limit on aggression in Article

10 but not on other forms of self-help, except for certain procedural restrictions in Articles 12, 13 and 15. The right of self-defence was not mentioned in the Covenant because at the time it was just one of the permissible ways of using armed force. In addition, the League's provisions for coercive measures were voluntary in that States had the option of deciding whether to impose sanctions or to take military measures against an aggressor when called upon to do so by the League.

The novel, but only partial, institutionalisation of the concept of collective security in the League of Nations gave way to the old system of competing interests and rival alliances. The defeat of the Axis powers by the Allies gave the victorious powers another chance to embed the concept of collective security more firmly in the new Organisation. Although there was agreement on the need for a new and improved collective security system, there was considerable disagreement on its nature. Churchill favoured a regional security system on the basis that only those States close to a conflict would be willing to take action to end it. Roosevelt on the other hand followed Wilson's idea that the victorious powers would act as the world's policemen, protecting the smaller States which would be gradually disarmed. Both of these ideas are to be found in the Charter in varying degrees, but each has within it the potential for dominance of the security system by a State or group of States. The only true global collective security system whereby all States would contribute to the maintenance of peace was suggested by Roosevelt's Secretary of State, Hull.[13]

One of the major problems at San Francisco was the reconciliation of the regional and more universal approaches to collective security. The provisions of Chapter VIII of the UN Charter establish the supremacy of the United Nations over regional bodies in the realm of enforcement action, although a regional organisation or any group of States acting in collective self-defence was permitted to use force without prior Security Council authorisation by the late insertion of Article 51 into the text of the Charter. Self-defence, whether individual or collective, was only permitted until the Security Council had 'taken measures necessary to maintain international peace and security'. States supporting regionalism[14] sought this limited escape clause because they foresaw that the composition and voting of the Security Council, the partial embodiment of Roosevelt's collective security concept, as leading to a stalled Security Council as the permanent members protected their pervasive interests by the often indiscriminate use of the veto.

Nevertheless, the UN Charter contained within it a far greater centralisation of coercive measures and machinery than did its predecessor. As well as containing quite elaborate provisions in Chapter VI for the pacific settlement of disputes, the 'teeth' of the Charter were contained in Chapter VII which granted the Security Council the unprecedented power to take mandatory economic and military action against an aggressor or to combat a situation which simply threatened international peace and security. If the Security Council acted under these mechanisms States would be obliged to take economic measures or to supply military forces under UN control. The potential power in the hands of the Security Council was enormous.

The potential of the Security Council was nullified for over forty years due to the intense ideological rivalry between the United States and the Soviet Union. In the place of a collective security system there was established a system of defensive alliances, principally the North Atlantic Treaty Organisation (NATO) dominated by the United States and the Warsaw Pact dominated by the Soviet Union, based on the concept of collective self-defence, namely that an attack on one party to the alliance was an attack against them all.[15] This rival system, which appeared to give some stability in the world, in the sense of preventing another global conflict, can be traced back to the old balance of power systems. Indeed, as with its predecessors, the post-1945 balance of power collapsed with the disintegration of the Soviet Union and the dissolution of the Warsaw Pact in 1991. The serious global instability that has resulted from these tumultuous events has only begun to be addressed by States, but it has already become apparent in the past few years that the Security Council is attempting to fill the vacuum. Whether it has done so successfully and whether it will do so in the future are issues to be addressed in the next few chapters.

Notes

1. Article 1(1) of the UN Charter.
2. Article 24(1), Chapters VI and VII of the UN Charter.
3. K. P. Sakensa, *The United Nations and Collective Security*, 8–10 (1974).
4. Articles 10, 11 and 16 of the League Covenant. UKTS 4 (1919), Cmnd 153.
5. See further B. B. Ferencz, *New Foundations for Global Survival: Security through the Security Council*, 88–91 (1994).
6. For text see R. B. Russell and J. E. Muther, *A History of the United Nations Charter*, Appendix C (1958).
7. For text see World Peace Foundation, *The United Nations in the Making: Basic Documents*, 9–10 (1945).
8. For text see United Nations Conference on International Organisations (UNCIO), vol. 3, 2–17.
9. See for example UNCIO, vol. 1, 502–3, delegate from Luxembourg.
10. See Article 27(3) of the UN Charter.
11. Message on the State of the Union, 6 January 1945.
12. L. A. Mander, *Foundations of a Modern World Society*, 59, 2nd ed. (1948).
13. Russell and Muther, *A History of the United Nations*, 96, 105.
14. See for example UNCIO, vol. 12, 687.
15. See further L. M. Goodrich, *The United Nations*, 168–76 (1960).

CHAPTER ONE

A geopolitical analysis of
the Security Council

Before analysing, in chapter two, the jurisdiction of the Security Council as contained in the Charter it will be helpful to identify the major geopolitical factors affecting the jurisdiction and operation of the Security Council. Factors arising, in particular, as a result of the global and strategic interests of the permanent members which often caused a paralysis in the Council in the past as those interests were protected by the veto during the Cold War between the United States and the Soviet Union of 1945–90. Latterly, however, the concert of Western powers on the Security Council, namely, France, the United States and the United Kingdom, has seized domination of the Council and has used the West's economic leverage to secure the support, or at least to avoid the veto, of China and the Soviet Union (since 1992, Russia).

It must be remembered, however, that the veto, along with another geopolitical limitation – regionalism – are both located in the Charter. In this sense they are legal limitations, but they must be realistically viewed as geopolitical limitations because they are manipulated for political motives. In addition the use of the power of veto and of the various regional organisations is often in contradiction to the express terms of the Charter so that it cannot really be said that they are legal as opposed to geopolitical limitations. It is true to say that with the end of the Cold War in the late 1980s these factors have had less of an impact on the Security Council. Free of these powerful limiting factors, the Security Council has been able to use the range of powers provided for in the Charter more readily, and indeed it has appeared in some instances to stretch those powers to breaking point. Moreover, this new-found freedom should not disguise the fact that the Security Council is, as shall be seen, still conditioned by political considerations, in that at the moment its actions correspond to the strategic, economic and political interests of the winners of the Cold War, the Western States.

The power of veto

The power of veto is contained in Article 27 of the Charter. After stating in paragraph 2 that 'decisions of the Security Council on procedural matters shall be made by an affirmative vote of nine members', paragraph 3 provides that 'decisions of the Security Council on all other matters shall be made by an affirmative vote of nine members including the concurring votes of the permanent members; provided that, in decisions under Chapter VI, and under paragraph 3 of Article 52, a party to a dispute shall abstain from voting'. Bailey lists those matters that the Council has treated as procedural in its practice, the most important of which are: inclusion of items on the agenda, removal of an item from the list of matters of which the Council is seized, rulings of the President, suspension and adjournment of meetings, invitation to non-members to participate in meetings, and convocation of an emergency special session of the General Assembly.[1] All non-procedural or substantive matters are potentially subject to a permanent member veto, which has been interpreted by the subsequent practice of the Council as requiring a negative vote. On this basis abstention by a permanent member on a substantive vote does not constitute a veto.[2]

The power of veto had its genesis in the desire to prevent the permanent members from being the potential objects of collective measures. However, Article 27(3) was drafted on a much wider basis after the Yalta Conference of 1945. It was clear after Yalta that Great Power unity was destined to be an unachieved ideal with the power of veto extending beyond the enforcement provisions of Chapter VII, to Chapter VI, which granted the Council general, recommendatory powers for pacific settlement, unless one of the permanent members was a party to the dispute.

Indeed, the Yalta formula, presented to the San Francisco conference in explanation of the right of veto, illustrated the permanent members' desire to leave no loopholes to prevent their use of the veto. The Yalta formula introduced the prospect of the 'double veto', which meant that any 'decision regarding the preliminary question as to whether or not such a matter is procedural must be taken by vote of [nine] members of the Security Council, including the concurring votes of the permanent members'.[3]

However, the smaller powers' objections at San Francisco were not directed at the double veto, but at the 'chain of events' theory outlined in the Yalta formula. The smaller powers demanded that the veto should be confined to questions concerning enforcement action. The Australian delegate argued that 'the Council has the duty rather than a right to conciliate disputants' and that it was essential that no member should have the right to veto resolutions aimed solely at pacific settlement of disputes.[4] The major powers stuck to the somewhat fallacious argument presented in the Yalta formula that any pacific measures 'may initiate a chain of events which might in the end require the Council under its responsibilities to invoke measures of enforcement'.[5] It might well be that such a chain of events could occur, but it did not appear necessary to allow the veto to occur at the pacific settlement stage as long as the permanent members could operate it at the enforcement stage. The 'chain of events' theory was, in reality, a mechanism whereby the whole field of Council action would be the subject of the veto. The smaller powers continued to object, but it became clear that Article 27 would have to be accepted as the 'Big Five decided to let it be known that unless the voting provision was accepted, there would be no Organisation'.[6] It was no longer a question of preserving Great Power unanimity but of preserving the Organisation.[7]

The applicability of the double veto and the chain of events theory peppered exchanges in the Council during its first decade. These have been thoroughly reviewed by Bailey[8] and it is not proposed to discuss them as a separate issue here. Such debates have, in any event, petered out in the face of the permanent members developing a practice which enabled them to use the veto to defeat any sort of proposal under Chapter VI or Chapter VII, unless it was clearly procedural.

In stating the chain of events theory the sponsoring powers still deferred to their obligation to abstain if they were parties to a dispute being dealt with by the Council under Chapter VI. In practice the permanent members have disregarded this provision thus destroying the general aim of this aspect of Article 27(3) to separate 'law as it is invoked by the claimants to the dispute and law as it is employed by [the Council] when passing its decision'.[9] The drafting of the provision allows a member to argue, if it wants, that it only has an 'interest' in the dispute which is insufficient to make it a 'party' or that the proposed resolution is only dealing with a 'situation' and not a 'dispute', [10] or does in fact envisage Chapter VII rather than Chapter VI action. In practice the permanent members rarely raise such arguments. The power of veto is exercised according to considerations of interests rather than in accordance with the letter of the Charter.

Permanent member, particularly superpower, interests and influences became so pervasive in the Cold War that the veto effectively debarred the Security Council from taking action or recommending measures of any sort in many areas of the globe. Indeed, in many cases, the superpowers operated the veto not to protect 'vital' interests but in order to curry favour with other States or as a reflex reaction to oppose the other superpower's voting intentions. The Soviet Union's veto of a proposed resolution that would have condemned the Indian invasion of Goa in 1961 and called for a cease-fire and an Indian withdrawal, is an example of the veto being used not for any vital protective purpose but, in this case, to express support for India, the Third World, and anti-colonialism.[11]

Even when a permanent member appears to be a 'party' to a 'dispute' within the meaning of Article 27(3), it has disregarded its obligation to abstain when faced with the possibility of being subject to a recommendatory Chapter VI-based resolution. The French and British could hardly deny that they were 'parties' to the Suez crisis in 1956, but they did not have to as they vetoed draft resolutions proposed by the United States and the Soviet Union calling for Israel to cease fire and withdraw. The proposers of the draft resolutions deliberately refrained from invoking Chapter VII for fear of justifying the imminent Anglo/French intervention. Nevertheless, the British and French vetoes were not challenged on the grounds of Article 27(3).[12]

During the Falklands crisis in 1982, the Panamanian representative thought that the last operative paragraph of resolution 502 placed it under Chapter VI, in that it called for pacific settlement of the dispute, in which case, he argued, the United Kingdom should be debarred from voting on the resolution. Sir Anthony Parsons, the British ambassador, stated that the resolution came under Chapter VII, namely Article 40, and so the obligation to abstain was not applicable.[13] Although no members challenged Sir Anthony further on this point, the very fact that he had to justify his right to vote was a rarity. Perhaps it can be explained by the fact that the Security Council approached the Falklands free from any overt superpower concern, and consequently discussions and resolutions were more clearly based on considerations of international and Charter law rather than on considerations of power and zones of interest.

Bailey has tabulated the number of vetoes in the period 1946–86.[14] The tally in this period was: China 22, France 16, Soviet Union 121, UK 26, and the USA 57. It is interesting to note that the Soviet Union cast 77 of its vetoes in the first ten years when the UN was Western dominated, whereas the United States cast 45 of its vetoes in the period 1976–86, when the Non-Aligned and Socialist blocs combined successfully in the UN. It is true to say that with the end of the Cold War in the late 1980s, the number of vetoes has decreased dramatically with very few being cast in the period 1990–96 as a whole.[15] Whilst this shows the new spirit of cooperation amongst the 'permanent five', there is as yet no sign that this indicates a new found respect for the limitations on the veto contained in Article 27(3). First of all, it is clear that although the veto has been largely removed from the formal meetings of the Security Council, it still operates in the informal meetings which are more prevalent in the post-Cold War period. In addition to this 'hidden veto', of which there is no formal record, there are still examples of the veto being used in open meetings. The United States used its veto twice following its military intervention in Panama in December 1989, first to prevent condemnation of the action and a call for a withdrawal of troops, and secondly to prevent a condemnation of its occupation of the Nicaraguan ambassador's residence in Panama in breach of the Vienna Convention on Diplomatic Relations.[16] Neither proposal envisaged Chapter VII action and clearly the United States was a party to the dispute.

The United States' military intervention in Panama clearly continued a pattern of such actions undertaken by the superpowers during the Cold War, and it is to these that we turn first before looking at the period of cooperation between the permanent members. The end of the Cold War unfortunately does not signify the end of geopolitical limitations although it is true to say that those limitations are much reduced.

Cold War limitations

In a world dominated by two superpowers with their own hemispheric or bloc domains there emerged a distinction between intra-bloc and inter-bloc conflicts. In intra-bloc conflicts such as Guatemala 1954 and Hungary 1956, the veto was operated by the relevant bloc leader to allow the dispute to be settled within that bloc, sometimes combined, in the case of the United States, with arguments in favour of the relevant regional organisation.

Inter-bloc conflicts often occurred on the 'power frontiers'[17] between the 'spheres of influence'[18] of the superpowers, usually as a consequence of a miscalculation by one of them as to the ambit of its hemispheric control. Good examples of such disputes were the Berlin blockade in 1948 and the Cuban missile crisis in 1962. In these cases, it will be argued, the Security Council did play a significant role. The polarised positions taken by each side before the Council were gradually whittled down behind the scene until a common ground was achieved. In inter-bloc conflicts the stark choice was between annihilation or 'peaceful coexistence'.[19] Both superpowers had to make concessions if peaceful coexistence was to continue.

Intra-bloc situations

During the initial Cold War period (1945–55), the United Nations was dominated by the West[20] which managed to manipulate the whole Organisation to further its political and strategic ends. The American-backed coup in Guatemala of 1954 is illustrative of how that manipulation often occurred to protect American interests. It also shows how the Soviet Union was often forced to use its veto in the early years because of the American dominance of the Council.

The Guatemalan episode involved the question of whether regional bodies should have priority over the world body. As shall be seen in this chapter, Articles 52(4) and 103 of the Charter clearly provide a negative answer and yet the Soviet Union was forced to use its veto to uphold this view after Brazil and Columbia had proposed a resolution which would have left the matter to the Organisation of American States (OAS).[21] The United States was in such a strong position in the Security Council that it did not have to use its veto to protect its interests – it merely relied on its allies on the Council to outvote any proposal which was deemed to be against Western interests. Its dominance of the Guatemalan debate was highlighted when the US President of the Council effectively prevented further consideration when he proposed to take a procedural vote on the question of whether to keep the item on the agenda. The item was duly removed despite the negative Soviet vote.[22]

As with several of the earlier intra-bloc disputes involving the United States, that country was so confident of its position on the Council that it did not feel it necessary to veto what appeared to be constructive Council resolutions on Guatemala. Resolution 104,[23] proposed by France, called for the 'immediate termination of any action likely to cause bloodshed, and requests all members to abstain from giving assistance to any such action'. It was essentially a neutral, valueless resolution but by voting for it along with the Soviet Union, the United

States reinforced the view that it was the upholder of the Charter even where the principles contained therein seemed to be operating against American interests, whereas the Soviet Union was portrayed as only voting for resolutions criticising the United States and as using its veto when there was even a hint of criticism of its own actions. Nevertheless, such illusions should not hide the real fact that the United States was manipulating the Council to protect its hemispheric interests. Its representative made this very clear by instructing the Soviet Union to stay out of the United States' 'hemisphere'.[24] This amounted to a reassertion of the Monroe Doctrine and constituted 'a declaration which reciprocal practice over the next two decades was to stamp with an almost jural quality'.[25]

The tacit agreement between the Great Powers at Potsdam in 1945 that Eastern Europe was within the Soviet Union's sphere of influence was put beyond doubt after the Soviet Union's military intervention in Hungary in 1956.[26] The Western powers were unwilling to help the Nagy government when it announced on 1 November the withdrawal of Hungary from the Warsaw Pact accompanied by a declaration of its neutrality, and requested the United Nations and the four other permanent members to defend its neutral status. The Soviet Union also saw it necessary to protect its interests by using its veto in the Security Council to defeat a United States-sponsored draft resolution calling for Soviet withdrawal and respect for 'the independence and sovereignty of Hungary'.[27] Ambassador Sobolev of the Soviet Union explained the action in terms of defence of the Soviet Union's strategic zone.[28]

Just as the United States saw, and probably still sees, the creation of a 'Communist' government – whether created by popular assent or by outside interference – as an attack on Western principles and interests, so the Soviet Union viewed 'capitalism' as an attack on its bloc solidarity. Both powers viewed the removal of each respective threat from their respective zones as a legitimate defence of their strategic interests. This form of defence is not recognised as legitimate under Article 51 of the UN Charter which only allows for self-defence in the face of an 'armed attack'.

Intra-bloc interventions were often challenged by the other superpower in the Security Council to show rhetorical, political support for the people of the country being intervened in. By allowing the other side to verbally vent its anger, it could be argued that the Security Council reduced the chance of that side counter-intervening leading to a global conflict.

The United States complained of Soviet intervention in Hungary in 1956. The compliment was repaid in 1965 when the Soviet Union complained of 'armed intervention' by the United States in the Dominican Republic.[29] The Soviets introduced a draft resolution condemning the intervention and demanding that the United States withdraw.[30] Western support was still strong enough in the Council to ensure that the proposal only secured two votes in its favour.[31] The United States treated the situation on a similar basis to Guatemala a decade earlier by allowing resolutions to be adopted calling for a cease-fire but not prejudicing the OAS's role in the situation.[32] Again the world saw the United States refraining from using its veto in contrast to the Soviet Union's use of its power to block resolutions on Hungary and later on Czechoslovakia.

Nevertheless, it is clear that the United States would have used its veto to prevent criticism of its action, or to prevent proposals for peaceful settlement of the situation, or to prevent the establishment of machinery to facilitate a cease-fire such as UN peacekeeping – in other words anything that would have vaguely hindered or criticised the US/OAS operation. According to Ambassador Stevenson 'the establishment of a communist dictatorship' in the Dominican Republic was a matter for 'hemispheric action only', thereby making it clear that the UN was precluded from taking any positive action.[33]

On 28 August 1968, Western States brought the situation in Czechoslovakia to the attention of the Council.[34] The Soviet Union's military intervention led to the enunciation of the Brezhnev Doctrine of limited sovereignty within the Socialist commonwealth,[35] paralleling the various interventionist doctrines expounded by American Presidents. Ambassador Malik made a weak attempt to justify the intervention by referring to it as defence against an 'imperialist' attack. However, in the same speech the real political reasons became apparent, in that 'the situation in Czechoslovakia affected the vital interests of the Soviet Union'.[36]

During the Cold War, the Soviet Union viewed the use of the veto in the Council to prevent criticism of its actions as a necessary corollary to the protection of its vital interests by intervention. There was no question even of allowing weak, neutral resolutions to be adopted, an attitude that probably can be explained by a 'knee-jerk' reaction produced by its minority position on the Council. In 1968, the Soviet Union vetoed a Danish draft which condemned Soviet 'armed intervention' as well as a Canadian draft which was aimed at achieving limited measures and took the form of a request to the Secretary General to send a representative to Prague 'to ensure the personal safety of the Czechoslovak leaders under detention'.[37]

The Soviet intervention in Afghanistan in December 1979 was different in geopolitical terms from its previous interventions in Czechoslovakia and Hungary because it represented the first time the Soviet Union had pushed its troops beyond the zone inherited after the Second World War. This was reflected in the large number of States – Non-Aligned as well as Western – which requested the convening of the Security Council to discuss the situation in Afghanistan.[38] A draft resolution was proposed by the Non-Aligned group on the Council which deplored the 'recent armed intervention' and called for 'the immediate and unconditional withdrawal of all foreign troops from Afghanistan'. The vetoed draft resolution also called for respect for Afghanistan's non-aligned status reflecting the Western view that the Soviet Union had stepped beyond its zone as well as the Non-Aligned movement's fear of its members being subjected to superpower intervention.[39]

Afghanistan illustrated the fine line between intra-bloc conflicts in which the other superpower will be content with rhetorical confrontation, and inter-bloc conflicts which may have escalated into a global military confrontation. The Carter Doctrine,[40] warned the Soviet Union not to advance any further towards the Gulf and drew the line at the Afghan border, suggesting that the United States was treating the intervention as politically allowable. However, President Reagan redrew the power frontier closer to the Soviet Union by authorising material support for the Afghan rebels.[41]

The intervention in Grenada in 1983, which was legally justified on three grounds by the United States, namely the protection of nationals (and wider arguments of humanitarian intervention to protect the whole population), the invitation of the Governor General and regional action by the Organisation of Eastern Caribbean States (OECS),[42] was, in reality, an application of the so-called Reagan Doctrine. This doctrine or policy encompassed support for anti-communists, whether established governments or rebels, not only in the American hemisphere but throughout the world. Consequently, the Reagan Administration supported the Contras fighting in Nicaragua,[43] the Khmer Rouge fighting the Vietnamese-imposed government in Kampuchea (Cambodia), the National Union for the Total Independence of Angola (UNITA) guerrillas fighting the Soviet/Cuban backed Popular Movement for the Liberation of Angola (MPLA) government in Angola, and the Afghan *mujahedin*. The Reagan Doctrine was offensive, its aim was to attempt to stand the dominoes back up.

In the debate over its intervention in Grenada, even the United States' closest ally, the United Kingdom, refused to support it in vetoing a draft resolution condemning the 'armed intervention' and calling for the withdrawal of foreign troops.[44] Unlike the cases of Guatemala and the Dominican Republic, the United States was unable to avoid using the veto to protect its interests. Indeed, the United States has continued to use its veto to protect its military interventions within its hemisphere as the blocking of a condemnation of its action in Panama in December 1989 shows. However, on this occasion the resolution was blocked by the triple veto of the Western permanent members,[45] indicating the recent increased cohesiveness on the Security Council of these States, a group now labelled the 'permanent three'.

With the Cold War drawing to a close by the late 1980s, the world witnessed a decreased global tension which enabled the UN to become increasingly involved in areas hitherto excluded from its purview. This period of cooperation among the permanent five will be examined later in this chapter but it is interesting to note that the United States has not renounced its policy of intervention within its bloc as the Panamanian intervention shows, although as shall be seen it has also allowed the UN to become involved in that region. Furthermore, Western dominance of the Security Council has enabled the United States to seek UN authority for its latest military intervention in its hemisphere, namely Haiti in 1994. With the collapse of Communism, the political justifications are now concerned with combatting drugs and terrorism, and supporting democracy, although the legal justifications remain the same, namely the protection of nationals and wider arguments of self-defence, with the recent addition of authorisation by the UN. It appears that whereas the winners of the Cold War reserve the power to intervene, the Warsaw Pact renounced the Brezhnev Doctrine in October 1989 and the Soviet Union refused to intervene within the Eastern bloc to prevent the collapse of Communist regimes in that year.[46]

Inter-bloc situations

The superpowers' pervasive global interests during the Cold War meant that there were very few areas in the world in which the Council could fully utilise the powers at its disposal. It is axiomatic that where there was a case of direct East–West confrontation there was little possibility of a Security Council resolution. Nevertheless, there was evidence to the effect that in these inter-bloc disputes, the Security Council did sometimes play a significant role, although the spotlight was normally on the Secretary General helping a negotiated solution using quiet diplomacy away from the verbal battleground of the Council chamber.

One must not underestimate the role of the Council in one of the most dangerous situations to threaten world peace since 1945. In 1962 the Americans purported to use the forum as a tactical measure with no real intention of using it to negotiate with the Soviets over the withdrawal of missiles from Cuba. The United States convened the Council and introduced a draft resolution which had little chance of being adopted. It reasserted its demand 'for immediate dismantling and withdrawal from Cuba of all missiles and other offensive weapons' and the dispatch to Cuba of a 'United Nations' observer corps to assure and report on compliance'. Only after the affirmative 'certification of compliance' would the quarantine imposed by the United States be terminated. The call for withdrawal of the missiles was expressly stated to be 'under Article 40', that is a 'decision' of the Council having binding force under Article 25.[47] The Soviet draft resolution was equally uncompromising in that it condemned the actions of the Americans and called for the immediate revocation of the 'decision to inspect the ships of other States bound for' Cuba, and for an end 'to any kind of interference in the internal affairs of' Cuba.[48]

There appeared little chance of settling the issue through these kind of polarised proposals, but the draft resolutions did overlap in one area; they both called for bilateral negotiations between the United States and the Soviet Union to remove the threat to the peace. Acting Secretary General U Thant seized on this common area in letters to Kennedy and Khrushchev in which he called for the 'voluntary suspension of all arms shipments to Cuba and also the voluntary suspension of the quarantine for a period of two to three weeks'.[49] On 26 October 1962 President Kennedy agreed to the proposal.[50] The Soviets indicated their willingness to accept by stopping the shipments. This eventually led to a tacit agreement by which the Soviets would remove their missiles already emplaced in Cuba in return for the American withdrawal of missiles from Turkey.

It may appear that it was the Secretary General's diplomatic moves which helped to settle the dispute, whereas moves in the Council were a failure. This view is founded on the belief that the Security Council is primarily an adjudicative body. The Council, being a political organ, very rarely acted in this fashion during the Cold War when the political inhibiting factors were strong. In these situations it established the often extreme positions of the parties, which obviously could not be reconciled in the public forum, so necessitating the supplementary aid of 'corridor' diplomacy.

The Cuban missile crisis of 1962 involved an inter-bloc dispute in the form of a direct confrontation between East and West. However, a large preponderance of modern warfare during the Cold War concerned the indirect involvement of the superpowers, in which one or both confronted the other by the use of proxy armies, often in the form of national liberation fronts.[51] In these situations the danger of escalation was less because the superpowers were effectively two steps away from all out war. Thus with this cushion the superpowers were less willing to compromise. As with the situation of direct East–West confrontation, this rendered the Security Council a barren place, but unlike direct inter-bloc disputes, there was often little possibility of diplomacy filling the vacuum. A good example of Council impotence was its paltry involvement in the Vietnam conflict.

The conflict in Vietnam had lasted in various forms from 1946 until 1975 when the North took over the South. It was a battle on the edge of the 'zones of influence', in this case the 17th parallel. The United States was determined to hold the line, for if Vietnam fell to Communism the 'domino theory'[52] suggested that neighbouring countries would fall as Communism spread through Indo-China. The United States did not distinguish between the Chinese and the Soviets who both supported the North Vietnamese, but with hindsight, the American defeat was seen as an expansion of the Soviet sphere.

The period 1946–54 saw France fighting the North Vietnamese Communist movement until the French were heavily defeated at Dien Bien Phu. Although the French were fighting to maintain their colonial empire in this period, by 1954 the conflict was taking on a Cold War aspect with the United States paying 75 per cent of the French costs in fighting the war. After Dien Bien Phu, a Conference was held at Geneva in July 1954 to consider the future of French Indo-China. A ceasefire agreement divided Vietnam at the 17th parallel, while the Final Declaration of the Conference provided for elections to be held leading to a single Vietnamese State.[53] The elections did not occur mainly because of South Vietnamese opposition, and so the scene was set for a conflict between North and South with Sino-Soviet aid to the former and American military commitment to the latter.

The Security Council, indeed the United Nations, had little to do either with the 1954 Conference or the preceding period.[54] After French involvement was replaced by American commitment, the Security Council played a peripheral role. It met inconclusively on four occasions, three of these concerned aspects of the war rather than the whole situation. In 1959, Laos complained of military incursions into its territory by the North Vietnamese.[55] The Security Council, using a procedural vote in the face of Soviet objections based on the 'double-veto' and the 'chain of events' principles, created an investigative sub-committee.[56] This committee reported that the fighting was of a 'guerrilla character' and so did not constitute a crossing of the frontiers of Laos by the North Vietnamese.[57]

In May 1964, the government of Cambodia complained to the Security Council of alleged acts of 'aggression' directed against it by South Vietnamese and United States' forces.[58] These two States denied the charge, and suggested that the non-demarcation of the boundary between Cambodia and South Vietnam was the reason. The United States' representative suggested that the answer would be a role for a United Nations' force, emplaced to observe the integrity of the boundary.[59] South Vietnam indicated its willingness to accept such an observer force on its territory, but Cambodia was opposed to having it on its side of the border. No observer or peacekeeping forces were sent.

In August 1964, the United States requested that the Council consider the attacks on American vessels in the Gulf of Tonkin by the North Vietnamese. The Hanoi regime was unwilling to state its case before the Council and declared via the Soviet Union that consideration of the problem did not lie with the Security Council, but with the members of the 1954 Geneva Conference.[60]

It was not until 1966 that an attempt was made to bring the whole situation before the Security Council when the United States requested a meeting of the Security Council and submitted a draft resolution calling for 'immediate discussions without preconditions', with the priority being the arrangement for a cessation of hostilities.[61] The Soviet representative objected to a Council meeting to discuss the Vietnam War. He stated that the move by the United States was a diversionary tactic to cover the expansion of its aggressive war in Vietnam as evidenced by the resumption of its 'barbaric' air raids on the North.[62] The overwhelming atmosphere of distrust between the superpowers meant that the American proposal was not even voted on.

Although many other complaints and correspondence were directed to the Security Council, Vietnam was only discussed by the body on the four occasions outlined above, in which no concrete measures were adopted. Yet the situation was so grave in Vietnam that although it was not on the agenda of the 21st session of the General Assembly, 107 out of 110 speakers referred to it. It was a virtual poll of international opinion. All of those who spoke on the subject recognised the conflict in Vietnam as a serious threat to international peace and security which had the potential to spread beyond south-east Asia and ignite a Third World War.[63]

There were certain factors which restricted the ability of the Security Council or General Assembly to deal with the threat to the peace which Vietnam posed. At the Geneva Conference in 1954, very few of the participants envisaged United Nations' involvement, particularly the North Vietnamese and Chinese.[64] These two countries maintained a strong desire to exclude the United Nations from being involved, seeing the United Nations as 'a tool for US aggression'.[65]

They had some justification for feeling this in that the West had dominated and, to a certain extent, had manipulated the United Nations in the early years particularly, as regards the Chinese, in the case of Korea in 1950. The United States had also prevented the Communist Chinese from taking the permanent seat until 1971. The Chinese and North Vietnamese, not being represented at the United Nations, felt a deep distrust for the Organisation, which when combined with the mutual distrust between the Soviet Union and the United States during the Cold War, had the result of giving the United Nations little possibility of taking positive steps to solve the conflict in Vietnam.

The United States relied on a similarity between the Korean War of 1950–53 and the conflict in Vietnam to justify its support for the South.[66] In the case of Korea, the United States was willing to turn its support for South Korea into a United Nations' action at the outset of the war, whereas in Vietnam, the United States only showed a willingness to involve the United Nations when the war was going against it, by which time the position of the opposing parties and their respective superpower backers had become too intransigent for the United Nations to intervene. While in the case of Korea, the Communist attack from the North was a clear violation of Article 2(4) and a 'breach of the peace' within Article 39, the Vietnamese situation was more complicated, evidenced by the fact that there was considerable support for the Vietcong in the South. There was no discernable initial aggression by the North and no significant event which would have enabled a collective response as in the case of Korea, and certainly the Soviet Union was not going to absent itself and so allow the collective response to become a collective United Nations' response. Vietnam could best be described as a gradually escalating, internationalised civil war which was a 'threat to the peace' rather than a clear 'breach of the peace' as in Korea. The gradual escalation of the conflict in Vietnam severely limited the potential of United Nations' action. It had not really dealt with the situation at its origin, either in 1946 or by participating in the 1954 Conference, and thereafter it was in the untenable position of having to deal with the conflict from the outside.

The Secretary General, U Thant, supported this view. In his New Year message in 1966, he pointed out that just as the parties to the conflict had decided in 1954 to negotiate the end of the war outside the framework of the United Nations, the conflict could not be settled in 1966 under the auspices of the United Nations because only the United States, of all the parties to the conflict, was a member of the United Nations. U Thant preferred diplomacy rather than open debate in the Security Council and at several points in the conflict made proposals for settlement.[67]

The Vietnam War only involved one superpower directly and so the other, the Soviet Union, was quite content to block any diplomatic moves initiated by the Security Council or in the United Nations as a whole, because by indirectly encouraging the North Vietnamese, it was partly tying up the United States militarily and politically, and also embarrassing it. The North Vietnamese showed considerable independence evidenced by the aid received from both the Soviet

Union and the Chinese, whereas the South Vietnamese were to all intents and purposes 'puppets' of the United States. The Soviets did not control the North Vietnamese. The asymmetry of the conflict in Vietnam, in other words the difference
in commitment between the two superpowers, meant that it was virtually impossible to solve in the United Nations.[68]

Regionalism

So far it has been shown how the influences and interests of the superpowers during the Cold War effectively precluded the Council from taking action in relation
to disputes within large areas of the globe. Another *de facto* limitation on the
Council's sphere of operation was regionalism, which was often, but not always,[69]
related to the spheres of influence claimed by the superpowers.

De jure, however, the United Nations' Charter does not permit regionalism to
be paramount over globalism. The Charter, in Chapter VIII Article 52(1), recognises 'the existence of regional arrangements or agencies for dealing with such
matters relating to the maintenance of international peace and security as are
appropriate for regional action'. It even provides, in Article 52(3), that the Security Council 'shall encourage the development of pacific settlement of local disputes through such regional arrangements'. However, the provisions of Chapter
VIII make it plain that the Security Council is supreme in matters relating to international peace and security. In relation to the pacific settlement of disputes, the
Council's paramountcy is maintained by Article 52(4), whilst Article 53(1) provides that 'the Security Council shall, where appropriate, utilise such regional
arrangements or agencies for enforcement action under its authority. But no
enforcement action shall be taken under regional arrangements or by regional
agencies without the authorization of the Security Council'.

Articles 52(4) and 53(1), together, mean that the Security Council retains
supremacy over matters coming within Chapter VI or Chapter VII. Any lingering
doubts about overall United Nations' supremacy are seemingly removed by
Article 103, which states that '[i]n the event of a conflict between the obligations
of the Members of the United Nations under the present Charter and their obligations under any other international agreement, their obligations under the present
Charter shall prevail'.

However, the compromise between regionalism and globalism attained in
Chapter VIII (and Article 103) is itself compromised by Article 51. The insertion
of this provision into the Charter at San Francisco arose from 'the fear that the
veto power' preserved in Article 53(1) 'might cripple the functioning of regional
arrangements'.[70] Consequently regional arrangements were granted the right of
collective self-defence in Article 51, a right which could be exercised 'until the
Security Council has taken measures necessary to maintain international peace
and security'. Whereas Article 53(1) allows the Security Council to veto any proposed enforcement action by a regional organisation, Article 51 effectively

removes action taken in collective self-defence from being vetoed, at least at the outset of the action.

Writers have tended to concentrate on the difference between regional bodies in the nature of collective self-defence pacts under Article 51 and regional organisations in the nature of 'arrangements' and 'agencies' under Chapter VIII, rather than looking to specific actions to see if they are of a defensive or enforcement nature.[71] This writer takes the view that organisations such as NATO and the former Warsaw Pact are not, *prima facie*, regional arrangements under Chapter VIII. Indeed, the treaties establishing these bodies seem to be clear that they are based on Article 51.[72] Such arrangements are probably confined to those which have similar functions and powers to the United Nations as regards international peace and perhaps as regards economic and social cooperation, except these powers are operated on a regional not a global basis. Organisations designed primarily to enhance the defence and military capabilities of power blocs do not fit this concept. This does not mean that such 'collective self-defence' pacts cannot undertake enforcement action, but if they do, it should be authorised by the Security Council under Article 53(1). On the other hand, if a regional organisation, which primarily appears to come within Chapter VIII operates, on occasions, solely in collective self-defence, it should not require such authorisation for it is acting under Article 51.

Designating that a regional organisation or body comes within Article 51 or Chapter VIII is only a *prima facie* presumption that its actions will be based on those provisions, it does not prevent that organisation from taking collective self-defence action under Article 51 even if it is a regional arrangement under Chapter VIII; nor does it prevent a *prima facie* collective self-defence pact from taking enforcement action under Article 53(1) as long as it is authorised by the Security Council. However, offensive action by a defensive alliance even if authorised under Article 53(1) may be incompatible with the terms of the defence pact itself. This, as shall be seen, has not prevented NATO taking action under UN authority in Bosnia from 1994. It is feasible to see the UN authorisation as not being directed at the defence pact itself, and therefore not involving defence treaty issues, but at the individual members of the pact, thus making the operation no different from the several other instances that have occurred of the UN delegating military enforcement action to a State or group of States. This post-Cold War development will be reviewed in chapter three.

Returning to the use of regional bodies during the Cold War. The OAS appears to be a regional organisation for the purposes of Chapter VIII, not simply because its Charter specifically states that it is, but also because it is designed to perform similar functions to the United Nations on a hemispheric level. Nevertheless, it can act solely within the terms of Article 51 as a defence pact, a fact envisaged by its Charter.[73] Be that as it may, unfortunately the OAS has sometimes been used when it was dominated by the United States to attempt to legalise interventions aimed at purging ideological non-conformity by one of the other American States.

The United States' intervention in the Dominican Republic in 1965 is illustrative of the manipulation of the OAS by the United States. Originally solely a United States' operation, the OAS authorised the use of its own force,[74] which remained mainly composed of United States' troops. Predictably the Soviet Union took the view that, 'in order to cover up its armed intervention in the Dominican Republic' the United States was 'once more trying to retreat behind the screen of the Organisation of American States, which it long ago placed in the service of its imperialist aims'.[75] The United States stated that the OAS action did not constitute 'enforcement' action within the meaning of Article 53(1) and so did not require prior Council authorisation, arguing instead that the organisation was undertaking a 'peacekeeping operation'.[76] It appears that peacekeeping operations, which, if properly based on basic legal principles of peacekeeping are conceptually distinct from enforcement actions, can be undertaken outside the United Nations without authorisation by the Security Council. The fact remains that, assuming that the OAS force was a true peacekeeping force, this could not somehow legitimate the initial unlawful intervention by the United States.[77]

The United States has advanced further arguments to attempt to circumvent Article 53(1). The quarantine imposed around Cuba by the United States and rubber stamped by the OAS during the Missile Crisis of 1962 was not undertaken in response to an 'armed attack', and as such it could not be considered as self-defence within the terms of Article 51. It was therefore enforcement action which, according to the United States, did not breach the authorisation requirement of Article 53(1) because that provision should be interpreted to allow regional enforcement action when the Council has failed to adopt a resolution, in effect allowing a permanent member to veto a resolution forbidding regional action, so freeing such action.[78]

Akehurst suggests that the United States' attempts at circumventing the Charter, attempts that do not appear to stand up to objective scrutiny, were merely designed to give the United States-inspired actions an air of reasonableness rather than legality, making them perhaps *politically* more acceptable to the rest of the world community.[79] However, United States' politicians occasionally seem to go further than this, evidenced by Robert Kennedy, then United States' Attorney General, commenting on the Cuban Missile Crisis: 'It was the vote of the Organisation of American States that gave the legal basis of the quarantine. It changed our position from that of an outlaw acting in violation of international law into a country acting in accordance with twenty allies legally protecting their position'.[80] This suggests that the United States believes that in American matters the OAS is paramount over the Security Council despite the provisions of the United Nations' Charter.

The relative sophistication of the United States' arguments put forward to attempt to justify the OAS operations during the Missile Crisis and in the Dominican Republic case in 1965 can be contrasted sharply with the former Soviet Union's quite spurious arguments based on collective self-defence when it intervened within its hemisphere. Its interventions in Hungary in 1956 and Czechoslovakia in 1968 were not even sanctioned by the former Warsaw Pact, and the arguments of self-defence, for instance that Czechoslovakia was under an imperialist attack in 1968,[81] were quite clearly false. Although actions in collective self-defence escape the requirement of Security Council authorisation by virtue of Article 51, it is quite clear that the action must be truly one of self-defence at the request of the victim State of an armed attack,[82] neither of which were present in the case of Czechoslovakia.

The development of quite independent foreign policies by most American States has meant that the United States is no longer guaranteed of being able to use the OAS to purport to justify its actions. Its intervention in Grenada was, as has been seen, accompanied by justifications based on authorisation by the more localised OECS and prevention of formal criticism by the Security Council by using its veto. The United States did not rely on regional machinery in its latest military intervention in Panama in 1989. Instead, it paralleled Soviet interventions, by relying on the right of self-defence, embodied in Article 51 of the UN Charter and Article 21 of the OAS Charter,[83] whilst vetoing condemnation in the Security Council. The falsity of this argument was evidenced by the fact that the intervention was not only condemned by the General Assembly of the United Nations but also by the OAS itself.[84]

However, the end of the Cold War has seen the ideology of the victors spreading through the world. One of the tenets of this ideology – democracy – has swept through most of the American States, resulting in the 1985 Protocol of Cartagena de Indias, which amended the OAS Charter to include support for representative democracy.[85] Resolutions of the OAS Assembly in 1991 envisaged the possible adoption of measures against States in which there had been a disruption of the democratic process.[86] This process was instituted for the first time in October 1991 when the government of President Aristide of Haiti, elected in December 1990 under joint OAS/UN supervision, was deposed by a military coup. The UN Security Council supported the OAS sanctions that were emplaced and imposed its own.[87] The concurrence of the OAS and UN responses to this situation is illustrative of the dominance of Western ideology with the end of the Cold War. It is to the Western dominance of the Security Council that we now turn.[88]

Cooperation and domination

The political changes in the United Nations in the post-Cold War period coincide with the dramatic changes in Eastern Europe and the Soviet Union that have occurred in the past few years. The coming to power of Mikhail Gorbachev in the Soviet Union in 1985 started a slow, sometimes imperceptible warming in East–West relations, until the dramatic climax which led to the collapse of the Soviet empire in Eastern Europe in the late 1980s, inevitably leading to the demise of the Warsaw Pact in 1991.[89] With the Soviet Union undergoing fundamental changes away from Communism we saw a period of cooperation between the

United States and the Soviet Union, starting in the late 1980s and ending in December 1991. During this period of cooperation in the Security Council the world saw almost a doubling of peacekeeping operations authorised by the Security Council as well as full-scale military and economic enforcement action taken against an aggressor, Iraq, after its invasion of Kuwait in August 1990.

The intense, hectic and, on occasions, ill-conceived Security Council activity of the past few years is set to continue even as the wind of change that blew through Eastern Europe has continued into the Soviet Union itself, leading to the collapse of that country and the emergence of the former republics of the Soviet Union as twelve new States. The Soviet Union was formally ended on 21 December 1991. It was replaced by a loose alliance of States known as the Commonwealth of Independent States (CIS). The former republics agreed that the Russian Federation (hereinafter referred to as Russia) should take over many of the functions of the Soviet Union, including the permanent seat on the Security Council, whilst the other republics (except Byelorussia, now known as Belarus, and the Ukraine, already members from 1945) would be supported in their applications for UN membership.[90]

In a letter dated 24 December 1991, Boris Yeltsin, the President of the Russian Federation, informed the UN Secretary General that the membership of the Soviet Union in the Security Council and all other United Nations organs was being continued by the Russian Federation with the support of the countries of the CIS. The letter went on to say that Russia remains responsible in full for the rights and obligations of the former Soviet Union under the United Nations Charter.[91]

Russia's claim to the permanent seat led to speculation that this would spark off a reassessment of those States entitled to hold a permanent seat, particularly France and the United Kingdom. However, the three Western permanent members appeared, with the acquiesence of China, to skilfully manage a Security Council summit, attended by Heads of State. The summit was held on 31 January 1992, ostensibly to make a general declaration on greater UN activity and effectiveness, but in reality to endorse Russia's claim to the permanent seat. President Yeltsin duly took part in the deliberations but no mention was made of the permanent seat.[92] The Security Council's acquiesence in this presumably met the requirements of Rule 15 of the Council's own rules of procedure, which provides that 'the credentials of representatives on the Security Council ... shall be examined by the Secretary General who shall submit a report to the Security Council for approval'.[93]

The Security Council thus treated Russia as continuing the membership of the Soviet Union rather than as a new member, which would have required a recommendation from the Security Council and acceptance by the General Assembly. This appears to accord to past practice as regards UN membership.[94] For example in 1947, India, an original member of the Organisation, broke into two States on independence. India was treated as continuing its UN membership without interruption, whereas Pakistan was treated as a new State having to apply for UN membership. However, such precedents have been recently ignored in the case of the Federal Republic of Yugoslavia (Serbia and Montenegro), which, the Security Council determined in 1992, could not continue membership of the State formerly known as the Socialist Federal Republic of Yugoslavia (former Yugoslavia).[95]

The Council's approach to the Russian claim to the permanent seat, although apparently smooth and avoiding any possibility of Security Council composition being called into question, has two drawbacks. First of all it confirms and enhances the perception of the Security Council by most States as an exclusive club, completely controlling its own membership, and secondly the process does not affect the Charter, Article 23 of which states that the permanent members of the Council include 'the Union of Soviet Socialist Republics'. Presumably any change of Article 23 will require the amendment procedure contained in Article 108 which requires a two-thirds vote in the General Assembly including all the permanent members.

The emplacement of Russia, and more importantly a Western friendly Russia, in the permanent seat represents a major change in the composition of the Security Council. Even a cooperative USSR in its later years represented a limited check on the dominance of that body by the three Western permanent members. For instance, the Soviet Union insisted on Iraq being given time to withdraw its troops from Kuwait before the US dominated Coalition of States could use force under UN auspices. The deadline of 15 January 1991 imposed in resolution 678 of 29 November 1990 was the Soviet price for supporting a resolution authorising the use of force. There is little evidence yet of Russia carving out an independent role in the Security Council as it struggles to cope with its new internal problems – a faltering market economy and an unstable democracy, as well as an attempted secession in Chechnya.

The ease with which Russia occupied the permanent seat can be usefully contrasted with the process by which the People's Republic of China only came to occupy the Chinese permanent seat in 1971, it being occupied for the first 22 years by the 'rump Kuomintang government which had taken refuge on Taiwan'.[96] Western domination of the United Nations, although in decline after the first decade, lingered for a sufficient period to keep the Communist Chinese out of the permanent seat. Eventually, the growth in members of the General Assembly enabled that organ to adopt a resolution by the requisite two-thirds majority which resolved to 'restore all its rights to the People's Republic of China ... and to expel forthwith the representatives of Chiang Kai-shek from the place which they unlawfully occupy'.[97] The Secretary General reported to the Council that he was satisfied under Rule 15 of the Rules of Procedure and the Council welcomed the Communist Chinese on 21 November 1971.[98] The United States had already started its process of *rapprochement* with the People's Republic earlier in 1971. The Republic of China (Taiwan) is no longer a member of the UN even though Article 23 still refers to the 'Republic of China' and not the 'People's Republic of China'.

With Russia now at least temporarily in the Western camp, it might be expected that the Chinese would act as a stop on Western dominance. However, since its accession to the permanent seat in 1971, the People's Republic has been loathe to use the veto, seeing it as a tool of the superpowers. Indeed, it has on many occasions preferred not to participate in the vote at all, a procedure designed to be 'an expression of slight disapproval greater than abstention but not great enough for the veto'.[99] However, in the past few years the number of Chinese non-participations and abstentions has decreased drastically, and it now supports the vast majority of resolutions adopted by the Security Council. Its increased cooperation seems to be the product of Western economic pressure and a desire for political rehabilitation after the Tiananmen Square massacre of June 1989. An exception was the resolution authorising the use of force by the Coalition of States gathered in the Gulf against Iraq. China abstained on this vote in that it supported a settlement of the problem by peaceful means but recognised that Iraq was being intransigent despite many overtures, by the Chinese amongst others.[100]

The informal and somewhat secretive way by which the transfer of power from the Soviet Union to Russia was carried out in the UN, is indicative of the new order at the United Nations. For instance the Security Council debates are no longer characterised by lengthy Cold War rhetoric by numerous invited non-members as well as the members, instead there are short meetings to formally approve resolutions previously negotiated and agreed upon informally behind closed doors. The absence of debate hides two very important elements: first, the political bargaining that has led to the compromise, and second an even greater lack of discussion about the legal basis for a particular Security Council resolution. It has become extremely difficult to gauge the political and legal movements in the Security Council, although it is true to say that the organ is now Western dominated. However, it is also true to say that the Council is working with more efficiency and alacrity than at any time in its existence. In addition, it has recently made some efforts to increase its transparency and accountability,[101] but not, as yet, its representation of the world community.[102]

In addition, despite domination by the 'permanent three' of the United States, the United Kingdom and France, it is true to say that the world has been opened up to Security action which sometimes takes the form of pacific settlement efforts as in the Middle East and Cyprus, sometimes peacekeeping as in Afghanistan, Namibia, Nicaragua, Angola, Western Sahara, El Salvador, Cambodia, Yugoslavia, Somalia, Mozambique, and between Iran and Iraq and Iraq and Kuwait, and sometimes enforcement action of an economic kind, for example embargoes against Libya, Haiti, Serbia and Iraq, as well as full-scale military action against the latter. More limited military enforcement actions have been authorised by the Security Council, for example in Haiti and Rwanda in 1994. This non-exhaustive list illustrates that the removal of the Cold War limitation has opened up the full range of Security Council powers from pacific settlement to military action. Cooperation amongst the permanent members appears even stronger with a pro-Western and Western dependent Russia occupying the permanent seat. The 'permanent three' seem set to dominate Security Council action, using that body to take action against so called anti-Western, 'pariah' States, for example Iraq and Libya, but also dealing with situations in which Western interests are not as strong, particularly when authorising peacekeeping forces. Although there is a danger of complete Western domination it must not be forgotten that Russia and China will not necessarily follow the Western line, nor will a sufficient number of the non-permanent members.[103] Most States seem economically and politically dependent on the West at the moment but as has been seen in the last few years, dramatic changes in the geopolitical shape of the world are possible. Indeed, relations between the three Western permanent members need not necessarily be so tight, particularly with possibly greater European integration, leading to France and the UK representing the European Union as much as themselves.[104]

One is faced with the paradoxical situation of welcoming the new found Security Council effectiveness, particularly in enforcement action, whilst at the same time remaining cautious of the fact that the Council, in its current period of relative Western domination, is not truly fulfilling the ideal of collective security, which requires the *impartial* enforcement of community norms. Time will tell whether the Security Council will combat aggression and threats to the peace wherever they may occur, or whether the end of the Cold War simply signifies that although there has been a vast increase in Council activity, it is still *selective* action against particular aggressors and situations which threaten peace, not against all such States and situations. Nevertheless, looking beyond enforcement action, to pacific settlement initiatives and to those peacekeeping operations listed above, it shall be seen that the Security Council has cast a very wide net in recent years, and that despite its manifest deficiencies, a working collective security system is far better than none at all. Indeed, despite the relative supremacy of the Western States at the moment, they still have to persuade a sufficient number of States in the Security Council to support them, which suggests that Security Council action is fulfilling some of the collective security ideals behind the Charter to the satisfaction of the majority of States. Nevertheless, the actions taken by the Security Council will increasingly 'be judged by standards of legitimacy and fairness, and that judgment will affect the capability of the decisions made to pull the community to compliance'.[105]

Whereas in the Cold War, the main problem was the fact that political rivalry between the superpowers restricted the Council's sphere of operations as well as stunting its use of powers, its ending has signified an expansion into new areas of the world, which is to be welcomed if the actions are designed to deal with genuine threats to or breaches of the peace when enforcement action is contemplated, or situations likely to endanger the peace when pacific settlement is foreseen. Its ending has also resulted in the Security Council using its powers to their fullest extent. Indeed, it does not require a great stretch of the imagination to see the Council overstepping the limitations imposed upon it by the Charter.[106]

Notes

1 S. D. Bailey, *The Procedure of the UN Security Council*, 199, 2nd ed. (1988). On con-voking Special Sessions of the General Assembly under Article 20, see chapter five.

2 S. D. Bailey, *Voting in the Security Council*, 69–73 (1969). See also *Legal Conse-quences for States of the Continued Presence of South Africa in Namibia (South West Africa) Notwithstanding Security Council Resolution 276 (1970)*, I.C.J. Rep. 1971, 16 at 22.

3 UNCIO, vol. 11, 713.

4 H. V. Evatt, *The United Nations*, 53 (1948).

5 UNCIO, vol. 11, 714.

6 See R. B. Russell and J. E. Muther, *A History of the Charter*, 766 (1958).

7 UNCIO, vol. 11, 592.

8 Bailey, *Voting*, 18–25, 33–7.

9 R. Higgins, 'The Place of International Law in the Settlement of Disputes by the UN Security Council' 64 *A.J.I.L.* (1970), 1 at 1.

10 But see J. P. Cot and A. Pellet, *La Charte des Nations Unies*, 607, 2nd ed. (1991).

11 SC 987–8 mtgs, 16 UN SCOR (1961). UN doc. S/5033 (1961).

12 SC 749 mtg, 11 UN SCOR 31 (1956). UN docs S/3710 (1956), S/3713/Rev. 1 (1956).

13 SC 2350 mtg, 37 UN SCOR (1982).

14 Bailey, *Procedure*, 209.

15 A. Roberts and B. Kingbury (eds), *United Nations, Divided World*, 11, 2nd ed. (1993). M. C. Wood, 'Security Council Working Methods and Procedures', 45 *I.C.L.Q.* (1996), 150 at 154–5. Wood records three vetoes being cast since 1990. See also the Chinese veto of 10 January 1997 on the sending of military observers to Guatemala on the basis of Guatemala's perceived support for Taiwan, UN SC 3730 mtg, 52 UN S/PV (1997). See further reports of a US veto in March 1997 of a proposal to condemn Israel's plan to build new Jewish settlements in East Jerusalem, *The Times*, 14 March 1997.

16 SC mtg, 23 December 1989; SC mtg, 16 January 1990.

17 J. Fawcett, *Law and Power in International Relations*, 67 (1982).

18 See P. Keal, *Unspoken Rules and Superpower Dominance*, 7–33 (1983).

19 See G. I. Tunkin, 'Coexistence and International Law', 95 *Recueil des Cours* (1958), 49.

20 See E. Luard, *A History of the United Nations: Vol. 1 The Years of Western Domina-tion 1945–1955* (1982).

21 UN doc. S/3232 (1954).

22 SC 676 mtg, 9 UN SCOR (1954).

23 SC Res. 104, 9 UN SCOR Resolutions 4 (1954).

24 SC 675 mtg, 9 UN SCOR (1954).

25 I. Dore, *International Law and the Superpowers: Normative Order in a Divided World*, 55 (1984).

26 See generally the report of the UN Special Committee on the problem of Hungary, 11 UN GAOR Supp. (No. 18) (1956).

27 UN doc. S/3730/Rev. 1 (1956).

28 SC 754 mtg, 11 UN SCOR (1956).

29 UN doc. S/6316 (1965).

30 UN doc. S/6328 (1965).

31 SC 1214 mtg, 20 UN SCOR (1965).
32 SC Res. 203 and 205, 20 UN SCOR Resolutions 10 (1965).
33 SC 1196 mtg, 20 UN SCOR 19 (1965); paralleling the Doctrine enunciated by President Johnson, 52 *US Dept of State Bulletin* (1965), 29.
34 UN doc. S/8758 (1968).
35 20 *Current Digest of the Soviet Press*, No. 46, 3–4.
36 SC 1441 mtg, 23 UN SCOR 8 (1968).
37 UN docs S/8761, S/8767 (1968), Denmark, Canada.
38 UN doc. S/13724 (1980).
39 UN doc. S/13729 (1980). SC 2190 mtg, 35 UN SCOR (1980).
40 16 *Weekly Compendium of Presidential Documents* (1980), 197.
41 See W. M. Reisman, 'Critical Defence Zones and International Law: The Reagan Codicil', 76 *A.J.I.L.* (1982), 589.
42 78 *A.J.I.L.* (1984), 645.
43 This support was unlawful according to the International Court of Justice in the *Case Concerning Military and Paramilitary Activities in and Against Nicaragua* hereinafter referred to as the *Nicaragua* case, I.C.J. *Rep* 1986, 14.
44 UN doc. S/16077/Rev. 1 (1983).
45 SC mtg, 23 December 1989.
46 *Keesing's* (1989), 36982.
47 SC 1022 mtg, 17 UN SCOR (1962). UN doc. S/5182 (1962).
48 UN doc. S/5187 (1962).
49 UN doc. S/5191 (1962). SC 1024 mtg, 17 UN SCOR 21 (1962).
50 UN doc. S/5197 (1962).
51 See generally J. F. Murphy, *The United Nations and the Control of International Violence*, 135–206 (1985).
52 See D. D. Eisenhower, *Mandate for Change*, 333 (1963).
53 Misc. 20 (1954), Cmnd 9239.
54 See generally M. S. Rajan and T. Israel, 'The United Nations and the Conflict in Vietnam', in the American Society of International Law, *The Vietnam War and International Law*, vol. 4, 114–43 (1976).
55 UN doc. S/4212 (1959).
56 SC Res. 132, 14 UN SCOR Resolutions 2 (1959). SC 847 mtg, 14 UN SCOR (1959).
57 UN doc. S/4236 (1959).
58 UN doc. S/5697 (1964).
59 SC 1126 mtg, 19 UN SCOR 11 (1964).
60 UN doc. S/5888 (1964).
61 UN doc. S/7106 (1966).
62 SC 1273 mtg, 21 UN SCOR 3 (1966).
63 See GA plen. mtgs 1411–14, 1416, 1418, 1420–4, 1426, 1430, 1432, 1434–8, 1440–7, 1501, 21 GAOR (1966).
64 See generally, *Documents on International Affairs*, 121–42 (1954).
65 *Peking Review*, 16 April 1965.
66 60 *A.J.I.L.* (1966), 565.
67 See *United Nations Yearbook* (1966), 147, 152. *UN Monthly Chronicle* (1967), 69.
68 For 1973 Paris Conference peace agreement, see 67 *A.J.I.L.* (1973), 389.
69 See for example B. Andemichael, *The OAU and the UN* (1976).

70 E. Berberg, 'Regional Organisations: A United Nations Problem', 49 *A.J.I.L.* (1955), 166 at 169.

71 H. Kelsen, 'Is the North Atlantic Treaty a Regional Arrangement?', 45 *A.J.I.L.* (1951), 162. A. L. Goodhart, 'The North Atlantic Treaty of 1949', 88 *Recueil des Cours* (1951), 187. E. W. Beckett, *The North Atlantic Treaty, the Brussels Treaty and the Charter of the United Nations* (1950).

72 See Article 5 of the North Atlantic Treaty 1949, 34 UNTS 243, and Article 4 of the Warsaw Pact 1955, 49 *A.J.I.L.* (1955), 194.

73 Articles 1–3 and 27 of the OAS Charter. 119 UNTS 4.

74 UN doc. S/6333/Rev. 1 (1965).

75 UN doc. S/6317 (1965).

76 SC 1200 mtg, 20 UN SCOR 33 (1965).

77 M. Akehurst, 'Enforcement Action by Regional Agencies with Special Reference to the OAS', 42 *B.Y.B.I.L.* (1967),175 at 213. See further SC 1221 mtg, 20 UN SCOR (1965), Cuba, USSR, Jordan, France, Uruguay.

78 A. Chayes, *The Cuban Missile Crisis*, 61 (1974).

79 Akehurst, 42 *B.Y.I.L.* (1967), 222.

80 R. Kennedy, *Thirteen Days*, 121 (1969).

81 SC 1441 mtg, 23 UN SCOR 8 (1968).

82 *Nicaragua* case, I.C.J. *Rep.* 1986, 14 at 104–5.

83 UN doc. S/21035 (1989).

84 GA Res. 44/240, 44 UN GAOR (1989), *New York Times*, 23 December 1989.

85 See 33 *I.L.M.* (1994), 981.

86 OAS doc. AG/Res. 1080 (XXI-0/91).

87 OAS doc. MRE/RES.2/91, supported in the UN GA Res. 46/7, 46 UN GAOR (1991). UN Security Council imposed sanctions in SC Res. 841, 48 UN SCOR (1993).

88 See further A. C. Arend, 'The United Nations and the New World Order', 81 *Georgetown Law Journal* (1993) 491 at 492–5.

89 *Keesing's* (1991), 38026.

90 *Keesing's* (1991), 38654.

91 UN doc. S/23319 (1991).

92 SC mtg 3046, 47 UN S/PV (1992).

93 UN doc. S/96/Rev. 7 (1982).

94 R. Mullerson, 'The Continuity and Succession of States by Reference to the Former USSR and Yugoslavia', 42 *I.C.L.Q.* (1993), 473 at 475–8; C. F. Amerasinghe, *Principles of the Institutional Law of International Organizations*, 111–14 (1996); H. G. Schermers and N. M. Blokker, *International Institutional Law*, 75, 3rd ed. (1995).

95 SC Res. 777, 47 UN SCOR Resolutions (1992). See Y. H. Blum, 'UN Membership of the "New" Yugoslavia: Continuity or Break?', 86 *A.J.I.L.* (1992), 830.

96 Bailey, *Procedure*, 156.

97 GA Res. 2758, 26 UN GAOR (1971).

98 SC 1599 mtg, 26 UN SCOR (1971).

99 D. Nicol, 'The People's Republic of China in the Security Council' in Nicol (ed.), *Paths to Peace*, 120 at 128 (1981).

100 SC 2963 mtg, 45 UN SCOR (1990).

101 Wood, 45 *I.C.L.Q.* (1996), 156–9.

102 See GA Res. 47/62, 47 UN GAOR (1992), and 48/26, 48 UN GAOR (1993). The lat-

ter established an Open-ended Working Group to consider the issue of equitable representation on the Security Council. For an example of proposals for reform see The Commission on Global Governance, *Our Global Neighbourhood*, 233–41 (1995).

103 See further W. M. Reisman, 'The Constitutional Crisis in the UN', 87 *A.J.I.L.* (1993), 83.

104 See Article B of the Treaty on European Union, signed at Maastricht, 7 February 1992.

105 T. M. Franck, 'The *Bona Fides* of Power: Security Council and Threats to the Peace', 240 *Hague Receuil* (1993, III), 189 at 190.

106 *Ibid*. See further T. M. Franck, *Fairness in International Law and Institutions* (1995).

CHAPTER TWO

The legal competence of the Security Council

Chapter one contained an examination of the geopolitical limitations on the competence of the Security Council. However, it would be wrong to say that these limitations are extra-legal, at least in origin. The pressure of the Cold War in the Security Council led to the exploitation and expansion beyond the express wording of the Charter of two legal limitations, namely the veto in Article 27(3) and the competence of regional organisations in Article 53(1). The extensive use and, on occasions, misuse of the power of veto in particular often deadlocked the Security Council when it should have been dealing with disputes and conflicts. With the end of the Cold War in the late 1980s and the demise of the Soviet Union in 1991, the opposing political pressures in the Security Council though not removed are much reduced, with the result that the veto is not so prevalent. The Council has been freed to use (and possibly misuse) the powers granted to it in the Charter. In this new political order international lawyers are faced with the novel situation of assessing the extent of Security Council powers. To a certain extent the current emphasis is on the limitations on the maximum extent of the Council's powers rather than with those limitations that prevented it operating at all.

This chapter examines the Charter provisions as to jurisdiction which provide the detail within the framework of the larger scale, global limitations elucidated in chapter one. The difference is essentially one of scale for it will be seen that many jurisdictional questions examined by the Security Council, for example the determination of a 'threat to the peace' within Article 39, are, in essence, political decisions. That is not to say that legal considerations do not play an important role on occasions, but such considerations only provide a counter-weight to the permanent members' interests which, if sufficiently strong, will predominate. This is still the case with the ending of the Cold War. The political pressures are different, and they are such that Council action is now more likely, but they still greatly influence the interpretation and development of the jurisdictional issues examined below.

This chapter will consider the relative openness of the Charter system regarding the maintenance of international peace and security through the Security

Council, in other words whether there is any equivalence between the norm of *jus cogens* contained in Article 2(4) and the situations contained in Article 39 which grant the Security Council jurisdiction under Chapter VII, containing the enforcement provisions. Perhaps this may help to distinguish between the type of situation, dispute or conflict which gives the Council competence under Chapter VI containing powers of pacific settlement, and the type which gives it jurisdiction under Chapter VII. It may be discovered that there is no essential difference and that what determines competence under each Chapter are political factors. To elucidate whether there is a distinct type of situation which is dealt with under Chapter VII an attempt will be made to find a consistent practice of the usage of, and perhaps even arrive at definitions of, the terms used in Article 39, namely 'threat to the peace', 'breach of the peace' and 'act of aggression'. The analysis will then be concerned with whether the domestic jurisdiction limitation contained in Article 2(7) has any effect on the Council's competence. Once a distinction has been made between the elements which initiate jurisdiction under Chapter VI and Chapter VII, the question of whether there is an essential difference in the nature of resolutions adopted under each Chapter will be examined. In essence, this will involve an examination of the recommendatory/mandatory dichotomy, and the nature of the Council's mandatory powers.

The essence of this chapter is to define the factors which grant, and the limitations upon, the Council's jurisdiction as contained in the Charter. It is not concerned with the powers that are at the Council's disposal once it has jurisdiction. An examination of the powers and effectiveness of the Council is left to chapter three. However, there is an assessment of the extent of the Council's powers at the end of this chapter, along with the related, and topical issue, of judicial review of the exercise of those powers.

The relevance of Article 2(4)

Article 2(4) is a peremptory norm of international law and a fundamental provision of the Charter. It states that all 'Members shall refrain in their international relations from the threat or use of force'. Since Article 2(4) purports to control the use of force by stating a norm of international law to which States must conform, and the Security Council is concerned with maintaining international peace by taking action against States using force in contravention of Article 2(4), it is plausible to examine the possibility of a correlation between Article 2(4) and the competence of the Security Council. One possible approach is to argue that the Security Council can only deal with actual or potential breaches of Article 2(4). Following from this, Chapter VI may be seen to empower the Council to deal with potential breaches, whereas Chapter VII allows it to deal with actual breaches, of Article 2(4). Indeed, further to this argument it may be possible to accept a direct relationship between 'threat or use of force' under Article 2(4) and a 'threat to the peace', 'breach of the peace' and 'act of aggression' under Article 39, which grants the Council jurisdiction under Chapter VII. In other words 'threat of force' corresponds with 'threat to the peace' and 'use of force' is equivalent to a 'breach of the peace' and 'act of aggression'. This necessarily would entail limiting the Security Council to situations which are breaches of Article 2(4). Such a thesis envisages that the Charter established a 'closed' rather than an 'open' system. The Security Council's competence would be defined, at its limits, by Article 2(4); to go beyond that and, say, determine that a situation was a 'threat to the peace' when it was not a 'threat of force' would be *ultra vires*.

Certainly the extreme thesis, equating as it does Article 2(4) with Article 39, pushes to one side potential breaches of Article 2(4) which may be caught under Chapter VI, where the general requirement is only a danger to international peace, or under Article 39 itself. The introduction of a wide, discretionary concept such as a potential breach of Article 2(4), weakens the argument beyond repair, because it would allow the Council to deal with a wide range of disputes that may theoretically breach Article 2(4) in time, but in reality are unlikely to do so.

The main advocate of a closed Charter system by which the Security Council's ultimate competence is defined by international law in the form of Article 2(4) is Arntz.[1] Kelsen, on the other hand, states that it is 'completely within the discretion of the Security Council as to what constitutes a threat to the peace'.[2] Kelsen and Higgins[3] state that because the Council is not fettered in its powers of determination under Article 39, such a determination, in a case where no obligation stipulated by customary international law or Charter law is breached, can create new law as to what constitutes a threat to or breach of the peace. It can be seen from this that the Council has a lawmaking role, but it does not necessarily follow that the Council is completely unfettered by international and Charter law. The issue of whether the international legal system embodies the concept of the rule of law, which means that all subjects of international law including international organisations, in particular the potentially powerful Security Council, are controlled by legal principles, is an underdeveloped area which will have to be properly addressed if the Security Council continues to expand its powers.[4] The possibility of judicial review by the International Court of Justice of Security Council actions will be considered at the end of this chapter.

As is to be expected from a politically orientated body, the Security Council has, in practice, manifested a preference for the open system. In particular it has applied the concept of a 'threat to the peace' in Article 39 to essentially internal situations. Arntz argues that internal situations are not within the ambit of Article 39 because they do not constitute a 'threat of force' against another State within the meaning of Article 2(4). He argues that the text of the Charter, particularly the Preamble and Article 1, indicate that 'peace' is the antithesis of war, and so the Charter only deals with threats to or breaches of inter-State or international peace, and not to intra-State or internal peace. However, the evidence is that if an internal situation or civil war is serious enough the Security Council will become involved, subject of course to political limitations. This is sufficient, in itself, to destroy the closed Charter theory.[5]

For instance, in 1966 the Council determined that the 'situation in Southern Rhodesia constitutes a threat to international peace and security'.[6] It cannot really be denied that the only 'threat or use of force' arose from the activities of the guerrillas infiltrating Rhodesia from the frontline African States. Nevertheless, the Council decided that the situation in Southern Rhodesia itself constituted a 'threat to the peace', evidenced by its policy of imposing sanctions against Rhodesia.

In 1977, the Security Council determined 'having regard to the policies and acts of the South African Government, that the acquisition by South Africa of arms and related matériel constitutes a threat to the maintenance of international peace and security'.[7] It could be argued that the 'acts' referred to were the frequent punitive attacks against the frontline countries of Botswana, Angola, Zambia, Zimbabwe, Mozambique and Lesotho, and so the 'threat to the peace' had the international character that Arntz's formulation requires. Indeed, the resolution made reference to South Africa's 'persistent acts of aggression against neighbouring States'. However, the resolution also referred to the 'policies' of the South African government and called for the elimination of apartheid and racial discrimination within the country. Given that the resolution was adopted against a background of riots and killing in the black townships, it is submitted that it was the internal system of apartheid that constituted the 'threat to the peace' with the border conflicts being manifestations of that threat.

A parallel can be drawn with the arrival of oil tankers at Beira carrying oil for Rhodesia, an event which the Security Council seemed to view, in resolution 221 of 1966, as being, in itself, a 'threat to the peace'.[8] However, the real threat was the situation in Southern Rhodesia itself, a fact later recognised by the Council in resolution 232. The Council initially made a limited finding of a threat because of political factors.[9] The same can be said of South Africa, where, during the apartheid years, the Western members refused to allow a general finding of a threat.[10]

It is often forgotten that the Council determined that there was a 'threat to the peace' arising from the crisis in the Congo after the situation had deteriorated so badly as to constitute a civil war in 1961.[11] It is arguable whether this was an internal situation as such, with Belgian support for Tshombe and Soviet aid to Lumumba. However, there was certainly no direct 'threat or use of force' by one State against another. At the time the Council determined that there was a 'threat to the peace' in resolution 161, the main foreign element of force consisted of the few hundred mercenaries employed by Tshombe to maintain Katanga's secession. The crisis had international repercussions in that the civil war could suck in outside forces including the superpowers and that was why the internal civil war in the Congo was a threat to international peace. The linkage of the civil war in the Congo and the threat to international peace was emphasised in resolution 161.

The situations in Southern Rhodesia, South Africa and the Congo involved international repercussions of varying degrees but it must be remembered that these repercussions derived from the internal situations themselves. To be sure, the Council has often refused to find a 'threat to the peace' in situations that seem to fit the Rhodesian model. Portugal's failure to implement the General Assembly's 'Declaration on the Granting of Independence to Colonial Countries and Peoples'[12] is one example. The Council went as far as to adopt a resolution in 1972 which found that the 'situation resulting from the policies of Portugal both in its colonies and in its constant provocations against neighbouring States seriously disturbs international peace and security'.[13] Although this falls short of a finding under Article 39 there is evidence to suggest that a finding of a 'threat to the peace' might eventually have been made as a result of international pressure against Western members had the Salazar regime survived in 1974.[14]

The above analysis suggests that a finding of a 'threat to the peace' is, to a large degree, a political decision on the part of the Council, and so such a finding as regards a wholly internal situation is not precluded. Generally, however, the permanent members are not going to exercise this discretion unless the situation has potential international repercussions which could affect their interests, or even involve them in an escalating conflict. The requirement that the internal situation has international consequences is also a convenient method of allowing the permanent members to hide behind the argument that a situation is purely internal and therefore not a threat when they want to protect their interests. Recent practice suggests that the requirement is something of a formality, and that the Council is in reality concerning itself with purely internal situations. In April 1991, the Council condemned the suppression of the Kurdish minority rebellion in the north of Iraq following the end of the war between the UN authorised army and Iraq in and around Kuwait, 'the consequences of which threaten international peace and security'. In an earlier paragraph the Council elaborated on those 'consequences', namely 'the massive flow of refugees towards and across international frontiers'.[15] Further, in January 1992 it found that the civil conflict in Somalia had 'consequences on the stability and peace in the region' the 'continuation' of which 'constitutes ... a threat to international peace and security'.[16] The perception is that the requirement for the threat to be against *international peace* as opposed to *internal peace* is being stretched to breaking point.

Danger or threat to the peace

Articles 33 and 34 of Chapter VI of the UN Charter refer to a 'dispute' or 'situation' which is 'likely to endanger the maintenance of international peace and security'. The remainder of Chapter VI, with the exception of Article 38, relates to the Council's powers of pacific settlement over disputes or situations of the nature referred to in Articles 33 and 34. The title to Chapter VII reads 'action with respect to threats to the peace, breaches of the peace, and acts of aggression'. These terms are repeated in Article 39 which makes it clear that the set of circumstances to be dealt with under Chapter VII, containing the Council's enforcement powers, are threats to or breaches of international peace.

This section will be concerned with determining whether there is any real difference between situations or conflicts dealt with under Chapter VI and those dealt with under Chapter VII, or whether the Security Council treats the powers contained in the two Chapters as one continuum, using them selectively and interchangeably as political factors, including the need for consensus, dictate. The main area of this analysis will concern the fine distinction, if one can be drawn, between a 'danger to international peace' and a 'threat to the peace'.

So close is the relationship between a 'danger' and a 'threat' that it will become clear from the following analysis that there is often no substantive factual distinction between the two. They are, in effect, often merely 'labels' put into the resolutions to indicate the political climate in the Council. Conceptually, however, there is a legal distinction between a 'danger' and a 'threat'. The latter, for example, is often used as a legal tool to facilitate the imposition of measures under Chapter VII, a function which the label 'danger' is not legally qualified to perform.

To say that there is little practical difference between a 'danger to international peace' and a 'threat to the peace' is not so radical as it may first appear. At San Francisco, the Dumbarton Oaks proposals had provided for a link between Chapters VI and VII. The proposals had a provision at the beginning of what emerged to be Chapter VII of the Charter which empowered the Council to find a 'threat to the maintenance of international peace and security' if the procedures in what is now Article 33(1) or recommendations in Article 36(1) had failed or had been ignored.[17] This implies that the scale or the nature of the conflict need not have altered significantly from when the Council had purported to deal with it under Chapter VI. The factor which converted a danger to international peace under Chapter VI to a threat to the peace under Chapter VII was not necessarily a change in the nature of the conflict (except its prolongation) but a failure by the Council to end it under Chapter VI. The provision was dropped at San Francisco not because it brought the concepts of danger and threat too close together, but because it fettered the Council's operation of its powers,[18] that is it might have prevented the complete unfettered discretion of the Council in determining whether a situation was a 'threat to the peace' or not. This was despite the fact that the proposed provision would have been of relative insignificance in practice, for it was itself discretionary.

Nevertheless, in its formative years the Council did seem to develop a jurisprudence purporting to differentiate between a danger and a threat to international peace, revealed most clearly by the Spanish question, 1946. The Council adopted a resolution establishing a sub-committee of five members to determine whether the existence and activities of the Franco regime in Spain endangered international peace and security.[19] The sub-committee reported that the situation was of 'international concern' but not yet a 'threat to the peace' within Article 39. There was a 'potential menace to international peace' and therefore 'a situation likely to endanger international peace' within the meaning of Article 34.

The sub-committee thus created a distinction between a potential threat to the peace which corresponds to a danger within Chapter VI and an actual or real threat within Article 39. There is no further development of the distinction in the report except the factual findings that Spain had no imminent warlike intentions which suggests that the test is the relative immediacy of the war or conflict. However, the probable reason for distinguishing between a potential and an actual threat was that the sub-committee was of the view that Chapter VII was a 'very sharp instrument' which enabled the United Nations to wage war if necessary. This belief meant that it was reluctant to find a threat unless there was a very real and immediate danger to international peace which there was not in Spain.[20]

The motivating factor behind the Council's finding or not finding a 'threat to the peace' remains, in most cases, the reluctance by some members to impose economic sanctions or to take military measures under Chapter VII of the Charter.

The development of the Security Council's arms embargo against South Africa is interesting for it reveals that often the difference between a potential threat and an actual threat or a danger and a threat is not an increase in the level of violence of a dispute or conflict, but the ephemeral motives and interests of the members of the Council. Until the southern African peace process which started in 1988 with the agreement by South Africa to withdraw from Namibia in return for the Cuban withdrawal from Angola followed by a reform process in South Africa itself, the Western permanent members saw the protection of their economic interests in South Africa as vital, and therefore their general aim was the prevention of a mandatory set of sanctions being imposed against the Pretoria government.

Nevertheless, the international pressure on South Africa and consequently on Western governments forced them to grant some concessions. Thus changing political factors affect the Council's jurisdictional finding often to a greater extent than any legal criteria.

In 1963 the Council called upon all States to cease the shipment of arms and military material to South Africa after expressing its conviction 'that the situation in South Africa is seriously disturbing international peace and security'.[21] The call was only voluntary with the phrase 'seriously disturbing' seemingly equivalent to 'likely to endanger'. As has been seen this was eventually made mandatory in 1977 with a determination that the supply of arms to South Africa constituted a 'threat to the peace'. The finding of a 'threat' accompanied by a specific embargo was delayed by the intransigence of Western States until 1977 mainly because it was not until this time that South Africa had become fully armed. There may have been a change in the nature of the situation due to an increased level of violence within South Africa which may have influenced the Council in its determination of a threat, though by far the most significant factors were the political interests of the Western States. The General Assembly had made its own determination that the situation within South Africa was a threat to the peace in 1965.[22]

The gradual change in the Council's collective will can be traced in the language of its resolutions on South Africa. By 1970, the determination was that, 'the situation resulting from the continued policies of apartheid and the constant build up of the South African military and police forces constitute a potential threat to international peace and security'.[23] The original draft resolution sponsored by the Non-Aligned members of the Council contained the phrase 'serious threat',[24] but with Western opposition the second and final draft amended this to 'potential threat'. The representative of the United Kingdom expressed the West's opposition to the earlier drafts using the language of Chapter VII, whereas the phrase 'potential threat' was not objectionable on those grounds.[25] With the prevention of entry into Chapter VII achieved, the resolution's call for an arms embargo was generally accepted to be only recommendatory, even though it also referred to a 'real threat to the security' of surrounding African States due to the arms build-up in South Africa.

'Likely to endanger international peace', 'seriously disturbing international peace', 'threats to the security' of neighbouring States, 'potential threat to international peace' and a 'threat to international peace' are terms used by the Council. They could be said to be arranged here in a scale of ascendancy with the last being the most serious and the only one which is recognised as representing an implied finding under Article 39. The factors which produce a move up or down the scale are a combination of factual and determinable change in the level and nature of the conflict and also political and strategic adjustments by the members of the Security Council, particularly the permanent members. Political factors being the stronger, the phraseology used should be seen as an indicator of a change in political will rather than providing any significant criteria by which one can legally define the difference between a danger to international peace and a threat to international peace.[26] Nevertheless, political factors primarily influence the timing of a finding of a 'threat to the peace'. Once a finding is made it is possible to determine why a situation is a 'threat to the peace' and to construct a legal definition. In so doing the political factors which influenced the designation of the situation as a threat to the peace at a particular time should be ignored, for it may well be that, legally speaking, such a threat had existed for many years prior to the finding.

The influence of political factors in finding a 'threat to the peace' in the Rhodesian situation illustrates the influence a solitary permanent member can have. Resolution 216 adopted on 12 November 1965 condemned the Unilateral Declaration of Independence (UDI) and called upon States not to recognise the 'illegal regime' or render any assistance to it. The resolution contained no determination of a danger to international peace nor of a threat to the peace because it arose from the desire to find a compromise between a British draft resolution which determined that the 'continuance of the resulting situation is likely to endanger the maintenance of international peace and security',[27] and a draft resolution proposed by the Ivory Coast which stated that the declaration of independence constituted a 'threat to international peace and security'.[28] The difference in terminology arose principally because of the British and Western view that Rhodesia should not be subjected to immediate punitive sanctions but to a policy of gradually escalating sanctions to urge peaceful change, whereas the Afro-Asian and Communist view was that Rhodesia should be the subject of immediate and punitive mandatory sanctions and possibly the use of military force.[29] This divergence was not primarily due to different perceptions of the nature of the situation in Rhodesia. According to the General Assembly a 'threat to the peace' had existed in 1963.[30]

Due to the United Kingdom's hold over the other members of the Council in the form of its veto, the Council's resolutions reflected the British policy rather than that of the Afro-Asian States. The Council gradually moved towards a finding of a threat to the peace with a corresponding move from voluntary to mandatory measures which were eventually made comprehensive. Resolution 217 adopted on 20 November 1965 determined that the 'continuance in time' of the Rhodesian situation 'constitutes a threat to international peace and security'. This phrase appears to be akin to a 'potential threat' and so it was no surprise when the Council found a 'threat to the peace' specifically in relation to the oil tankers arriving at Beira, then a general finding of a 'threat to the peace' as regards the Southern Rhodesian situation as a whole, accompanied by the imposition of mandatory sanctions which were later made comprehensive.

An intermediate finding of a potential threat is generally indicative of the Council members' first consensual step towards an implied finding under Article 39. Ambassador Goldberg of the United States summarised the state of the Council's deliberations when voting on resolution 217, stating that it did 'not mention whether Chapter VI or Chapter VII is brought to bear. My Government agrees with this interpretation of the text'. This bizarre comment merely reflects the midpoint between the polarised views of the other Council members. For example, the Ivory Coast believed that resolution 217 imposed mandatory sanctions, whereas the British viewed it as 'not falling under Chapter VII'.[31]

The phrase 'potential threat', which conceptually appears to be no different to a 'danger to the peace', is a product of the Cold War which forced members to achieve consensus by appeasing all sides. If some members desired a finding of a threat accompanied by Chapter VII action, whilst others, for equally political reasons, desired only a finding of a danger and a recommendation of peaceful settlement under Chapter VI, in order to produce some sort of resolution a compromise was often achieved by the use of 'potential threat' accompanied perhaps by voluntary measures. If a compromise was not achieved the veto was inevitably used.

In the two examples given, a slow march by the Security Council towards a finding of a threat to the peace combined with the undertaking of enforcement action can be perceived. In other instances, during the Cold War the process was much more likely to halt before the Council reached Chapter VII as the all pervasive political limitations intervened. With the ending of the Cold War, this slow process is less evident, and as shall be seen, the Council more freely enters upon Chapter VII, often avoiding any preliminary steps such as the determination of a danger or potential threat to the peace. Indeed, the evidence of the last three years is that the increasingly dynamic Council is not, for the moment, concerned with concepts such as potential threat. Resolutions appear now to be mainly clearly within Chapter VII, and increasingly containing enforcement measures, or not within Chapter VII. The jurisdictional phraseology of Chapter VI seems to have become generally subverted to the need for the Security Council to react rapidly to situations without the need to consider the legal niceties. The most important jurisdictional distinction in the post-Cold War era is that between Chapter VII resolutions, which normally are mandatory, and Chapter VI resolutions, which normally are recommendatory.

Occasionally, the Council will find a threat to the peace without taking any mandatory action, as when it found that the consequences of the suppression of the Kurdish rebellion threatened international peace and security in resolution 688 of April 1991. Normally, however, it signifies its use of Chapter VII not only by making a finding of a threat to or breach of the peace within the terms of Article 39, but by actually stating that the resolution, or the relevant part of a resolution, is adopted under Chapter VII. For example, in September 1991, the Security Council determined in a preambular paragraph of its resolution that 'the continuation of' the fighting in Yugoslavia and its effects on neighbouring countries constituted 'a threat to international peace and security'. It then decided 'under Chapter VII of the Charter' that all States immediately implement a complete arms embargo against Yugoslavia.[32]

Indeed, unlike the Security Council's laborious approach to the Rhodesian and South African situations, its post-Cold War approach generally gives States little chance to prepare themselves for Council action. In January 1992, the Western dominated Council turned its attention to Libya, long seen as a 'pariah' State in the West, and with the end of the Cold War, without many friends either inside or outside the Council chamber. The Council did urge in resolution 731 that the Libyan government effectively respond to the requests of France, the United States and Britain for extradition of the Libyan nationals allegedly behind acts of terrorism, specifically the sabotage of the Pan Am flight over Lockerbie in Scotland in 1988. However, the same resolution made it clear that this was not the only action the Council was prepared to take if necessary, by stating in the Preamble that certain acts of terrorism constituted 'threats to international peace and security'. This effectively opened the door for Chapter VII action in the future if the Libyan government did not respond to the satisfaction of the Council, or more correctly, the Western permanent members. During the Cold War, it may have taken many months, possibly years, for the Council to take further action, if at all. It was just over two months later on 31 March 1992 that the Council adopted resolution 748, in which the Council stated that it was 'acting under Chapter VII of the Charter' in imposing an arms and air embargo against Libya.

Whereas the Cold War encouraged the proliferation of phrases such as 'potential threat' which may have indicated the general direction of the Council towards Chapter VII, its ending in the late 1980s has removed these nuances in Council language. The new approach is a simple one, namely a clear distinction between a determination of a 'threat to the peace' which, alongside 'breach of the peace' and 'act of aggression', form the gateway to Chapter VII action, and other disputes or situations which are not, at that moment, to be dealt with under Chapter VII but under Chapter VI or under the Council's increasingly developed declaratory powers.[33] Generally, the formal requirement of a finding of a 'danger to international peace' does not now seem necessary for a resolution to bear the mark of a Chapter VI resolution, it simply must lack the necessary finding under Article 39. However, occasionally still the Security Council does make an express finding of a danger to international peace. For instance in April 1993, the Council determined that Armenia's invasion of a district of Azerbaijan endangered international peace and security while demanding a cease-fire and withdrawal of Armenian forces.[34] Despite the fact that, as was pointed out in the resolution itself, the conflict not only involved a transborder use of armed force (*prima facie*, therefore, constituting a 'breach of the peace' or 'act of aggression'), but also raised the issue of displaced civilians and breaches of humanitarian law (issues, which as shall be seen in the next section, have been deemed to be 'threats to the peace'), the Council failed to make a determination under Article 39.[35] The exercise of its discretion by making it clear in this instance that the conflict was to be dealt with under Chapter VI, is indicative that the lack of political will in the Council is often the deciding factor in its opting for Chapter VI in cases where the conflict seems to be ripe for a determination (followed by action) under Chapter VII.

Threat to the peace

It has been seen in the above section that because of a delay caused by political factors in a finding of a 'threat to the peace' there appears to be little factual difference between a situation 'likely to endanger international peace' and a 'threat to the peace'. Undoubtedly, a 'threat to the peace' is a very flexible concept covering anything from intra-State situations to inter-State disputes. Nevertheless, ignoring for a moment the confusion caused by political delay, it can be seen that the term 'threat to the peace' is taking on a conceptual form.[36]

Earlier practice of the Council does not reveal the same usage of 'threat to the peace' as does later practice, which is probably a reflection of change in the type of dispute or conflict occurring in the post-1945 world order. In early years, a finding of a threat to the peace was viewed as a preliminary to a finding of a breach of the peace. The invasion of Palestine by the surrounding Arab countries after the proclamation of the State of Israel on 14 May 1948, eventually led the Council to classify the situation as a 'threat to the peace within the meaning of Article 39', and to order that 'pursuant to Article 40', there should be a cessation of hostilities which should take place 'not later than three days from the date' of the resolution. Any failure to comply 'would demonstrate the existence of a breach of the peace within Article 39'.[37] The Council was not declaring that the Arab countries were threatening to breach the peace for hostilities had already begun, it was the continuance in time of the conflict which would convert a threat into a breach of the peace.

Later practice shows the term being modified to deal with intra-state situations and conflicts rather than the traditional inter-State conflict, for which the other terms in Article 39 are more applicable. One of the most extensive uses of the term, undoubtedly, was during the meetings of the Security Council between 1965 and 1968, although very few of the speakers explained why the situation in Southern Rhodesia was a threat to the peace. Perhaps the decision was a political one requiring no rational or conceptual deliberations by the members of the Council. However, the meeting of 16 December 1966, at which the first mandatory resolution of a more general nature was adopted, reveals that at least some of the representatives had applied their minds as to why an essentially internal situation was a threat to the peace. The representative of Jordan stated that the UDI amounted to 'an invasion of the rights of the majority. It is an act of aggression that cannot be condoned. The answer to such invasion and aggression is Chapter VII'.[38] Superficially he appeared to be referring to an inter-State conflict rather than an internal situation; however, the 'invasion of the rights of the majority' clearly shows that the primary reason for the situation being a threat to the peace was the denial of the right to self-determination of the people of Southern Rhodesia, although another element in a threat to the peace is the potential spillover effect, the likelihood of internal violence spreading to become international violence. This writer believes that the spillover element in a finding of a threat is overplayed because any situation where there is a denial of self-determination or a significant deprivation of human rights has the potential to ignite international violence, for example through misconceived or misapplied unilateral humanitarian intervention.

During the apartheid years in South Africa, there was little doubt that the denial of the South Africans' right to self-determination constituted a 'threat to the peace'. The Council did not make such a finding in general terms, although resolutions passed in condemnation of the system of apartheid said as much without using the term. For example resolution 473 of 13 June 1978 reaffirmed that, 'the policy of apartheid is a crime against the conscience and dignity of mankind and is incompatible with the rights and dignity of man, the Charter of the United Nations and the Universal Declaration of Human Rights and seriously disturbs international peace'. The last phrase appears to be added to keep the resolution within the bounds of Chapter VI. Nevertheless designating apartheid as a 'crime against mankind' and a 'crime against humanity'[39] must surely have brought the whole situation, and not just the acquisition of arms by South Africa, within the concept of a 'threat to the peace'. The decision to keep the situation within the terms of Chapter VI was a political one on the part of the Western permanent members who were not willing to subject the regime to a more comprehensive embargo.[40]

It appears that a 'threat to the peace' is the term the Council has shaped to use in situations of non-traditional international violence in which the main danger to international peace is not a conflict between two or more States, instead it arises primarily from the internal events in one State, which may, as in the case of South Africa, manifest itself in the form of attacks upon other States.[41] Whereas South Africa and Rhodesia were concerned with the denial of self-determination by racist regimes, the crisis in the Congo was more akin to a civil war situation. The problems of civil strife and human suffering were, in themselves, sufficient to warrant a finding of a threat to the peace, although the Council tended to combine this with the menace caused by Belgian and mercenary military intervention.[42]

In other conflicts the question of civil strife is often overshadowed by foreign intervention. In 1974 a Greek backed coup against Archbishop Makarios followed by the Turkish invasion of the northern part of Cyprus led the Council to adopt resolution 353, which stated that there was a 'serious threat to international peace and security' and demanded 'an end to foreign military intervention' in Cyprus.[43] The threat to international peace was inherent in the civil strife between the Greek and the Turkish Cypriots, a fact recognised by resolution 186, adopted in 1964, which classified the violent eruptions on the island as 'likely to threaten international peace'. The Turkish invasion in 1974 was a manifestation and realisation of the threat.

The term 'threat to the peace', it can be seen, is being applied increasingly to internal situations. In 1969, Ireland requested a meeting of the Security Council to consider the situation in Northern Ireland with a view to sending a United Nations' peacekeeping force to the province because of the serious disturbances caused by the alleged denial of civil rights to the Catholic community.[44] Although the question was not even adopted on the agenda, it is interesting to note that Lord Caradon was sufficiently perturbed by Irish references to southern Africa that he not only relied on Article 2(7) as would be expected, but also denied that the situation in Northern Ireland was a threat to international peace.[45]

The Northern Ireland situation illustrates that the concept of a 'threat to the peace' was restricted during the Cold War to denials of self-determination or civil wars, which is not the case in Northern Ireland, with the additional requirement that the situation must have consequences for international peace, in terms of destabilising neighbouring States or drawing in outside powers. Recent post-Cold War practice when the Council has been more willing to enter Chapter VII illustrates this point. As has been pointed out the civil conflicts in Iraq, Yugoslavia and Somalia[46] were all designated threats to the peace within 1991–2, not only because of the massive scale of destruction in each of these conflicts but also because of their adverse effects on neighbouring States. Further examples of such findings are to be found in the Council's resolutions of 1992 and 1993 dealing with the civil wars in Liberia[47] and Angola.[48] The international repercussions of some of these internal conflicts were limited, in particular those in Somalia and Angola.

The extension of the concept of a 'threat to the peace' into what are essentially internal situations involving 'extreme violence'[49] has not been without controversy. It is interesting to note that resolution 688 of 5 April 1991, which found that the consequences of the Iraqi repression of the Kurds mainly in the form of a 'massive flow of refugees' towards and over the Iranian and Turkish frontiers, threatened international peace, was the least supported of the Council's resolutions on the Gulf Crisis following Iraq's invasion of Kuwait in August 1990. The resolution received only ten votes in favour, with three against (Cuba, Yemen, Zimbabwe), and two abstentions (China and India). Many of those States which could not support the resolution expressed alarm at the intrusion into another State's internal affairs.[50] On the other hand the resolutions on Yugoslavia and Somalia received unanimous votes. The difference appeared to be that resolution 688 concerned the suppression of a section of the population by the legitimate government of Iraq, a move that clearly would bother members of the Council themselves guilty of suppression, whilst the other States, Yugoslavia and Somalia, were completely factionalised by the time the Council determined that there was a threat to the peace. The resolutions were not directed against an established government and therefore could be supported by all members.[51]

The unifying feature in most of the Council practice discussed so far as regards 'threat to the peace', is that the situations have at their core the use of armed force, either internal or international. The integrity of the concept has been maintained by many of the recent uses of the terms by the Security Council, covering issues such as threats of force (provocative action directed by Iraq against Kuwait),[52] widespread violations of international humanitarian law (including 'ethnic cleansing' in Bosnia),[53] massive humanitarian crises (caused by the genocide in Rwanda in 1994 which led to related problems in Burundi and Zaire in 1996),[54] and breach of a Security Council arms embargo (relating to Rwanda).[55]

The 1992 Council resolutions against Libya, which represent a new development of the concept of a 'threat to the peace' to cover aspects of terrorism, raised the question of whether these departed too far from the core of the concept. Building on a general resolution of June 1989, which determined 'to encourage the promotion of effective measures to prevent acts of terrorism', and specifically condemned 'all acts of unlawful interference against the security of civilian aviation',[56] the Western members satisfied the Council of the complicity of the Libyan government in acts of air sabotage and gained Council support for their demand that Libya respond immediately and effectively to the requests of the three Western permanent members that Libya cooperate in the 'legal procedures', namely the extradition of alleged terrorists to the West. Resolution 731, adopted unanimously on 21 January 1992, was not mandatory in that there was no reference to Chapter VII within it, but it contained within it the possibility of further action in the future when it affirmed 'the right of all States ... to protect their nationals from acts of terrorism that constitute threats to international peace and security'. Little was said in the Council meeting at which this resolution was adopted to further explain this development of the term 'threat to the peace'.[57]

Although Libya did respond by offering to try the alleged terrorists in Libya, and thereby purporting to comply with its obligations under Article 7 of the Montreal Convention on the Suppression of Unlawful Acts against the Safety of Civil Aviation of 1971,[58] this did not satisfy the Council, which on 31 March 1992 adopted resolution 748 by a majority of ten votes to nil with five abstentions – China, Cape Verde, India, Morocco and Zimbabwe. The Council, after recalling Article 2(4) of the Charter, determined 'that the failure of the Libyan Government to demonstrate by concrete actions its renunciation of terrorism and in particular it failure to respond fully and effectively to the requests in resolution 731 (1992) constitute a threat to international peace and security'. It then went on to impose enforcement measures under Chapter VII with the aim of obtaining Libya's compliance with the requests and its renunciation of terrorism.

The Security Council debate was inconclusive as to the exact nature of the threat in this case, although at one point the British representative said, 'terrorists … have as their objective the undermining of efforts … to seek peaceful solutions to international disputes. They represent, in fact, one of the greatest threats to peace around the world, and that includes peace in the Middle East'.[59] The concept of threat to the peace although expanded from its immediate post-1945 meaning has generally been restricted to civil wars and denials of the right to self-determination (usually involving some degree of armed struggle). The invocation of Article 2(4) in resolution 748 may have been intended to give the resolution that necessary reference to armed force, which appears essential if the Security Council is to embark upon enforcement action in its collective security role for the maintenance of international peace and security. Extensive support for terrorism can obviously affect international peace, although it might be suggested that the impact has to be quite serious to merit the finding of a 'threat to the peace'. Resolution 748 reflected the General Assembly's 1970 Declaration of Friendly Relations[60] when it stated that 'every State has the duty to refrain from organizing, instigating, assisting or participating in terrorist acts against another State or acquiescing in organized activities within its territory directed towards the commission of such acts, when such acts involve the threat or use of force'.

Although there were doubts raised about the Council's determination of a 'threat to the peace' in the context of Libya's support for terrorism,[61] the Council entrenched this development with subsequent practice in 1996 in relation to the Sudan which refused to hand over three suspects wanted in connection with the assassination attempt on President Mubarak of Egypt in June 1995 as demanded by the Security Council.[62] After reiterating that the 'suppression of acts of international terrorism, including those in which States are involved, is essential for the maintenance of international peace and security', the Security Council determined that Sudan's failure to comply constituted a threat to international peace and security and imposed mandatory diplomatic, and later air, sanctions against that State.[63]

Although the concept of a 'threat to the peace' is flexible, and very much motivated by political factors, which were clearly in play in the case of Libya, the imposition of specific sanctions against that State following a determination that its alleged support for terrorism was a threat to the peace seems to be a new departure from past practice. It was a development that needed to be entrenched by subsequent practice by the Security Council; this seems to have been achieved by its resolutions against Sudan. Having pushed the concept of 'threat to the peace' in a new direction, the P3 have utilised their dominance on the Security Council to push further items on the Western agenda on to the agenda of the Security Council.

In 1993 the Security Council determined first that the humanitarian crisis and the problem of refugees in Haiti,[64] and then that the failure by the military authorities in Haiti 'to fulfil obligations under the' Governor's Island Agreement, by which the military regime agreed to the restoration of democracy',[65] constituted threats to peace and security in the region.[66] In its later resolution authorising a United States led military operation 'to facilitate the departure from Haiti of the military leadership', the 'unique character' of the situation in Haiti was reiterated,[67] in an attempt to assuage those members with grave misgivings about intervention in Haiti to restore democracy.[68] Although the resolution authorising the use of armed force referred to the plight of the Haitian refugees, thereby giving the determination the required international element,[69] it is clear that the refugee problem was not of the scale of the Iraqi, Rwandan or Zairean situations.[70] Furthermore, the members of the Security Council, in its later meetings, discussed the situation solely in terms of the brutality of the regime, its denial of democracy, and its defiance of the Security Council's will.[71] The representative of Uruguay represented the views of the minority when he stated that 'we do not believe that the internal political situation in Haiti projects externally in such a way as to represent a threat to international peace and security'.[72]

The current domination of the Council by the Western States may lead in time to further expansion of the concept, moving it away from international threats of force and internal situations of 'extreme violence', towards drug trafficking, armament, and environmental matters.[73] The latter two possibilities were mentioned in the statement issued by the President of the Security Council following its meeting of Heads of State and Government of January 1992.[74]

Breach of the peace

In practice, a breach of the peace has rarely been found, the recent preference being for findings of aggression. This is surprising for aggression is merely a special case of breach, Article 1(1) of the Charter mentioning 'acts of aggression or other breaches of the peace'. Although a finding of aggression is much more condemnatory, often, as shall be seen, it produces little by way of sanctioning measures. 'Breach of the peace', although a much more neutral expression when applied to traditional international violence has, on the four occasions on which it has been found, been accompanied by positive Council action.

The Australian representative attempted a definition of a breach of the peace during discussion of the Indonesian question, when he assumed that it meant 'a breach of international peace and applies to cases where hostilities are occurring, but where it is not alleged that one particular party is the aggressor or has committed an act of aggression'.[75] He advocated such a finding in relation to the conflict occurring in Indonesia.

The Dutch representative objected on the grounds that, 'what happened in Indonesia was not a breach of international peace but rather a breach of internal peace. Breaches of internal peace are and remain the exclusive responsibility of the Members of the United Nations on the territory of which those unfortunate occurrences take place'.[76]

A finding of a threat to the peace may have been more applicable if the situation was indeed a breach of internal peace. As will be seen later, a finding under Article 39 identifies the situation as an international, not merely domestic, matter and, as such, beyond the scope of Article 2(7). However, the Council did not make such a finding, neither at the beginning of the conflict nor at any stage throughout it, in order to gain Dutch consent to its resolutions. Council practice in the late 1940s had not evolved the wider concept of a threat to the peace, which in retrospect could have been applied to the Indonesian question.

There have been four findings of a breach of the peace in conflicts brought to the attention of the Council. The first concerned the conflict in Korea in 1950. On 25 June, the Council was rapidly convened at the request of the United States, after a substantial North Korean force had crossed the 38th parallel which had divided the country since the Japanese surrender to Soviet forces north of that line and to American forces south of it.[77] The Soviet Union had been absent from the Council since 30 January 1950 in protest of the failure to install the Chinese Communists in the permanent seat instead of the Nationalists. If the Soviet Union had been present any Council moves would probably have been vetoed, possibly on the grounds that the armed conflict in Korea was a civil war or war of national liberation involving only that country. However, the rest of the Council viewed the North Korean attack as a 'breach of the peace'.[78] The resolution referred to the 1949 General Assembly resolution (293) which recognised the government of the Republic of Korea based in South Korea, and so the Council was able to view the attack as akin to an armed attack by one State against another. Following this line of argument, it is probably correct to say that the North Korean attack was an 'act of aggression', a view taken by the United States.[79] The Council drew back from making a damning determination and opted for the more neutral concept of a 'breach of the peace' as being sufficient for it to proceed to take military enforcement action against North Korea.

It was not until 1982 that the Council made its next formal determination that international peace had been breached. On 3 April, after Argentina had invaded the Falklands, the British introduced resolution 502 which determined that there was a 'breach of the peace in the region of the Falkland Islands'. The resolution did not condemn Argentinean 'aggression' to ensure that it did not incur the veto of an otherwise indifferent Soviet Union. It then introduced certain provisional measures which although not complied with were, in the circumstances, probably the best that could be expected.

The third occasion upon which the Security Council determined that a breach of the peace existed was on 20 June 1987 when it unanimously adopted resolution 598. The breach was found in relation to the Gulf War between Iran and Iraq which had been continuing for seven years before the Council found that a clear case of inter-State conflict came within Article 39. This illustrates the political nature of such a finding because during those years the Council was unwilling to step into Chapter VII.

The Security Council acted with much greater alacrity when Iraq invaded Kuwait on 2 August 1990. Within hours the Council had convened and had adopted resolution 660 which condemned the Iraqi 'invasion' of Kuwait after determining that 'there exists a breach of international peace and security as regards the Iraqi invasion of Kuwait'. Again the more condemnatory term 'aggression' appeared more suitable to a clear violation of Article 2(4) within the terms of Article 3 of the Assembly's 1974 Definition of Aggression. Although some members of the Council condemned the Iraqi aggression, others seemed to hope that a more neutral determination, whilst giving the Security Council the option of taking further action under Chapter VII, would not make the Iraqis more intransigent, when in the days following the invasion there appeared to be the possibility of the Iraqis withdrawing voluntarily.[80]

'It would seem logical that any resort to armed force would come within the meaning of the phrase' 'breach of the peace'.[81] Even if the phrase is defined more narrowly as referring to international and not internal peace,[82] it appears, at the very least, incongruous, that a body established with primary responsibility for international peace and security has found a breach of the peace on only four occasions. The conflicts between Ethiopia and Somalia in 1977, Tanzania and Uganda between 1978 and 1979, India and Pakistan between 1947 and 1949, again in 1965 and 1971, Vietnam and Cambodia in 1978, China and the Soviet Union in 1969, India and China in 1962, the Arab–Israeli wars of 1948–49, 1956, 1967, 1973, the Israeli invasions of Lebanon in 1978 and 1982, the Soviet armed interventions in Hungary in 1956, Czechoslovakia in 1968 and Afghanistan in 1979, the United States' incursions into Guatemala in 1954, the Dominican Republic in 1965, Grenada in 1983 and Panama in 1989, are just some of the most obvious breaches of international peace in the sense of direct inter-State armed conflict, on which the Council failed to make a determination under Article 39, or, in some instances, did not even discuss the matter. Clearly many of these conflicts involved the superpowers and so any condemnation would have been vetoed. It was to be hoped that the end of the Cold War would have freed the Council to make such determinations and take action much more readily. However, it has failed to make such determination in relation to many post-Cold War inter-State uses of armed force (one example being the conflict which broke out between Ecuador and Peru in February 1995), with the exception of Iraq's invasion of Kuwait, perhaps indicating the Council's reservation of the phrase for serious breaches of inter-State peace which have international repercussions.

Act of aggression

As has been suggested above an act of aggression is a special form of a breach of the peace, in particular it labels or condemns one of the States involved in a conflict as the guilty party. There is also the possibility of individual as well as State responsibility attaching to an aggressor under customary international law as the Nuremberg trials of German leaders after the end of the Second World War showed.[83] Whilst it is not surprising that the term 'aggression' is used quite frequently in exchanges in the Council chamber, the body as a whole is unlikely to agree to use it on a regular basis. Although the Council is not adverse to acting as a quasi-judicial body on occasions, particularly after the ending of the Cold War, the potential consequences of a finding of aggression at the initial stages of a conflict, and the fact that such a determination will not encourage the accused State to withdraw, signify that there has been very limited Council practice on the term 'act of aggression'.

Indeed, before the adoption of a definition of aggression in 1974,[84] there had been no formal findings of aggression; since, there have been several against apartheid in South Africa[85] and Israel.[86] However, Western members' caution has only allowed findings of aggression against two friendly States, not the imposition of punitive or coercive measures. These States have eased their consciences, as well as deflecting international pressure to introduce sanctions against these countries, by allowing the occasional condemnatory but paper resolution to be adopted.

It is interesting to note that the condemnations so far do relate to quite limited *acts* of aggression, such as the Israeli bombing of the Palestine Liberation Organisation's headquarters in Tunis in 1985, and not to wider *wars* of aggression, in the form of full-scale attacks or invasions. Attempts have been made in the Security Council to make formal findings of aggression in relation to full-scale armed conflicts but none have succeeded. In 1967, during the Six Day War, the Soviet Union submitted a draft resolution condemning Israeli aggression and demanding the immediate withdrawal of Israeli troops from the Arab territories occupied by the Israelis.[87] This attempt to introduce a binding resolution under Chapter VII after an implied finding under Article 39 was too much for the pro-Israeli members of the Council. After much negotiation a consensus was reached on a recommendatory resolution, with no condemnatory overtones.[88]

During the drafting of the Charter at San Francisco, both Bolivia and the Philippines proposed to include a definition of aggression.[89] The Bolivian definition was similar to the Soviet proposal submitted to the Disarmament Conference in 1933,[90] in that it combined the enumeration of acts of aggression with a recognition of the Council's power to determine that other acts also constitute aggression.

At San Francisco, the committee concerned rejected the idea of a definition, stating that it would not be able to envisage or encompass new developments in warfare, besides which it might lead to the 'premature application of enforcement measures' through 'automatic Council action'.[91] Despite these objections the United Nations struggled for years to find an acceptable definition of aggression. When this finally happened on 14 December 1974 in the General Assembly, the formulation was similar to the Bolivian proposal.

The definition was a compromise between those States which favoured a generic definition and those which favoured an enumerative approach. The problem was resolved by the adoption of a mixed definition. Article 1 contains the generic definition: 'Aggression is the use of armed force against the sovereignty, territorial integrity or political independence of another State, or in any other manner inconsistent with the Charter of the United Nations'. This is similar to Article 2(4) of the Charter. Unlike Article 2(4), the definition makes it clear that for the purposes of a determination under Article 39 of aggression the Council is considering the use of armed force only.

Article 3 enumerates the acts that may qualify as aggression. Invasion, attack, bombardment, blockade and occupation are cases of direct aggression, whereas allowing territory to be used by another State to perpetrate aggression against a third State, and the sending of armed bands to carry out acts of force against another State are really cases of indirect aggression. The latter are additions to the already well settled cases of direct aggression, and meet, to a great extent, the objection made at San Francisco that a definition would not be able to encompass modern methods of warfare.

However, although the definition introduces indirect aggression, it has never been found in a Security Council resolution, for as Broms, chairman of the Special Committee on the Definition of Aggression, points out, 'the case of aggression must be exceptionally clear and reprehensible before the term aggression has a chance of being adopted by consensus'.[92] Cases of indirect aggression are more likely to be unclear, although guidance on the interpretation of Article 3(g) of the definition, which defines indirect aggression, can be found in the *Nicaragua* case.[93]

Articles 2 and 4 of the definition preserve the discretionary powers of the Council. Article 2 states that the 'first use of armed force by a State in contravention of the Charter shall constitute *prima facie* evidence of an act of aggression' although the Council, in the light of all the evidence, may decide otherwise. Article 4 further states that acts enumerated in Article 3 'are not exhaustive and the

Security Council may determine that other acts constitute aggression under the provisions of the Charter'.

Although the use of the term aggression in Council resolutions has increased since 1974, the definition has not resulted in a consistent application of the term. The findings are mainly motivated by selective, discretionary and political factors and so the fears expressed by some[94] that the definition would lead to a proliferation of unhelpful, condemnatory resolutions have not been realised. The loopholes provided in the definition by retaining a balance in favour of the discretion of the Council have proved sufficient to save the Council the embarrassment of making clear determinations of aggression when faced with them.

Although the Council may have appeared to be acting within the definition when it condemned South Africa and Israel, it is being somewhat selective because, irrespective of their treatment of blacks and Palestinians within their countries or territories under their occupation, they too were being subjected to armed force of an indirect nature which the Council ought to have examined to see if it amounted to indirect aggression. However, although formal findings of 'aggression' are sparse, the appearance in Council resolutions of terms which are used to define aggression in Article 3 of the definition have an increased significance since the 1974. When the Council condemned the Iraqi 'invasion' of Kuwait on 2 August 1990 in resolution 660, it was, in effect, determining that Iraq was the aggressor. Given this implicit determination, it can be argued that the Council should no longer be afraid of making formal declarations of aggression.

The relevance of Article 51

It has been stated by the Chairman of the Special Committee on the Definition of Aggression, that most members thought that in defining armed aggression they were also providing a definition of 'armed attack' in Article 51.[95] This view is reinforced by an examination of the French text of Article 51 which uses the term 'aggression armée'.[96] Article 51 is, alongside Article 2(4), one of the most important provisions concerning the use of force in international law. It states that '[n]othing in the present Charter shall impair the inherent right of individual or collective self-defence if an armed attack occurs against a Member of the United Nations, until the Security Council has taken measures necessary to maintain international peace and security. Measures taken by Members in the exercise of this right of self-defence shall be immediately reported to the Security Council ...'.[97] It is this provision which attempts to define the competence of the Security Council *vis-à-vis* the traditional right of self-defence and to a certain extent it parallels municipal systems which outlaw the use of force by members of that society except in limited self-defence, combined with a centralisation of coercive powers. It is quite clear that the Charter admits only two exceptions to the use of force in international law, first the right of self-defence in response to an armed aggression, and second the authorisation of the use of military measures by the Security

Council under Chapters VII and VIII of the Charter in response not only to aggression but to wider situations that threaten or breach international peace. It follows that it is important to determine the relationship between the two exceptions *in the case of an armed attack or armed aggression occurring against a State*.

The truncation of the Council's powers during the Cold War signified that there was no real or potential overlap between the two exceptions. The rivalry between the two superpowers led to a system of defensive alliances, whilst the collective security system was frozen. The military option was only used once in the Cold War period in response to an armed attack, in the case of the North Korean invasion of the South in 1950. This illustrates how close the two exceptions are on occasions in that the United States sent troops to the aid of the South immediately, an action obviously in collective self-defence although not stated as such.[98] This response was then transformed into a UN operation by the Security Council recommendation, in the absence of the Soviet Union, that States assist the South to resist the attack. Collective self-defence became collective security in this instance. The complications this caused will be looked at in chapter three.

The significant phrase in Article 51 in this context, is the requirement that the right of self-defence exists until the Security Council has taken 'measures necessary to maintain international peace and security'. Article 51 was inserted at a late stage at San Francisco in order that action in collective self-defence by regional organisations should not require Security Council authorisation under what was to become Article 53 of the Charter. However, the delegates were not prepared to allow a completely decentralised right of self-defence and so the phrase was inserted that would permit self-defence until the Security Council took over the role of combatting the aggression.[99]

The problem remained mainly theoretical during the Cold War and only surfaced in the Gulf Crisis which started with the Iraqi invasion and occupation of Kuwait in August 1990. In the Falklands conflict of 1982, the Argentineans did argue at one point that the United Kingdom was precluded from acting in self-defence following the adoption of Security Council resolution 502 on 3 April which contained a mandatory demand that Argentina withdraw from the islands.[100] The resolution was clearly based on Article 40 of the UN Charter, but it would appear unacceptable that a demand for compliance with a mandatory provisional measure has the effect of precluding a State from acting in self-defence, since such a resolution cannot by itself be a sufficient alternative to the victim State's right to meet and repulse the aggression. Although a resolution containing 'measures', it did not contain 'measures necessary' to restore international peace and security. It seems clear that 'measures' within the meaning of Article 51 must be either the authorisation of armed force or the imposition of mandatory sanctions (or both) by the Security Council. Furthermore, there are doubts about whether the imposition of sanctions by the Security Council can constitute measures that can be said to be 'necessary' to maintain, or more properly restore, international peace and security.[101]

Measures within the meaning of Article 51 must be those that can effectively replace the State's right of self-defence, that is they must stop the aggression and remove the aggressor from the victim State's territory. Whereas self-defence is generally restricted to a proportionate response to the armed attack, military action in pursuit of collective security objectives can extend further, possibly to remove the source of the aggression. This issue was raised both in the Korean War of 1950–53 and in the Gulf Crisis of 1990–91. A realistic interpretation of Article 51, and one that does not leave the victim State defenceless, is to say that only those measures that will be 'effective'[102] in removing the aggression can be said to *suspend* the right of self-defence. The right must revive if the measures prove ineffective for to argue otherwise would again leave a victim State defenceless and still occupied. In the absence of collective security machinery which acts effectively to combat aggression, the system must permit States to protect themselves. International law has advanced to the stage where the wider doctrine of self-help has been reduced to a quite limited right to self-defence. It would appear premature, even with the recent resurgence in effective activity at the UN, to limit that right even further.

The Charter, in Article 39, states that the Council 'shall … decide what measures shall be taken in accordance with Articles 41 and 42, to maintain international peace and security'. Articles 41 and 42 contain the express power to decide on economic measures and military measures respectively. Obviously if the Security Council undertakes military action to repel aggression then the right of self-defence is lost, unless the action proves ineffective. In this respect, the United Nations effectively replaced the right of self-defence on behalf of South Korea in 1950 and Kuwait in 1991 when it authorised the use of force against North Korea and Iraq.[103]

The major problem, which was highlighted for the first time during the Gulf Crisis of 1990–91, was the question whether the right of self-defence can be said to be suspended when the Council has taken 'measures' in the form of mandatory economic sanctions within the terms of Article 41, Chapter VII of the UN Charter. By resolution 661 of 6 August 1990, the Security Council imposed mandatory economic sanctions against Iraq with the aim of forcing Iraqi compliance with the terms of resolution 660, which had demanded Iraqi withdrawal from Kuwait. In other words the 'measures' were imposed to remove Iraq from Kuwait, which would have been the objective of an action in self-defence of Kuwait. However, the United States-led Coalition forces from Western and Arab States were gathering in the Gulf in August to act in collective self-defence of Saudi Arabia if the Iraqi expansion continued, and in collective self-defence of the occupied State of Kuwait, at the request of the rulers of those countries.[104] The two main Coalition States, the United States and the United Kingdom, argued that their right of defence was not curtailed by the adoption of a resolution imposing sanctions, in particular one that affirmed 'the inherent right of individual or collective self-defence, in response to an armed attack by Iraq against Kuwait, in accordance with Article 51'.[105] The other permanent members, although far less vociferous, seemed to insist that Article 51 signified that the right of self-defence was lost as long as the Council was purporting to deal with it under Article 41, and that the only way that armed force could be used against Iraq was for the Security Council to take the next step up its ladder of powers and authorise military action.[106] Eventually, the United States sought the authorisation of the Security Council for limited force to be used against vessels suspected of breaching the embargo against Iraq,[107] and eventually the use of full-scale force to evict the Iraqis from Kuwait.[108] However, in doing so, the United States seemed to imply that it was seeking authorisation in order to make the operations politically acceptable to the world community, not out of any legal requirement in the Charter. Both the United Kingdom and the United States thought the authorisations were unnecessary, they simply gave the operations an 'additional' legal basis.[109]

It is difficult to see an answer to these views, particularly in the light of the limited debate in the Council on such issues. The answer appears to depend to a great extent on the effectiveness or otherwise of sanctions in removing aggression. An empirical analysis of sanctions and their impact will be left until chapter three. If it is concluded that they are an effective alternative to military coercion in removing an aggressor then it is arguable that they are 'measures' within the meaning of Article 51 and the right of self-defence ceases. However, the *prima facie* evidence is not strong. It can be seen, without looking in detail, that sanctions are a blunt instrument, perhaps more suitable to addressing threats to the peace within countries rather than acts of aggression, in that they are directed at the aggressor State's economy which will only very slowly affect its military capacity to hold on to the victim State's territory. It then becomes a question of how long the world community is prepared to wait for the possible withdrawal of an aggressor whilst all the time the victim State is under military occupation. On the other hand to allow self-defence as well as sanctions might end in an even more devastating conflict. There is no simple solution, although it is a problem that will be returned to in the next chapter.

The domestic jurisdiction limitation

Article 2(7) of the Charter provides that '[n]othing contained in the present Charter shall authorise the United Nations to intervene in matters which are essentially within the domestic jurisdiction of any State or shall require the Members to submit such matters to settlement under the present Charter'; 'but this principle shall not prejudice the application of enforcement measures under Chapter VII'. The meaning of Article 2(7) is unclear. It has been argued that the limitation was intended to exclude all Security Council review, whether discussion or resolution, either under Chapter VI or by its recommendatory powers under Chapter VII when the situation it is faced with is essentially internal.[110] The provision expressly allows for enforcement measures which as has been discussed above would be economic and military measures under Articles 41 and 42 of the Charter.

An examination of the drafting process of the provision in Article 2(7) whereby enforcement action is expressly permitted, shows the delegates intended a wider exception. In the immediate aftermath of the Second World War and the atrocities committed against civilian populations by Germany, France had wanted to confine the domestic jurisdiction limitation further by proposing that it would apply 'unless the clear violation of essential liberties and human rights constitutes itself a threat capable of compromising peace'.[111] The problem was finding the correct words to express the view that 'it would be proper in the interests of peace and justice, and in the preservation of human rights to interfere in the internal affairs of Member States'.[112] The Australian amendment that the domestic jurisdiction principle 'shall not prejudice the application of enforcement measures under Chapter VII' was rather clumsy. It did not fully express the views of the delegates and has given rise to technical difficulties.

In practice, the Security Council has developed its own interpretation as to what constitutes intervention and domestic jurisdiction. Of course a finding under Article 39 accompanied by the application of enforcement measures under Article 41 or Article 42 is exempt by the terms of Article 2(7) itself. The Council has taken the next logical step by adopting the practice that any finding under Article 39, whether or not combined with enforcement measures, is sufficient to internationalise the situation and so escape the grasp of Article 2(7). In fact this probably does no more than the delegates at San Francisco had in mind for Article 2(7).

For example, it has been argued that if it is accepted that the UN Operation in the Congo (ONUC) was authorised pursuant to Article 40 (which is the non-enforcement provision of Chapter VII) it should have been subject to the domestic jurisdiction limitation.[113] It must be remembered that the Council eventually made a finding of a threat to the peace in relation to the situation within the Congo.[114] Resolution 169 referred to resolution 161 which contained the finding of a threat while authorising the Secretary General to take vigorous action including the requisite measure of force in order to 'apprehend all foreign troops and mercenaries'.[115] The resolution also declared that 'all secessionist activities against the Republic of the Congo are contrary to the *Loi Fondementale* and Security Council decisions' and specifically demanded 'that such activities which are now taking place in Katanga shall cease forthwith'. This certainly appears to be interference in the internal affairs of the Congo which is the sort of activity *prima facie* prohibited by Article 2(7). Certain members expressed reservations about setting a dangerous precedent for the future, by putting the United Nations 'at the beck and call of any State faced with a problem of a dissident minority within its own borders'.[116]

The International Court advised that ONUC was not an enforcement measure under Article 42,[117] which leaves open the question considered in chapter eight whether it came instead within the terms of Article 40. If Article 40 is the correct Charter base for ONUC, according to a literal reading of Article 2(7), the exception to the domestic jurisdiction limitation for enforcement measures is inapplicable. However, this ignores the fact that when a situation is designated a threat to the peace it is inevitably taken out of the domestic realm and put into the international sphere. Any action within Chapter VII, whether enforcement or not, is not limited by Article 2(7).

Furthermore, it is also true to say that the domestic jurisdiction limitation contained in Article 2(7) is circumvented not only by a finding of a threat to the peace, but also by the finding that the situation is one of 'international concern'. As Professor Higgins states, 'this doctrine of international concern has seen service in the guise of a potential threat to the peace'.[118] Thus a finding of a potential menace can be seen not only as a link between Chapters VI and VII, but also as a means by which the Council can utilise the provisions of Chapter VI and the power to ask for voluntary measures in the face of the provisions of Article 2(7).

Indeed, as early as 1946, the Council interpreted Article 2(7) as allowing it to establish a Commission of Investigation under Article 34 in order to report on aspects of the Greek civil war.[119] Further, in the Spanish question, the Security Council set up a sub-committee to investigate the situation in Spain.[120] These two early examples highlight the fact that an investigation to ascertain the facts and, in the latter, to make substantive recommendations, does not constitute examples of intervention. The sub-committee found the situation in Spain to be of 'international concern' and a 'potential menace to international peace'. It recommended action under Chapter VI in the form of a voluntary termination of diplomatic relations. Although no such resolution was adopted, the view that Article 2(7) was inapplicable in cases of international concern prevailed, the proposed resolution being vetoed by the Soviet Union on the different ground that the situation was a threat to the peace and should have been dealt with by mandatory measures.[121]

Another example of the Council using its recommendatory powers in a superficially domestic situation was as regards South Africa during the years of the apartheid regime. As has been stated, the Council did not find a general threat to the peace in relation to the system of apartheid in South Africa. However, it adopted many resolutions of a recommendatory nature including a call for selective voluntary measures[122] after 1985 witnessed killings in the townships, further political detentions, suppression of freedom and the declaration of a state of emergency. South African objections based on Article 2(7) proved fruitless,[123] because by characterising apartheid as a 'crime against humanity', the Council recognised the situation as one of sufficient international concern to warrant collective intervention using recommendatory measures.

Article 2(7) was a rather clumsy attempt to reconcile the doctrine of State sovereignty with the need to intervene in cases of international concern, which historically connotes the gross deprivation of human rights. However, it has been pointed out that the concepts of international concern and domestic jurisdiction are 'incapable of capture and crystallisation for all time. What is truly domestic today will not necessarily be so in five years' time'.[124] Human rights abuses certainly appear to be of international concern, but even with the ending of the Cold War, there is still a disinclination to intervene within States guilty of quite serious human rights abuses. Although the doctrine of State sovereignty has been relatively unaffected by the end of superpower rivalry, there is increasing evidence that the Security Council is more willing to intervene in situations traditionally seen as internal.

One of the first examples of this new found freedom occurred in the aftermath of the war between Iraq and the Coalition acting under Security Council authority. The rebellion by the Kurds in the north and the Shias in the south was put down with extreme brutality by the still powerful Iraqi army. As we have seen the Security Council adopted resolution 688 on 5 April 1991 which was not supported by five members, including China and India, on the grounds that it constituted interference in the internal affairs of Iraq. This was despite the fact that although the resolution found that the repression threatened international peace, it did not impose sanctions. However, the Security Council maintained sanctions against Iraq under the auspices of the permanent cease-fire resolution, 687 of 3 April, which provided for a review every sixty days of the continuance of most sanctions 'in the light of the policies and practices of the government of Iraq'.

The Kurdish issue suggested greater UN involvement in internal affairs, particularly when the Western troops sent to northern Iraq to protect the Kurds in April and May 1991 were replaced by UN guards. However, whereas the Iraqis did not consent to the Western troops they gave formal consent to the UN guards,[125] illustrating the UN's fundamental respect for the sovereignty of a State. The apparent exceptional nature of the Kurdish crisis was underlined in the special summit meeting of the Security Council on 31 January 1992 at which heads of State and government issued a general declaration on the future role of the Council. It was anticipated that the statement would contain mention of greater humanitarian intervention by the Security Council, but consensus requirements did not allow for this. Western members of the Council, in the individual speeches made references to human rights and democracy as being the bedrock of the international community, but other members, including Russia, concentrated on other areas, including disarmament. The Chinese Prime Minister made a pointed reference to the importance of the principle of non-intervention in the internal affairs of States.[126]

There were signs that after resolution 688 on Iraq, the Council would not make any further inroads into the internal affairs of States. Resolution 688 on Iraq can be contrasted with the refusal of the Council to even have a meeting over the strife in Haiti in September 1991 after the elected government in that country had been overthrown by a military dictatorship. The Ambassador of Haiti, a representative of the deposed government, had requested a meeting under Article 35 of the UN Charter. Members of the Council decided that it was an internal affair in which the Council should not become involved.[127] However, as has been seen, the Council did eventually designate the situation in Haiti to be a 'threat to the peace' in 1993 and went on to impose mandatory economic sanctions, and authorise the use of military force under Chapter VII of the Charter in 1994.

It appears that the Council, having made a giant leap in the case of Iraq, teetered on the brink of further encroachment into domestic issues with the danger that it might fall back into the traditional pitfall of respect for sovereignty. It is with the expansion of the concept of 'threat to the peace', reviewed above, into situations of starvation (Somalia), genocide and serious humanitarian crises (Rwanda, Burundi, and Zaire), and civil wars (Liberia and Angola), as well as its most controversial action to restore democracy (Haiti), that the Security Council has seriously eroded the effectiveness (in terms of protecting a State) of Article 2(7), despite lip-service paid to the principle of non-intervention in many of the resolutions,[128] or expressions of the 'uniqueness' of the situation being intervened in.[129] Agreement must be made with the statement by Ruth Gordon that:

The United Nations is, and will increasingly be called upon to intervene in many more internal conflicts, on a much broader scale and in a more proactive fashion than has been the case in the past. This reflects changed perceptions regarding such concepts as: domestic jurisdiction, which seems to have further shrunk; 'threat' to the peace, which appears to be an ever-broadening category; and the Mission of the Organization in internal conflicts … To such an extent that in the type of situations reviewed above and in new cases of wide-scale human rights abuses 'intervention by the Organization should no longer be objectionable on domestic jurisdiction grounds'.[130]

The Council's mandatory power

One of the major improvements on the League of Nations was the investment of the primary UN organ with mandatory powers. A resolution adopted in pursuance of these powers creates an international legal obligation on all members of the United Nations. Article 25 of the UN Charter provides that '[t]he Members of the United Nations agree to accept and carry out the decisions of the Security Council in accordance with the present Charter'.[131] Although the provision of mandatory powers is unusual, it is clearly a binding treaty obligation for those States that are members of the United Nations. Given that most States are members of the Organisation, a mandatory decision of the Security Council can have a wide ranging impact. Treaty law would *prima facie* prohibit treaty obligations extending to non-party States.[132] However, Article 2(6) of the Charter provides that '[t]he Organization shall ensure that States which are not Members of the United Nations act in accordance with these Principles so far as is necessary for the maintenance of international peace and security'.

It is possible to reconcile Article 2(6) of the Charter with general treaty law by concentrating on the Principles of the UN Charter in Article 2 which in particular contain the now customary provisions banning the use of force in international relations. A State violating these principles is not only in breach of its Charter obligations which may result in mandatory measures by the Security Council, but is also in breach of customary international law binding on all States.[133] All States therefore are under an obligation to refrain from recognising or assisting in the illegal act. In this respect non-member States of the UN are bound to follow the Security Council's decisions if they are concerned with enforcing the basic provisions of customary law concerning peace and security. The World Court recognised this in the *Namibia* case in 1971. In discussing the obligations imposed by Security Council resolution 276 of 1970 which terminated South Africa's mandate, declared the South African occupation of South West Africa/Namibia illegal, and called on 'all States' to refrain from any dealings with South Africa which were inconsistent with its illegal presence, the Court opined that although non-member States were not bound by virtue of Articles 24 and 25 of the Charter, 'the termination of the mandate and the declaration of the illegality of South Africa's presence in Namibia are opposable to all States in the sense of barring *erga omnes* the legality of a situation which is maintained in violation of international law'. Given that the resolution of the Security Council was furthering international law and it was adopted pursuant to the UN powers as supervisory authority over mandated territories as successor to the League, it was for non-member States 'to act in accordance with those decisions'.[134]

A similar approach can be taken to the mandatory sanctions imposed by the Security Council against Iraq following its invasion of Kuwait in resolution 661 on 6 August 1990. The resolution was legally binding on member States by virtue of Article 25 of the UN Charter. Non-members were obliged by customary international law not to recognise as legal the Iraqi invasion and subsequent annexation and not to take any action which would encourage the Iraqis in their illegal acts.[135] One could go further and argue that since Iraq's aggression was a breach of a customary obligation *erga omnes*, customary international law required all States to take measures to remove it, or at least to not take action which would undermine measures taken by other States and by the UN to remove it. This argument comes close to making Security Council resolutions binding on all States, which was certainly the *prima facie* purpose of resolution 661 which called upon 'all States, including States non-members of the United Nations, to act strictly in accordance with the provisions of the present resolution'. However, few States on the Security Council thought that this imposed a legal obligation on non-member States, others seemed to opine that it was simply an encouragement for those States to comply.[136] Customary law obliges non-members *not* to take measures that would encourage the illegal acts. If the circumstances so require, this may oblige the non-member State to take economic sanctions if they are necessary to fulfil this customary requirement, but these sanctions may be much more limited than those required by the Security Council. For instance in the case of Iraq, non-members were probably only obliged to take measures that would have ensured that there was no tacit recognition or encouragement of the Iraqi annexation such as not dealing with oil produced in Kuwait while under Iraqi occupation and not allowing Iraq to use any of Kuwait's assets overseas. Further measures, designed for wider purposes as may be set by the Security Council, would appear to be optional for non-members under international law.[137]

Furthermore, in the case of 'threats to the peace' within the meaning of Article 39, which are not always centred on violations of *erga omnes* customary obligations, the arguments for making mandatory resolutions of the Security Council binding on non-members is less strong. However, as has been seen above, threats to the peace have predominantly focused on violations of human rights norms often of a fundamental nature (for instance, genocide, grave breaches of humanitarian law, and the denial of self-determination).

Having looked at the external impact of the mandatory decisions of the Security Council, the exposition will now turn to the constitutional issue of the extent of those mandatory powers. The concern is with the issue of whether the Council's use of mandatory decisions is limited to Chapter VII. Article 25 itself is not found within the confines of Chapter VII but is located in Chapter V of the Charter containing the general powers of the Council, in particular Article 24(1) which confers on that body primary responsibility for the maintenance of international peace and security. Furthermore, a close reading of the specific powers of the Security Council will illustrate that although Chapter VI powers, concerning the pacific settlement of disputes, are mainly recommendatory, provision is made for 'decisions' in Article 37(2), while within Chapter VII we find provision for non-binding 'recommendations' in Article 39 amidst the more frequent provisions for binding 'decisions'.

Different factions of the Security Council have interpreted Article 25 in varying ways. The situation in Namibia highlighted the controversy over Article 25. During a Council debate on the situation, the British representative stated that 'as a matter of law, my Government considers the Security Council can only take decisions generally binding on Member States only when the Security Council has made a determination under Article 39', 'only in these circumstances are decisions binding under Article 25'.[138] In this statement he was disagreeing with the advisory opinion of the International Court of Justice on Namibia. The Court opined that Article 25 was not restricted in its application to Chapter VII since it was not located in Chapter VII, besides which Articles 48 and 49 of Chapter VII secured a binding effect for resolutions adopted under its auspices.[139] The Council resolution to which the British objected was resolution 269 of 12 August 1969 which 'decided' that the continued occupation of the Territory of Namibia by the South African authorities constituted an aggressive encroachment on the authority of the United Nations after reminding members of the content of Article 25. The resolution did not contain an express or implied determination under Article 39 in spite of the suggestion that the United Nations was in some way the object of some sort of aggression. An express determination would, for example, be 'an act of aggression within the meaning of Article 39'. An implied finding would merely refer to an 'act of aggression'. Similar language, for example, 'an aggressive encroachment' is not usually sufficient to constitute an implied finding. Nevertheless the resolution invoked Article 25. All the Western powers on the Council abstained on this resolution indicating that the collective view of the West is to equate Article 25 with Chapter VII. Nevertheless, the World Court in advocating an approach of careful scrutiny of Security Council resolutions to discover whether they are binding, opined that resolution 269 was 'adopted in conformity with the purposes and principles of the Charter and in accordance with its Article 24 and 25' making it binding on all members of the United Nations including those States either abstaining or voting against.[140]

The views of the United States were also enunciated in the initial Council dealings with Namibia after the termination of South Africa's mandate by the General Assembly.[141] Initially, the Council concerned itself with the essentially peripheral matter of the trials by the Pretoria government of members of the South West African People's Organisation (SWAPO). Although resolutions 245 and 246 originally contained references to Article 25,[142] these were deleted on the insistence of the United States, whose representative explained that 'among these changes is the omission of the reference to Article 25 of the Charter which we would have regarded as inappropriate for a resolution which was to be adopted under Chapter VI'.[143]

The Western view is probably based on the desire to provide a rough and ready, convenient and simple guide to the drafting of resolutions, which through constant reiteration by its adherents has taken on, for them, the status of international law.[144] Other States seem to adopt a more flexible position more in line with the World Court's approach. The former Soviet Union adopted this approach in 1973 during the debates of the Council on the Yom Kippur War. The East–West deadlock which had prevented the Council acting at the beginning of the war was overcome by the invitation of Secretary of State Kissinger to Moscow. The result was a resolution virtually forced through the Council by the superpowers which simply called on the parties to the conflict to 'terminate all military activity' no later than 12 hours after the adoption of the resolution, followed by the implementation of resolution 242 of 1967.[145] Non-compliance with the cease-fire resulted in another joint superpower sponsored resolution which confirmed the Council's 'decision' in the previous resolution and urged the combatants to 'return to the positions they occupied at the moment the cease-fire became effective'.[146] Although both resolutions had the appearance of being provisional measures under Article 40, an application of the Western view would mean that without a finding under Article 39, there can be no decision within the meaning of Article 25 and consequently the resolution can only be a recommendation adopted within the parameters of Chapter VI. The Soviet Union, while not actually citing Article 25, seemed to view both the resolutions as binding decisions,[147] although it must be pointed out that it was in the political interests of the Soviet Union to refer to 'decisions' in order to put pressure on Israel to comply because at the time the Arab States, favoured by the Soviet Union, were in retreat.

Higgins has pointed out that the British view of Article 25 would effectively re-title Chapters VI and VII as 'Recommendations for the settlement of disputes' and 'Decisions with respect to the breakdown of peace' respectively. She suggests that although this may provide a good working basis an equally good working basis would be 'achieved by looking to see whether a resolution was intended as a recommendation or a decision'.[148] If a resolution simply 'calls upon', 'urges' or generally is asking for voluntary cooperation or compliance then it is probably a recommendation, whereas in the Middle East crisis in 1973, the Council, particularly the sponsors, intended resolutions 338 and 339 to be binding without aggravating the situation by making a determination of a threat to or breach of the peace. Often political compromise will not allow a finding to be made under Article 39 of Chapter VII. However, this absence does not, on occasions, prevent the production of a resolution which is a binding decision. Similarly a recommendation can be made under Article 39. This is expressly provided for in that provision.

Nevertheless, Western States seem to have maintained their position and with their current dominance of the Council many recent resolutions bear the mark of their approach to Chapter VII. Many of the resolutions dealing with the Iraqi invasion of Kuwait, whilst referring to the initial resolution, 660, which determined that the invasion was a breach of international peace within the meaning of Article 39, then simply stated that the Council was 'acting under Chapter VII of the Charter'. While this meets the formal requirements of the Western approach, an examination of the contents of the resolutions reveals the development of the Council's powers beyond the literal meaning of Articles 39–42. Although as shall be seen in chapter three, the Council used its economic and military powers as well as demanding a withdrawal under Article 40, it also adopted resolutions 'under Chapter VII' which demanded that Iraq release third State nationals from Iraq and Kuwait,[149] demanded that Iraq comply with its obligations as regards foreign diplomats,[150] reminded Iraq of its international responsibility for its invasion and occupation,[151] condemned Iraq for its attempt to alter the demographic composition of Kuwait,[152] as well as imposing far reaching cease-fire conditions upon Iraq after the war ended in April 1991.[153] There are many other examples of actions taken by the Security Council under Chapter VII which are not readily reconcilable with the provisions contained therein – the establishment of International Criminal Tribunals in the former Yugoslavia in 1993 and in Rwanda in 1994[154] reviewed in chapter three are good examples.

The Western insistence that only Chapter VII resolutions are binding has resulted in an artificial approach to the Charter.[155] The resolutions listed above are really examples of the Council's general powers to maintain and restore international peace and security derived from Article 24 which are clearly intended to be binding by Article 25. The Western States may have been advised to use the Council's general mandatory powers as identified by the World Court in the *Namibia* case rather than attempting to squeeze the resolutions into Chapter VII.

The extent of the Council's power

As has been seen when looking at the Council's development of the concept of a 'threat to the peace', the practice of that organ is hugely important in examining the meaning of a particular provision. Subsequent practice is a valid method of interpreting treaty provisions,[156] particularly so in the case of constituent treaties of international organisations, which are living instruments and are subject to natural, dynamic development.[157] The importance of this will become clearer when the powers and practice of the Security Council are examined in chapter three. In this section, the inquiry is simply the identification of the extent of the power of the Security Council, and, in the following brief section, whether any limitations upon its power are practical or theoretical ones. In addition to considering the ambit of the Council's powers, these final sections will also contain discussion of the extent of the Assembly's powers, since in many of the cases looked at the issues involved both organs. The implications of these deliberations for the Assembly will be picked up again in Part Two.

It appears to be accepted in the practice of the UN and in decisions of the principal judicial organ of the UN, the International Court of Justice, that the political organs of the UN have implied, as well as express, powers. Early in the life of the United Nations, the World Court accepted such a doctrine in the *Reparation* case when it stated:

The Court must therefore begin by inquiring whether the provisions of the Charter concerning the functions of the Organization, and the part played by its agents in the performance of those functions, imply for the Organization power to afford its agents the limited protection that would consist in the bringing of a claim on their behalf for reparation for damage suffered in such circumstances. Under international law, the Organization must be deemed to have those powers which, though not expressly provided in the Charter, are conferred upon it by necessary implication as being essential to the performance of its duties.[158]

The Court deemed that it was necessary for the UN to be able to bring a claim on behalf of its employees, though it did not state from which express (sometimes called 'delegated') power this implied power derived. It appeared to be derived more from the general nature and purposes of the UN as a body aimed at securing international peace and security, an aim requiring the extensive use of personnel in dangerous situations.[159] Judge Hackworth, in his dissenting opinion, pointed to the problem with the Court's approach:

There can be no gainsaying the fact that the Organization is one of delegated and enumerated powers. It is to be presumed that such powers as the Member States desired to confer upon it are stated either in the Charter or in complementary agreements concluded by them. Powers not expressed cannot freely be implied. Implied powers flow from a grant of expressed powers, and are limited to those that are 'necessary' to the exercise of powers expressly granted. No necessity for the exercise of power here in question has been shown to exist. There is no impelling reason, if any at all, why the Organization should become the sponsor of claims on behalf of its employees.[160]

The difference in the approach of the majority and Judge Hackworth embodies the doctrinal confusion of what exactly is meant by implied powers. The approach inevitably adopted by the UN in interpreting its treaties is to imply powers not only from the express powers of the Charter, but also from its purposes and principles outlined[161] in the Preamble and in Articles 1 and 2, and furthermore, the requirement of 'necessity' seems to have been liberally interpreted both by the Security Council (and as shall be seen in Part Two, the General Assembly), and by the World Court.

The International Court of Justice has adopted a very generous view of the doctrine of implied powers, not only in the *Reparation* case but in the *Expenses* and *Namibia* cases. In the latter case, the International Court found that the General Assembly's termination of South Africa's mandate[162] was within its competence. It pointed to no specific Charter provisions but made the more general proposition that 'the United Nations as a successor to the League, acting through its competent organs, must be seen above all as the supervisory institution, competent to pronounce, in that capacity, on the conduct of the mandatory with respect to its international obligation, and competent to act accordingly'. The action of the Assembly in terminating the mandate was viewed by the Court 'as the exercise of the right to terminate a relationship in the case of a deliberate and persistent violation of obligations which destroys the very object and purpose of that relationship', in accordance with the general principles of international law governing termination of a treaty relationship for breach.[163]

As to the legal basis of Security Council resolution 276, which affirmed the Assembly's 'decision' to terminate South Africa's mandate over Namibia and declared that the continued presence of South Africa was illegal and therefore all actions taken by the South African authorities in Namibia were illegal and invalid, the Court stated that:

Article 24 of the Charter vests in the Security Council the necessary authority to take action such as that taken in the present case. The reference in paragraph 2 of this Article to specific powers of the Security Council under certain chapters of the Charter does not exclude the existence of general powers to discharge the responsibilities conferred in paragraph 1. Reference may be made in this respect to the Secretary General's Statement, presented to the Security Council on 10 January 1947, to the effect that 'the powers of the Council under Article 24 are not restricted to the specific grants of authority contained in Chapters VI, VII, VIII and XII ... [T]he Members of the United Nations have conferred upon the Security Council powers commensurate with its responsibility for the maintenance of peace and security. The only limitations are the fundamental principles and purposes found in Chapter I of the Charter'.[164]

The Court's approach is liberal and functionalist 'so that powers *relating* to the purposes and functions specified in the constitution can be implied', rather than narrow and formalist whereby 'one can imply only such powers as arise by necessary intendment from the constitutional provisions'.[165]

Such a liberal approach is exemplified in the *Expenses* case when the Court did not stop to consider whether the development of a power to create and mandate peacekeeping forces by the General Assembly was *necessary* for the fulfilment of the express provisions of the Charter.[166] On the issue of the General Assembly's power, the Court stated that 'the provisions of the Charter which distribute functions and powers to the Security Council and to the General Assembly give no support to the view that such distribution excludes from the powers of the General Assembly the power' to adopt measures designed to maintain peace and security. The emphasis is not on the implication of powers necessary to make an express provision effective as in the *Reparation* case, but on the absence of any provision in the Charter prohibiting the exercise of such a power. The only limitation on the powers of the General Assembly in the field of peace and security is that, according to the Court, only the Security Council can 'order coercive action'.[167] In effect, the General Assembly's powers are only limited by provisions in the Charter which clearly prohibit such acts, in the case the restriction was that only the Security Council could order enforcement action under Chapter VII. Furthermore, in discussing the creation of the Congo force (ONUC) by the Security Council, the Court did not feel it necessary to identify the provisions of the Charter from which peacekeeping could be derived, it simply stated that 'the Charter does not forbid the Security Council to act through instruments of its own choice', and that ONUC was not a 'preventive or enforcement' action under Chapter VII and therefore did not come within the sole ambit of the Security Council but could be mandated by the General Assembly.[168]

The Court certainly seemed to accept the British view on the creation of the United Nations Emergency Force (UNEF), contained in a Minister's response in the House of Commons to the question of which article of the Charter had the Force been created under. The response was in terms of UNEF not being created under any express provisions, but under a resolution of the General Assembly which was not prohibited by the Charter. The narrow view of the Soviet Union that the only express mention made of the creation of any type of armed forces in the Charter was in Chapter VII, where only the Security Council was authorised to act, was rejected.[169] With the emphasis on UN organs having the power to undertake any action within the UN's purposes as long as the Charter does not expressly prohibit it, the Court, in many ways, seemed to have moved away from the doctrine of implied powers to that of inherent powers as argued for by Professor Seyersted.

Indeed, it appears that while intergovernmental organizations, unlike States, are restricted by specific provisions in their constitutions as to the aims for which they shall work, such Organizations are, like States, in principle free to perform any sovereign act, or any act under international law, which they are in a factual position to perform to attain these aims, provided that their constitutions do not preclude such acts. While a minority of the members will always have the right to challenge the legality, from an internal point of view, of acts performed to attain aims other than those defined in the constitution, the minority cannot challenge acts performed in order to attain aims covered in the constitution merely on the basis that such acts were not 'essential' or 'necessary' to attain these aims. Thus it is

not necessary to look for specific provisions in the constitution, or to resort to strained interpretations of texts and intentions, or to look for precedents or constructions to justify
legally the performance by an intergovernmental organisation of a sovereign or international act not specifically authorized in its constitution. As an intergovernmental organization it has an *inherent power* to perform such acts.[170]

From Seyersted's view of the personality and powers of international organisations, it follows from this that 'they have an inherent capacity (not implied in any
particular articles of their constitution) to perform any sovereign or international
act which they are in a practical position to perform and which is not precluded by
any provisions of their constitution. Their position thus differs from states in fact
rather than in law'.[171]

Judicial review

Having established that despite the justificatory terminology of 'implied powers'
being used by the World Court, the real extent of the Council's competence is its
'inherent powers'. The doctrine of inherent powers has two advantages over other
approaches. First, it satisfies the functionalist agenda by allowing the United
Nations to fulfil its aims and not be hidebound by the legal niceties of its individual, and often obscurely drafted, compromise provisions; and secondly it enables
Courts and commentators to review the actions of the Organisation quickly and
accurately since there are only two real legal controls on the actions of the Organisation – that the action in question aims to achieve one of the purposes of the
Organisation, and that it is not expressly prohibited by any of the provisions of the
constitution. Only if either of these legal thresholds is crossed can an international
court, jurist or member State, claim that the action is *ultra vires*.

The issue to be discussed here is whether the doctrine of *ultra vires* is a practical limitation on the activities of the UN – in particular the now active Security
Council (though several of the cases examined here look at the same issue as
regards the General Assembly). In recent years this has raised the issue of whether
the International Court has the power of judicial review.

The problem is there is no established procedure in the UN Charter or in the
Statute of the International Court for decisions of the organs of the UN to be
reviewed by the Court. The International Court may be given an opportunity to
comment on the legality of UN resolutions either if so requested, directly or indirectly, in a non-binding, and therefore non-enforceable, advisory opinion in accordance with Article 65 of the International Court's Statute, or if the matter arises in
contentious proceedings between States under Article 36 of the Statute. Article 65
provides that 'the Court may give an advisory opinion on any legal question at the
request of whatever body may be authorised by or in accordance with the Charter
of the United Nations to make such a request'. All the principal organs of the UN,
excluding the Secretariat, have been authorised 'by or in accordance with the

Charter' to request advisory opinions as have most of the specialised agencies and a handful of other functional organisations. However, this mechanism is not used on a regular enough basis, and in particular is not so used to enable the World Court to review the legality of decisions taken by the UN or other authorised organisations. Furthermore, in the rare instances when the Court has the chance to act as a constitutional court, it has usually steered clear of declaring institutional acts as *ultra vires* and therefore illegal. Here, the main instances of this approach will be examined.

In the *Certain Expenses* case, after analysing the structure and powers of the two principal UN organs and finding that the General Assembly was indeed empowered to create and mandate peacekeeping forces, the Court then tested whether the expenditures were compatible with the purposes of the UN (as requested by the Assembly). The Court then summarised the broad purposes set out in Article 1 of the Charter and stated:

These purposes are wide indeed, but neither they nor the powers conferred to effectuate them are unlimited. Save as they have entrusted the Organization with the attainment of these common ends, the Member States retain their freedom of action. But when the Organization takes action which warrants the assertion that it was appropriate for the fulfilment of one of the stated purposes of the United Nations, the presumption is that such action is not *ultra vires* the Organization.[172]

It must be stressed that the Court is prepared only to *presume* that the action is *intra vires* and that it leaves itself the option of being able to declare future actions *ultra vires*, if given the opportunity. The difficulty is that it rarely has the opportunity, hence the presumption. It would make for a totally inefficient security system if every resolution of the Security Council or General Assembly had question marks as to its legality hanging over it. States wanting to deny their obligations to the UN would simply maintain opposition to the resolutions on the basis of their alleged illegality, as France and the Soviet Union had done over the expenses crisis, and very little could be done to prevent this. However, if the decisions are presumed to be lawful until declared otherwise, States are under an undeniable obligation to comply.

The Court points out that there is no established procedure for judicial review in the structure of the United Nations unlike 'in the legal systems of States' where 'there is often some procedure for determining the legality of ... a legislative or governmental act'. The fact that there is an absence of judicial review procedure in some municipal legal systems with their much more efficient centralised powers, strengthens the contention that it is unnecessarily legalistic and perhaps detrimental to expect such a procedure in an underdeveloped, quasi-centralised, international system. Such a procedure may be put in place once an efficient supranational structure is established as in the European Communities. On occasions, though, in advisory opinions, the Court may have the opportunity to comment on the constitutionality of UN actions.[173]

It must be stressed, however, that in the *Expenses* case, the World Court was prepared to examine the legality of the General Assembly's action in terms of its competence under the UN Charter; it did not abdicate its responsibility as the judicial organ of the UN in deference to the political power of the Assembly. However, what it did do, as has been seen above, was to adopt a very liberal attitude to Charter interpretation. In effect the approach was to assert its ability to examine the actions of the Assembly but to do so in a very lenient way with the end result that the General Assembly was found competent. Perhaps this lenient approach is an inevitable consequence of the presumption against *ultra vires*.

A similar attitude can be found in the World Court's judgment in the *Namibia* case, following the Security Council's request for an advisory opinion on the question of the legal consequences for States of the continued presence of South Africa in Namibia notwithstanding the adoption by the Security Council of resolution 276 of 1970. As has been seen, this request clearly raised vital constitutional issues, namely the power of the General Assembly to make decisions terminating mandates and the power of the Security Council to adopt a decision on illegality which is binding on member States in the absence of a determination of a threat to the peace or breach of the peace under Chapter VII of the Charter.

The World Court adopted a similar, somewhat contradictory, approach evidenced in the *Expenses* case, in that it stated first that 'a resolution of a properly constituted organ of the United Nations which is passed in accordance with that organ's rules of procedure, and is declared by the President to have been so passed, must be presumed to have been validly adopted'; and further that the Court 'does not possess powers of judicial review or appeal in respect of the decisions taken by the United Nations organs concerned';[174] but at the same time it did review the actions of the two organs and in so doing again adopted a very generous approach to the powers of the UN. As in the *Expenses* case, the opinion seemed to assume that the actions are lawful but proceeded to examine them with a view to justifying that assumption. The Court upheld the power of the General Assembly to terminate South Africa's mandate despite the fact that the Charter does not explicitly grant the Assembly powers to make binding decisions beyond budgetary and membership matters. In addition, the Court found that the Security Council's declaration of illegality and call to States not to have dealings with South Africa was a binding decision under Article 25 notwithstanding the approach of Western members that mandatory decisions could only be made under Chapter VII.[175]

Judges Gros and Fitzmaurice dissented in the *Namibia* case basically on the grounds that the organs of the UN lacked competence to act in the fashion that they did. Judge Fitzmaurice was at pains to state that the Court could and should have reviewed the actions of, *inter alia*, the Security Council and declared them *ultra vires* when he stated that 'limitations on the powers of the Security Council are necessary because of the all too great ease with which any acutely controversial international situation can be represented as involving a latent threat to peace and security, even where it is really too remote genuinely to constitute one. Without these limitations, the functions of the Security Council could be used for purposes never originally intended …'. Furthermore, he made it clear that he would be prepared to examine Security Council determinations of a 'threat to the peace' or 'breach of the peace' under Article 39 (although none were made in the case) to see if they were genuine for there was a very great danger of the Council 'artificially creat[ing a threat] as a pretext for the realisation of ulterior purpose'.[176] He was prepared to look behind the wording of UN resolutions at the motives of those voting for them whilst the majority appeared to accept the resolutions at their face value.[177] Only the two dissenting judges would have been prepared to determine whether there really existed a 'threat to the peace', and if none existed, they would have been prepared to declare the resolution *ultra vires*.

The very issue of the Court being prepared to exercise true review powers to see if there really was an abuse of power by the Security Council in determining that there existed a 'threat to the peace' arose in the *Lockerbie* cases of 1992. The cases arose out of the bomb explosion on board Pan Am flight 103 which caused the death of all those on board over Lockerbie in Scotland on 21 December 1988. Two Libyan nationals and State employees were indicted in the United States and charged in Scotland for planting the bomb. In a joint declaration on 27 November 1991, the United States and Britain requested that Libya surrender the suspects for trial.[178] Lack of a satisfactory response to this led to the two Western countries proposing what was to become resolution 731 of 21 January 1992, which urged Libya 'immediately to provide a full and effective response to those requests so as to contribute to the elimination of international terrorism'. This resolution did not appear to be mandatory, it certainly was not adopted under Chapter VII, but during the debates leading to its adoption, both Western States mentioned the adoption of further resolutions imposing sanctions if Libya failed to comply.[179]

It was this threat which led to Libya instituting proceedings before the International Court on the basis of Article 14(1) of the 1971 Montreal Convention, alleging that the United States and Britain had breached the 1971 Convention relying, *inter alia*, on Article 5(2) which obliges State parties to either try an alleged terrorist in their jurisdiction or extradite them to a State willing to exercise such jurisdiction. Libya asserted that it had submitted the case to the relevant Libyan authorities for the purpose of prosecution. Libya requested that the Court grant provisional measures enjoining the United States and the United Kingdom from taking action to compel or coerce Libya into surrendering the accused and to ensure that no steps be taken that would prejudice Libya's rights pending the outcome of the case.[180]

The Court heard the request for provisional[181] measures between 26 and 28 March. On 31 March 1992 the Security Council determined that 'the failure by the Libyan Government to demonstrate by concrete actions its renunciation of terrorism and in particular its continued failure to respond fully and effectively to the requests in resolution 731 (1992) constitute a threat to international peace and security', and acting under Chapter VII of the Charter, decided that Libya must comply with the extradition requests and renounce all forms of terrorism by 15 April 1992 or suffer sanctions. The Court delivered its opinion denying interim measures on 14 April and sanctions were imposed the next day.

The decision of the Court denying Libya's request for provisional measures was extremely short and lacked any real explanation.

Whereas both Libya and the United States, as Members of the United Nations, are obliged to accept and carry out the decisions of the Security Council in accordance with Article 25 of the Charter; whereas the Court, which is at the stage of proceedings on provisional measures, considers that prima facie this obligation extends to the decision contained in resolution 748 (1992); and whereas, in accordance with Article 103 of the Charter, the obligations of the parties in that respect prevail over their obligations under any other international agreement, including the Montreal Convention.[182]

Decisions of the Security Council under Chapter VII appear to be in general beyond the purview of any review by the Court, at least at the provisional measures stage, because they are binding obligations which prevail over any other treaty commitment. The Court is certainly not willing to look behind the motives of the sponsors of resolution 748 in order to determine whether there really existed a threat to the peace from an incident that has occurred over three years previously.[183]

However, the case still leaves open the possibility of review at the merits stage,[184] as does the 1993 application by the Bosnian government for provisional measures in order to halt the acts of genocide allegedly being committed by Serbia and Montenegro, in which the Bosnian government argued that the Security Council's mandatory arms embargo against the whole of Yugoslavia imposed in resolution 713 of 1991, after the Council had determined that the situation in the former Yugoslavia constituted a threat to the peace, prevented it from defending itself from the commission of these acts of genocide.[185] Only *ad hoc* Judge Lauterpacht thought that, although the Court had no power to review Council determinations of threats to the peace, since there was a conflict between members' obligations under Article 25 of the Charter and a norm of *jus cogens* (that prohibiting genocide), the latter obligations prevailed and that resolution 713, being contrary to an established rule of *jus cogens*, might be legally null and void.[186]

The separate and dissenting judgments in the *Lockerbie* cases again provide more fertile ground for those seeking some sign of judicial willingness to question the activities of the Security Council. Judge Lachs refers to the Court as 'the guardian of legality for the international community as a whole, both within and without the United Nations',[187] though this is certainly not precise enough to be interpreted as promising judicial review in the future. Judge Shahabuddeen simply asks a series of questions on this issue:

whether a decision of the Security Council may override the legal rights of States, and if so, whether there are any limitations on the power of the Council to characterize a situation as one justifying the making of a decision entailing such consequences? Are there any limits to the Council's powers of appreciation? Is the equilibrium of forces underpinning the structure of the United Nations within the evolving international order, is there any conceivable point beyond which a legal issue may properly arise as to the competence of the Security Council to produce such overriding results? If there are any limits, what are those limits and what body, if other than the Security Council, is competent to say what those limits are?[188]

Although seeing these as important issues to be discussed the judge is unsure as to how far the Court can enter into the debate. Judge Bedjaoui, on the other hand, appears adamant that the Court should be able to review the acts of the Security Council, not simply to determine their legal effects, but to assess their very legal core, namely their compatibility with the UN Charter. Referring to Article 24 of the Charter, which by reference to Article 1(1) provides that the Security Council must take measures 'in conformity with principles of justice and international law', he cites Judge Fitzmaurice in the *Namibia* case to the effect that the Security Council is as much a subject of international law as any member State, although he also seemed to recognise that generally the Court should not be used as a Court of Appeal from Security Council decisions, unless the Security Council was attempting to subvert the integrity of the Court. Further he seemed to accept the presumption that Security Council resolutions were valid unless the resolution was an attempt to deprive the Court of its jurisdiction.[189] Judge Weeramantry agreed that the Court was not vested with 'review or appellate jurisdiction', but when issues involving the interpretation of the Charter come before the Court it 'acts as guardian of the Charter and international law for, in the international arena, there is no higher body charged with judicial functions and the determination of questions of interpretation and application of international law'. However, this guardianship does not go to questioning the discretion of the Security Council under Article 39 of the Charter to determine that a 'threat to the peace' exists.[190]

As with its previous decisions there appears to be an undercurrent in the Court in favour of seizing the rare opportunities for enhancing review of the legality of UN actions, but on balance this is a minority view, and in many respects those judges advocating it do not present very coherent or logical arguments in trying to balance assertions of the Court's 'guardianship' of the Charter against respect for the Security Council's freedom to act in the field of peace and security. Very few judges are prepared to question the competence of the Security Council in the area which has most impact on States, namely determinations under Article 39 which may lead to enforcement action under Chapter VII. Without that power, the World Court cannot be seen as a constitutional court in the true sense.[191]

However, it has been seen that the Court is prepared to comment on the competence of the Security Council and General Assembly in other matters raised, in particular, in advisory opinions examined in the preceding section. It acts as a limited check on unlawful expansionism by the Security Council, along with other international tribunals which may have the chance of pronouncing on the legality of Security Council actions.[192] Furthermore, 'judicial review often does not arrive' in legal systems 'fully formed, heralded and portentous; aspects of review are more likely to emerge incrementally, unannounced and, sometimes, unnoticed', so that while it is accurate to state that the World Court is not currently a constitutional court, it is inaccurate to state that it will never be one.[193]

Notes

1 J. Arntz, *Der Begriff der Friendensbedrohung in Satzung und Praxis der Vereinten Nationen*, (1975).

2 H. Kelsen, *The Law of the United Nations*, 727 (1951).

3 R. Higgins, *The Development of International Law through the Political Organs of the United Nations*, 266 (1963).

4 See dissenting opinion of Judge Weeramantry, *Case Concerning Questions of Interpretation and Application of the 1971 Montreal Convention arising from the Aerial Incident at Lockerbie (Libyan Arab Jamahiriya v USA)*, hereinafter referred to as the *Lockerbie* case (provisional measures) I.C.J. Rep. 1992, 114 at 163–81. The Court delivered an almost identical judgment in the Libyan case against the UK, I.C.J. *Rep.* 1992, 3.

5 J. P. Cot and A. Pellet (eds), *La Charte des Nations Unies*, 655, 2nd ed. (1991).

6 SC Res. 232, 21 UN SCOR Resolutions 7 (1966).

7 SC Res. 418, 32 UN SCOR Resolutions 5 (1977).

8 SC Res. 221, 21 UN SCOR Resolutions 5 (1966).

9 J. C. Nkala, *The United Nations, International Law and the Rhodesian Independence Crisis*, 77–90 (1985).

10 See for example, UN doc. S/18785 (1987), vetoed on 9 April 1987; see SC 2747 mtg, 42 UN SCOR (1987).

11 SC Res. 161, 16 UN SCOR Resolutions 2 (1961).

12 GA Res. 1514, 15 UN GAOR Supp. (No. 16) 66 (1960).

13 SC Res. 312, 27 UN SCOR Resolutions 10 (1972).

14 See SC 1639 mtg, 27 UN SCOR 14 (1972), India.

15 SC Res. 688, 46 UN SCOR Resolutions 31 (1991).

16 SC Res. 733, 47 UN SCOR Resolutions 55 (1992).

17 UNCIO, vol. 3, 13.

18 R. B. Russell and J. E. Muther, *A History of the United Nations Charter*, 669–70 (1958).

19 SC Res. 4, 1 UN SCOR Resolutions 8 (1946).

20 Report of the Sub-Committee on the Spanish Question, 1 UN SCOR Special Supp. (No. 2) 4–5 (1946).

21 SC Res. 181, 18 UN SCOR Resolutions 7 (1963).

22 GA Res. 2054, 20 UN GAOR Supp. (No. 14) 26 (1965).

23 SC Res. 282, 25 UN SCOR Resolutions 12 (1970).

24 UN doc. S/9882 (1970).

25 SC 1549 mtg, 25 UN SCOR 3 (1970).

26 But see R. Gordon, 'United Nations Intervention in Internal Conflicts: Iraq, Somalia

and Beyond', 15 *Michigan Journal of International Law* (1994), 519 at 563–8.

27 UN doc. S/6928 (1965).

28 UN doc. S/6929 (1965).

29 H. Strack, *Sanctions: The Case of Rhodesia*, 23–36 (1978).

30 GA Res. 1889, 18 UN GAOR Supp. (No. 15) 46 (1963).

31 SC 1265 mtg, 20 UN SCOR 15, 6, 16 (1965).

32 SC Res. 713, 46 UN SCOR Resolutions 42 (1991).

33 But see Gordon, 15 *Michigan Journal of International Law* (1994), 569.

34 SC Res. 822, 48 UN SCOR Resolutions (1993).

35 See further SC Res. 853, 874, 48 UN SCOR Resolutions (1993).

36 See R. Cryer, 'The Security Council and Article 39: A Threat to Coherence?', 1 *Journal of Armed Conflict Law* (1996), 161.

37 SC Res. 54, 3 UN SCOR Resolutions 22 (1948).

38 SC 1340 mtg, 21 UN SCOR 4 (1966).

39 SC Res. 556, 39 UN SCOR Resolutions 4 (1984).

40 UN doc. S/18087 (1986), vetoed at SC 2686 mtg, 41 UN SCOR (1986).

41 See SC Res. 567, 571, 574, 40 UN SCOR Resolutions 16–18 (1985).

42 SC Res. 161, 16 UN SCOR Resolutions 2 (1961).

43 SC Res. 353, 29 UN SCOR Resolutions 7 (1974).

44 UN doc. S/9394 (1969).

45 SC 1503 mtg, 24 UN SCOR 1 (1969).

46 See also SC Res. 794, 47 UN SCOR Resolutions 63 (1992), which 'determined that the magnitude of the human tragedy caused by the conflict in Somalia, further exacerbated by the obstacles being created to the distribution of humanitarian assistance, constitutes a threat to international peace and security'. See further SC Res. 814, 48 UN SCOR Resolutions (1993).

47 SC Res. 788, 47 UN SCOR Resolutions 99 (1992).

48 SC Res. 864, 48 UN SCOR Resolutions (1993).

49 B. Simma (ed.), *The Charter of the United Nations: A Commentary*, 611 (1994). See also A. C. Arend, 'The United Nations and the New World Order', 81 *Georgetown Law Journal* (1993), 491 at 529.

50 SC 2982 mtg, 46 UN SCOR (1991).

51 SC 3009 mtg, 46 UN SCOR (1991); SC 3039 mtg, 47 UN SCOR (1992). But see H. Freudenschuss, 'Article 39 of the UN Charter Re-visited: Threats to the Peace and the Recent Practice of the UN Security Council', 46 *Austrian Journal of Public International Law* (1993), 1 at 21–2.

52 SC Res. 949, 49 UN SCOR Resolutions (1994).

53 SC Res. 827, 48 UN SCOR Resolutions (1993).

54 SC Res. 929, 49 UN SCOR Resolutions (1994). See also SC Res. 1049, 51 UN S/PV (1996) re Burundi; SC Res. 1078, 51 UN S/PV (1996) re Zaire.

55 SC Res. 1053, 51 UN S/PV (1996).

56 SC Res. 635, 44 UN SCOR Resolutions (1989).

57 SC 3033 mtg, 47 UN SCOR (1992).

58 UKTS 10 (1974), Cmnd 5524.

59 SC 3063 mtg, 47 UN S/PV 72 (1992).

60 GA Res. 2625, 25 UN GAOR Supp. (No. 28) 121 (1970).

61 See the *Lockerbie* cases (provisional measures), I.C.J. *Rep*. 1992, 114, reviewed more

fully below.

62 SC Res. 1044, 51 UN S/PV (1996).

63 SC Res. 1054, 1070, 51 UN S/PV (1996).

64 SC Res. 841, 48 UN SCOR Resolutions (1993).

65 UN doc. S/26063 (1993).

66 SC Res. 873, 48 UN SCOR Resolutions (1993).

67 SC Res. 940, 49 UN SCOR Resolutions (1994). See also SC Res. 841, 48 UN SCOR Resolutions (1993).

68 SC 3413 mtg, 49 UN S/PV, Spain.

69 See Canada and Venezuela, SC 3238 mtg, 48 UN S/PV (1993) re SC Res. 841.

70 Freudenschuss, 46 *Austrian Journal of Public International Law* (1993), states at 27 that the Dominican Republic, most affected by the refugee problem, stated that it did not consider there to be a threat to the peace.

71 SC 3413 mtg, 49 UN S/PV, Russia and UK.

72 *Ibid.* See also Brazil and China.

73 Freudenschuss, 46 *Austrian Journal of Public International Law* (1993), 28; Cryer, 1 *Journal of Armed Conflict Law*, 185–6.

74 UN doc. S/23500 (1992).

75 SC 171 mtg, 2 UN SCOR (1947).

76 SC 417 mtg, 4 UN SCOR (1949).

77 SC 473 mtg, 5 UN SCOR (1950).

78 SC Res. 82, 5 UN SCOR Resolutions 4 (1950).

79 SC 473 mtg, 5 UN SCOR 3–7 (1950).

80 SC 2932 mtg, 45 UN SCOR (1990).

81 L. M. Goodrich, E. Hambro and P. S. Simons, *The Charter of the United Nations*, 296, 3rd ed. (1969).

82 Simma (ed.), *The Charter*, 609.

83 41 *A.J.I.L.* (1947), 172.

84 GA Res. 3314, 29 UN GAOR Supp. (No. 31) 142 (1974).

85 Three examples are: See SC Res. 387, 31 UN SCOR Resolutions 10 (1976) re Angola; SC Res. 466, 35 UN SCOR Resolutions 17 (1980) re Zambia; SC Res. 568, 40 UN SCOR Resolutions 20 (1985) re Botswana.

86 SC Res. 573, 40 UN SCOR Resolutions 23 (1985) re PLO base in Tunis; SC Res. 611, 43 UN SCOR Resolutions (1988), re assassination of Abu Jihad.

87 UN doc. S/7951/Rev. 2 (1967).

88 SC Res. 242, 22 UN SCOR Resolutions 8 (1967).

89 See UNCIO, vol. 3, docs 577–9, 535–42.

90 See 5 Records of the Conference for the Reduction and Limitation of Armaments, League of Nations publication, Ser. D, 535–42.

91 UNCIO, vol. 12, doc. 505.

92 B. Broms, 'The Definition of Aggression', 154 Recueil des Cours (1977), 299 at 378.

93 *Case Concerning Military and Paramilitary Activities in and Against Nicaragua*, I.C.J. *Rep.* 14 at 103–4.

94 For example, J. I. Garvey, 'The UN Definition of Aggression: Law and Illusion in the Context of Collective Security', 17 *Virginia Journal of International Law* (1977), 177 at 178.

95 Broms, 154 *Recueil des Cours* (1977), 370.

96 Cot and Pellet, *La Charte*, 772.

97 On the reporting requirement see D.W. Greig, 'Self-Defence and the Security Council: What does Article 51 Require?', 40 *I.C.L.Q.* (1991), 366 at 367, 387.

98 Statement by President Truman, 27 June 1950, *United States Policy in the Korean Crisis*, 18 (1950).

99 Russell and Muther, *History of the UN Charter*, 699–706. UNCIO, vol. 12, 687. But see E. V. Rostow, 'Until What? Enforcement Action or Collective Self-Defense?', 85 *A.J.I.L.* (1991), 506 at 510.

100 SC 2360 mtg, 37 UN SCOR (1982).

101 But see J. Quigley, 'The United States and the United Nations in the Persian Gulf War: New Order or Disorder?', 25 *Cornell International Law Journal* (1992), 1 at 41; Simma (ed.), *The Charter*, 677.

102 *Ibid.*, Sir Anthony Parsons, UK. T. Stein, 'Decentralized International Law Enforcement: The Changing Role of the State as Law Enforcement Agent', in J. Delbrück, *Allocation of Law Enforcement Authority in the International System*, 113 (1995).

103 But see Rostow, 85 *A.J.I.L.* (1991), 506–10; O. Schachter, 'United Nations Law in the Gulf Conflict', 85 *A.J.I.L.* (1991), 452 at 459–60.

104 UN docs S/21492, S/21501 (1990).

105 See for example, Prime Minister Thatcher's statement in the House of Commons, *Hansard*, H.C., 6th series, vol. 7, 737. For US position see SC 2937 mtg, 45 UN S/PV 33 (1990). See also Oppenheim's International Law, 9th ed. vol. 1, p. 423 n. 22 (1992); Schachter, 85 *A.J.I.L.* (1991), 458–9.

106 *The Independent*, 9 November 1990, USSR; *The Observer*, 11 November 1990, France and China. See also *The Independent*, 9 November 1990 for statement to this effect by the Secretary General.

107 SC Res. 665, 45 UN SCOR Resolutions 21 (1990).

108 SC Res. 678, 45 UN SCOR Resolutions 27 (1990).

109 SC 2938 mtg, 45 UN S/PV 26, 47 (1990).

110 D. R. Gilmour, 'The Meaning of Intervene Within Article 2(7) of the United Nations Charter' 16 *I.C.L.Q.* (1967), 330 at 349.

111 UNCIO, vol. 3, 386.

112 Report of the Conference held at San Francisco by the Rt Hon Peter Frazer, Chairman of the New Zealand delegation, NZ Dept of External Affairs publication, No. 11, 28.

113 N. T. Kasser, 'The Legal Limits on the Use of International Force through United Nations Practice', 35 *Revue Egyptienne de Droit International* (1979), 163 at 207.

114 SC Res. 161, 16 UN SCOR Resolutions 2 (1961).

115 SC Res. 169, 16 UN SCOR Resolutions 3 (1961).

116 SC 976 mtg, 16 UN SCOR para.15 (1961), UK.

117 *Certain Expenses of the United Nations Case*, I.C.J. Rep. 1962, 151.

118 Higgins, *The Development of International Law*, 77.

119 SC Res. 15, 1 UN SCOR Resolutions 8 (1946).

120 SC Res. 4, 1 UN SCOR Resolutions 8 (1946).

121 SC 47 mtg, 1 UN SCOR (1946).

122 SC Res. 569, 40 UN SCOR Resolutions 8 (1985).

123 See GA 401 plen. mtg, 7 UN GAOR 332 (1952).

124 Higgins, *The Development of International Law*, 61.

125 UN doc. S/22513 (1991).

126 SC 3046 mtg, 47 UN S/PV (1992).
127 SC 3011 mtg, 46 UN S/PV (1991).
128 See for example SC Res. 688 which reaffirmed the 'commitment of all Member States to the sovereignty, territorial integrity and political independence of Iraq'; see further representative of the U.S who stated that '[i]t is not the role or intention of the Security Council to interfere in the internal affairs of any country' – SC 2982 mtg, 46 UN SCOR (1991).
129 See for example SC Res. 841, 48 UN SCOR Resolutions (1993).
130 Gordon, 15 *Michigan Journal of International Law* (1994), 522.
131 For debate as to the meaning of the phrase 'in accordance with the present Charter', see Simma (ed.), *Charter*, 413–14.
132 Articles 34 and 35 of the Vienna Convention on the Law of Treaties 1969.
133 See further V. Gowlland-Debbas, 'Security Council Enforcement Action and Issues of State Responsibility', 43 *I.C.L.Q.* (1994), 55.
134 *Legal Consequences for States of the Continued Presence of South Africa in Namibia (South West Africa) Notwithstanding Security Council Resolution 276 (1970)*, I.C.J. Rep. 1971, 16 at para. 126.
135 SC Res. 662, 45 UN SCOR Resolutions 20 (1990), para. 2.
136 SC 2933 mtg, 45 UN S/PV (1990).
137 UN doc. S/21585 (1990). But see Simma (ed.), *Charter*, 414.
138 SC 1598 mtg, 26 UN SCOR 5 (1971). France expressed a similar view at 2.
139 *Namibia* case, I.C.J. *Rep.* 1971, 16 at para. 113.
140 *Ibid.*, paras 114–15.
141 GA Res. 2145, 21 UN GAOR Supp. (No. 16) 2 (1966).
142 SC Res. 245 and 246, 23 UN SCOR Resolutions 1–2 (1968).
143 SC 1397 mtg, 23 UN SCOR (1968).
144 R. Higgins, 'The Advisory Opinion on Namibia. Which UN Resolutions are Binding under Article 25 of the Charter?', 21 *I.C.L.Q.* (1972), 270 at 283.
145 SC Res. 338, 28 UN SCOR Resolutions 10 (1973).
146 SC Res. 339, 28 UN SCOR Resolutions 11 (1973).
147 SC 1751 mtg, 28 UN SCOR 8–10 (1973).
148 Higgins, 21 *I.C.L.Q.* (1972), 283.
149 SC Res. 664, 45 UN SCOR Resolutions 21 (1990).
150 SC Res. 667, 45 UN SCOR Resolutions 23 (1990).
151 SC Res. 674, 45 UN SCOR Resolutions 25 (1990).
152 SC Res. 677, 45 UN SCOR Resolutions 27 (1990).
153 SC Res. 687, 707, 715, 46 UN SCOR Resolutions 11, 22, 26 (1991).
154 SC Res. 827, 48 UN SCOR Resolutions (1993); SC Res. 955, 49 UN SCOR Resolutions (1994).
155 Simma (ed.), *Charter*, 410.
156 Article 31(3)(b) of the Vienna Convention on the Law of Treaties 1969.
157 See *(Second) Admission of a State to the United Nations*, I.C.J. *Rep.* 1950, 23 (Judge Azevedo) and 18 (Judge Alvarez).
158 *Reparation for Injuries Suffered in the Service of the United Nations*, I.C.J. *Rep.* 1949, 174 at 182.
159 But see M. Rama-Montaldo, 'International Legal Personality and the Implied Powers of International Organizations', 44 *B.Y.B.I.L.* (1970), 111 at 130–1.

160 I.C.J. *Rep.* 1949, 198.
161 D. W. Bowett, *The Law of International Institutions*, 337, 4th ed. (1982).
162 GA Res. 2145, 21 UN GAOR Supp. (No. 16) (1966).
163 I.C.J. Rep. 1971, 46–7, 49–50.
164 *Ibid.*, 52.
165 Bowett, *International Institutions*, 337–8.
166 *Ibid.*, 338.
167 *Certain Expenses of the United Nations*, I.C.J. *Rep.* 1962, 151 at 163–4.
168 *Ibid.*, 177.
169 F. Seyersted, *United Nations Forces*, 133–4 (1966).
170 *Ibid.*, 155.
171 Bowett, *International Institutions*, 338.
172 *Certain Expenses of the United Nations*, I.C.J. *Rep.* 1962, 151 at 168.
173 *Ibid.* See also separate opinion of Judge Spender, 197; dissenting opinion of Judge Bustamente, 304; and dissenting opinion of Judge Morelli, 217. See J. Crawford, 'The General Assembly, the International Court of Justice and Self-Determination', in V. Lowe and M. Fitzmaurice (eds), *Fifty Years of the International Court of Justice* (1996), 585 at 590; C. F. Amerasinghe, *Principles of the Institutional Law of International Organizations*, 178–9 (1996).
174 *Namibia* case, I.C.J. *Rep.* 1971, 16 at 21–2, 45. See further M. Bedjaoui, *The New World Order and the Security Council: Testing the Legality of its Acts*, 24–5 (1994).
175 *Ibid.*, 51–3.
176 *Ibid.*, 294.
177 G. P. McGinley, 'The ICJ's Decisions in the Lockerbie Cases', 22 *Georgia Journal of International and Comparative Law* (1992), 577 at 598.
178 *Lockerbie* case, *Libya* v *UK*, I.C.J. *Rep.* 1992, 3 at 11.
179 SC 3033 mtg, 47 UN SCOR (1992).
180 *Lockerbie* case, *Libya* v *UK*, I.C.J. *Rep.* 5–7.
181 See Article 41 of the ICJ Statute.
182 *Lockerbie* case, *Libya* v *US*, I.C.J. Rep. 1992, 114 at 126.
183 See dissenting opinion of Judge Bedjaoui, *ibid.*, 153.
184 *Lockerbie* case, *Libya* v *US*, 126–7. See further L. Caflisch, 'Is the International Court Entitled to Review Security Council Resolutions Adopted under Chapter VII of the United Nations Charter?', in N. Al-Nauimi and R. Meese (eds), *International Legal Issues Arising under the United Nations Decade of International Law* (1995), 633 at 660–1.
185 *Application of the Convention on the Prevention and Punishment of the Crime of Genocide, Provisional Measures, Order of 13 September 1993*, I.C.J. *Rep.* 1993, 325 at 332.
186 *Ibid.*, 439–42.
187 *Lockerbie* case, *Libya* v *US*, I.C.J. *Rep.* 1992, 138 (separate opinion).
188 *Ibid.*, 142 (separate opinion).
189 *Ibid.*, 143 (dissenting opinion).
190 *Ibid.*, 165–6, 176 (dissenting opinion). Judge Oda based his separate opinion on the fact that the Court could not challenge the Council's competence to determine a 'threat to the peace' and take action under Chapter VII, *ibid.*, 129.
191 But see T. M. Franck, 'The "Powers of Appreciation": Who is the Ultimate Guardian

of UN Legality?', 86 *A.J.I.L.* (1992) 519. For further discussion see: B. Graefrath, 'Leave to the Court What Belongs to the Court: The Libyan Case', 4 *European Journal of International Law* (1993), 184; E. McWhinney, 'The International Court as Emerging Constitutional Court and the Co-ordinate UN Institutions (Especially the Security Council): Implications of the Aerial Incident at Lockerbie', 30 *Canadian Yearbook of International Law* (1992), 261; M. W. Reisman, 'The Constitutional Crisis in the United Nations', 87 *American Journal of International Law* (1993), 83; G. Watson, 'Constitutionalism, Judicial Review, and the World Court', 34 *Harvard International Law Journal* (1993), 1; M. Koskenniemi, 'The Police in the Temple. Order, Justice and the United Nations: A Dialectical View', 6 *European Journal of International Law* (1995) 325; R. Kennedy, 'Libya v United States: The International Court of Justice and the Power of Judicial Review', 33 *Virginia Journal of International Law* (1993), 899; V. Gowlland-Debbas, 'The Relationship between the International Court of Justice and the Security Council in the Light of the Lockerbie Case', 88 *A.J.I.L.* (1994), 643.

192 See the Appeals Chamber of the International Tribunal for the Former Yugoslavia in the case of *The Prosecutor* v *Tadic*, IT-94-1-AR72, 2 October 1995.

193 J. E. Alvarez, 'Judging the Security Council', 90 *A.J.I.L.* (1996), 1 at 7 and 2–4.

CHAPTER THREE

Powers, practice and effectiveness
of the Security Council

Having examined the limitations on the competence of the Security Council, both in terms of politics and law, the examination will now turn to the development and use of the Council's powers, bearing in mind those limitations. As has been suggested in chapter two, there has been some blurring of the distinction between Chapters VI and VII and this will be reflected in the analysis below. Nevertheless, the basic structure of the Charter in terms of the Council's powers remains intact after fifty years of that body's practice. The array of powers available to the Security Council has been described in terms of 'une gradation d'intensité des pouvoirs',[1] culminating in the provisions of Chapter VII.

The development of the Charter provisions concerning collective measures was the main preoccupation of the sponsoring powers at San Francisco in their quest for collective security. As has been seen the contents of Chapter VII were not greatly questioned by the smaller powers. The only significant amendments to the Dumbarton Oaks proposals were the removal of the provision linking Chapter VI to Chapter VII; and to readily accept a Chinese proposal for the insertion of a provision enabling the Council to call for the adoption of provisional measures. The proposals regarding pacific settlement were to prove more novel and problematic both to the sponsoring powers and to the other delegates at San Francisco.

Chapter VI of the United Nations' Charter arose out of Chapter VIII A of the Dumbarton Oaks proposals. The latter had 'the doubtful distinction of being regarded as one of the most poorly drafted sections' which necessitated a multitude of amendments.[2] In fact the amendments probably created more confusion than the untouched proposals. The proposals were firmly based on the concept of the Security Council as a policing organisation. This was emphasised in the proposals by placing the Council's powers of investigation at the head of the section containing powers of pacific settlement.

The main action the Council could take under the proposals for pacific settlement was primarily to call on the parties to the dispute to settle it by the peaceful means enumerated in the third paragraph of Chapter VIII A. If the dispute continued the Council could then utilise its powers in paragraph 5 to 'recommend appro-

priate procedures or methods of adjustment' or move into the enforcement powers contained in section B by means of paragraph 1 of section B.

The original proposals did recognise a 'situation' as well as a 'dispute' but the
possible measures outlined above only applied to 'disputes'. The amendments to
the proposals extended to the Council powers to give it a somewhat quasi-judicial
or arbitral role. One of the amendments to this effect was to empower it to 'recommend appropriate procedures and methods of adjustment' to 'situations' as
well as 'disputes' in Article 36(1) of the Charter. Theoretically it is the Council
only which can recognise a 'situation likely to endanger the maintenance of international peace and security' in Article 34, for the obligation placed on members
to settle their disputes by peaceful means contained in Article 33 only applies to
'disputes'. This extends the Council's powers of determining the nature of events
that endanger peace and hence is an enhancement of its judicial powers. Practically, however, States will often refer situations as well as disputes to the Council
under Article 35, and although the Council could, by itself, determine jurisdiction
under Article 34, it rarely does so, nor has it attempted to distinguish between a
dispute and a situation.

Goodrich, Hambro and Simons summarise the major changes in the Dumbarton Oaks proposals for pacific settlement made at San Francisco. The proposals
were rearranged so as to 'give pride of place to the obligation of the parties to seek
a solution to their disputes by peaceful means'.[3] The primary emphasis of the
members' obligation to settle in Article 33(1) not only recognises that without
some cooperation by the parties to the dispute settlement will be hard to obtain, it
also illustrates the greater emphasis on the envisaged judicial role of the Council.
If the parties fail to settle out of the Council, they may be subject to settlement not
necessarily by the Council but with the (perhaps unwelcome) help of the Council;
a process broadened by the second major amendment of enabling the Council to
recommend 'terms' as well as 'procedures' for settlement embodied in Article
37(2). In fact, the addition of Articles 37 and 38 to the proposals were intended to
invest the Council with quasi-judicial powers. The confusion is created because
the change of emphasis from policeman to judge did not involve a wholesale revision of the Dumbarton Oaks proposals, instead the judicial provisions were tacked
on so that the fundamental role the Council should play in relation to international
disputes is unclear. Only an examination of the Council's practice will help us to
understand the role it has created for itself.

Supervision of the obligation to settle peacefully

Article 33(1) of the Charter imposes upon members an obligation to settle disputes 'the continuance of which' are 'likely to endanger the maintenance of international peace and security', by peaceful means. It lists some examples of
methods whereby this obligation could be fulfilled such as negotiation, mediation,
arbitration and resort to regional arrangements.[4] Article 33(2) states that, 'the

Security Council shall, when it deems necessary, call upon the parties to settle their disputes by such means' as contained in paragraph (1). Despite the inclusion of the word 'shall' instead of 'may', this provision does not purport to impose a mandatory obligation on the Council to enforce in some way the provisions of Article 33(1), for it only operates when the Council deems it necessary, which in theory should be when it has found the basic requirement of a danger to international peace and security. The Council's role under Article 33 is one of supervision of the obligation to settle placed on members.

The effective use of this power would not only act as a reminder to States of their duties under the Charter, but also as a warning of future Council action under the other provisions of Chapter VI or, if the States concerned continue to be in breach of their obligation, of the possibility of Council action under Chapter VII. A Presidential statement, made with the unanimous support of all the Council, is often preferable, for it can be made quickly and is illustrative of the mood of the Council towards a continuance of the conflict, or if the Council is purporting to take preventive measures, towards future breaches.

In 1982, with an Argentinian invasion of the Falklands imminent, the President of the Council made a statement on the same day that the Council was convened at the request of the United Kingdom.[5] It called upon Britain and Argentina 'to exercise the utmost restraint at this time and in particular to refrain from the use or threat of force in the region and to continue to search for a diplomatic solution'.[6] Although a balanced reminder, the statement was a warning to Argentina not to invade. The Argentinians needed a fair degree of international support if they were to maintain their hold on the islands, but the statement reflected unanimous Council opposition to invasion. The Argentinians misread the signs and carried out their threat to the almost unanimous condemnation of the Council.[7]

The Council then found a breach of the peace and demanded withdrawal,[8] which although not complied with, effectively put Argentina in the wrong, helped to isolate it internationally, and contributed to Argentina's defeat in that it tacitly supported the British stance in support of principles of international law, though not necessarily the use of force in defence of those principles.

During the Cold War, the use of Article 33(2) was sometimes the only measure available to the Council. In 1983, the United States' objection to any Security Council interference in the Central American region relaxed slightly with the introduction of the OAS supported Contadora group's peace efforts. This proved to be sufficient regionalisation to enable the United States to support resolution 530 which expressed the Council's concern at 'the danger of military confrontation between Honduras and Nicaragua'.[9] Although the resolution was similar to the previously vetoed draft resolution,[10] it put more emphasis on the efforts of the Contadora group and so represented a particular application of the Council supervising the obligation imposed by Article 33(1), namely of 'resort to regional agencies or arrangements'. It represented a minimum measures resolution aimed at securing the support of the United States.

Sometimes this attitude was taken to extremes, most notably during the horrific and prolonged Gulf War between Iran and Iraq. Although the initial Council call in 1980 to Iran and Iraq within the meaning of Article 33(2)[11] was supplemented by other recommendatory Chapter VI resolutions,[12] it took seven years of bloody conflict before the necessary consensus could be achieved to enable the Council to unanimously adopt resolution 598 on 20 July 1987 which contained a mandatory demand for a cease-fire within the terms of Chapter VII.

With the Cold War over it was hoped that such procrastination would cease. The obligation to settle disputes peacefully is primarily to be fulfilled before conflict breaks out, when there is a danger to the peace but not yet a breach of the peace.[13] To extend the Council's supervision of the obligation into the conflict stage would appear to be an abrogation of the Council's responsibility to deal with a breach of the peace, unless it is a prelude to more positive action. A recommendation that belligerents settle their disputes by peaceful means is going to be ignored. Such a call *before* the outbreak of hostilities could act as a warning to States not to use force, which may be particularly powerful with the current co-operation between the permanent members which may more readily indicate that the call will be followed by enforcement measures.

It may be hypothesised that such a veiled warning on 1 August 1990, when the talks between Iraq and Kuwait on oil quotas and disputed territory broke down and the Iraqis massed 100,000 troops and 300 tanks on the border between the two countries, might have indicated to Iraq the consequences of any invasion. Unfortunately, the Council only met after the invasion and immediately adopted resolution 660 within the terms of Articles 39 and 40. Interestingly the resolution also called upon Iraq and Kuwait 'to begin immediately intensive negotiations for the resolution of their differences and supports all efforts in this regard, and especially those of the League of Arab States'. This call would have had a greater impact if it had been made one day earlier. The Gulf Crisis revealed a new edge to the Council's resolve to combat aggression, but it did not reveal any great development in post-Cold War preventive diplomacy.

Although there has been a proliferation of Security Council calls for peaceful settlement of conflicts in the post-Cold War period, almost all of these have occurred during hostilities, or at best are made during lulls in the conflict,[14] or to remind the parties to carry out agreements purportedly settling the conflict.[15] Although the obligation to settle persists during hostilities,[16] the effectiveness of the Security Council resolution or Presidential statement[17] calling on the parties to fulfil that obligation is much reduced if it comes after the outbreak of hostilities.

Investigation

The Council's preventive function would be greatly increased if it was supplied with a constant update of information on potential conflict zones and if it met without relying on one of the disputants bringing the matter to the attention of the

Security Council under Article 35 of the UN Charter.[18] Alternatively the Secretary General could more readily use his powers under Article 99 of the Charter 'to bring to the attention of the Security Council any matter which in his opinion may threaten the maintenance of international peace and security'.

Investigatory bodies established by the Security Council to ascertain the facts of a dispute are relatively rare. The Charter basis for such bodies is to be located in a combination of Articles 34 and 29, although they are rarely cited in the enabling resolutions. Often the body's function will go beyond mere fact finding and enter the realm of good offices and peacekeeping. In this section an attempt will be made to keep the discussion centred on investigatory bodies, the true basis of which is Article 34. Good offices committees and peacekeeping bodies have different constitutional bases and are discussed later. Article 34 provides that 'the Security Council may investigate any dispute or any situation in order to determine whether the continuance of the dispute or situation is likely to endanger the maintenance of international peace and security'.

During the early years of Council practice, some confusion arose from the fact that this provision did not confer a general power of investigation on the Council. The power appears to be confined to ascertaining whether the dispute or situation came within the parameters of Chapter VI. Indeed, the sub-committee on the Spanish question established in 1946 was directed to ascertain whether the activities of the Franco regime constituted a situation within the meaning of Article 34 or Article 39.

However, very soon after, the Council showed its willingness to go beyond a strict interpretation of Article 34 when, in 1946, it established a Commission of Investigation to examine certain frontier incidents on the Greek borders.[19] The Commission not only ascertained the facts but made several wide ranging recommendations,[20] which were not adopted by the Council because of Soviet opposition.[21]

A method used to circumvent the superpower veto in the Cold War was by applying a procedural vote to the establishment of such a body. This was done in 1959 to establish a sub-committee to investigate a complaint by Laos despite the negative Soviet vote. The legality of this method is doubtful and it has not become an established feature in the practice of the Security Council.

Another problem as regards fact finding during the Cold War was that even in the areas beyond the superpowers' interests where Council investigation was possible, the body established to undertake the task was often faced with a *fait accompli*. After alleged attacks by Portuguese forces on the independent African States of Guinea in 1970 and Senegal in 1971, the Council established Special Missions to ascertain whether such attacks had occurred.[22] The Missions' report on Guinea led to the Council determining that the attack constituted a threat to the peace.[23] However, since the attacks were over, the Council could only condemn them, warn Portugal against further attacks, and demand that Portugal pay compensation to Guinea.

Often in these cases where the aggression was short-lived and the *status quo* had been re-established, the investigation's only purpose was to find the guilty party which proves virtually impossible in the case of mercenary aggression and difficult in the case of guerrilla activities. After a mercenary attack in 1977 aimed at overthrowing the government of Benin, a Special Mission could only report that the attackers worked for pecuniary motives and that the financiers could not be found.[24] This resulted in a general Council condemnation of mercenary aggression.[25]

Although there were other examples of fact finding during the Cold War, they can be characterised generally as being selective and often ineffectual,[26] although on other occasions they did form the basis of a later peaceful settlement or at least a stabilisation of the conflict with the assistance of a UN peacekeeping force.[27] As early as 1988, with superpower relations beginning to thaw, there was an indication of greater fact finding by the Security Council, when a mission was sent to Nicaragua,[28] and was a foretaste of the regional settlement process started by the Guatemala Accords of 1987, and culminating in the UN supervision of peaceful elections in Nicaragua in 1990.

Nevertheless, fact finding by the Security Council is not undertaken as a matter of course, it often relies on a patchwork of sources including established peacekeeping or observation teams, the Secretary General and his staff, and the occasional formal fact finding body mandated by a Security Council resolution. For instance in April 1996 the Security Council, while calling for a cease-fire in the Lebanon between Israel and Hezbollah, deplored the shelling of a UNIFIL base at Qana in Lebanon[29] which resulted in over 100 deaths (mainly civilians sheltering from the hostilities). No determination was made as to the extent of Israel's guilt in committing this atrocity, nor did the Council formally dispatch a commission of inquiry to undertake such a task. Instead the Secretary General sent his military adviser to investigate. Despite the military adviser's report stating that 'it is unlikely that gross technical and/or procedural errors led to the shelling of the United Nations compound',[30] no action was taken against Israel.

Whatever the source, fact finding can only be undertaken with the consent of the State or States involved in the dispute. The Security Council has not attempted to invoke a mandatory power to send a fact finding mission into a State, although it shall be seen that in the Gulf Crisis, after the conflict between Iraq and the Coalition forces ended in March 1991, Iraq was subjected to very intrusive missions. Although Iraq consented to them when it agreed to the permanent cease-fire in Security Council resolution 687 on 3 April 1991, it really had little choice given the threat of further military actions against it.

Without a mandatory power to order a State to accept a fact finding mission, and in view of the fact that the Gulf Crisis was exceptional in the sense that military action *preceded* the missions when normally they should be one of the first steps taken by the Council, fact finding is not going to be properly institutionalised. If all members of the Security Council accepted that it did have the power to oblige States to accept a fact finding mission by making it clear in the enabling resolution that it was a binding resolution under Articles 34 and 25, there does not appear to be any legal limitation on this power.[31] Article 34 itself is not restricted to recommendations, although if one accepts the Western view that it is only under Chapter VII that binding decisions can be made then such a power is not contained in the Charter.

As has been seen from the introduction to this chapter, the Security Council has an inherent quasi-judicial power, one that it has used sparingly for most of its life as the political pressures of the Cold War led to resolutions based on compromise rather than on judicial-type rulings. However, with the end of the Cold War the Council has increasingly used this power to condemn States for breaches of international law, rather akin to the General Assembly. Any basic judicial process would commence with a determination of the facts before moving on to the judicial decision,[32] yet in the Security Council, the facts are often not clarified, or if they are, the Council has already condemned.

Following disturbances in Jerusalem on 8 October 1990 which resulted in the deaths of several Arabs, the Security Council, on this occasion, unanimously condemned the acts of violence committed by the Israeli Security forces while calling on Israel to abide by the Fourth Geneva Convention Relative to the Protection of Civilian Persons in Time of War of 1949,[33] as well as supporting the Secretary General's decision to send a mission to examine the circumstances surrounding the events in Jerusalem and to report on ways to protect Palestinian civilians under Israeli occupation.[34] Not surprisingly Israel refused consent and was condemned for its intransigence by the Council.[35] Indeed, the judicial process seemed to be completely reversed when nearly one month after the shootings and the Council's condemnation of Israel, the Security Council watched an amateur video tape submitted as evidence that the shootings were unprovoked.[36] An even clearer instance of lack of proper fact finding by the Security Council, perhaps indicating that in the post-Cold War period investigation is sidelined to an even greater extent than before, is cited by Quigley:

In 1992, the Security Council's handling of a complaint that Libya planted a bomb on a commercial airliner raised sharply the adequacy of Security Council fact-finding. Without undertaking its own investigation, the Council imposed sanctions on Libya on the strength of information supplied by the United States and Britain.[37]

It is questionable whether this rather summary approach to justice will be improved as a result of a recent General Assembly resolution, supported by all member States, entitled the Declaration on Fact Finding by the United Nations in the Field of the Maintenance of Peace and Security, adopted without a vote on 17 January 1992, following a report of the Sixth Committee which in turn was based on work by the Special Committee on the Charter.[38] Although the resolution recognised 'that the ability of the United Nations to maintain international peace and security depends to a large extent on its acquiring detailed knowledge about the factual circumstances of any dispute or situation', and that the competent organs of the UN should endeavour to undertake fact finding activities that should be 'comprehensive, objective, impartial and timely', it still recognised that 'the sending of a United Nations fact finding mission to the territory of any State requires the prior consent of that State'. Although the Assembly encouraged States to adopt 'a policy of admitting ... fact finding missions to their territory', the UN's respect for the sovereignty of its members undermines the proper institutionalisation of fact finding, whether it be by the Security Council, the General Assembly, or the Secretary General.

The fact is that even when States consent to such missions, they are often too late to contribute to prevent a conflict breaking out, and if a conflict is already underway, they do little towards its peaceful settlement. The sending of a fact finding mission in May 1992 to the disputed enclave of Nagarno Karabach, which is in Azerbaijan but is claimed by Armenia, was endorsed by the Security Council months after the dispute, which had been a long running dispute between Soviet Republics, had become internationalised with the break-up of the Soviet Union in December 1991.[39] This tendency to establish fact finding missions late in the day has been put to better use in the case of the former Yugoslavia and Rwanda where in 1992[40] and 1994[41] respectively Commissions of Experts were dispatched to investigate violations of international humanitarian law in those countries as a prelude to the establishment of International Criminal Tribunals (reviewed below). Although an applaudable development, it is not one which increases the Council's preventive function.

The settlement of disputes

Article 36(1) of the Charter provides that 'the Security Council may, at any stage of a dispute of a nature referred to in Article 33 or of a situation of a like nature, recommend appropriate procedures or methods of adjustment'. Paragraph 2 of the Article directs the Council to 'take into consideration any procedures for the settlement of the dispute which have already been adopted by the parties'. This is a reversal of the procedure envisaged by Article 33 but it is also a recognition that the Security Council can recommend 'appropriate procedures or methods of adjustment' to 'situations' as well as 'disputes'.

The terms of Article 36 can be applied to a variety of situations in the absence of any statement in the resolution of its Charter base. Non-mandatory resolutions calling for a cease-fire and withdrawal of troops can be seen as 'appropriate procedures or methods of adjustment' as can recommendations of settlement. This latter power can also be derived from Article 37(2) which empowers the Council to recommend 'such terms of settlement as it may consider appropriate'. When the Council makes a recommendation for settlement it does not state which provision in the Charter it is using and so it must be assumed that, in practice, the Council's powers as regards settlement have been amalgamated. However, it could be said that Article 36 empowers the Security Council to establish the modalities for settlement or the framework within which a settlement process may be undertaken, whereas Article 37 enables it to recommend the terms of settlement directly.

Before examining the Council's use of these powers, it is worth mentioning the little utilised[42] but potentially wide power conferred on the Council by Article 38, which provides that the Council 'may, if all the parties to any dispute so request, make recommendations to the parties with a view to a pacific settlement of the dispute'. The dispute does not have to cross the threshold of being a danger to international peace and security. However, despite the fact that by means of this provision the Council could involve itself in any kind of dispute as a mediator or conciliator, at the parties' request, it has not been used in this way. During the Indonesian question, the Council appeared to have Article 38 in mind when it adopted resolution 31 on 21 August 1947, which resolved to tender the Council's 'good offices' in the form of a Committee of Three if the parties so requested. There can be little doubt, however, that the Indonesian situation was, at the very least, a danger to international peace and security, although the Council did not make such a determination, nor did it make one under Article 39.

Good offices

The phase of the Indonesian question which ended with a truce between the Netherlands and Indonesia with the signing of the Renville Agreement[43] in 1948 represented a relative early success for the Council in its role as a peacemaker. Resolution 27 of 1 August 1947 called for a cease-fire and called on the parties 'to settle their disputes by arbitration or by other peaceful means'.[44] The Council then began to build on the fragile cease-fire that ensued. Resolution 30 noted with satisfaction the steps taken by the parties to implement resolution 27, steps which included a Dutch statement that it intended to implement the Linggadjati Agreement.[45] It also noted the request by Indonesia for the creation of a commission of observers. On this last point the Council acted quickly by requesting, in the same resolution, that governments with consuls in Batavia jointly prepare reports on the state of the cease-fire for the Council. Then came the creation of the Committee of Three by resolution 31. The Council was creating the machinery to facilitate the reaching of an agreement; it did not, at this stage, recommend one itself, although its resolutions implicitly favoured the implementation of the Linggadjati Agreement. After clarifying the meaning of the earlier resolutions, the Council urged the Committee of Three (alternatively called the Committee of Good Offices) to help the parties reach an agreement.[46]

On 24 December 1947, the Committee of Good Offices addressed an informal message to the parties containing suggested terms for a truce agreement. The Renville Agreement between the Netherlands and Indonesia provided for an immediate cease-fire, the establishment of demilitarised zones, and the supervision of arrangements by the military assistants of the Committee of Good Offices.

It also contained principles governing negotiations towards a political settlement. The effectiveness of the Council depended, to a great extent, on the participation and cooperation in good faith of both parties to the dispute. The Dutch, although still denying the Council's jurisdiction, viewed use of the Council as the only viable means of achieving a peaceful solution.[47] Good offices resolutions do not work when the parties refuse to cooperate or give only token cooperation. This may be a truism, but it illustrates the inherent and unavoidable weakness of the Council in its pacification role as a whole.

Sometimes the parties to a dispute may appear willing to reach an agreement with the help of the United Nations. In the Cyprus question the two main disputants, Greece and Turkey, have consented, as has the Cypriot government, to the good offices of the Secretary General.[48] However, ever since the Secretary General commenced his task, the Turkish government has gone about consolidating its grip on the northern part of the island. 'Good offices' implies that the Secretary General should help the parties to reach an agreement. In the Cyprus case, it is the Secretary General who has, so far, made proposals for settlement. Several plans have failed. The disputants have so far displayed token, not genuine, consent to the settlement process.[49]

In 1964, the Security Council emplaced a peacekeeping force in Cyprus to stabilise the situation whilst encouraging the Secretary General in a good offices mission to seek a peaceful solution.[50] This was quite usual during the Cold War and as shall be seen when examining peacekeeping in Part Three of this book, it can lead to a stalling of the peace process as parties are reluctant to change the *status quo* for something that could possibly be worse. The increase in peacekeeping forces since 1988 has been remarkable as the UN penetrates areas of the world hitherto denied to it by superpower political and economic hegemony. This has led to a new approach to old disputes where peacekeeping and pacific settlement are combined, so that the State or States involved not only accept the peacekeeping force to maintain a cease-fire and if necessary supervise a withdrawal of foreign troops, but also accept a peace plan which may involve, if the situation is internal, the supervision of elections in that country. Such an approach has been successful in Namibia and Nicaragua for example.

However, in other situations or disputes the old approach has persisted with the Secretary General being urged to seek a solution to disputes or conflicts in which the UN may or may not have emplaced a peacekeeping force. For example, peacekeeping was not linked to peacemaking in the conflict between Iran and Iraq and was not linked to peacemaking in Yugoslavia. Iran and Iraq finally accepted the Security Council's mandatory demand for a cease-fire in August 1988,[51] over a year after the demand had been made, and nearly eight years after the conflict had broken out. A peacekeeping force was emplaced under the provisions of the cease-fire as mandated in resolution 598 of 1987. The same resolution encouraged the Secretary General to find a permanent peaceful solution to the conflict. For several years it appeared that the peacekeeping force was having a stalemating

effect on peace talks. Fortuitously, Iraq's invasion of Kuwait in August 1990 and
the build-up of Coalition forces against it in the Gulf, signified that Iraq had to
concede to Iranian terms on 15 August 1990,[52] to enable its forces to be concentrated in and around Kuwait.

In Yugoslavia, the Security Council authorised the emplacement of a peacekeeping force between Croatia and Serbia in resolution 743 adopted on 21 February 1992. In the same resolution the Security Council could only encourage the
European Community's attempts at negotiating a peaceful break-up of
Yugoslavia. As will be seen in Part Three, the UN Protection Force (UNPRO-
FOR) was dragged into the conflict in the former Yugoslavia, particularly Bosnia,
the most ethnically mixed republic. Peacemaking attempts by the EC and the UN
proved unsuccessful, until UN authorised NATO airstrikes against the Bosnian
Serbs, and a change in the military balance of power in favour of Croatia, led to
the US-brokered Dayton Peace Agreements of November 1995.[53] The Agreements provided for a heavily armed Implementation Force (IFOR) to be provided
by NATO not the UN, although the Security Council sanctioned it.[54] The failure
of the UN to settle the conflict led to disenchantment with the UN's ability in this
area, evidenced by the fact that UNPROFOR was replaced by IFOR, and the Dayton Agreements delegated the electoral supervisory function to the Organisation
on Security and Cooperation in Europe (OSCE) rather than the more experienced
UN.

The quasi-judicial role of the Security Council

Although it has been stated above that some of the provisions of Chapter VI and
the general principles contained in Article 1(1) create a quasi-judicial role for the
Council, an examination of most Council debates leading to the adoption of a recommendation towards the pacific settlement of a dispute illustrates that it is often
arrived at by political consensus, and that law is often merely a 'tactical device'
and a 'weapon in the armoury of rhetoric'.[55] The law of nations could be said to
play a residual role in the work of a political body such as the Security Council,
although the ending of the Cold War has witnessed an increase in judicial-type
determinations by the Security Council.

The contention that although the Council does not decide cases in accordance
with international law as does the World Court, it is constrained by a 'broad
framework of legally acceptable solutions',[56] did appear to be somewhat flawed
during the Cold War, in that some Security Council inspired pacification attempts
sought solutions which appeared to contradict the tenets of international law. For
example, the Council-supervised negotiations on the Gulf War were premised on
the non-identification of the aggressor, namely Iraq.[57] Indeed, this neutral
approach persisted with Security Council inaction as regards the Iran–Iraq Gulf
War despite the fact that the Secretary General apportioned responsibility to Iraq
for its attack on Iran in 1980 in a report to the Security Council in *1991*.[58] This attitude appears even more inexplicable in the light of Iraq's new found 'pariah'

status since its invasion of Kuwait in 1990, although it may be that the West has not yet fully accepted Iran into the international community. It can be seen from this that despite the ending of the Cold War that political influences can still cloud the Council's legal judgment.

Alternatively, it may be argued that the Security Council fails to identify breaches of international law but it does not adopt resolutions which are themselves in breach of international law. However, this is a long way from the position that law plays an important role in the Council's pacification function.

The Council's failure to establish a solution is mainly due to it often being faced with the situation of an aggressor country gaining, with little possibility of it handing back its gains when faced with a Council recommendation. This is an inevitable flaw in any system based on recommendation and voluntary acceptance. Nevertheless, in order to ensure that the recommendation has a chance of success, it should be clear and unambiguous. Unfortunately, the necessities of consensus dictate that clarity is often unattainable. Resolution 242, adopted on 6 November 1967, five months after the Israeli victory in the Six Day War, is an example of an ambiguous recommendation. The resolution stated, *inter alia*, that the Council,

Affirms that the fulfilment of Charter principles requires the establishment of a just and lasting peace in the Middle East which should include the application of both the following principles:
(i) Withdrawal of Israeli armed forces from territories occupied in the recent conflict;
(ii) Termination of all claims or states of belligerency and respect for and acknowledgement of the sovereignty, territorial integrity and political independence of every State in the area and their right to live in peace within secure and recognised boundaries free from threats or acts of force.

This appears to be a reasonable framework for the settlement of the Middle East problem, although the two principles outlined in the resolution miss the root of the problem, namely the homeless Palestinians. Nevertheless, the resolution is based on legal principles, namely, the implication that Israel has the right to exist, the non-use of force, and the return of territories occupied by Israel in the Six Day War. However, the fact that the resolution does not state whether this means 'all' or 'some' of the territories detracts from its value. Law and justice point to the former interpretation, otherwise the Israelis would be gaining by the use of force, although it could be argued that the occupied territories, or at least some of them, are essential for the security and defence of Israel. Although Perry argues that if an advisory opinion of the International Court were sought, there would be no doubt that resolution 242 would be interpreted to mean 'all' the territories,[59] the doubt and confusion created by the British-proposed text has not helped to end the conflict. Besides although the World Court may opt for this solution, it is not unforeseeable that the Council may promote peace on the basis of Israel handing back some of its territories but not all. It must not be forgotten that international law is greatly tempered by political considerations in the Council forum.

Generally, when attempting to settle a dispute the Security Council tends to adopt recommendations which are aimed at not causing offence to either party in order to induce them to come to an agreement. Determinations of legal guilt may come later if the parties remain recalcitrant. The initial recommendations are usually based on broad principles of international law and justice centred around the *jus cogens* contained in Article 2(4) and the principle that a State should not gain from its breach. It may be argued that more concrete legal determinations should be made even under purely recommendatory Chapter VI resolutions. There are both pitfalls and advantages in this approach. A 'once and for all' legal determination may make a State more intransigent and so work against the settlement process, and at the same time it may mobilise international opinion which will work in its favour.

However, with the end of the Cold War, the Council has been more willing to make legal determinations even if they might inhibit the settlement process by branding one of the disputants as the guilty party. Part of the reason for this is that the Council is more willing to enter into the enforcement provisions of Chapter VII if the parties do not comply with the determination. Although this approach is somewhat selective and is mainly directed at the so-called 'pariah' States, it must be remembered that these States have usually breached international law.

The 'balanced' approach to the situation in the Israeli Occupied Territories evidenced in resolution 242 of 1967, was maintained in the Security Council right up until the end of the 1980s by Israel's ally, the United States, using its veto to prevent consistent declaratory resolutions condemning Israel's actions of repression as a breach of the Fourth Geneva Convention of 1949. However, since mid-1989 the Security Council has consistently condemned such acts in a series of resolutions[60] which may have led, in part, to Israel entering into negotiations on settlement in the Middle East. Although as has already been pointed out, there are defects in the Council's judicial approach, in that it is of a somewhat selective and summary nature, in the Middle East, where settlement without consistent condemnations has not occurred, there is a strong argument for supporting the Council's more assertive approach.

The post-Cold War practice of the Council has not only taken on greater judicial overtones, but has increasingly extended to enforcement of its determinations utilising the powers of Chapter VII of the UN Charter.[61] This has particularly been the case as regards Iraq following its aggression against Kuwait in August 1990, Libya for its support for terrorism, and the remnants of the Yugoslavian State (Serbia and Montenegro) for its intervention in the neighbouring former Yugoslav Republic and emerging State of Bosnia in May 1992.[62] In these instances, as shall be seen in subsequent sections, the Security Council condemned the State in question and then went on to enforce that decision using its economic, and in the case of Iraq, its military powers under Chapter VII of the Charter.

A recent instance of the Security Council using its judicial power, but not yet its legislative/enforcement powers under Chapter VII, followed the shooting down on 24 February 1996 of two small civil aircraft by Cuba while infringing into Cuban airspace. The Security Council condemned this action as a violation of the International Convention on Civil Aviation 1944,[63] but only in July 1996,[64] after the International Civil Aviation Organisation (ICAO) had conducted its investigation and delivered its report to the Security Council[65] as requested in a Security Council Presidential statement issued immediately after the incident.[66] This incident illustrates the Security Council acting with more propriety and restraint in its judicial capacity, despite the fact that Cuba is a 'pariah' State, at least from the Western perspective.

Binding settlement

Articles 36 and 37 are firmly premised on the Security Council simply having the ability to recommend terms of settlement. There has been little suggestion that the Council has the power to impose a mandatory settlement by a combination of Article 25 and Chapter VI. Nevertheless, on occasions, the Council's recommendations for settlement based on a combination of Article 24 and Chapter VI, are more comprehensive and detailed so that they suggest a more intense and concerted effort by the Council to achieve a settlement than on other occasions. However, they are not binding on non-complying parties.

The conclusion of the Renville Agreement of 1948 between the Netherlands and Indonesia represented a success for the Security Council and its Committee of Good Offices. However, although the truce arrangements were put into effect, the political discussions broke down despite the efforts of the above mentioned Committee. In December 1948, a Dutch surprise attack enabled it to capture most of the principal cities in the territory of the Republic, which, when combined with a more intransigent approach by the Dutch, signified that the Council could no longer persevere with its good offices approach. Nor did it venture into Chapter VII. Instead it adopted resolution 67 on 28 January 1949 which represented a much more comprehensive approach by the Council aimed at achieving a political solution.

The resolution uses, in its Preamble, the language of Article 24, and then goes on to outline a more detailed recommendation for settlement presumably with Article 36 or Article 37 in mind. The use of Article 24 was possibly to impress upon the intransigent parties the desire of the Council to fulfil its primary responsibility. By the resolution the Council established the United Nations' Commission for Indonesia in the place of the Good Offices Committee, a move which indicated the Council's increased commitment to a more comprehensive settlement. In operative paragraph 3 the Council recommended the establishment of an interim federal government which was to have internal powers until the transfer of sovereignty by the Netherlands to be achieved by 1 July 1950. Elections for the Indonesian Constituent Assembly were to be completed by 1 October 1949. The Commission was established to help the parties implement the resolution.

   The resolution was recommendatory only but it had the value of being so comprehensive that it was almost 'decision like' in its content. Nevertheless, the Belgian representative made it clear that the resolution remained a recommendation
under Chapter VI.[67] However, the combination of Article 24 and the obvious commitment of the Council to the independence of Indonesia led to the Dutch government notifying its general acceptance of the resolution with a few exceptions.[68]
On 27 December 1949 the Netherlands transferred sovereignty to the Republic of
Indonesia.

   In the Namibian situation, the Council 'decided' in 1969 that the 'continued
occupation of the Territory of Namibia by the South African authorities' was illegal and that its mandate over the territory was terminated.[69] However, this was
only a decision on legality, it was not a political solution, although it provided a
basis for the United Nations' plan for Namibia contained in Security Council resolution 435 adopted on 29 September 1978. This resolution endorsed the proposals in the Secretary General's report providing for internationally supervised
elections leading to the independence of the disputed territory,[70] a plan which after
over a decade of South African inspired frustration, came to fruition on 21 March
1990 with the independence of Namibia. It took an accord negotiated outside the
United Nations and containing concessions towards South Africa, particularly by
linking Cuban withdrawal from Angola with South African withdrawal from
Namibia, before South Africa would agree to the United Nations' plan.

   The Security Council, itself, was unable to coerce the South Africans into
implementing the plan because Western members were unwilling to back the UN
plan with anything more than voluntary measures of a limited nature called for in
resolution 566 of 1985. The original text supported the implementation of mandatory sanctions against Pretoria if the Namibian Independence Plan had not been
put into operation by a certain date, but the United Kingdom and the United States
could not support this and they later vetoed a Non-Aligned draft which would
have determined that the 'continued illegal occupation of Namibia by South
Africa constitutes a breach of international peace and an act of aggression', and
would have imposed mandatory sanctions against South Africa under Article 41,
Chapter VII.[71]

   The use of Chapter VII action to enforce the provisions of a settlement proposal
ostensibly made under Chapter VI and Article 24 would have represented the
most effective method of operation for the Council short of the use of force. The
two Western powers did not commit themselves to this, when, paradoxically, they
were two of the original drafters of the Namibian Plan for Independence.[72]

   Although the provisions of Chapter VI do not expressly allow for the Council
to impose a mandatory settlement, it is able to use a combination of powers under
Chapters VI and VII to the same effect if it determines that the situation or conflict is a threat to or breach of the peace. Indeed, the gateway to Chapter VII,
Article 39, provides that the Security Council can 'make recommendations' for
settlement 'or decide what measures shall be taken in accordance with Article 41

and 42'. This appears to allow the Council to propose pacific settlement, and if it is not accepted, to take economic or military action. Such a combination of powers amounting to the attempted enforcement of a settlement is tantamount to a *binding* settlement. Part Three will show the Security Council using a combination of powers in order to make the emplacement of a peacekeeping force conditional on the parties accepting the terms of a settlement, but it has not yet fully utilised a combination of settlement and mandatory sanctions.

However, the Security Council has come close to this in the break up of Yugoslavia, when it imposed sanctions against the Serbian-led remnants of that State for interfering in the emerging neighbouring State, and former Yugoslav republic, of Bosnia, in May 1992.[73] Following a peaceful settlement on Bosnia agreed to by the parties at Dayton, Ohio in November 1995,[74] sanctions were formally terminated in October 1996 following elections in Bosnia.[75] However, it took a combination of NATO airstrikes and the emplacement of a rapid reaction force on the ground in August 1995, both authorised by the Security Council,[76] combined with a successful military offensive in the west by the Croats and Muslims, to finally coerce the Serbs into negotiating peace in Bosnia at Dayton. The Security Council welcomed the Peace Agreement in a resolution adopted under Chapter VII, a resolution which recognised 'that the parties shall cooperate fully with all the entities involved in the implementation of the peace settlement', in particular the NATO-led IFOR, which the parties agreed could use 'necessary force to ensure compliance with Annex 1-A of the Peace Agreement'. Although the Dayton Accords were formally a product of the consent of the parties, they were in reality arrived at, in part, as a result of the legitimate coercion authorised by the Security Council, and are being complied with because of the threat of further Council sanctioned coercion by IFOR and its replacement SFOR (Stabilisation Force).[77]

The Security Council effectively imposed terms of settlement on Iraq in 1991 following the successful prosecution of a UN authorised war against it to counter the Iraqi invasion of Kuwait in August 1990. This is the reversal of the normal process whereby the Council proceeds in a faltering incremental fashion from settlement proposals to enforcement action. The Iraqi aggression, as shall be seen later in this chapter, was met with economic and military enforcement action authorised by the Security Council. With the Iraqis in Kuwait defeated in March 1991, the Security Council imposed the most draconian measures seen in the organ's lifetime. Resolution 687 was adopted on 3 April 1991 by twelve votes to one (Cuba) with Yemen and Ecuador abstaining. Its Preamble contained, *inter alia*, an affirmation of the 'sovereignty, territorial integrity and political independence of Kuwait and Iraq' and called on States taking military action under UN authority to 'bring their military presence in Iraq to an end as soon as possible'.

Although this statement satisfied sufficient members that the Council's intention was not to overthrow the Iraqi regime, the thrust of the resolution was to oblige Iraq to compensate for its aggression, to severely curtail that regime's ability to wage further aggressive wars by intrusive disarmament provisions, and also, by maintaining the sanctions regime, to gradually undermine its grip on the country. It also demanded that Iraq and Kuwait respect the 'inviolability of the international boundary and the allocation of islands' as agreed by them in 1963.[78] It authorised the Secretary General to make arrangements to demarcate the boundary between Iraq and Kuwait, and finally decided to guarantee the inviolability of the demarcated international boundary. This, as with the rest of the resolution, was a measure taken under Chapter VII and therefore binding on Iraq. The disputed boundary had been used as an excuse by Iraq for its invasion and so the Council was coercing the Iraqis into settling their dispute with Kuwait to prevent it being so used again. The Iraqis had no choice but to accept this and all the other aspects of the resolution.[79] A Boundary Commission was established in May 1991 with three independent experts and a representative each from Iraq and Kuwait. Despite Iraq's complaints about the legality of the Council's imposition of a boundary,[80] the Commission completed its task and its demarcation was endorsed by the Security Council.[81]

On the issue of responsibility, resolution 687 reaffirmed that Iraq 'is liable under international law for any direct loss, damage … or injury to foreign Governments, nationals and corporations, as a result of Iraq's unlawful invasion and occupation of Kuwait', reaffirming its resolution 674 of 29 October 1990. This clearly shows the Council acting in a judicial capacity. It also decided to establish a fund to pay compensation and a Compensation Commission to administer it.[82] The Secretary General was requested to report with a recommendation for 'mechanisms for determining the appropriate level of Iraq's contribution to the fund based on a percentage of the value of the exports of petroleum and petroleum products … taking into account the needs of the people of Iraq'. In resolution 705 adopted on 15 August 1991, the Security Council decided that the figure should be that suggested by the Secretary General of 30 per cent.[83]

It is clear from the above that Iraq's ability to fully comply with its obligation to compensate depended upon it resuming exports of oil, which it could not do since resolution 687 maintained the sanctions regime, first imposed by resolution 661 of 6 August 1990. On 15 August 1991 the Security Council adopted resolution 706, which authorised States to allow the import of petroleum products from Iraq for a period of six months to an amount not exceeding $1.6 billion.[84] The purpose of this resolution was to allow Iraq to purchase foodstuffs and medicines under the exceptions to the sanctions regime, but also to pay 30 per cent of that amount into the Compensation Fund. For several years Iraq refused to sell any oil, not on the grounds that it was unwilling to comply with its obligations under resolution 687 but on the basis that because it was willing to fulfil its obligations under that resolution, sanctions should no longer be applied against it.[85]

However, desperate humanitarian need led to Iraq finally accepting an 'oil for food' agreement in May 1996,[86] whereby the Security Council authorised States to import up to $1 billion in Iraqi oil every 90 days.[87] Although the primary aim of the resolution was to meet 'the humanitarian needs of the Iraqi population', 30 per cent of the funds raised were still to be paid into the Compensation Fund. With the implementation of this resolution being delayed by the Iraqi government's incursion into the Kurdish safe-haven in the north of Iraq in September 1996,[88] oil did not legitimately flow out of Iraq until December 1996.

In addition to a continuing arms embargo against Iraq, resolution 687 included a decision that 'Iraq shall unconditionally accept the destruction, removal or rendering harmless, under international supervision' of its chemical and biological weapons, development and support systems, as well as 'all ballistic missiles with a range greater than 150 kilometres'. Iraq was put under an obligation to fully report, within fifteen days, on its weapons systems and to undertake not to develop ones in the future. A Special Mission was created to inspect and verify the destruction of these weapons as well as to develop a plan for the ongoing monitoring of the state of Iraqi armament. Furthermore, resolution 687 decided that 'Iraq shall unconditionally agree not to acquire and develop nuclear weapons' and to report to the International Atomic Energy Agency (IAEA) within fifteen days on its nuclear weapons facilities. Iraq was also obliged to allow the IAEA to remove, render harmless or destroy such facilities and weapons, and to develop a plan for the ongoing monitoring of Iraq's nuclear programme.

The disarmament of Iraq pursuant to resolution 687 has been a long and so far uncompleted task. It has involved a slow process, with the Special Commission's inspectors and the IAEA officials gradually gaining access to weapons facilities not revealed in Iraq's initial response to resolution 687. Destruction and removal of many weapons and facilities has been achieved but neither the Special Commission nor the IAEA has yet fulfilled their tasks.[89] The Secretary General has pointed out that a three stage process is involved, namely 'inspection and survey, disposal of weapons of mass destruction and the facilities for their production, and ongoing monitoring and verification of Iraq's compliance with its obligations under' resolution 687. The Security Council has adopted further mandatory decisions in order to obtain Iraqi compliance with its disarmament demands. The Security Council condemned Iraq's failure to comply fully with its obligations contained in resolution 687, in resolution 707 adopted on 15 August 1991, and demanded that Iraq allow the Special Commission and the IAEA inspectors access to all weapons facilities and demanded that Iraq cease concealing some of those facilities. It also determined that 'Iraq retains no ownership interest in items to be destroyed, removed or rendered harmless pursuant to' resolution 687.

As regards the future monitoring of Iraq's compliance with resolution 687, the Security Council adopted a mandatory resolution on 11 October 1991. Resolution 715 approved the plan submitted by the Secretary General and the IAEA and demanded that Iraq meet unconditionally all the obligations under that plan. The plan provides for inspections, aerial overflights of Iraq and submission of reports by Iraq so that the Special Commission and the IAEA will be able to monitor and verify that no nuclear, chemical or biological weapons or ballistic missiles or other items prohibited by resolution 687 are acquired anew by Iraq.[90]

The Special Commission and the IAEA both reported in 1996[91] that they were much nearer to completing their tasks of accounting for and disposing of the proscribed weapons and programmes, and although Iraq was still not fully forthcoming on information, and was occasionally obstructive towards the inspectors,[92] the emphasis was changing somewhat towards putting in place monitoring mechanisms. In this regard the Security Council adopted a resolution in March 1996 approving of import/export monitoring mechanisms aimed at preventing Iraq from re-establishing its programmes proscribed by resolution 687.[93]

Despite the problems the Security Council has encountered in trying to remove the threat to the peace constituted by the high level of Iraqi armament, it has achieved a remarkable success in gradually wearing down the Iraqi resistance to its disarmament programme. Whether the programme will be fully completed remains to be seen, but the progress so far has been astounding. Iraqi compliance has been faltering but has been eventually given as it suffers from continuing sanctions and from the threat of further devastating military action. The Council has a general power to formulate plans for disarmament in Article 26 of the UN Charter, but there is no evidence that this was intended to be a mandatory power. Ironically if the West's view is accepted that it is only under Chapter VII that mandatory resolutions can be adopted, there appears little room to imply such a power. However, if a more flexible attitude is taken, mandatory resolutions can be adopted outside the confines of Chapter VII if the resolutions clearly show such an intention and the implication of such a power does not breach the express provisions of the Charter. Resolution 687 and those adopted to further its aims were expressly stated to be adopted under Chapter VII, and Article 26 is not expressly confined to recommendations. It therefore appears that the Council has this power.

However, looking at its imposition of a settlement as regards the issues of compensation and the frontier dispute, it appears more difficult to impute a mandatory power to the Security Council. Those provisions of Chapter VI that allow the Council to propose terms of settlement, namely Articles 36 and 37, allow for recommendations only, yet resolution 687 is expressly adopted under Chapter VII. The Iraqi acceptance of resolution 687 may be pointed to as pushing to one side the problem of the binding nature of the resolution, but this does not overcome the fact that the Council intended the resolution to be binding, and it may have been for this reason that Iraq accepted it.[94] It appears unavoidable to conclude that whereas the Council's disarmament programme for Iraq is a legitimate implied power derived from Article 26 to fulfil the Council's primary responsibility for international peace and security under Article 24, its development of its quasi-judicial powers to punish Iraq and determine its border with Kuwait appear more problematic.

It may be that such a development will be entrenched by consistent subsequent practice on the part of the Council. It is perhaps possible to reconcile this approach with the International Court's doctrine of implied powers as stated in the *Repara-*

tions case of 1949 when it stated 'the rights and duties of an entity such as the Organization must depend upon its purposes and functions as specified or implied in its constituent documents and developed in practice'.[95] Or it may be that States, particularly the permanent members, have adopted a more open, 'living instrument', approach to the Charter, allowing it to evolve to cope with changes in international relations leading to the development of powers which fulfil the purposes of the UN even if it is not possible to imply such powers from the particular provisions of the instrument, as long as the power does not breach any of the express provisions of the Charter.[96] This approach is more akin to the controversial doctrine of 'inherent' powers.[97]

Whether the 'implied' or 'inherent' approach is accepted, it is possible to see the imposition of mandatory settlements as a development of the Council's express powers to recommend settlement under Chapter VI and not as a breach of those provisions, as well as being more generally an expression of its lawmaking competence under Chapter VII.[98]

Reference to the International Court

Article 36(3) of the Charter states that 'in making recommendations under this Article the Security Council should also take into consideration that legal disputes should as a general rule be referred by the parties to the International Court'.

Many factors act against increased reference by the Council to the International Court. Many countries are not willing to gamble losing a dispute in an all or nothing legal ruling; they prefer, if anything, political compromises. In addition a strict delineation between the Council and the International Court on the basis of whether the dispute is political or legal fails to take account of the fine and often blurred distinction between law and politics and the fact that the Council has, by other provisions in Chapter VI, a quasi-judicial role anyway.

In fact the Council has made little use of Article 36(3). In the dispute between Albania and the United Kingdom over aspects of passage through the Corfu Channel in 1947, the Security Council recommended that the parties 'immediately refer the dispute' to the International Court.[99] That the Council, under Article 36(3), can do no more than make a recommendation which the parties are free to accept or reject was made clear by the World Court. The United Kingdom argued that the Council's resolution had established the Court's jurisdiction. Although the Court found it unnecessary to rule on this point, a majority pointed out that Article 36(3) did not introduce a new case of compulsory jurisdiction.[100]

The only other use of Article 36(3) by the Council occurred in 1976 when Greece complained of 'flagrant violations by Turkey of the sovereign rights of Greece on its continental shelf in the Aegean' which has 'created a dangerous situation threatening international peace and security'.[101] Resolution 395 was adopted on 25 August 1976 by consensus; it called for negotiations and invited the parties to refer the question to the International Court.[102]

Article 36(3) is really an example of settlement by pacific means and so should be associated with Article 33(1). It is not generally used by the Security Council because it only entails a recommendation. If the parties are willing to refer their dispute to the International Court they do not generally need the Council to remind them to do so. The infrequent use of Article 36(3) is a consequence of the limited use of the World Court in resolving conflicts and also the wider consideration that both these organs of the United Nations, the International Court and the Security Council, seem to prefer not to interfere in the other's perceived competence.[103]

International Criminal Tribunals

The end of the Cold War not only saw the expansion of the use of established powers by the Security Council, but also the development of new implied and inherent powers. There is no express mention in the Charter of a power to create international criminal tribunals to try individuals charged with breaches of international humanitarian law, and yet in February 1993 the Security Council decided 'that an international tribunal shall be established for the prosecution of persons responsible for serious violations of international humanitarian law committed in the territory of the former Yugoslavia since 1991', after concluding that 'widespread violations of international humanitarian law' constituted a threat to international peace and security,[104] and after having established in October 1992 a Commission of Experts to collect evidence.[105] After requesting and receiving a report from the Secretary General on the structure and functions of the tribunal,[106] the Security Council, 'acting under Chapter VII of the Charter', established the International Criminal Tribunal for the Former Yugoslavia (ICTY).[107]

The Security Council took the similar steps of 'condemnation; publication; investigation; and by establishing the tribunal, punishment',[108] as regards the genocide occurring in Rwanda in 1994. A Commission of Experts was established in July 1994,[109] and the International Criminal Tribunal for Rwanda (ICTR) was established under Chapter VII of the Charter in November 1994 'for the sole purpose of prosecuting persons responsible for genocide and other serious violations of international humanitarian law committed in the territory of Rwanda and Rwandan citizens responsible for genocide and other such violations committed in the territory of neighbouring States, between 1 January 1994 and 31 December 1994', after determining that 'genocide and other systematic, widespread and flagrant violations of international humanitarian law' committed in Rwanda constituted a threat to international peace and security'.[110] Although the tribunals are separate with the ICTY having its seat at the Hague and the ICTR at Arusha, a single Appeals Chamber was established 'to ensure that the international norms of international humanitarian law, crimes against humanity and genocide will be interpreted and applied consistently by both new international tribunals, whose case law will have considerable impact on the development of these norms'.[111]

One of the first tasks undertaken by the ICTY was to consider its own constitutional basis. In the *Tadic* case, the defendant was indicted in February 1995 charged with responsibility for the killings within and outside the Omarska camp between May and August 1992.[112] He challenged the jurisdiction of the ICTY on several grounds, the first (and the one considered here) being the illegal foundation of the tribunal. The defendant argued that the 'International Tribunal should have been created either by treaty, the consensual act of nations, or by amendment of the Charter … not by resolution of the Security Council', particularly because the Security Council did not possess the power to create a judicial body under Chapter VII.[113]

The Trial Chamber dismissed all the defendant's arguments against its jurisdiction. In relation to the argument as to the constitutionality of the tribunal, the Trial Chamber was of the opinion that decisions taken by the Security Council under Chapter VII were not subject to judicial review, besides which the ICTY was not empowered by its statute 'to question the legality of the law which established it'.[114] The Appeals Chamber, in dismissing the appeal on other grounds, thought that the tribunal did have the power to review its own legal basis as a necessary first step to establishing its jurisdiction over the case before it.[115]

The Appeals Chamber examined Chapter VII of the Charter, in particular Article 39, and stated:

It is clear from this text that the Security Council plays a pivotal role and exercises a very wide discretion under the Article. But this does not mean its powers are unlimited. The Security Council is an organ of an international organisation, established by a treaty which serves as a constitutional framework for that organisation. The Security Council is thus subjected to certain constitutional limitations, however broad its powers under the constitution may be.[116]

The Appeals Chamber then considered that the Security Council had acted within that constitution in determining that the situation in the former Yugoslavia constituted a threat to the peace on the basis of 'the subsequent practice of the membership of the United Nations at large' that an internal armed conflict can be so categorised.[117] As to the constitutional basis of the tribunal itself, the Appeals Chamber stated that it was not merely a subsidiary organ of the Security Council within Article 29 of the Charter but that it fell 'squarely within the powers of the Security Council under Article 41'.[118] The fact that the measures expressly mentioned in Article 41 do not include the establishment of a tribunal was dismissed on the basis that 'the measures set out in Article 41 are merely illustrative examples which obviously do not exclude other measures'.[119] In effect the Appeal Chamber stated that Article 41 allows the implication of other measures, thus adopting an implied, rather than an inherent, powers approach. Article 41, along with Article 29, seems to have been recognised by jurists as the Charter base of the ICTY (and therefore the ICTR as well).[120]

If the Appeals Chamber had adopted an inherent powers approach it would not have had to somewhat artificially tie down the creation of the tribunal to a specific

Charter provision, but it would have had to examine whether the creation of it fulfilled the purposes of the UN, primarily the maintenance of international peace and security. The Appeals Chamber did make the rather anodyne statement that 'the Security Council has resorted to the establishment of a judicial organ in the form of an international criminal tribunal as an instrument for the exercise of its own principal function of maintenance of peace and security',[121] reflecting the Security Council's own determinations that this was the case.[122] The defendant had argued that the creation of the tribunal did not contribute to the maintenance of international peace and security and was therefore beyond the competence of the UN.[123] Essentially this contention is based on the premise that the establishment of a tribunal does not contribute to the solution to a dispute, indeed that there is an incompatibility between negotiating peace with individuals and trying them for war crimes (though this does not apply to Tadic who allegedly was a camp guard of sorts).[124] However, the subsequent Dayton Peace Accords of November 1995 somewhat belie this contention, though the problem of war criminals may yet unravel the peace process. In addition, it must be noted that the purposes of the UN are not solely directed at peace and security but include the promotion of respect for human rights and the establishment of the 'conditions under which justice and respect for the obligations arising from treaties and other sources of international law can be maintained'.[125]

It is too early to evaluate the effectiveness of the two tribunals in prosecuting individuals for breaches of international criminal law. Inevitably, there have been considerable problems leading to a delay of eighteen months before the ICTY issued its first indictment, a delay which 'hurt the credibility' of the tribunal.[126] Although further indictments have been made by both the ICTY and the ICTR, and trials are underway in both,[127] the tribunals have been the subject of great criticism.[128] One weakness which is inherent in the creation of an international judicial body amidst independent sovereign States, or more conceptually, the creation of a 'monist institution in a dualist world',[129] is the need for the cooperation of States to enable the tribunals to function effectively. Article 29(2) of the ICTY Statute provides that 'States shall comply without delay with any request for assistance or an order issued by a Trial Chamber', including, *inter alia*, 'the arrest or detention of persons', and 'the surrender or transfer of the accused to the International Tribunal'.[130] Nevertheless, both Statutes are backed by mandatory decisions of the Security Council and the evidence is that States are complying with the tribunals' orders.[131] Ultimately the compliance of States with the tribunal depends on the Security Council backing up its mandatory decisions with coercive measures if necessary.

It has also been argued that 'the Bosnian Serbs are not subject to the orders of the Tribunal. They are not even subject to the decision of the Security Council in this regard, since they are not a state (yet?)'.[132] Since a number of individuals charged and indicted with breaches of international criminal law are Bosnian Serbs, a major stumbling block appears to be the arrest of these individuals while they remain within the Serb-controlled areas of Bosnia. The Dayton Accords overcome this to some extent in that the Bosnian Serbs (the Republika Srpska) is a party to them, and is therefore under a duty to cooperate with the ICTY.[133] Furthermore, it is arguable that the Security Council authorised military operation in Bosnia – IFOR (now SFOR) – should arrest suspected war criminals in accordance with its residual powers of enforcement under the Dayton Accords, and on the basis of the obligation placed on States, including members of NATO, by the Security Council to cooperate with the ICTY.[134] However, NATO does not seem to have clearly accepted this obligation, or at least has taken few steps to actively fulfil its duty.[135]

It is arguable that NATO's reluctance to capture war criminals is in part due to its unwillingness to possibly jeopardise the peace process in Bosnia, which in turn illustrates the divergent, and perhaps conflicting, aims of the Security Council. Nevertheless, the trial and punishment of individuals guilty of breaching international criminal law is a laudable aim, which the Security Council is attempting to make part of its collective security function. It remains to be seen whether this approach is successful in the two tribunals which have been established, and, if so, whether this power will be developed by subsequent practice, or whether a permanent international criminal court will be established for the task.[136]

Provisional measures

In the *Tadic* case, the Appeals Chamber of the ICTY stated that the tribunal could not be viewed as a provisional measure within the meaning of Article 40, because '[t]hese measures as their denomination indicates, are intended to act as a "holding operation", producing a "stand-still" or a "cooling-off" effect ...'.[137] Article 40 provides that,

In order to prevent the aggravation of the situation, the Security Council may, before making the recommendations or deciding upon the measures provided for in Article 39, call upon the parties concerned to comply with such provisional measures as it deems necessary or desirable. Such provisional measures shall be without prejudice to the rights, claims, or position of the parties concerned. The Security Council shall duly take account of a failure to comply with such provisional measures.

By placing this provision in Chapter VII which deals mainly with mandatory measures, there has been a tendency to view recommendations of provisional measures (usually a call for a cease-fire and withdrawal) as coming within Chapter VI, usually Article 36, with Article 40 measures being exclusively mandatory following a finding under Article 39 or by the invocation of Article 25.[138] However, as has been seen, provisional measures can be binding without references to Article 39 or Article 25 if the language of the resolution is peremptory and the discussions in the Council so indicate.

Once some degree of flexibility in the nature of provisional measures as developed in the practice of the Security Council is accepted, it can be seen that

Article 40 is the natural basis for them whether their invocation is recommendatory or in the form of a decision under Article 25, just as Article 41 is the basis for
sanctions whether voluntary or mandatory. The reason why the Council so often
has to resort to cease-fire calls is due to the fact that it is badly prepared. Often the
cease-fire resolution is the first Council action in a conflict whereas if it had
heeded the warnings it could have attempted to defuse the situation at an earlier
stage. The Middle East is again illustrative of the Council's poor crisis management. In the build-up to the outbreak of the Six Day War on 5 May 1967, the
Council showed an unwillingness to prevent what appeared to be at least 'a very
serious potential threat to the peace'.[139]

The withdrawal of UNEF and the military build-up of Egyptian, Syrian and Jor-
danian forces appeared to be a threat to the peace but pro-Arab members of the
Council blocked any attempted move to prevent war.[140] Yet when the war broke
out the Council managed to adopt a unanimous resolution which called upon 'the
Governments concerned as a first step to take forthwith all measures for an immediate cease-fire'.[141] This was disregarded so on 7 June the Soviet Union, concerned
about Arab losses, proposed a more forceful draft which was adopted as resolution 234. In it the Council demanded a cessation of hostilities. A similar resolution was adopted when fighting intensified on the Syrian front.[142] By 10 June all
the disputants had accepted the cease-fire.

These later resolutions appear to have been more effective, perhaps because of
the greater use of peremptory language. However, this is deceiving for the Israelis
only accepted the cease-fire when they had gained the Sinai, the West Bank and
the Golan Heights, whereas the Arabs were in no position to refuse when their
armies started losing severely. Cease-fire resolutions are often combined with or
are followed by a call for the withdrawal of occupying troops. In the case of the
Six Day War it was some months before the Council adopted resolution 242,
which, *inter alia*, called for Israeli withdrawal.

The Middle East illustrates how the Council is often unable to step beyond the
establishment of a cease-fire. Even compliance with such a call is illusory of
Council effectiveness, in that it will only be accepted when both sides are simul-
taneously ready because of their relative military positions. Withdrawal calls are
not generally complied with because the party in the strongest position will lose
most. Settlement in terms of international law or justice is unlikely while
countries are able to benefit territorially by the use of force.

Potentially, the Security Council's role in a conflict, if excluding for the
moment mandatory enforcement measures, can be summarised as calling for or
demanding a cease-fire, then a withdrawal to prior positions and then an outline
of settlement. The first two stages may be facilitated by the interpositioning of a
peacekeeping force. On several occasions the Council has been unable to go
beyond a cease-fire call. For example, the sole Council resolution on a post-
colonial armed clash between France and Tunisia in 1961 concerning the remaining French base at Bizerta, was a recommendatory call 'for an immediate cease-

fire and a return of all armed forces to their original positions'.[143] Similarly, for many years the Council called on Iran and Iraq to cease firing in the Gulf War.[144]

On 20 July 1987 the Council finally adopted a mandatory demand for a cease-fire between Iran and Iraq in resolution 598 after expressly referring to Articles 39 and 40 of Chapter VII as well as determining that there existed a 'breach of the peace as regards the conflict between Iran and Iraq'. The evidence was that a mandatory call for provisional measures was more effective since a cease-fire was established in August 1988. However, the cease-fire was as a result of the failure of the Iranian offensive and of economic exhaustion which led it to accept the cease-fire, Iraq having already accepted resolution 598 because of its tenuous position. The mandatory call may have provided the necessary diplomatic handle for both parties to grasp, but they were only prepared to grasp it when they both realised that the war was truly stalemated.

Mandatory resolutions may be marginally more successful than their recommendatory counterparts, but they still have the same inherent flaw when they are successful; they do not provide any basis for a permanent solution nor, if they are simply cease-fires, do they always secure a return to the *status quo ante* as they are intended to do. A simple cease-fire call if complied with will tend to freeze the dispute and usually to the advantage of one of the parties, usually the one which has gained by the use of force. Even fairly rapidly arrived at resolutions, although sometimes effective, work to the advantage of one of the parties. When violence erupted between the two Cypriot communities in 1974, the Council was rapidly convened on 16 July. With a Turkish invasion occurring, the Council adopted resolution 353 which found a 'serious threat to international peace and security' and demanded an 'end to foreign military intervention'.[145] The resolution called for both a cease-fire and for the cooperation of the parties with the peacekeeping force present since 1964. The cease-fire was eventually complied with after the call had been reiterated.[146] Further measures created a security zone between Turkish forces in the north of the island and Greek Cypriot forces to the south.[147] The effect of this was to cement the solution sought by Turkey and the Turkish Cypriots by the partition of the island, and seemed to be contrary to the non-prejudicial nature of provisional measures.

The drafters of the Charter inserted the provisional measures provision as an optional stop-gap before the application of enforcement measures under Articles 41 and 42. The Security Council has mainly used Article 40 more in the way of a holding measure while pacific settlement is sought. The Secretary General's attempts at mediation in the Cyprus situation have been mentioned. In the Falklands War, the Council speedily adopted a call for provisional measures after a finding of a breach of the peace and then encouraged the Secretary General in his good offices mission.[148] Although the call for provisional measures was quickly adopted in the Falklands War, it was ignored by Argentina. This is probably because the Council's past record showed that it usually had not taken further measures to ensure compliance.

The one main exception to that during the Cold War was in the case of the North Korean invasion of the South in 1950: the Council quickly found a breach of the peace and called for a cessation of hostilities and a withdrawal of North Korean forces to the 38th parallel.[149] This call was also ignored, but was backed up, as shall be seen, by the Council recommending military action against North Korea. The end of the Cold War, whilst not revealing any greater preventive peacemaking by the Council, has shown it willing to back up calls for provisional measures with enforcement action if necessary, and so in this respect acting closer to the intention of the drafters of the Charter, although this approach is by no means guaranteed.

Immediately after Iraq had invaded Kuwait in August 1990, the Council demanded that Iraq withdraw from Kuwait in a mandatory resolution expressly adopted under Articles 39 and 40 of the Charter.[150] Iraqi non-compliance was resolutely met with first economic sanctions under Article 41 then military action. Similarly on 15 May 1992, the Security Council unanimously adopted resolution 752 which demanded an end to the fighting in the former Yugoslav Republic of Bosnia-Herzegovina, in particular by the remnants of the Yugoslav National Army, dominated by Serbia. As shall be seen in the section below, when this demand was not complied with the Security Council imposed a range of quite hurtful mandatory sanctions against it. Again as shall be illustrated in the following sections, mandatory cease-fire demands directed at the Bosnian Serbs were eventually backed up by coercive mechanisms (economic sanctions and military measures) including the deployment of a rapid reaction force.[151] Another example is the cease-fire demanded by the Security Council in Rwanda following the outbreak of violence there in 1994 which was accompanied by a mandatory arms embargo,[152] followed, as shall be seen, by the authorisation of military action. However, both of these recent examples illustrate the weakness even of enforced provisional measures, given that the action was too little and too late for many Bosnian Muslims caught in the 'safe areas', and thousands of Rwandan Tutsis.

Nevertheless, the greater willingness of the Security Council to enforce its demands for provisional measures may increase States' willingness to comply with the demands more immediately in the future instead of calling the Council's bluff as happened in the past. Furthermore, the end of the Cold War has increased the effectiveness of the Council's provisional measures not only because of the greater use of enforcement action but also, as shall be seen in Part Three, by an increased use of peacekeeping to facilitate the adoption of provisional measures in combination with peacemaking in the form of a settlement of the dispute.

Economic sanctions

Article 41 of the United Nations' Charter reads,

The Security Council may decide what measures not involving the use of armed force are to be employed to give effect to its decisions and it may call upon the Members of the

United Nations to apply such measures. These may include the complete or partial interruption of economic relations and of rail, sea, air, postal, telegraphic, radio, and other means of communication, and the severance of diplomatic relations.

The powers contained in Article 41 were intended to allow for the imposition of mandatory enforcement measures following a finding of a threat to or breach of the peace under Article 39. However, on many occasions, the Council has been unwilling to take mandatory action with the consequence that it has settled for a call for voluntary measures or sanctions. Such action can be viewed as a re-interpretation of Article 41 to allow for recommendations, or as merely a recommendation under Chapter VI, or a recommendation of enforcement action under Article 39. Although the Charter base for such powers is inconclusive there is no doubt that the Council has developed such a power, the evolution of which lies in political compromise. In almost every case in which voluntary measures have been called for, Western powers have objected to a finding under Article 39 combined with mandatory sanctions. Voluntary sanctions, as the term implies, are breached with impunity and so are relatively ineffective except for a certain symbolic role.

In the Rhodesian situation the Council called for an arms, oil and petroleum embargo to be imposed against the Smith regime in 1965.[153] The Western powers viewed this as a voluntary call, although others thought that it was 'only under Chapter VII that economic sanctions are mentioned'.[154] With at least two of the permanent members regarding the call as voluntary, the resolution must be regarded as recommendatory.

International pressure sometimes has the effect of turning voluntary measures into mandatory ones. In the case of Rhodesia this happened relatively quickly when the Council first imposed selective mandatory sanctions in 1966 and then more comprehensive sanctions in 1968.[155] Nevertheless, over two years elapsed between the call for voluntary measures and the call for comprehensive mandatory measures, a fact that decreased the effectiveness of the sanctions for it allowed the Rhodesian economy time to prepare. It was almost as if certain members were dragging their feet to allow this to happen. The same can be said as regards the arms embargo placed on South Africa. This was originally a voluntary call made in 1963,[156] fourteen years later it was made mandatory,[157] giving the Pretoria regime ample time to stockpile and to work out alternative supply routes.[158]

Other than Iraq where sanctions were imposed, at least initially, to combat *aggression*, the Security Council has deployed the mandatory sanctions weapon in the following instances of *threats to the peace*: comprehensive regimes against Southern Rhodesia from 1968–79, Yugoslavia (Serbia and Montenegro) from 1992–96, and the Bosnian Serbs from 1994–96; more selective regimes against Libya from 1992, Haiti 1993–94, Sudan from 1996, and UNITA held areas of Angola from 1993; and arms embargoes against South Africa from 1977–94, against Somalia and Liberia from 1992, and against Rwanda from 1994–95. It is clear from this list that during the Cold War the Council was greatly reluctant to use its full powers under Article 41, but with the freeing of the Council from the chains of the superpower veto, the Council has used the power contained in Article 41 quite frequently. The fact that the Council has increased the use of its mandatory powers to impose sanctions indicates that it feels that they are effective in a collective security role. The purpose here will be to review the use and effectiveness of sanctions to combat and control threats to and breaches of the peace.

There have been varying assessments of the effectiveness of the mandatory economic measures imposed against Rhodesia. The figures produced by the Security Council's Committee established to monitor reports on the effect of the sanctions regime suggest that, after initially struggling, from 1968 the Rhodesian economy improved.[159] This data provides *prima facie* evidence to deny the effectiveness of economic measures.[160] Nevertheless, there is evidence to suggest that after 1974 with the combined effects of Mozambique's independence (Portugal, the colonial power, was a major sanction breaker), the guerrilla war and the sanctions regime, the Rhodesian domestic situation as a whole began to decline. Although the application of sanctions did not immediately achieve the primary goals of the Security Council of either ending UDI by forcing Smith to negotiate, or ruining the Rhodesian economy and thus forcing internal change, it did achieve certain subsidiary goals which must be viewed as a success. These were namely, the prevention of an all out civil war in Rhodesia after the proclamation of UDI, the prevention of foreign military intervention to end UDI, and the encouragement of the white regime to negotiate.

Nevertheless, in the Rhodesian case, sanctions were mandatory and so binding on member countries. The question remains as to why the Rhodesian economy was not affected more rapidly. One major reason for this is the poor timing of the imposition. Pokalas summarises the effect of this in the case of Rhodesia.

Such anticipatory actions as stockpiling materials, developing alternative supply sources to obviate over-dependence on any one source, diversifying domestic production, planting crops that were readily exportable, conserving key commodities and establishing new trade routes were utilised by Southern Rhodesia even prior to Security Council action.[161]

Comprehensive economic sanctions were imposed several years after UDI by the Smith regime in 1965, which in terms of the United Nations was relatively quickly. However, it was six years since the United Nations had taken cognisance of the situation,[162] giving the regime ample time to prepare. For sanctions to be given the chance of being effective they must be immediate, mandatory and comprehensive. In other words a resolution should have been adopted by the Council on the day of UDI or even before containing a determination of a threat to the peace and the imposition of mandatory, comprehensive measures. In the Rhodesian situation sanctions were applied in a 'gradual crescendo of severity' creating many loopholes which the Security Council gradually filled in a piecemeal fashion.[163] Above all, for sanctions to be effective, they must have the full support of the members of the United Nations, in particular the permanent members of the Security Council.

Furthermore, the sanctions in the Rhodesian situation were by no means watertight, and sanction breakers went unpunished in many instances which led the Council to adopt resolution 333.[164] This called for the 'enactment and enforcement of legislation providing for the imposition of severe penalties on persons natural or juridical that evade or commit breach of sanctions'. Admittedly, in the case of Rhodesia the two countries which openly defied sanctions, South Africa and Portugal, were, at the time, international pariahs, over which the rest of the international community had little hold. In addition to South Africa and Portugal, other prominent sanction breakers during the Rhodesian crisis were multinational corporations. These proved to be the most difficult to prevent because of their diverse locations and their economic and political power. Multinationals are mainly based in the West and so it is natural that they should have been the responsibility of Western members of the United Nations. In particular, supervision of compliance with the sanctions regime should have been coordinated by the three Western permanent members on the Council.[165]

Another main sanction breaker during the Rhodesian situation was the United States which in 1970 defied the Security Council by passing the Byrd Amendment enabling it to trade with Southern Rhodesia in strategic materials.[166] The Council, with the United States merely abstaining, censored that country in resolution 320 of 1972.[167] The Rhodesian economy could not but benefit from such illegal activities evidenced by its economic growth in conjunction with the reported number of sanction violations. By 1968 there had been 13 violations; this had increased to 73 by 1970 and 346 by 1976. The United States had committed 46 violations by 1978.[168] The United States had ignored a mandatory decision of the Security Council and had therefore abrogated its treaty obligations and breached Charter law. The lead given by the United States led to the initial vigilance of other States being relaxed with the result that the mandatory measures were then treated like voluntary measures, as a token gesture to be ignored with impunity.

Despite the weaknesses of the sanctions regime, the Smith government eventually negotiated majority rule and the Security Council lifted the sanctions in 1979.[169] Sanctions had an effect although Rhodesia was relatively strong in an economic sense. It was self-sufficient in agriculture, had abundant minerals including gold and a strong industrial base, but it still needed trade and investment. This is why the Council should have implemented a total embargo against the country, for as Pokalas points out 'had the embargo been properly implemented by States' legislation, strictly enforced by States' administration and judicial sectors, and diligently coordinated by the Committee, the Rhodesian economy would have floundered and ultimately collapsed'.[170]

The Rhodesian experience was not a conclusive 'experiment' in the use of sanctions to remove a threat to the peace. The rather ambiguous attitude to sanctions shown by member States undermined their effectiveness. In the case of Iraq, sanctions were first imposed by resolution 661 of 6 August 1990, following Iraq's refusal to comply with the Council's mandatory cease-fire call in resolution 660 of 2 August 1990, the day of its invasion of Kuwait. Immediately it can be seen that sanctions in this case were imposed very quickly and, as the terms of resolution 661 show, they were comprehensive. Resolution 661 prohibited the import of goods from, and the export of goods to, Iraq and Kuwait, except in the latter situation for 'supplies intended strictly for medical purposes, and, in humanitarian circumstances, foodstuffs', as well as a freeze on financial arrangements with Iraq and its overseas assets. The Council also decided to establish 'a Committee of the Security Council consisting of all the members of the Council', to examine reports on the progress of implementation of sanctions by member States. In analysing these reports, Bethlehem concludes that support for resolution 661 reached well over 80 per cent of the membership of the UN. Many non-members responded positively, although at least one, Switzerland, stated that it was not under a legal obligation to impose sanctions against Iraq.[171]

The sanctions regime against Iraq appeared relatively watertight. As Bethlehem states,

From the outset, Iraq appeared to be uniquely placed to be influenced by sanctions: it was a one product economy that had recently emerged from a punishing war against Iran; the movement of its principal export commodity, oil, was relatively easy to track and interdict; Iraq imported between 60–70 per cent of its basic food requirements; with the possible exception, in the early stages of the crisis, of Jordan, it could not count on support from any of its immediate neighbours to circumvent sanctions; in an unprecedented show of solidarity, virtually the entire international community had condemned the Iraqi action which had been the cause of the crisis. In short, if sanctions as a means of enforcing international law were not to succeed here, they would not be likely to succeed elsewhere.[172]

Indeed, the Security Council adopted a series of resolutions to fine tune the embargo,[173] including, as shall be seen in the next section, the authorisation to navies in the Gulf to intercept ships suspected of sanction breaking. Sanctions were imposed in August 1990, by January 1991, when the UN authorised military campaign started against Iraq, sanctions did not appear to have weakened Iraq's resolve to hang on to Kuwait, although they may have affected Iraq's military capacity to resist the overwhelming military action launched against it. Nevertheless, question marks must be raised against the effectiveness of sanctions and their capacity to act as an alternative to military action. Sanctions were continued against Iraq by resolution 687 of 3 April 1991 after military action successfully ousted Iraq from Kuwait. The purpose of the continuing sanctions regime was to secure Iraq's compliance with the resolution's provisions on disarmament and compensation, although the hidden agenda must have been to undermine the regime of Saddam Hussein. Resolution 687 provides for a review of the sanctions regime against Iraq 'every sixty days in the light of the policies and practices of the Government of Iraq'. Although the sanctions regime remains in place, it has been seen above that the 'oil-for-food' agreement between Iraq and the United Nations allows Iraq to export $1 billion of oil every 90 days from December 1996.

Turning to the effectiveness of sanctions, a fundamental flaw can perhaps be perceived. The aim of sanctions was expressly stated not to be to starve the people of Iraq into submission, but initially to weaken Iraq's hold on Kuwait and then, following its defeat in Kuwait, to force it to comply with its obligations to disarm and to compensate States and individuals for its aggression. This was made clear from the outset by resolution 661 adopted on 6 August 1990 and elaborated upon by resolution 666 of 13 September 1990. The latter resolution outlined a mechanism whereby the Sanctions Committee would monitor the food situation in Iraq and make determinations of how particular needs ought to be met. The Committee struggled to achieve the aim of not using 'starvation as a weapon'.[174] Nevertheless, whereas some States, including the United States, thought that the sanctions regime prohibited foodstuffs unless there was clear evidence of humanitarian need, other States on the Council, particularly Cuba, argued that there was a general humanitarian need in Iraq and therefore all foodstuffs should be allowed into Iraq without any particular proof being required.[175] It appears that the direct effect of sanctions was not on the regime's grip on Kuwait, and when removed from that country in March of 1991, on its grip over its own people, but upon the Iraqi people.

The Security Council was not unresponsive to these negative effects. In resolution 687, 3 April 1991, which contained the terms of settlement imposed on Iraq, the Security Council formalised the 'no-objection' procedure which had come to replace the necessity for proof of humanitarian need in the Council's Sanctions Committee. This meant that the export of foodstuffs or other materials or supplies for essential civilian needs was permitted as long as the Committee was notified, and there were no objections to the cargoes in that Committee.

Iraq must blame itself for the suffering of its people by its unwillingness to comply fully with resolution 687. In addition, it must not be forgotten that it was Iraq which had clearly violated international law in August 1990. Nevertheless, it appears that the sanctions regime is not a sufficiently sharp weapon to point directly at those responsible for the invasion, namely the Iraqi regime of Saddam Hussein. The ordinary Iraqi citizens appear to be the ones suffering, more particularly those elements, the Kurds in the north and the Shias in the south, that revolted against the regime and are now suffering themselves from an internal embargo imposed by the Iraqi government as punishment.

It can be argued that the sanctions weapon, although a blunt instrument and not capable of removing aggression, is more suitable to remove threats to the peace in that it is directed at those who must change the internal situation, both rulers and ruled. However, the Iraqi experience shows that the people who suffer the most are those who are not responsible for the unlawful acts, namely the ordinary citizens.[176] Furthermore, the effect is not only on the citizens of Iraq or the target State, but also on the peoples and governments of States that have traditionally traded with the target State. The sanctions regime against Iraq illustrates that the Security Council was really powerless to address the immediate economic plight of other States such as Jordan, even though Article 50 of the UN Charter provides that such States have 'the right to consult the Security Council with regard to a solution of those problems'.[177]

Whether or not sanctions provoke a change in the Iraqi regime, either by fostering discontent in the population, or by eventually forcing the regime to fundamentally change in a way acceptable to the Security Council, the sanctions experiment against Iraq appears to suggest that economic coercion is not an effective alternative to military coercion *per se*, and that sanctions alone are not an adequate enough weapon on which to base a system of collective security. Sanctions should be given time to work, and should suspend the taking of military action in self-defence in response to *aggression*, but if unsuccessful after a reasonable period of time the Security Council ought to consider the use of armed force, or if not, allow States their right of self-defence.[178] If no aggression has been committed but the situation is a *threat to the peace*, then the Security Council alone has the right and the duty to consider whether to use military force to supplement the imposition of sanctions. It may decide that military action is unnecessary or it may not find the political consensus to authorise military action, in which case sanctions will continue in the hope that they will eventually help to remove the threat to the peace as in the Rhodesian situation. This approach accords with the wording of Article 42, which, in the original Charter plan, was the basis for military action. Article 42 opens with the words 'should the Security Council consider that measures provided for in Article 41 would be inadequate or have proved inadequate' it may consider taking military action.

Turning now to look at some more recent sanctions regimes. Although the evidence on the effectiveness of these embargoes is preliminary it might be suggested that the sanctions experiences against Rhodesia and Iraq show that the only potentially successful method of ensuring that the weaknesses of the relatively strong target State's economy are exposed is to impose an immediate comprehensive embargo.[179] Limited embargoes are insufficient because even if they are aimed at those areas of weakness the other unsanctioned areas of the economy will develop to compensate. Nevertheless, as has been pointed out, there are humanitarian considerations to be taken into account when a full embargo is imposed.

The use of an arms embargo against South Africa was questionable because South Africa's strong economy and natural resources supply enabled it to produce its own weapons. However, an effectively policed arms embargo may be successful against a country totally dependent on outside States providing arms, particularly when there is no real prospect of that country being able to produce its own arms, as with the arms embargo against war-torn Somalia imposed by the Council in resolution 733 of 23 January 1992. However, the resolution contained no machinery for the monitoring of arms shipments, and without that the Council is simply relying on a member's sense of obligation towards a mandatory decision of the Council. The Council's mandatory arms embargo against Liberia imposed by resolution 788 of 19 November 1992[180] seems to have had a greater impact on the peace process in that ravaged country although by far the major factor seems to be the military activities of the Economic Community of West African States (ECOWAS) 'peacekeeping' force, which is exempted from the embargo. The effect of a mandatory oil and arms embargo against another extremely poor country, Haiti, by resolution 841 adopted on 17 June 1993 seems to have been more dramatic, with the military regime agreeing to the restoration of democracy under the deposed President on 2 July 1993. However, there was a subsequent lack of implementation of the agreement with the result that the Security Council reimposed the oil and arms embargo in October 1993, accompanied by the authorisation to member States to stop suspected sanctions-breaking ships.[181] Although sanctions were further expanded in May 1994,[182] it took the threat, in July 1994,[183] of a UN authorised United States' military operation for the military dictatorship in Haiti to step down in October 1994, consenting to a US and then a UN force to oversee the return to democracy. Sanctions were lifted on 16 October 1994.[184] Again it seems that sanctions alone, without the threat or use of military force, were inadequate for the tasks.

Nevertheless, these instances provide limited evidence that sanctions imposed to combat internal situations designated threats to the peace can be effective if the target State is very weak, and that it does not necessarily require a comprehensive embargo to make these effective. Indeed, a comprehensive embargo against a State whose population is below the poverty line would seem inhumane in the extreme. A slightly different approach has been taken as regards the civil war in Angola following the breakdown in the peace process, with the Security Council imposing a mandatory arms and oil embargo only against UNITA held areas of Angola.[185] This approach was later adopted in September 1994 when the Security Council imposed a more comprehensive regime against the Bosnian Serbs.[186] In these cases, sanctions are directed at the faction responsible for the continuation of the internal conflict, but this more 'just' approach is only possible in a State which is not only divided politically or ethnically but also geographically.

A more comprehensive embargo was imposed against the remnants of the war-torn State of Yugoslavia by resolution 757 of 30 May 1992. The Council condemned the continued intervention by Yugoslavia (Serbia and Montenegro) and Croatia in the former Yugoslav Republic, and emerging State, of Bosnia, and determined that the situation there constituted a threat to international peace and security. Despite the fact that both Serbia and Croatia were intervening in Bosnia in support of the factions there, the Security Council implicitly blamed Serbia when it imposed mandatory sanctions against it on the import or export of commodities except for 'supplies intended for medical purposes and foodstuffs' notified to the Council's Committee on Sanctions against Yugoslavia, established by resolution 724 of 15 December 1991, as well as a freeze on financial and other transactions with Yugoslavia (Serbia and Montenegro).

The resolution built on the mandatory arms embargo imposed against the whole of Yugoslavia by resolution 713 of 25 September 1991. Clearly the aim of the arms embargo resolutions against Somalia, Haiti, Liberia and the former Yugoslavia, was to prevent the escalation of the civil wars which would occur if outside States supplied arms to one faction or the other. One problem with this approach is that it leaves the most poorly armed faction, in the latter instance, the Muslims in Bosnia, in a very vulnerable position. An attempt to lift the arms embargo to allow the Bosnian Muslims to receive arms was defeated on 29 June 1993 by a vote of six in favour to none against with nine abstentions in the Security Council.[187]

The aim of the more comprehensive sanctions regime against Serbia was to prevent its forces assisting the Bosnian Serbs in their struggle to gain more territory in Bosnia. Unlike the arms embargo which was to prevent escalation, the aim of the sanctions regime against Serbia was to punish it for its intervention and support for the policy of ethnic cleansing, and to coerce it into withdrawing its military support for the Bosnian Serbs, as well as forcing that faction to agree to the proposals for the peaceful settlement of the conflict in Bosnia. Sanctions did have a dramatic effect on Serbia and Montenegro with hyper-inflation, unemployment and many shortages leading in part to Serbia's agreement to close its border with Bosnia in return for the suspension of some of the economic sanctions against it in September 1994.[188] However, it took NATO airstrikes and a Croatian/Muslim military offensive to force the Bosnian Serbs into accepting the Dayton Accords in November 1995, again illustrating the inadequacy of sanctions *per se*.[189]

One final point to note in this catalogue of UN sanctions regimes is the mandatory arms and air embargo imposed against Libya in resolution 748 of 31 March 1992. This followed a determination by the Council that Libya's support for terrorism constituted a threat to international peace and security and was designed to coerce Libya into not supporting terrorism, in particular, to hand over the two suspected of the Lockerbie bombing. So far the resolution has not had its desired effect. In response, the Security Council ordered States to freeze Libyan assets abroad and also not to supply any oil related equipment.[190] Again the Council is adopting an incremental approach but has so far stopped short of a mandatory oil embargo. A less punitive approach has been adopted so far by the Security Council as regards the imposition of sanctions against Sudan in April 1996 for its support for terrorism, primarily in refusing to extradite three suspects wanted in connection with the assassination attempt on President Mubarak of Egypt. The Council decided that all States 'shall significantly reduce the number and level of staff at Sudanese missions and consular posts', as well as controlling the movement within their territories of such staff. In addition, States were obliged to restrict entry into their territories of members of the Sudanese government, government officials and members of the Sudanese armed forces. Continued non-compliance by Sudan led the Council to impose aircraft sanctions under Chapter VII in July 1996.[191]

Military measures

As with the UN's use of sanctions, the use of military force to achieve collective security goals has an uneven track record, although the evidence seems to suggest that military measures are more effective in removing aggressors, illustrated by the limited success against North Korea in 1950, and the greater success against Iraq in 1991. The evidence is less clear cut as regards threats to the peace where there is not often a clear 'enemy', although the threat of force against the military rulers in Haiti was successful in removing them without the need to use force in 1994. In other cases of threats to the peace, particularly in Bosnia and Somalia, the use of force proved ineffective, in particular in Somalia where UNOSOM II (United Nations Operation in Somalia) was withdrawn in March 1995 leaving the civil strife to continue in that country.

Although the effectiveness of military measures will be further considered in this brief review, it is necessary to concentrate on a more important issue of principle – namely whether the military actions authorised by the UN fulfil the principle of collective security or do they constitute unacceptable delegations of power to dominant States?

The Organisation's collective security role was premised, in 1945, on the ability of its primary organ, the Security Council, ultimately to use military measures to enforce the peace. The Council's ultimate weapon and deterrent was contained in Article 42.

Should the Security Council consider that measures provided for in Article 41 would be inadequate or have proved to be inadequate, it may take such action by air, sea or land forces as may be necessary to maintain or restore international peace and security. Such action may include demonstrations, blockade, and other operations by air, sea, or land forces of Members of the United Nations.

Article 43 then details the mechanism whereby armed forces are to be made available, namely by 'special agreements' made by members of the UN, detailing the numbers, location and the state of readiness of such forces. These agreements were to be reached as soon as possible.

The agreements foreseen by Article 43 were not arrived at because the Second World War unity of the Allies soon collapsed into a bitter ideological struggle between East and West. Nevertheless, the Security Council did manage to instruct the Military Staff Committee, established under Article 47 of the UN Charter and consisting of the Chiefs of Staff of the permanent members, to report to the Council by April 1947 on the basic principles that should govern the UN's armed forces.[192] The Committee's report did contain draft articles detailing such basic principles. Unfortunately, only half of these had been accepted by all the permanent members.[193]

The major areas of agreement were that the initial contributions of armed forces should come from the permanent members, with other members contributing at a later stage. It was also agreed that the members' forces should be under the command of the contributing nation except when they were being utilised by the Security Council, when they would come under the overall political control of the Security Council, and under the operational and military command of the Military Staff Committee. Although these were indeed significant initiatives towards the collective security ideal concerning the control of UN forces which has been singularly lacking in the UN military operations to date, there were disagreements on practical issues such as the size of the force and the contributions from each permanent member, with the Soviet Union preferring a small force with equal contributions.

Furthermore, the Soviet Union was of the opinion that the UN armed forces could not be used against any of the permanent members, an argument which though undermining the collective security ideal as well as the ideal of the rule of law,[194] seemed to be supported by the practical consideration that the voting system agreed upon by the permanent members at Yalta and embodied in Article 27 of the Charter, allowed any permanent member to veto a proposed military action, including, and especially, one aimed at the permanent member in question. Yet the United States, as well as preferring a much larger army, thought that the force could be used against a permanent member guilty of aggression. Furthermore, the United Kingdom stated that the problem of the veto could be avoided by meeting aggression committed by a permanent member by combining Article 43 and Article 51, not Articles 42 and 43.[195] In other words, aggression could be met by the UN army, minus the aggressor State's troops, in an action in collective self-defence rather than as authorised by the Security Council. Indeed, when coming to examine the UN military operations to date which have been directed at combatting aggression, such a confusion of the right of collective self-defence and the concept of collective security is apparent.[196] Nevertheless, in terms of Charter law it must be true that Articles 42 and 43 are within the exclusive competence of the Security Council, and as such must be utilised by the Security Council voting for such an operation in accordance with the voting rules as laid down by Article 27 as interpreted by subsequent practice.

With no likelihood of consensus between the permanent members, at least during the Cold War, the idea of a standing army was shelved, although the Military Staff Committee continued its formal, and unproductive, meetings. It is generally thought that in the absence of agreements reached under Article 43, the Council is unable to 'decide' on the use of military measures under Article 42.[197] Articles 39 and 42 seem to envisage the Council having the power to make binding, mandatory decisions directed at member States to take military action against a transgressor. Without the agreements under Article 43, it would seem difficult for the Council to impose an obligation on member States to provide armed forces when the Council demands them. A counter-argument would be to point to Article 41 which empowers the Security Council to impose mandatory sanctions against a State, a decision binding on all member States without the requirement for any prior agreements between the member States and the Organisation beyond that contained in Article 25. However, the rationale behind Article 43 was the recognition that for the Council to undertake military action requires a much higher degree of coordination and logistical organisation. Without that a mandatory demand that States provide military forces would appear vacuous. Furthermore, Article 106 of the Charter permits the permanent members to make transitional arrangements for military action 'pending the coming into force of such special agreements referred to in Article 43 as in the opinion of the Security Council enable it to begin the exercise of its responsibilities under Article 42'. This implies that the agreements in Article 43 are a prerequisite to the utilisation of Article 42 by the Security Council.[198]

However, it is incorrect to state that there is an inextricable link between Articles 42 and 43 in the sense that it would be a misuse of power for the Council to decide on the use of military measures under Articles 39 and 42 without any *a priori* agreements under Article 43.[199] It would appear acceptable for the Council to use the power granted to it in Article 42 without the mechanisms that were designed to make the imposition of military coercion a practical option. If an alternative practical option emerges such as an *ad hoc* coalition prepared to act under UN authority then it would appear to be *prima facie* lawful. During the Cold War the possibility of the Council acting under Article 42 with or without the agreements under Article 43 was such a remote possibility that Article 42 was effectively a dead letter. However, with the ending of the Cold War, there is the possibility of the Security Council utilising Article 42. Furthermore, there have been suggestions of having at least a small UN force ready to take military action. At the special Security Council Summit of Heads of State and Government on 31 January 1992, President Mitterand of France offered to make 1,000 troops available to the UN under the control of the Military Staff Committee.[200]

Although it may be argued that the agreements under Article 43 are not necessary to make the Council's military option under Article 42 a practicality, the Charter does strongly indicate that UN control of such military operations is an essential prerequisite for the legality of military action by the Security Council. This appears to be made clear by Articles 46 and 47(3) which provide that 'plans for the application of armed force shall be made by the Security Council with the assistance of the Military Staff Committee', and 'the Military Staff Committee shall be responsible under the Security Council for the strategic direction of any armed forces placed at the disposal of the Security Council ...'. Strategic control by the Military Staff and overall political control by the Security Council appear necessary for the achievement of the collective security concept, in that they embody the centralisation of the collective use of force. This argument can be used to criticise the Security Council's practice in the use of the military option, when it has simply delegated authority and control to a State or group of States.

A counter-argument would be to state that if the Security Council simply authorises a State to use force to achieve an objective within the ambit of the UN's security role, despite the fact that it is being performed by one State, it is still a *collective* use of force, in that it is being performed to carry out the collective will of the Security Council on behalf of the United Nations. This is all the more so when the Security Council authorises a group of States to carry out such a function. The question remains whether control by the Security Council and the Military Staff Committee is essential to properly fulfil the collective security function. It could be argued that the provisions of Articles 46 and 47(3) as well as Article 43 are simply formalities which if in operation would facilitate the use of the power contained in Article 42. They can be seen as just one method of allowing the Council to fulfil its collective security role. Following from this it would appear to be unnecessary to make these formalities a prerequisite to the use of military enforcement action by the Security Council.

The answer lies somewhere between these poles. It probably would be too formalistic and bureaucratic to require control by UN Committee, though it must be pointed out that enforcement of sanctions is put under the control of a Committee of the Security Council. Nevertheless, a complete delegation of command and control[201] of a military operation to a member State or a collection of States would lack that degree of centralisation legally necessary to designate a particular military action as a *United Nations* military action, as opposed to a unilateral or multilateral, and probably illegal, use of force outside the umbrella of the UN. The minimum legal requirement for a military action to be a UN military action, is first of all a resolution authorising the use of force, and second, that resolution and subsequent resolutions should specify clearly the extent, nature and objectives of the military action. Problems of lack of continuous control can be overcome by a clear and unambiguous mandate at the outset. If States using force under this authority then wish to use more or less force, they must seek a change in mandate from the Security Council.[202]

Such a legal requirement ensures that the UN Security Council is in control of military operations undertaken under its authority, it does not prevent dominant groups within the Security Council using that organ to achieve their ends as well as the UN's. Use of centralised power to achieve the ends of a dominant individual or group within any society is not necessarily unlawful, if that power is channelled correctly through the institutional structures. Current dominance by the West in the Security Council does not mean that when the West uses that organ to protect Western interests it is automatically a misuse of power as long as the military action achieves the collective security purposes of the Organisation as well.[203]

The result, however, is an erratic collective security system, stuttering into life only when the interests of the West are affected, but is that not better than none at all? Indeed, arguments of self-interest may embarrass the West into agreeing that the Council can be used to fulfil purposes beyond narrow Western interests – witness the use of NATO under the authority of the UN in Bosnia and UN authorised actions in war-torn Somalia. However, in these conflicts there are still some doubts about the commitment of the powerful States to the resolution of the crisis. Whether the development of the military option is viewed as a power implied from Article 39 or 42, or both, is not of great importance, if the power is used to fulfil the purposes of the UN and is clearly formulated at the outset of the operation. What is clear at the moment is that the Security Council has not yet 'decided' to use military force, it has simply recommended or authorised that States, on a voluntary basis, use force in particular situations and for particular purposes.

The initial failure of UN operations to provide humanitarian assistance to the starving people of Somalia in 1992 led to the Secretary General outlining the options the Council had in order to create conditions for uninterrupted delivery of relief supplies to Somalia.[204] The final choice from these options vividly illustrates the changing nature of UN operations in civil conflicts, away from simple humanitarian provision towards enforcement. The options were: first, a continued deployment of UNOSOM under the existing principles of peacekeeping. The Secretary General stated that this option 'would not in present circumstances be an adequate response to the humanitarian crisis in Somalia'. Second, to abandon the use of international military personnel to protect humanitarian relief, withdraw UNOSOM's military elements and leave humanitarian agencies to negotiate with faction leaders. This option was favoured by some of the humanitarian agencies but the Secretary General stated that he was 'more than ever convinced of the need for international military personnel to be deployed in Somalia'. Finally, that force should be used either by UNOSOM, in a limited area or country wide, or by a group of States under Security Council authorisation.[205]

As regards the last option, while favouring the development of enforcement action under the command and control of the United Nations in the future, the Secretary General recognised that at that time, the UN did not have the capacity to mount such an operation within the time frame required. The Secretary General concluded that the only option was to resort to Chapter VII of the Charter. Again although stating a preference for UN command and control of such an operation, he stated that a Council authorised operation undertaken by member States would be acceptable as long as the aims of the operation were precisely defined and limited in time to enable post-conflict peacekeeping and peacemaking.

The Secretary General concluded that the US Secretary of State had informed him that if the Council would authorise the use of force to ensure aid delivery, the United States was willing to lead such an operation.[206]

On 3 December 1992, the Council unanimously adopted resolution 794 'under Chapter VII', authorising the 'Secretary General and Member States cooperating to implement the offer' by the United States 'to use all necessary means to establish as soon as possible a secure environment for humanitarian relief operations in Somalia', after determining that the 'magnitude of the human tragedy caused by the conflict in Somalia, further exacerbated by the obstacles being created to the distribution of humanitarian assistance, constitutes a threat to international peace and security'. The Council demanded that the parties comply with a cease-fire and cooperate with the force to be established. The resolution contained very little concerning the command and control of the force, indeed it implicitly left it to the United States by authorising 'the Secretary General and the Member States concerned to make the necessary arrangements for the unified command and control of the forces involved, which will reflect the' United States' offer. The resolution did not mention a time frame nor specific tasks for the US-led Unified Task Force (UNITAF) beyond the establishment of a 'secure environment for humanitarian relief operations in Somalia'.

Under the initial phase of 'Operation Restore Hope', UNITAF was composed of 28,000 US personnel, later to be supplemented by 17,000 personnel from 20 other States. UNITAF was emplaced on 9 December 1992 and it immediately adopted a fairly aggressive stance towards disarming the various factions in the country and in opening up humanitarian aid routes. It was not afraid to use substantial force beyond that required for self-defence. The United States started to reduce its troop commitment in February 1993, even before the Security Council approved the Secretary General's proposal[207] for a 28,000 strong UN force (UNOSOM II) under Chapter VII of the Charter on 26 March 1993. Resolution 813 authorised the use of force if necessary to ensure the delivery of humanitarian assistance, but also stressed the need to restore peace, to disarm factions, and to protect relief workers, suggesting the possible wider use of force. The force would also be responsible for returning hundreds of thousands of refugees, clearing land mines, setting up a police force, and helping to rebuild the economy.

UNITAF handed over responsibility, effectively for the policing of Somalia, on 4 May 1993. The new force attempted to continue the aggressive approach of the US-led force and in so doing lost any semblance of neutrality in the conflict, by taking forceful actions against one of the factions, the Somali National Alliance, and under Security Council authority, seeking the arrest of that faction's leader for attacks against UNOSOM II.[208] The UN effectively became one of the factions in a civil war on which it could not impose its will. In this 'no-win' situation the UN force ignominiously withdrew from Somalia in March 1995.

The collective action in Somalia not only illustrates the dangers of a peacekeeping force being converted or being supplemented by an enforcement action (reviewed more fully in Part Three), it also highlights the problem of using volunteers to enforce the will of the international community: that those volunteers may withdraw their services as with the withdrawal of the US forces from UNITAF and their replacement by what was essentially a peacekeeping force with an enforcement mandate. This cannot be prevented unless the Security Council binds the States to act, a power envisaged in the original Charter scheme but not activated, as also evidenced by the US withdrawal from the NATO naval patrol in the Adriatic in November 1994. Although the sanctions against the former Yugoslavia were mandatory and binding on all States including the US, the request that they be enforced by NATO and Western European Union (WEU) warships was simply a recommendation,[209] not binding on the US or any other contributing State.

In addition, in all the instances when the Security Council has authorised the use of force by a State or group of States on behalf of the UN – Korea, the Gulf, Somalia, Yugoslavia, Haiti, Rwanda, Zaire – there has been a legal defect, namely insufficient centralisation of the aims and objectives of the authorisation.

For instance, its authorisations of naval forces to take necessary measures to enforce sanctions regimes against Rhodesia in 1966,[210] Iraq in 1990,[211] and Yugoslavia in 1993, did not specify what levels of force were to be used, for example firing across the bows or firing at the suspected sanctions-busting ship. This raises question marks about whether the authorisation to use force was adequately centralised. Despite the lack of centralisation in these limited naval operations, there is no evidence to suggest that the States concerned in any way interpreted the language of the enabling resolutions to enable them to pursue national aims beyond those stated by the Security Council. There is of course a far greater danger of this happening when the Security Council authorises the full-scale use of force against an aggressor.

The first instance of this was set in motion when on 25 June 1950, 100,000 North Korean troops crossed the 38th parallel that had divided the country after the Second World War. The Communist North Korean aim was to unite the country by force. The United States requested a meeting of the Security Council, and with the Soviet representative absent in protest at the continued presence of Nationalist China in the permanent seat, the Council adopted a US proposal. Resolution 82 of 25 June determined that the 'armed attack' by North Korea constituted a 'breach of the peace', and called for an immediate cessation of hostilities and a withdrawal of North Korean forces to the 38th parallel. North Korea ignored this demand with the result that the United States sent combat forces to South Korea.[212] Although not specified as an action in collective self-defence, the United States' action could only have been justified as such at this early stage in the war.[213]

However, the United States sought to utilise the other exception to the ban on armed force contained in Article 2(4), namely the use of force under the auspices of the Security Council, by proposing what was to become resolution 83 of 27 June 1950. This recommended 'that the Members of the United Nations furnish such assistance to the Republic of Korea as may be necessary to repel the armed attack and to restore international peace and security in the area'. Secretary General Lie wished for some form of central UN control of this force,[214] but the United States rejected this idea. Instead the Council adopted a French and British proposal as resolution 84 on 7 July 1950. This recommended 'that all Members providing military forces ... make such forces available to a unified command under the United States of America'. The resolution also authorised the use of the UN flag concurrently with the flags of the contributing States, and finally requested the United States to provide the Security Council with regular reports 'on the course of action taken by the unified command'.

The British representative, Sir Gladwyn Jebb, explained the military action in Korea as coming under Article 39 of the Charter on the basis that in the absence of agreements made under Article 43, the Council could not 'decide' on military action within the terms of Article 42, but could call on States to volunteer to help.[215] This appears to be an acceptable implication of power but it cannot involve a total delegation of authority to a single State without adequate safeguards that prevent the obvious national interests motivating the State to volunteer its forces outstripping the collective security interests of the Security Council. Resolution 84 appeared to simply delegate or even abdicate responsibility to the United States, which supplied 90 per cent of the force. The force was not controlled by the UN, instead its commander, General MacArthur, was appointed by the United States and took his orders from the White House.

When Ambassador Malik of the Soviet Union returned to the permanent seat at the end of July 1950, thereby preventing the United States from adopting any further substantive resolutions on the war, the United States war effort was well under way and did not require any further enabling resolutions. Resolution 82, mandating the military action, was sufficiently ambiguous that it was not clear whether it simply authorised the pushing back of North Korea, or whether the elliptical phrase 'to restore international peace and security to the area', allowed the US-led army to push into North Korea. In any event the Western-dominated General Assembly adopted a resolution on 7 October 1950 calling for stability throughout Korea and for steps to be taken for the establishment of a unified Korea. Furthermore the resolution stated that UN forces should stay in Korea until these objectives were fulfilled, implicitly authorising the crossing of the 38th parallel.[216]

Unfortunately, the crossing of the parallel did not restore peace and security to Korea. Instead when the UN forces pushed towards the Chinese frontier, the People's Republic of China responded with massive force. The war then swung towards the Communists until the UN forces eventually managed to hold them around the 38th parallel by July 1951. Negotiations between the United Nations Command, in fact the United States,[217] and a North Korean and Chinese delegation eventually produced an armistice in July 1953 dividing the country, an agreement which has lasted until the present day.

It can be strongly argued that the UN operation in Korea was an unconstitutional delegation of authority to the United States enabling it to use the Organisation to go beyond the collective objectives of the body to fulfil the national objectives of the United States in its attempts to fight Communism. However, such an argument is difficult to prove in that combatting aggression is one of the prime aims of the Organisation as embodied in Article 1(1) of the Charter. Doubts about whether the objectives of the operation were sufficiently collective could have been allayed, either by more control of the armed forces by means of a Committee established by the Security Council, or by being much more specific in the war aims of the UN response. Presumably the Security Council can authorise action going beyond simply the defensive. There appears no restriction on the Security Council authorising offensive action if that is what is required to maintain or restore international peace and security.[218] However, if the Council is going to authorise offensive force then the resolution, or subsequent resolutions, should clearly state as such. If there are doubts then the response should be limited to a defensive action. In this respect the UN action is akin to an action in collective self-defence although its legal basis remains distinct, deriving from Article 39 (and possibly 42) rather than Article 51 of the Charter.[219] This argument signifies that the American decision to push into North Korea went too far, putting American war aims above those of the United Nations. However, the United States did gain the somewhat ambiguous support of the General Assembly. The question whether the General Assembly has the power to authorise the use of force will be examined in Part Two.

Limitations on the extent of the use of force under UN authority seem to have influenced the US-led action against Iraq, in that coercion was used in January and February 1991 principally to remove Iraq from Kuwait in a mainly defensive operation.[220] Between the Iraqi invasion of Kuwait on 2 August 1990 and the authorisation to use force on 29 November 1990, the Security Council had used its powers to demand Iraqi withdrawal under Articles 39 and 40, and had imposed comprehensive mandatory sanctions under Articles 39 and 41. In addition, the Council adopted numerous other resolutions which were either of a condemnatory quasi-judicial character, for instance the declaration that the Iraqi annexation of Kuwait was 'null and void', and the demand that Iraq release the foreign nationals it was holding in Iraq and Kuwait,[221] or were resolutions aimed at improving the embargo imposed by resolution 661 on 6 August 1990.

On 7 August 1990, the United States and Saudi Arabia agreed that American troops were to be sent to Saudi Arabia to prevent any further Iraqi advance in accordance with Article 51 of the UN Charter.[222] This was the basis of the defensive posture adopted by the United States and various allies that gathered in Saudi Arabia and the Gulf in the months after the Iraqi aggression. The United States and the United Kingdom also stated that they had the option of acting in collective self-defence of Kuwait at the request of the deposed rulers of that country even though the Security Council had imposed sanctions. This contention has been dealt with in chapter two above.

As with Korea, the United States decided that it was politically necessary to have the support of the Security Council in order to make any military operation internationally acceptable. It managed to persuade twelve members of the Security Council to vote for a resolution authorising the use of force, with Cuba and Yemen voting against on the basis that the resolution granted 'authority without accountability', and 'carte blanche' to the United States and its allies to use military force. China abstained on the grounds that it preferred that a peaceful solution be sought to the crisis.[223] Indeed, resolution 678 was very ambiguous in its direction to States in that it appeared first of all to be an ultimatum to the Iraqis and only secondly an authorisation to use force. The time delay was inserted at the insistence of the Soviet Union in the hope that the mere threat of force would compel the Iraqis to withdraw. Operative paragraph 2 of resolution 678 of 29

November 1990, authorised 'Member States co-operating with the Government of Kuwait, unless Iraq on or before 15 January 1991 fully implements … the foregoing resolutions [of the Council on the crisis], to use all necessary means to uphold and implement Security Council resolution 660 and all subsequent resolutions and to restore international peace and security in the area'.

The unnecessarily ambiguous language of this resolution can be cleared up in part by statements made by some of the members of the Council and not objected to by others. The representative of Malaysia stated that the resolution did 'not provide a blank cheque for excessive and indiscriminate use of force' and warned against any action 'purportedly taken under this resolution that would lead to the virtual destruction of Iraq'. Mr. Hurd, the UK Foreign Minister, stated that Iraq was required to 'withdraw all its forces unconditionally to the positions on which they stood on 1 August … If not, then Member States … are authorised to use such force as may be necessary to compel compliance'.[224] Indeed, it could be argued that the phrase 'necessary' implies proportionality within the customary law of self-defence, so that the resolution simply authorised a defensive action. However, the fact was that debate about the extent of the UN's war aims in resolution 678 would not have been necessary if a far more detailed resolution was adopted excluding or at least clarifying the phrase 'to restore international peace and security in the area', which, by itself, suggests the possibility of offensive force to remove the source of the aggression.

A clear enabling resolution would have dispelled doubts about the delegation of control to the United States, which contributed two-thirds of the troops of the 750,000 strong army from 29 States, making the action little different to the Korean War. As with the Korean War, the war against Iraq served American interests, in this case the protection of Western oil supplies. However, this does not mean that the authorisation to use force to expel Iraq was an abuse of power if that authorisation was fulfilling carefully defined UN aims. Prevention of aggression is a legitimate and indeed ultimate aim of a collective security system, but the methods of achieving it need to be clearly stated and approved.

There should have been detailed discussions, either in the Military Staff Committee, or in less formal forums about the extent of the armed force to be applied against Iraq *before* it was used. Security Council approval of the Coalition's war plan should have been sought immediately before the deadline against Iraq ran out. As it was the Security Council did not convene formally after the adoption of resolution 678 until the deadline of 15 January 1991 had run out.[225] The only obligation in the period of the ground and air campaign was to provide regular reports to the Security Council during the campaign which related to events in the war *after* they had occurred and not to the strategy and plans of the Coalition.[226] There was an obvious need not to inform Iraq of the Coalition's every move beforehand, but this should not have prevented overall UN control of the objectives of the action, after all it was meant to be a UN operation.

The need for greater UN control of the operation does not necessarily signify that the operation was contrary to the UN Charter. The use of force needs to be assessed to see if it achieved those aims set out in resolution 678 as restrictively interpreted above. The Coalition of forces operating under the umbrella of the UN, but not on this occasion using its flag, started its air campaign against Iraq on 16 January 1991 soon after the deadline in resolution 678 ran out. The ground offensive for the liberation of Kuwait started on 24 February 1991 and was successful in achieving the liberation of Kuwait within five days. It appears that, individual actions in the campaign apart which must be judged by the laws of war,[227] the Coalition did adopt a reasonable interpretation of resolution 678 limiting the military action to the enforcement of resolution 660 and other resolutions of the Security Council aimed at securing the withdrawal of Iraq from Kuwait. Although the air campaign did penetrate deep into Iraq and was aimed at industrial as well as military targets, and the ground offensive included a large part of southern Iraq, as well as a temporary occupation of part of the south after the war, these actions appeared necessary to achieve the successful liberation of Kuwait without the need for a long drawn out and even more destructive war between Iraq and the Coalition.

The campaign against Iraq was limited to UN objectives, it was not hijacked for Western purposes beyond those that coincided with Western purposes, and so did not lead to the overthrow of the aggressive regime in Iraq advocated by some in the West.[228] Although it is probable that the Security Council could authorise an offensive war involving the overthrow of a regime, such as that in Iraq, with a record of aggression, such an aim should be clearly spelt out in the enabling resolutions. Nevertheless, the defeat of Iraq enabled the Security Council to impose a temporary cease-fire on Iraq in mandatory resolution 686 of 2 March 1991, which, *inter alia*, forced Iraq to rescind its annexation of Kuwait, accept its liability for damages caused by its aggression, release third State nationals and prisoners of war, return all property seized in Kuwait, and to provide information on all mines and weapons left in Kuwait. Iraq complied and also agreed to the even more stringent mandatory resolution providing for a permanent cessation of hostilities, resolution 687, adopted on 3 April 1991 which has been reviewed above. The Security Council, in effect, decided that it would maintain pressure on the Iraqi regime by the use of sanctions rather than the use of force, although Western States have undertaken limited military strikes against Iraq in January 1993 and September 1996, purportedly, though not convincingly, taken under existing Security Council resolutions.[229]

Despite the success of the operation in the Gulf, question marks hang over the extent that the UN simply delegated its power to a group of willing volunteers. In order to combat these doubts it must be admitted that whereas the prevention of aggression is indeed a legitimate and ultimate aim of a collective security system, the methods of achieving it need to be clearly stated and approved if the action itself is going to comply with the principle of collective security and also the rule of law.

Similar accusations of lack of centralisation of the use of force can be found in the military operations authorised by the UN for combatting 'threats to the peace'. In addition to its authorisation for a US-led force in Somalia, the Security Council authorised a gradually increasing level of NATO involvement in Bosnia.[230] The fact that the NATO treaty has not been altered to allow it to take a wider security, as opposed to defensive, role, has not prevented the Security Council calling on NATO to undertake certain enforcement tasks in Bosnia. While NATO clearly could not have undertaken this role unilaterally, it can do so under Security Council authority. Legally speaking this can be seen either as an authorisation under Article 53(1) of the Charter with the Security Council treating NATO as a regional arrangement, or as an authorisation of the individual members of NATO to take enforcement action under Chapter VII of the Charter. The latter interpretation overcomes the defects in the NATO treaty by recognising that the authorisation is not directed at NATO but at individual States. Legally speaking, the individual members of NATO could have volunteered for the task, just as the French volunteered for limited enforcement action in Rwanda, and the United States in Haiti.

The Security Council started to bring NATO into the Bosnian theatre of war in resolution 770 of 13 August 1992, in which the Security Council, 'acting under Chapter VII of the Charter of the United Nations', called 'upon States to take nationally or through regional agencies ... all measures necessary to facilitate in coordination with the United Nations the delivery by relevant United Nations humanitarian organisations and others of humanitarian assistance to Sarajevo and wherever needed in other parts of Bosnia ...'. The phrase 'all measures necessary' has been used in the past by the Security Council to authorise military operations. Furthermore, the Council, in resolution 781 of 9 October 1992 imposed a no-fly zone over Bosnia. Authorisation to enforce this no-fly zone was granted by the Security Council in resolution 816 of 31 March 1993. Safe havens were established by resolutions 819 of 16 April 1993, 624 of 6 May, 836 of 4 June, and 844 of 22 June under UNPROFOR protection, including the use of force if necessary. Limited use of air power by member States was also authorised by resolution 836.

Initially, limited coercion was used by NATO under these provisions: NATO threatened air strikes against the Bosnian Serbs surrounding Sarajevo in February 1994 if they failed to withdraw their heavy weapons; NATO planes shot down four Serb warplanes above Bosnia in the same month; and NATO planes bombed Serb airbases in Croatia in November 1994,[231] and Serb ammunition dumps near Pale, the Bosnian Serb 'capital', in May 1995. In this limited enforcement period, with UNPROFOR vulnerable on the ground, there was a considerable amount of control over NATO operations by the UN Secretary General's representative and UNPROFOR commanders, with NATO air strikes only taking place at the request, or with the consent of, UNPROFOR – the so-called 'dual key' approach.[232] A greater use of air power by NATO, in consultation with the Secretary General, and the emplacement of a rapid reaction force on the ground at the end of August 1995 followed Bosnian Serb attacks against the UN safe areas of Srebrenica and Zepa.[233]

The peace agreements secured at Dayton, Ohio in November 1995[234] as a result partly of NATO actions, provided for UNPROFOR in Bosnia to be replaced by a NATO-led IFOR, which was granted the power to oversee and enforce the agreements without the need to seek further approval from the Secretary General. The London Peace Implementation Conference on Bosnia of 9 December 1995 summarised the primary functions of IFOR as ensuring compliance with the cease-fire, ensuring withdrawal and separation of forces, and the secondary functions as the creation of conditions in which humanitarian tasks could be performed by other organisations and bodies, to prevent interference with the return of refugees, and to assist in the clearing of minefields.[235]

The UN Security Council endorsed the creation and emplacement of IFOR in what amounted to a greater degree of delegation to NATO than had occurred in Bosnia before,[236] but little different to the delegation to member States to undertake potentially offensive military operations in Rwanda, Haiti and Somalia. Resolution 1031 of 15 December 1995, authorised IFOR 'to take all necessary measures to effect the implementation of and to ensure compliance with' the agreement and, 'stresses that the parties shall be held equally responsible for compliance ... and shall be equally subject to such enforcement action by IFOR as may be necessary to ensure implementation ... and takes note that the parties have consented to IFOR's taking of such measures'. Although IFOR has been consented to by the parties it is not a traditional form of peacekeeping. IFOR (now SFOR)[237] performs a traditional peacekeeping role while the accords are being complied with, but will become an offensive operation if the accords are broken. Indeed, even while it is performing a basic peacekeeping function, the threat of enforcement action if the peace is broken, combined with the much greater military capacity of IFOR, makes it a much more capable military operation than UNPROFOR, which for all practical purposes, despite Security Council attempts at tinkering with its mandate, was a traditional peacekeeping force (see Part Three).

As regards the Security Council authorisation for the United States to use force in Haiti in 1994, the resolution simply said that the Council 'acting under Chapter VII of the Charter ... authorises Member States to form a multinational force under a unified command and control and, in this framework, to use all necessary means to facilitate the departure from Haiti of the military leadership ...' and to create the conditions for the restoration of democracy.[238] This is arguably an unacceptable delegation of power to the United States shown by the fact that the removal of the military dictatorship was finally achieved by US negotiators led by Jimmy Carter and had nothing to do with the UN.

Similar problems arose with the Security Council's authorisation of France's 'Operation Turquoise' in Rwanda in 1994 following the genocide there. Although the resolution stressed the 'strictly humanitarian character' of the operation 'which shall be conducted in an impartial and neutral fashion',[239] France's connection with the Hutu government, responsible for the genocide directed at the Tutsis, cast grave doubts about the collective goals of the operation. Lessons seemed to be learnt from this when the crisis in the Great Lakes region, fuelled by the huge flows of refugees displaced from Rwanda, caused a grave humanitarian crisis for these refugees in eastern Zaire in October 1996. This led to the authorisation of a multi-national force (to be drawn mainly from the P3 but commanded by Canada) mandated 'to facilitate the immediate return of humanitarian organisations and the effective delivery by civilian relief organisations of humanitarian aid to alleviate the immediate suffering of displaced persons, refugees and civilians at risk in eastern Zaire, and to facilitate the voluntary, orderly repatriation of refugees by the United Nations High Commissioner for Refugees'.[240] Although overcoming to a certain extent the perceived illegitimacy of authorising a unilateral military intervention,[241] the multinational force was not finally deployed to eastern Zaire as the rather lacklustre military preparations were overtaken by events which led to the return of a significant number of refugees. A reluctance, by the United States and the United Kingdom in this case, to commit troops to an area beyond their vital interests is inevitable in a decentralised collective security system, particularly where the costs of such operations are not generally funded collectively by the UN, but by the contributing States themselves in addition to voluntary contributions.

There are, undoubtedly, problems with relying on a system of volunteers to uphold collective security ideals, not the least of which is the erratic nature of such a method in that aggression or threats to the peace will only be met by force when there are volunteers to be found. States will generally only volunteer when it will serve their purposes as well as the UN's. Political considerations apart, the legality of these UN authorised operations is still a matter of heated debate, but there are now, within the UN's terms, several precedents for recommendatory military action, and it is arguable that the Security Council has by its practice established a power to authorise States to take 'necessary measures' with regard to a particular conflict or situation. On the other hand, it is arguably legally unacceptable to imply a power which goes against the express provisions of the Charter which clearly envisage collective security in the form of the centralisation of armed force. In this respect the Council authorisations to use force to date, when there is often neither a clear and relatively precise enabling resolution nor UN control of these operations, undermine the constitutionality of the resolutions in this crucial area of UN practice.

Although there are some doubts about the constitutionality of UN military operations, there has been an increase in the number of successes since the end of the Cold War. However, the inconsistent responses of the world community, inevitable in a system which relies simply on the recommendation of military action, illustrate that as yet the UN cannot claim to embody the collective security ideal.

Notes

1 J. P. Cot and A. Pellet, *La Charte des Nations Unies*, 629, 2nd ed. (1991).

2　R. B. Russell and J. E. Muther, *A History of the United Nations Charter*, 657 (1958).

3　L. M. Goodrich, E. Hambro and P .S. Simons, *The Charter of the United Nations*, 258, 3rd ed. (1969).

4　On the various methods of peaceful settlement see B. Simma (ed.), *The Charter of the United Nations: A Commentary*, 510–11 (1994). See generally J. G. Merrills, *International Dispute Settlement*, 2nd ed. (1991).

5　See UN doc. S/14942 (1982).

6　SC 2345 mtg, 37 UN SCOR (1982).

7　SC 2349 mtg, 37 UN SCOR (1982).

8　SC Res. 502, 37 UN SCOR Resolutions 15 (1982).

9　SC Res. 530, 38 UN SCOR Resolutions 10 (1983).

10　UN doc. S/14941 (1982).

11　SC Res. 479, 35 UN SCOR Resolutions 23 (1980).

12　See for example SC Res. 582, 41 UN SCOR Resolutions 13 (1986).

13　Goodrich, Hambro and Simons, *The Charter*, 161. But see A. C. Arend, 'The Obligation to Pursue Peaceful Settlement in International Disputes during Hostilities', 24 *Virginia Journal of International Law* (1983), 97.

14　For example S/PRST/1995/42 re Tajikistan.

15　For example SC Res. 1088, 51 UN S/PV (1996), re the implementation of the Dayton Accords of November 1995 in Bosnia.

16　B. Simma (ed.), *The Charter*, 508.

17　See for example SC Res. 1036, 51 UN S/PV (1996) re Georgia, and SC Res. 1040, 51 UN S/PV (1996) re Burundi.

18　See J. Quigley, 'Security Council Fact Finding: A Prerequisite to the Effective Prevention of War', 7 *Florida Journal of International Law* (1992), 191.

19　SC Res. 15, 1 UN SCOR Resolutions 6 (1946).

20　UN doc. S/360/Rev. 1 (1947).

21　SC 136 mtg, 2 UN SCOR (1947).

22　SC Res. 289, 25 UN SCOR Resolutions 13 (1970) re Guinea; SC Res. 294, 26 UN SCOR Resolutions 2 (1971) re Senegal. See also SC Res. 568, 40 UN SCOR Resolutions 20 (1985) re South African attacks on Botswana; and SC Res. 57, 40 UN SCOR Resolutions 16 (1985) re South African incursions into Angola.

23　SC Res. 290, 25 UN SCOR Resolutions 13 (1970). But see SC Res. 302, 26 UN SCOR Resolutions 3 (1971) re Senegal.

24　32 UN SCOR Special Supp. (No. 3) (1977).

25　SC Res. 419, 32 UN SCOR Resolutions 18 (1977).

26　See also SC Res. 189, 19 UN SCOR Resolutions 11 (1964) to investigate alleged aggression against Cambodia; SC Res. 496, 36 UN SCOR Resolutions 11 (1981) to investigate mercenary aggression against the Seychelles.

27　See SC Res. 377, 30 UN SCOR Resolutions 7 (1975) for the investigation which started the Western Saharan peace process; SC Res. 39, 3 UN SCOR Resolutions 2 (1948), for the investigation which led to the cessation of hostilities in Kashmir and the emplacement of an observer force.

28　SC 2802 mtg, 43 UN SCOR (1988).

29　SC Res. 1052, 51 UN S/PV (1996).

30　UN doc. S/1996/337 (1996).

31　Simma (ed.), *The Charter*, 525.

32 E. Lauterpacht, *Aspects of the Administration of International Justice*, 42 (1991).
33 75 UNTS 31.
34 SC Res. 672, 45 UN SCOR Resolutions 7 (1990).
35 SC Res. 673, 45 UN SCOR Resolutions 7 (1990). See UN doc. S/21219 (1990).
36 SC 2953 mtg, 45 UN SCOR (1990).
37 Quigley, 7 *Florida Journal of International Law* (1992), 192.
38 GA Res. 46/59, 46 UN GAOR Supp. (No. 49) 290 (1992).
39 SC mtg, 12 May 1992.
40 SC Res. 780, 47 UN SCOR Resolutions (1992).
41 SC Res. 935, 49 UN SCOR Resolutions (1994). See also SC Res. 1012, 1013, 50 UN
    SCOR Resolutions (1995) establishing international commissions of inquiry to inves-
    tigate violence in Burundi and the supply of arms to the troops of the former Rwandan
    government.
42 Cot and Pellet, *La Charte*, 641.
43 UN doc. S/649/Rev. 1 (1947).
44 SC Res. 27, 2 UN SCOR Resolutions 6 (1947).
45 SC Res. 30, 2 UN SCOR Resolutions 6 (1947).
46 SC Res. 36, 2 UN SCOR Resolutions 9 (1947).
47 UN doc. S/537 (1947).
48 SC Res. 593, 41 UN SCOR Resolutions 16 (1986).
49 See doc. S/1994/262. Also SC Res. 902, 49 UN SCOR Resolutions (1994), which
    'reiterates that the maintenance of the status quo is unacceptable'.
50 SC Res. 186, 19 UN SCOR Resolutions (1964).
51 SC 2823 mtg, 43 UN SCOR (1988).
52 UN doc. S/21803 (1990).
53 35 *I.L.M.* (1996), 75.
54 SC Res. 1031, 50 UN SCOR Resolutions (1995).
55 R. Higgins, 'The Place of International Law in the Settlement of Disputes by the UN
    Security Council', 63 *A.J.I.L.* (1970), 1 at 4.
56 *Ibid*. See also O. Schacter, 'The Quasi-Judicial Role of the Security Council and the
    General Assembly', 58 *A.J.I.L.* (1964), 960.
57 UN docs S/20093, S/20242, S/20442 (1988).
58 UN doc. S/23273 (1991).
59 G. Perry, 'Security Council Resolution 242: The Withdrawal Clause', 31 *Middle East
    Journal* (1977), 413 at 432.
60 See for example SC Res. 799, 47 UN SCOR Resolutions 6 (1992).
61 K. Harper, 'Does the United Nations Security Council have the Competence to Act as
    a Court and a Legislature?', 27 *New York University Journal of International Law and
    Politics* (1994), 103 at 106. On the question of the propriety of the Security Council
    acting as a court and a legislature see 129–55.
62 The Security Council also condemned the Bosnian Serbs for their violations of inter-
    national humanitarian law: SC Res. 819, 48 UN SCOR Resolutions (1993); SC Res.
    941, 49 UN SCOR Resolutions (1994); SC Res. 1034 50 UN SCOR Resolutions
    (1995). See also SC Res. 851, 48 UN SCOR Resolutions (1993), for a similar con-
    demnation as regards UNITA in Angola.
63 15 UNTS 295.
64 SC Res. 1067, 51 UN S/PV (1996).

65 UN doc. S/1996/509.
66 S/PRST/1996/9.
67 SC 417 mtg, 4 UN SCOR (1949).
68 UN doc. S/1274 (1949).
69 SC Res. 269, 24 UN SCOR Resolutions 2 (1969).
70 UN doc. S/12857 (1978).
71 UN doc. S/17633 (1985).
72 UN doc. S/12636 (1978).
73 SC Res. 757, 47 UN SCOR Resolutions 13 (1992). See also SC Res. 942, 49 UN SCOR Resolutions (1994), which extended sanctions to the Bosnian Serb held areas of Bosnia.
74 35 *I.L.M.* (1996), 75.
75 SC Res. 1074, 51 UN S/PV (1996).
76 SC Res. 816, 836, 48 UN SCOR Resolutions (1993); SC Res. 998, 50 UN SCOR Resolutions (1995).
77 SC Res. 1088, 51 UN S/PV (1996).
78 485 UNTS 321.
79 UN docs S/22465, S/22480 (1991).
80 UN doc. 23 May 91. 28(3) *UN Chronicle* (1991), 15.
81 SC Res. 833, 48 UN SCOR Resolutions (1993).
82 See 30 *I.L.M.* (1991), 1703 (on the status of the Commission); 31 *I.L.M.* (1992), 1009 (on criteria for claims); 34 *I.L.M.* (1995), 235 (first awards of compensation); 35 *I.L.M.* (1996), 939 (further awards).
83 UN doc. S/22661 (1991).
84 See also SC Res. 712, 46 UN SCOR Resolutions 24 (1991).
85 UN doc. S/23514 (1991).
86 35 *I.L.M.* (1996), 1095.
87 SC Res. 986, 50 UN SCOR Resolutions (1995).
88 See generally N. D. White, 'Commentary on the Protection of the Kurdish Safe-Haven: Operation Desert Strike', 1 *Journal of Armed Conflict Law* (1996), 197.
89 UN docs S/1995/1017.
90 UN docs S/22871/Rev. 1, S/22872/Rev. 1 (1991).
91 UN docs S/1996/258, S/1996/261.
92 UN doc. S/1996/182.
93 SC Res. 1051, 51 UN S/PV (1996).
94 See further L. D. Roberts, 'United Nations Security Council Resolution 687 and its Aftermath: The Implications for Domestic Authority and the Need for Legitimacy', 25 *New York University Journal of International Law and Politics* (1993), 593 at 613–14.
95 *Reparation for Injuries Suffered in the Service of the United Nations*, I.C.J. *Rep.* 1949, 174 at 198. See chapter two.
96 See the dissenting opinion of Judge Alvarez, *Competence of the General Assembly for the Admission of a State to the United Nations*, I.C.J. *Rep.* 1950, 4 at 15–19. See further N. D. White, *The Law of International Organisations*, 128–33 (1996).
97 F. Seyersted, *United Nations Forces: In the Law of Peace and War*, 154–5 (1966). See chapter two.
98 H. Kelsen, *The Law of the United Nations*, 727 (1951); R. Higgins, *The Development*

of International Law through the Political Organs of the United Nations, 266 (1963). But see Roberts, 25 *New York University Journal of International Law and Politics*, 614–21.

 99 SC Res. 22, 2 UN SCOR Resolutions 3 (1947).

100 *Corfu Channel Case*, I.C.J. *Rep.* 1949, 15 at 31–2.

101 UN doc. S/12167 (1978).

102 See *The Aegean Sea Continental Shelf Case*, I.C.J. *Rep.* 1978, 3.

103 *Lockerbie* case (provisional measures), I.C.J. *Rep.* 1992, 114.

104 SC Res. 808, 48 UN SCOR Resolutions (1993).

105 SC Res. 780, 47 UN SCOR Resolutions 36 (1992).

106 UN doc. S/25704 (1993).

107 SC Res. 827, 48 UN SCOR Resolutions (1993).

108 J. C. O'Brien, 'The International Tribunal for Violations of International Humanitarian Law in the Former Yugoslavia', 87 *A.J.I.L.* (1993), 639 at 640.

109 SC Res. 935, 49 UN SCOR Resolutions (1994).

110 SC Res. 955, 49 UN SCOR Resolutions (1994).

111 J. Karhilo, 'The Establishment of the International Tribunal for Rwanda', 64 *Nordic Journal of International Law*, (1995), 683 at 697.

112 16 *H.R.L.J.* (1995), 223.

113 Case No. IT-94–1-T, 10 August 1995, para. 2.

114 *Ibid.*, paras 7–8.

115 Case No. IT-94–1-AR72, para. 20.

116 *Ibid.*, para. 28.

117 *Ibid.*, para. 30.

118 *Ibid.*, paras 15 and 36.

119 *Ibid.*, para. 35.

120 M. C. Bassiouni and P. Manikas, *The Law of the International Criminal Tribunal for the Former Yugoslavia*, 239 (1996); V. Morris and P. Scharf, *An Insider's Guide to the International Criminal Tribunal for the Former Yugoslavia*, 42–3, vol. 1 (1995); O'Brien, 87 *A.J.I.L.* (1993), 643; G.H. Aldrich, 'Jurisdiction of the International Criminal Tribunal for the Former Yugoslavia', 90 *A.J.I.L.* (1996), 64 at 65. But see A. Rubin, 'An International Criminal Tribunal for the Former Yugoslavia', 6–7 *Pace International Law Review* (1994), 1 at 8–10.

121 Case No. IT-94–1-AR72, para. 19.

122 SC Res. 827, 48 UN SCOR Resolutions (1993); SC Res. 955, 49 UN SCOR Resolutions (1994).

123 Case No. IT-94–1-T, para. 2.

124 T. D. Mak, 'The Case Against an International War Crimes Tribunal for the Former Yugoslavia', 2 *International Peacekeeping* (1995), 536 at 555–6.

125 Article 1(3) and the Preamble of the UN Charter.

126 Karhilo, 64 *Nordic Journal of International Law* (1995), 696.

127 UN doc. S/1995/728, Annual Report of the ICTY.

128 See for example *The Guardian*, 10 January 1997. See UN doc. A/51/789 (1997) for a scathing UN report on the ICTR.

129 Mak, 2 *International Peacekeeping* (1995), 554.

130 Article 27 of the Statute on detention shows the need for cooperation in that imprisonment of convicted individuals will take place in consenting States' prisons.

131 *Keesing's* (1996), 40890, 40986, 41018.
132 Rubin, 6–7 *Pace International Law Review* (1994), 8.
133 35 *I.L.M.* (1996), 75, Annex 1-A, Article X.
134 *Ibid.*, Article VI(4); SC Res. 827 48 UN SCOR Resolutions (1993).
135 N. Figa-Talamanca, 'The Role of NATO in the Peace Agreement for Bosnia and Herzegovina', 7 *European Journal of International Law* (1996), 174.
136 See J. Crawford, 'The ILC's Draft Statute for an International Criminal Court', 88 *A.J.I.L.* (1994), 140.
137 Case No. IT-94–1-AR72, para. 33. Simma (ed.), *The Charter*, 619.
138 Cot and Pellet, *La Charte*, 617–18. Simma (ed.), *The Charter*, 620.
139 UN doc. S/7906 (1967).
140 See SC 1341–1346 mtgs, 22 UN SCOR (1967).
141 SC Res. 233, 22 UN SCOR Resolutions 2 (1967).
142 SC Res. 235, 22 UN SCOR Resolutions 3 (1967).
143 SC Res. 164, 16 UN SCOR Resolutions 9 (1961).
144 For example SC Res. 588, 41 UN SCOR Resolutions 13 (1986).
145 SC Res. 353, 29 UN SCOR Resolutions 7 (1974).
146 SC Res. 354, 29 UN SCOR Resolutions 7 (1974).
147 SC Res. 355, 29 UN SCOR Resolutions 8 (1974).
148 SC Res. 502, 505, 37 UN SCOR Resolutions 15–17 (1982).
149 SC Res. 82, 5 UN SCOR Resolutions 4 (1950).
150 SC Res. 660, 45 UN SCOR Resolutions 19 (1990).
151 SC Res. 998, 50 UN SCOR Resolutions (1995).
152 SC Res. 918, 49 UN SCOR Resolutions (1994).
153 SC Res. 217, 20 UN SCOR Resolutions 8 (1965).
154 SC 1265 mtg, 20 UN SCOR 15 (US) 16 (UK) 6 (Ivory Coast) (1965).
155 SC Res. 232, 21 UN SCOR Resolutions 7 (1966); SC Res. 253, 23 UN SCOR Resolutions 8 (1968).
156 SC Res. 181, 18 UN SCOR Resolutions 7 (1963).
157 SC Res. 418, 32 UN SCOR Resolutions 5 (1977).
158 The arms embargo was terminated by SC Res. 919, 49 UN SCOR Resolutions (1994).
159 See UN doc. S/12265 (1975).
160 J. A. Sigmon, 'Dispute Resolution in the United Nations: An Inefficient Forum?', 10 *Brooklyn Journal of International Law* (1984), 437 at 450.
161 J. Pokalas, 'Economic Sanctions: An Effective Alternative to Military Coercion?', 4 *Brooklyn Journal of International Law* (1980), 289 at 312.
162 See GA Res. 1747, 17 UN GAOR Supp. (No. 17A) 3 (1962).
163 Pokalas, 4 *Brooklyn Journal of International Law* (1980), 312.
164 SC Res. 333, 28 UN SCOR Resolutions 14 (1973).
165 J. C. Nkala, *The United Nations, International Law, and the Rhodesian Independence Crisis*, 81 (1985).
166 H. R. Strack, *Sanctions: The Case of Rhodesia*, 162–4 (1978).
167 SC Res. 320, 27 UN SCOR Resolutions 9 (1972).
168 Pokalas, 4 *Brooklyn Journal of International Law* (1980), 314.
169 SC Res. 460, 34 UN SCOR Resolutions 15 (1979).
170 Pokalas, 4 *Brooklyn Journal of International Law* (1980), 306.
171 D. Bethlehem (ed.), *The Kuwait Crisis: Sanctions and their Economic Consequences*,

xxxiv–xxxvi (1991). UN doc. S/21585 (1990). See further Simma, *The Charter*, 627.

172 *Ibid.*, xliii. See further C. Joyner, 'Sanctions, Compliance and International Law: Reflections on the United Nations' Experience against Iraq', 32 *Virginia Journal of International Law* (1991), 1.

173 SC Res. 666, 669, 670, 45 UN SCOR Resolutions 22, 24 (1990).

174 Provisional record of the fifth meeting of the Sanctions Committee, 31 August 1991, USSR, Bethlehem, *The Kuwait Crisis: Sanctions*, 797.

175 See for example argument between Cuba and the United States over a cargo of powdered milk, *ibid.*, 809–10.

176 F. L. Kirgis, 'The Security Council's First Fifty Years', 89 *A.J.I.L.* (1995), 506 at 536.

177 On this see SC Res. 669, 45 UN SCOR Resolutions 24 (1990). Bethlehem, *Kuwait Crisis*, ch. 3.

178 R. Lavalle, 'The Law of the United Nations and the Use of Force, under the Relevant Security Council Resolutions of 1990 and 1991, to Resolve the Persian Gulf Crisis', 23 *Netherlands Yearbook of International Law* (1992), 3 at 13.

179 Joyner, 32 *Virginia Journal of International Law* (1991), 38.

180 See also SC Res. 918, 49 UN SCOR Resolutions (1994), on the arms embargo against Rwanda. Terminated in SC Res. 1011, 50 UN SCOR Resolutions (1995).

181 SC Res. 874, 875, 48 UN SCOR Resolutions (1993).

182 SC Res. 917, 49 UN SCOR Resolutions (1994).

183 SC Res. 940, 39 UN SCOR Resolutions (1994).

184 SC Res. 948, 49 UN SCOR Resolutions (1994).

185 SC Res. 873, 48 UN SCOR Resolutions (1993).

186 SC Res. 942, 49 UN SCOR Resolutions (1994).

187 The UN General Assembly requested that the Security Council lift the arms embargo against the Bosnian Muslims in GA Res. 48/88, 48 UN GAOR (1993), by 109 votes to 57.

188 SC Res. 943, 49 UN SCOR Resolutions (1994).

189 Sanctions were formally terminated against Serbia and the Bosnian Serbs by SC Res. 1074, 51 UN S/PV (1996).

190 SC Res. 883, 48 UN SCOR Resolutions (1993).

191 SC Res. 1054, 1070, 51 UN S/PV (1996).

192 SC 105 mtg, 2 UN SCOR (1947).

193 Special Supp. (No. 1), 2 UN SCOR (1947).

194 See generally R. A. Falk, 'The United Nations and the Rule of Law', 4 *Transnational Law and Contemporary Problems* (1994), 611; I. Brownlie, 'The Decisions of Political Organs of the United Nations and the Rule of Law', in R. Macdonald (ed.), *Essays in Honour in Wang Tieya* (1994), 91.

195 Goodrich, Hambro and Simons, *The Charter*, 323.

196 See O. Schacter, 'United Nations Law in the Gulf Conflict', 85 *A.J.I.L.* (1991), 425 at 459–60.

197 Cot and Pellet, *La Charte*, 709–11.

198 But see J. Quigley, 'The United States and the United Nations in the Persian Gulf War: New Order or Disorder?', 25 *Cornell International Law Journal* (1992), 1 at 33–7.

199 Simma, *The Charter*, 633.

200 SC 3046 mtg, 47 UN S/PV 18 (1992).

201 See generally J. W. Houck, 'The Command and Control of United Nations Forces in

the Era of "Peace Enforcement"', 4 *Duke Journal of Comparative and International Law* (1993), 1.

202 T. Stein, 'Decentralized International Law Enforcement: The Changing Role of the State as Law Enforcement Agent', in J. Delbrück, *Allocation of Law Enforcement Authority in the International System* (1995), 107 at 125. A.C. Arend, 'The United Nations and the New World Order', 81 *Georgetown Law Journal* (1993), 491 at 507–11.

203 But see T. M. Franck, 'The *Bona Fides* of Power: Security Council and Threats to the Peace', 240 *Hague Recueil* (1993 III), 189.

204 UN doc. S/24868 (1992).

205 30(1) *UN Chronicle* (1993), 13–16.

206 UN doc. S/24868 (1992).

207 UN doc. S/25168 (1993).

208 SC Res. 837, 48 UN SCOR Resolutions (1993). See further chapters eight and nine.

209 SC Res. 787, 47 UN SCOR Resolutions 29 (1992).

210 SC Res. 221, 21 UN SCOR Resolutions 5 (1966).

211 SC Res. 665, 45 UN SCOR Resolutions 21 (1990).

212 See statement by President Truman, 27 June 1950, *United States Policy in the Korean Crisis*; 18 (1950).

213 But see the Secretary General's view, T. Lie, *In the Cause of Peace*, 332 (1954).

214 *Ibid.*, 334.

215 SC 477 mtg, 5 UN SCOR (1950).

216 GA Res. 376, 5 UN GAOR (1950).

217 L. Goodrich, 'Korea: Collective Measures against Aggression', 494 *International Conciliation* (1953), 157 at 178.

218 J. N. Singh, *Use of Force under International Law*, 82 (1984).

219 But see J. Stone, *Legal Control of International Conflict*, 234–7 (1954).

220 But see Quigley, 25 *Cornell International Law Journal* (1992), 17–19.

221 SC Res. 662, 664, 45 UN SCOR Resolutions 20–1 (1990).

222 UN doc. S/21492 (1990).

223 SC 2963 mtg, 45 UN SCOR (1990).

224 *Ibid.*

225 E. V. Rostow, 'Until What? Enforcement Action or Collective Self-Defense', 85 *A.J.I.L.* (1991), 506 at 509.

226 A. Parsons, 'The UN and the National Interests of States', in A. Roberts and B. Kingsbury (eds), *United Nations Divided World*, 2nd ed. (1993), p. 121; Quigley, 25 *Cornell International Law Journal* (1992), 15–17. See also SC 2977 mtg, 46 UN SCOR (1991).

227 N. D. White and H. McCoubrey, 'International Law and the Use of Force in the Gulf', 10 *International Relations* (1991), 347 at 359–73.

228 But see the imposition of air exclusion zones by Western States over northern Iraq in March 1991, and over southern Iraq in August 1992. There appears to be no explicit Council authority for these measures, although they were justified by Western leaders as coming under UN cease-fire terms, and under resolution 688, respectively. See *Keesing's* (1991), 38081.

229 See White, 1 *Journal of Armed Conflict Law* (1996), 197.

230 See generally T. M. Franck, 'The United Nations as Guarantor of International Peace

and Security: Past, Present and Future', in C. Tomuschat (ed.), *The United Nations at Fifty: A Legal Perspective* (1995), 25 at 31–2.

231 SC Res. 958, 49 UN SCOR Resolutions (1994).

232 Security Council resolutions authorising NATO air strikes simply required 'close coordination' with the UN Secretary General and UNPROFOR. They did not explicitly state that UN consent was necessary before each strike, though this was the interpretation put on them in practice.

233 UN doc. S/1995/987.

234 UN docs S/1995/999, 1995/1021, 1995/1029. 35 *I.L.M.* (1996), 75.

235 UN doc. S/1995/1029.

236 Article 1(1)(b) of Annex 1A of the Dayton Agreement.

237 SC Res. 1088, 51 UN S/PV (1996).

238 SC Res. 940, 49 UN SCOR Resolutions (1994).

239 SC Res. 929, 49 UN SCOR Resolutions (1994).

240 SC Res. 1080, 51 UN S/PV (1996). Only an advance contingent of 350 troops had been sent under the auspices of this resolution by the end of March 1997.

241 See generally H. Freudenschuss, 'In Between Unilateralism and Collective Security: Authorisation of the Use of Force by the UN Security Council', 5 *European Journal of International Law* (1994), 492 at 528–9. See also SC Res. 1101, 28 March 1997, by which a multinational force was authorised to 'facilitate the safe and prompt delivery of humanitarian assistance' to Albania.

PART TWO

The General Assembly

CHAPTER FOUR

The political context

Whereas the Security Council's position as the primary body responsible for the maintenance of international peace and security is reasonably well established and defined, the General Assembly's role in this context is nebulous and ill-defined. The drafting of the provisions of the UN Charter relating to the General Assembly's functions and powers was a source of contention between the smaller States represented at San Francisco and the sponsoring powers. The latter group's Dumbarton Oaks proposals gave the Assembly no real power. At San Francisco, the smaller States insisted that all the power should not be in the hands of the Council, or more specifically in the hands of the veto-wielding members. As a result Chapter IV, which contains the powers of the General Assembly, became a compromise between the provisions granting generous powers to the Assembly to placate the smaller nations, namely Articles 10 and 14, and provisions attempting to restrict the powers and competence of the Assembly, that is Articles 11 and 12.

The result is an example of political compromise, an ambiguous set of provisions which have been interpreted advantageously by and for the benefit of whichever group or groups of States is dominating the Assembly at a particular time. In the early years of the Organisation the body was Western dominated. With the advent of rapid decolonisation in the late 1950s and during the 1960s the whole complexion of the Organisation changed with the Non-Aligned movement seizing virtual control of the Assembly. Unlike the Security Council, where the Cold War was a relatively constant factor in limiting the use and development of the Council's powers, there were two distinct phases in the Cold War influences on the General Assembly.

The Cold War era

During the early years the Soviet Union protected its interests by the use of the veto in the Security Council and was fiercely critical of any attempt to give the Western dominated Assembly more than subsidiary powers in the field of international peace, basing its objections on a narrow interpretation of the relevant

Charter provisions. Nevertheless, the West used its dominant position to introduce procedures and bodies to circumvent the paralysis in the Council brought on by the Soviet veto, using a liberal interpretation of the Charter.

An example of this wide interpretation of the Charter was the adoption by the Western dominated Assembly in 1950 of the Uniting for Peace Resolution, a Western initiative which purported to allow the Assembly to recommend the use of military action to combat breaches of the peace when the Council was unable to act because of the veto. The aim was to allow the General Assembly to take over the role of the Council in the maintenance of peace, and it was made even more poignant in that it was adopted against the background of the Korean War, the first UN authorised military operation. The United States, realising that Security Council authorisation of military action was unlikely to re-occur as long as the Cold War continued, wanted to allow the Assembly to authorise Korean-type operations in the future. The legality of this resolution and other Western ploys adopted during the Assembly's first decade will be discussed in chapter five. It is worth emphasising at this point, that the clear Cold War motivations behind such initiatives do not *ipso facto* render them unlawful. Most laws or interpretations of laws are politically motivated. Furthermore, a politically motivated interpretation of the Charter, if constitutional, can be used by subsequent political groupings to the detriment of the original sponsors of the interpretation.

This happened to a certain extent in the next phase of the General Assembly's life during the Cold War, in that after the end of the period of Western domination, 1945–55, the new majority in the Assembly used Western-type interpretations of the Charter to further their political goals, though in the absence of military or economic might in this group, the achievements were more rhetorical than coercive. In 1945 the membership of the United Nations numbered 51 whereas by the end of the Cold War this had increased to 159. The bulk of this increase consisted of the 100 or so members of the Non-Aligned (sometimes called the Group of 77) new States emerging from the decolonisation process, dramatically altering the balance of power in the Assembly. During this period, the then Socialist States cleverly adopted similar stances to the Non-Aligned on such issues as colonialism and self-determination, which understandably were and still are of considerable concern to the Non-Aligned. Paradoxically, the West, which might be expected to dominate questions of freedom and self-determination (though not in colonial contexts), was not able to align itself on these issues with the newly independent States. Thus it was the erstwhile colonial powers and their allies (namely the 'West') which were, in the majority of discussions and votes, in the minority in the Assembly. Consequently, the West withdrew its liberal interpretation of the Charter which it used so successfully in the early years, and argued instead on a narrow constitutional basis that the Security Council was the primary body, where, predictably, the number of Western vetoes in protection of Western interests increased dramatically, and further that the General Assembly had a limited discursive, and moreover, subsidiary, role.

Relatively, the number of Western and Socialist bloc countries remained constant during this period; the variable factor was the group of newly independent States without a permanent member from within its ranks, on the Security Council protecting its interests. Consequently, there was an increasing divergence on similar issues between the views of the Assembly where a majority of two-thirds could adopt a resolution on 'important questions' such as those concerning international peace,[1] and those of the Council where the overriding consideration was one of compromise in order to avoid the veto. In the early years the West dominated both bodies and so used the Assembly as a means of dealing with issues on which the Soviet Union was sensitive. Nevertheless, there was still a link between the Assembly and the Council during the Cold War period. The Cold War intensified during the 1950s and 1960s, but the introduction of a third factor, the newly independent States, meant that the link between the Assembly and the Council became increasingly tenuous. The Assembly began to take initiatives and became antagonistic towards the Council.

The new majority viewed the Council as a private club protecting the interests of the superpowers and their allies,[2] a view highlighted by the decreasing representation in the Security Council of the membership of the Organisation. In 1945 the ratio of members of the Security Council to members of the Organisation was 11:51 (21.6 per cent). In 1985 this percentage had decreased to 9.4 (15:159). It would have taken a Security Council of thirty-three members to reproduce the original ratio in 1985, and a non-permanent member could hope for election to the club once every sixteen years.[3] As shall be seen in the next section, the membership of the Organisation has increased even further so that the Security Council has become even less representative. At the end of 1996 it would have taken a Security Council of forty members to re-create the original balance between the general membership and membership of the executive organ. These figures emphasise the decreasing ties between the Council and the Assembly with the latter acting with increasing independence in the field of international peace and security, with a subsequent expansion in the *de facto* competence of the Assembly, particularly in the Cold War period. Whether this expansion breached the *de jure* restrictions in the Charter will be examined in the next chapter, but the flexible nature of the Charter must be borne in mind, a fact particularly apparent in Chapter IV concerning the General Assembly.

Luard accurately summarises the implications and importance to the Non-Aligned of its political power in the General Assembly.

If the West had been tempted to use its votes to force through its own views with little thought of negotiations to impose the tyranny of the majority, how much more would the third world when it came to power, be tempted to do so? The West at least had possessed alternative means of securing the ends it cherished, overwhelming military power, widespread diplomatic opportunities, huge economic strength, unrivalled political leverage. The third world had none of these assets. It had no military power, little diplomatic experience, negligible economic strength, and insignificant political leverage. For these countries, it appeared, the one weapon at their disposal was the UN, which not long after [the period of Western domination] they knew to be permanently at their disposal. It is scarcely surprising that, armed with this weapon, and inspired by the example presented by their predecessors, they proceeded, over the coming decades, to exploit, to the best of their ability, the one asset at their disposal.[4]

It will be illustrated in chapters five and six that the Non-Aligned and Socialist majority used its voting power to adopt resolutions on a wide range of situations and issues concerning international relations. However, this was not a revolution-ary development, for at San Francisco, the smaller States had made proposals for wide ranging competence, to authorise the Assembly to consider, for example, 'any matter within the sphere of international relations' or 'affecting international relations'.[5] However, at the time, such provisions were not specifically included, although the compromise that was achieved left sufficient loopholes for the Assembly to develop its powers in a direction similar to that envisaged by the smaller States in 1945.

It is important to note, however, that it was neither envisaged at the time, nor has it emerged since, that the Assembly has any formal mandatory powers along the lines of those possessed by the Security Council under Chapter VII. Although the Assembly has been assertive, 'demanding' and 'deciding', as well as 'recom-mending' and 'calling', there is no real suggestion that the Assembly can adopt anything more, in Charter terms, than a recommendation on matters of interna-tional peace and security. One issue that will emerge in chapter five is that the Assembly, while not having a mandatory power conferred upon it by the Charter, can adopt resolutions that are binding in the sense that they are based on estab-lished principles of international law. However, the Assembly is in this instance simply acting as a focal point for States' views on international law, an important function, but not one that can be said to create a mandatory power, and certainly not one that grants the Assembly a coercive power to *order* economic or military enforcement measures.

After the Cold War

The decolonisation process can be seen to have continued in an altered form to span the divide between the world order before and after the end of the Cold War. New States emerged out of the collapse of the Soviet Union and the Socialist bloc in general. In 1989 the membership of the United Nations was 159 and had been relatively stable for a number of years following the rapid expansion in the 1950s and 1960s with the admittance of newly independent African and Asian States. By 31 December 1996 the membership of the Organisation had increased to 185.

One can see nearly all the new member States as part of the 'fall-out' from the end of the Cold War. The former Soviet Republics of Armenia, Azerbaijan, Georgia, Kazakhstan, Kyrgyzstan, Moldova, Tajikistan, Turkmenistan, and

Uzbekistan,[6] as well as the more recent acquisitions to the former Soviet empire, the Baltic States of Latvia, Lithuania and Estonia, are clear examples. The same can be said about those new States emerging from the collapse of the Communist regime in Yugoslavia, namely, Bosnia and Herzegovina, Croatia, Slovenia, and the Yugoslav Republic of Macedonia, in addition to the new member States of Namibia, the Democratic People's Republic of Korea, the Republic of Korea, Eritrea, the Czech Republic and Slovakia. The remainder of the new membership in the post-Cold War era, namely, the Federated States of Micronesia, Liechtenstein, the Marshall islands, San Marino, Monaco, Andorra, and Palau are all so-called 'micro-States'.

The West's victory in the Cold War is confirmed in part by the fact that many of the new States, particularly the Baltic States, several of the former Yugoslav republics and some of the former Soviet republics, all have Western aspirations, alongside those States in Eastern Europe which once formed part of the Communist bloc but are now taking faltering steps towards Western-style governments and economies. These States have not continued to take an anti-Western stance in the General Assembly with the result that the Assembly's condemnations of South Africa and Israel, which during the Cold War were overwhelming, are either not so strongly supported, or are not so vehement in their condemnatory tones.

The voting patterns are changing in the General Assembly. Although the Non-Aligned group of developing States do still command a sufficient majority for such resolutions to be adopted, the force of these resolutions is less impressive often with a significant minority now abstaining or voting against. In addition, with many of the Non-Aligned in effect dependent on economic aid from the West, there appears to be less possibility of the General Assembly challenging the Security Council as the organ dealing with a situation or dispute that endangers or threatens international peace and security. Whereas during the Cold War the Assembly did usurp the primary responsibility of the Security Council on quite a number of occasions, it now appears to be a subsidiary organ. In addition, given the resurgence in the Security Council's activities, the Assembly has often little choice but to take a secondary or silent role. The overwhelming, and more importantly, unchallenged economic, military and political strength of the West in the post-Cold War era has led to a resurgent Security Council and a curtailed General Assembly. It has not resulted, however, in a return to the situation that existed in the first decade when both organs were dominated by the West, with the Non-Aligned States still forming the majority in the General Assembly.

Indeed, given the collapse of the bipolar world, it seems a little incongruous to talk about Non-Alignment, which essentially was a position somewhere between the Western and Eastern blocs. Instead we have a rough division of the world along North–South lines, with the richer nations of the northern hemisphere being pressured in international forums for a more equitable distribution of wealth and technology. This conflict is reflected in the debates and resolutions adopted by the General Assembly as a result of recommendations by the membership in the Second Committee of the General Assembly relating to Economic and Financial matters, but does not fully impinge on the Assembly's role in the maintenance of international peace and security. Indeed, the attitude of the majority appears at the moment to be one of leaving the Security Council to deal with situations concerning peace and security even though the Council may be pursuing Western policy. Furthermore, there is evidence of a developing trend in which the General Assembly adopts resolutions tentatively supporting the Security Council's efforts to resolve a dispute or deal with a situation that threatens the peace or has actually breached it. This phenomenon will be more fully examined elsewhere, though one or two examples will be pertinent here.

Even though Iraq invaded Kuwait shortly before the General Assembly opened its 45th annual session in September 1990, the Assembly essentially took a back seat during the Gulf Crisis of 1990–91. It did provide some limited support for the Security Council when it adopted a resolution on 28 November 1990, condemning the acts of violence against diplomatic and consular commissions.[7] This was obviously directed at Iraq and indeed that country cast the sole vote against the resolution, but it failed to mention Iraq by name although it recalled those Security Council resolutions that had condemned Iraq's violations of diplomatic law. It must be noted also that the resolution was adopted the day before the Security Council adopted resolution 678 which authorised the Coalition to use force against Iraq to remove it from Kuwait. It can be seen that the General Assembly has maintained its independence in that the same resolution also called upon States 'to make use of the means for the peaceful settlement of disputes'. This was obviously not deemed to be a tacit condemnation of the proposed use of force against Iraq for Western States were able to support the resolution as well, but it cannot be construed as amounting to anything more than limited support for the Security Council's approach to Iraq. In a later resolution at its 45th session, the General Assembly did condemn Iraq for its human rights violations in Kuwait and against third State nationals.[8] During its 46th session on 17 December 1991, it adopted a resolution supporting the Security Council's condemnation of the Iraqi suppression of sections of its own people in Council resolution 688 of 5 April 1991.[9] Furthermore, despite the continuation of the hurtful sanctions regime against Iraq, the Assembly has in recent years squarely blamed Iraq, in terms of it having 'sole responsibility', for the dire situation in the country as well as the widespread abuse of human rights committed by the regime.[10]

There is also limited evidence that the Assembly may be starting to support Western ideals more in its resolutions. Following the overthrow of the government of Haiti on 29 September 1991 which had been elected under UN observation on 16 December 1990, the General Assembly adopted a resolution without a vote on 11 October 1991 condemning the coup and expressing its support for 'the development of democracy in Haiti'.[11] This may be seen as support for the Western concept of democracy as well as its position on Haiti, although it did follow the initial refusal of the Security Council to deal with the dispute despite the protestations of the deposed President of Haiti on 3 October 1991 before the Council.[12] Furthermore, it had been the General Assembly that had supported Haiti's original request for observation in the December 1990 elections. The Assembly had authorised the observers on 10 October 1990,[13] although the Secretary General ensured that the Security Council approved of the General Assembly's action first in an exchange of letters with the President of the Security Council in September and October 1990.[14]

Indeed, with the Security Council adopting mandatory sanctions against Haiti in 1993 supported by the General Assembly, the two organs appeared to be in harmony,[15] although in contrast to the Assembly resolutions on Iraq, it took the lead during the initial phase of the Haitian crisis. Arguably since the matter, at least at the outset, was primarily one of human rights rather than collective security, the Assembly was justifiably involved. It was only when the Security Council deemed it to be a threat to the peace and used its coercive powers (both economic and military under Chapter VII), that it assumed primary responsibility for the crisis. Again, as with the UN's actions against Iraq, although both organs were involved they were acting in concert with the Assembly playing a subsidiary role in the realm of collective security, while continuing to emphasise its competence in the field of human rights.

Although the two organs seemed to be in accord, this is not necessarily evidence that the General Assembly has simply adopted the Western agenda. The fact is that it pushed the Western dominated Security Council into taking action against the Haitian military rulers. Furthermore, the Assembly's general support for greater democratisation within States seemingly reflects the views of the whole membership,[16] rather than the grudging acceptance of a majority under pressure from a minority of Western States.

Although it is possible to see the post-Cold War Assembly simply adopting or mimicking the ideology of the West, its continued independence of mind, though much suppressed, is still evident in its calls for the ending of the economic embargo imposed against Cuba by the United States,[17] as well as its call for exempting Bosnia from the arms embargo imposed on the whole of the former Yugoslavia by the Security Council, to enable the government of Bosnia to defend itself from the Bosnian Serbs.[18] The fact that the resolution on Cuba was opposed by the United States, while the resolution on Bosnia was supported by the United States, shows that the Assembly is perhaps no longer dogmatic but forms a view on the merits of each dispute or situation brought before it.

Before turning to the question of whether the Assembly has the legal competence to adopt such resolutions, it must be noted that the division outlined above, where the Assembly consisted of three blocs during the Cold War – Western, Non-Aligned and Socialist, and two divisions since – North and South, is too simplistic a view. The General Assembly consists of many sub-divisions based loosely on regions such as the Group of Western States, League of Arab States, Group of African States, Group of Asian States, and the Group of Latin American States.

Sometimes these become more definitive and take the form of regional organisations from which one member is chosen from each to represent its views in the
Assembly. The European Union, the Organisation of African Unity, the Organisation of American States, the Organisation of the Islamic Conference, the Organisation of South East Asian States are examples of regional bodies which are
represented in the General Assembly, each with a different degree of cohesiveness.

However, the Assembly is not like a political party system as found in a democratic society.[19] Nevertheless, in the course of examining and voting upon problems involving the use of force in international relations during the Cold War, the
Assembly very regularly divided into the three blocs discussed above. East–West
relations were of great significance in the maintenance of peace through the
United Nations, and the Non-Aligned united on this issue on so many occasions
because its militarily weak members were so often the victims of the use of force
in which a superpower was involved. Whether the Non-Aligned movement can
maintain itself as a significant coalition and as a united advocate of the non-use of
force in international relations remains to be seen now the Cold War has ended,
and the General Assembly is once again redefining its 'subsidiary' role in the
maintenance of international peace and security.

The indications are that it will continue to adopt resolutions condemning the
illegal use of force by the United States, evidenced by its condemnation of the
American military intervention in Panama in 1989,[20] but it is significant that it
failed to adopt a resolution directly condemning the Iraqi invasion of Kuwait in
1990. This contrast is perhaps illustrative of the North–South divide creeping into
the actions of the General Assembly, in that it was prepared to condemn an unlawful use of force by a developed State, but was not so prepared when that act was
committed by a developing State. Such an approach, if it continues, will undermine the considerable credibility the General Assembly has in its consistent condemnations of unlawful acts of aggression. In defence of the Assembly's
approach, it could be argued that the Security Council did condemn the use of
force against Kuwait, but obviously not against Panama, necessitating an Assembly response only in the latter case. It may be that these two instances simply point
to the more subservient approach of the Assembly to collective security matters
rather than double standards.

Notes

1 See Article 18(2) of the Charter.
2 GA Res. 1991, 18 UN GAOR Supp. (No. 15) 21 (1963), established the composition
   of the Council as follows: 5 permanent members, 5 from Afro-Asian States, 1 from
   Eastern Europe, 2 from Latin America, 2 from Western European and other States.
3 D. Nicol, *The United Nations Security Council: Towards Greater Effectiveness*, 4
   (1982).

4 E. Luard, *A History of the United Nations: vol. 1 The Years of Western Domination (1945–1955)*, 383 (1982).

5 See for example the delegates from New Zealand and Australia, UNCIO, vol. 9, 272, 266.

6 Belarus, formerly Byelorussia, and the Ukraine have been members since 1945 originally at the insistence of the Soviet Union, in order to provide some balance in the Organisation between the two power blocs.

7 GA Res. 45/39, 45 UN GAOR Supp. (No. 49) 360 (1990).

8 GA Res. 45/170, 45 UN GAOR Supp. (No. 49) 283 (1990).

9 GA Res. 46/134, 46 UN GAOR Supp. (No. 49) 206 (1991).

10 See for example GA Res. 50/191, 50 UN GAOR Supp. (No. 49) 254 (1995).

11 GA Res. 46/7, 46 UN GAOR Supp. (No. 49) 13 (1991).

12 SC 3011 mtg, 46 S/PV (1991).

13 GA Res. 45/2, 45 UN GAOR Supp. (No. 49) 12 (1990).

14 UN docs S/21845, 21847 (1990).

15 Supported in GA Res. 48/27, 48 UN GAOR Supp. (No. 49) 29 (1993); GA Res. 49/27, 49 UN GAOR Supp. (No. 49) 32 (1994).

16 GA Res. 51/31, 51 UN A/PV (1996).

17 See for example GA Res. 50/10, 50 UN GAOR Supp. (No. 49) 17 (1995).

18 GA Res. 47/121, 47 UN GAOR Supp. (No. 49) (1992); GA Res. 48/88, 48 UN GAOR Supp. (No. 49) 40 (1993). See also the resolution adopted on 13 March 1997 by the Assembly calling on Israel to refrain from building a new settlement in East Jerusalem by 130 to 2 (US and Israel) with 2 abstentions, following a US veto of a similar text in the Security Council on 7 March 1997.

19 S. D. Bailey, *The General Assembly*, 23 (1960).

20 GA Res. 44/240, 44 UN GAOR (1989).

CHAPTER FIVE

The subsidiary powers of the General Assembly

The idea that Articles 10, 11, 12 and 14 of the UN Charter, containing the source of the General Assembly's powers, can be subject to varying interpretations has already been raised in the introductory section to this Part when it was stated that the Western governments have changed their position from that of favouring a wide interpretation of these provisions giving the Assembly wide powers in the field of international peace, to a more narrow constitutional position in later years. The West still maintains this position despite the ending of the Cold War and its current dominance of the Security Council due to the fact that it is still in the minority in the subsidiary body.

General powers

Proponents of a wide view of the competence of the General Assembly would point to Articles 10 and 14 of the Charter. According to Article 10:

The General Assembly may discuss any questions or any matters within the scope of the present Charter or relating to the powers or functions of any organs provided for in the present Charter, and, except as provided in Article 12, may make recommendations to the Members of the United Nations or to the Security Council or to both on any such questions or matters.

Article 10 establishes a general competence for the Assembly to discuss any matter within the jurisdiction of the United Nations as determined by the Charter.[1] This power indeed makes the Assembly the 'town meeting place of the world', and 'the open conscience of humanity', as intended.[2] Its power to make recommendations on any such matter must also cover the same area as the more concrete recommendatory powers of the Security Council under Chapters VI and VII as regards the maintenance of international peace and security. Hence Article 10 is subject to Article 12 which attempts to delineate between the functions of the Assembly and those of the Security Council.

Once it is established that Article 10 creates the widest possible sphere of competence for the Assembly subject to Article 12, then the other provisions defining the powers of the Assembly are to some extent unnecessary unless they detract from the powers contained in Article 10. Article 11 deals more specifically and in a more limited fashion with the Assembly's role in the maintenance of international peace, but is subject to paragraph 4 which states that 'the powers of the General Assembly set forth in this Article shall not limit the general scope of Article 10'.

If Article 10 is insufficient to grant the Assembly the full range of recommendatory powers, Article 14 re-emphasises its potentially wide jurisdiction with specific reference to international security by providing that:

Subject to the provisions of Article 12, the General Assembly may recommend measures for the peaceful adjustment of any situation, regardless of origin, which it deems likely to impair the general welfare or friendly relations among nations, including situations resulting from a violation of the present Charter setting forth the Purposes and Principles of the United Nations.

Article 14 with its jurisdictional threshold of a situation deemed 'likely to impair the general welfare or friendly relations among nations' appears to give the Assembly access to a much wider range of situations in the field of international peace and security than the Security Council which technically requires a danger to international peace, a threat to or breach of the peace or an act of aggression to act under Chapter VI or VII.[3] The test under Article 14 covers the whole spectrum of situations which might impair peace, whereas the provisions contained in Articles 34 and 39 deal with the more important, global, and potentially explosive, situations. The Assembly can, under Articles 10 and 14, discuss situations covered by Articles 34 and 39, but to prevent any clash between the work of the Security Council, which is primarily concerned with such situations, and the General Assembly, Article 14, as well as Article 10, is subject to the limitation contained in Article 12.

Despite the fact that Article 14 is rarely cited in Assembly resolutions,[4] it, along with Article 10, forms the basis of most resolutions directed towards the maintenance of international peace and security, enabling the Assembly to suggest measures or sanctions against States and enabling it to by-pass the domestic jurisdiction limitation contained in Article 2(7).[5]

Goodrich, Hambro and Simons state that Article 14 has formed the basis of Assembly resolutions dealing with fundamental human rights and self-determination 'in the face of arguments that the questions being dealt with are matters of domestic jurisdiction'.[6] The above authors cite the report of the Special Commission set up by the Assembly in 1953 to study the apartheid policies of South Africa. The Commission interpreted the scope of Article 14 as covering cases which 'were likely to bring interests into conflict with one another'.[7] This epitomises a rather more relaxed approach to Article 2(7) in the General Assembly compared to the Security Council, where the situation must usually be a threat to the peace or of international concern before intervention, in the form of a resolution, takes place.

The reference in Article 14 to the purposes and principles of the United Nations indicates that perhaps one of the major roles of the General Assembly is to deal with the right to self-determination contained in Article 1(2). Also Articles 1(3) and 13(1)(b) contain references to 'human rights and fundamental freedoms'. These provisions combined with the Assembly's role as regards the maintenance of international peace and security contained in Articles 10, 14 and indeed Article 11, suggest that the General Assembly has a major, if not primary role in situations concerning either human rights or the question of self-determination, or both, even when the situation also concerns the maintenance of international peace.

Whether it could be said that the proper division of functions between the Security Council and the General Assembly as regards the maintenance of international peace and security depends on whether the situation is predominantly one of human rights and self-determination (in which case the General Assembly is perhaps the organ jurisdictionally competent to deal with it) will be examined later. For the moment it is sufficient to say that this view is practice based.[8]

Division of competence between the Security Council and the General Assembly according to the Charter

Articles 10 and 14 empower the General Assembly to discuss and make recommendations on matters which may be a danger to international peace within the meaning of Article 34, Chapter VI, or which constitute a threat to or breach of the peace within the meaning of Article 39, Chapter VII. Since these are the jurisdictional thresholds to the Security Council's competence in the field of international peace and security clearly there is a large area of overlap between the two organs. It is clear from Article 24(1) that the Security Council has 'primary responsibility' for peace and security, a position which Articles 11 and 12 of the UN Charter attempt to elaborate upon.

Article 11, in paragraphs 2 and 3, attempts to clarify the relationship between the Assembly and the Security Council as regards questions which come within Chapter VII or situations under Chapter VI. Nevertheless, these provisions of limitation must be read subject to paragraph 4 of Article 11, whereby Article 10 is stated not to be subject to the restrictions contained in Article 11, which suggests that Article 11 has no effect on the division of competence at all. This confusing situation may be explained by the compromise that brought these provisions about between the smaller States advocating wide powers and the sponsoring States attempting to limit these powers.[9]

Article 11(2) and (3) attempts to refine the wide area of overlap between the two organs created by Articles 10 and 14. Article 11(3) deals specifically with a situation which comes within Chapter VI, as defined by Article 34. 'The General Assembly may call the attention of the Security Council to situations which are likely to endanger international peace'. Article 11(3) seems to envisage the possibility of concurrent jurisdiction between the two organs in that it does not place an obligation on the Assembly to refer any such situation to the Council.

Article 24(2) refers to Chapter VI as containing 'specific powers granted to the Security Council' for the discharge of its primary responsibility, and all the Articles, except Article 35, seem to envisage exclusivity of operation to the Security Council. Nevertheless, Articles 10 and 14 empower the Assembly to make recommendations for pacific settlement similar to those contained in Chapter VI. Article 11(3) operates as a safety valve in that the Security Council is the body designed to deal with such situations. Article 11(3) does perform this function to a certain extent as evidenced by the fact that it is one of the rare Charter provisions actually cited in Assembly resolutions, for example as regards the situation in South Africa,[10] but it cannot be said to operate to oblige the General Assembly to refer such matters to the Security Council, it simply appears to be a rule of guidance which the Assembly can ignore if it wishes. Article 24(2) also states that Chapter VII contains the specific powers of the Security Council, and, indeed, its power conferring provisions (Articles 39–42) do not mention the Assembly nor seem to envisage the Assembly entering into Chapter VII. Article 11(2) is an attempt to provide an answer to the conundrum of whether the Assembly can utilise Chapter VII by providing,

The General Assembly may discuss any questions relating to the maintenance of international peace and security brought before it by any Member of the United Nations, or by the Security Council, or by a State which is not a Member of the United Nations in accordance with Article 35, paragraph 2, and, except as provided in Article 12, may make recommendations with regard to any such questions to the State or States concerned or to the Security Council or to both. Any such question on which action is necessary shall be referred to the Security Council by the General Assembly either before or after discussion.

Article 11(2) enables the General Assembly to find a 'threat to the peace', a 'breach of the peace' or an 'act of aggression' and to make recommendations thereon to restore international peace, a power concurrent with that of the Security Council under Article 39. It is a recommendatory power only, any coercive measures under Chapter VII requiring a mandatory decision can only be adopted by the Security Council.[11]

This interpretation of Article 11(2) is supported to a limited extent by the International Court in the *Expenses* case, when the Court stated,

The Court considers that the kind of action referred to in Article 11, paragraph 2, is coercive or enforcement action ... The word 'action' must mean such action as is solely within the province of the Security Council. It cannot refer to recommendations which the Security Council might make, as for instance under Article 38, because the General Assembly under Article 11 has a comparable power ... If the word 'action' in Article 11, paragraph 2, were interpreted to mean that the General Assembly could make recommendations only of a general character affecting peace and security in the abstract, and not in relation to specific cases, the paragraph would not have provided that the General Assembly may make recommendations on questions brought before it by States or by the Security Council.[12]

Although ambiguous, in that this does not make clear whether coercive or enforcement 'action' within the meaning of Article 11(2) is of a mandatory character or not, the tenor of this section of the judgment suggests that the General Assembly has a similar recommendatory power to the Security Council. Indeed, earlier in the judgment the Court seems to make it clear that the Security Council has a monopoly only on *mandatory* coercive action, not voluntary or recommendatory measures, when it states that 'only the Security Council ... can *require* enforcement by coercive action' and further that 'it is the Security Council which, exclusively, may *order* coercive action'.[13] It follows from this that the Assembly can go so far as to recommend action by the Security Council, or to suggest voluntary sanctions, or further to recommend military measures.[14] There is a limited amount of General Assembly practice to support this contention, although the power to recommend military measures has not been utilised in the full sense, and in the current post-Cold War climate, has become even more a theoretical, rather than, practical issue.[15] The fact remains, however, that the General Assembly does appear, on balance, to have this power and it is not impossible to envisage a situation in which its future use may be considered.

Kelsen thought that the limitation in Article 11(2) precluded the recommendation of enforcement action, but considered that in any case Article 10 could be used.[16] Indeed on the assumption that Article 10 contains the *lex generalis* and Article 11 and, to a certain extent, Article 14, contain the *lex specialis*, the provisions of Article 11 are to a certain extent unnecessary under the principle that the extent of the Assembly's powers is defined by the general and in this case wider, rather than the specific, and in this case narrower, provisions. Nevertheless, the power of the Assembly to recommend economic or military action is controversial in that in the original Charter scheme the only way in which the United Nations could undertake economic or military action was by a mandatory decision of the *Security Council* under Articles 41 or 42. It is argued that since the UN has the power to order military action, then it must have the lesser power to recommend military action, and once this recommendatory power is recognised there is nothing in the Charter which prohibits the Assembly as well as the Council from exercising it. This contention, however, disguises the fact that recommendatory military action allows for the potential of greater abuse by member States (see chapter three), but it is the model adopted by the UN.

Despite these misgivings, it is submitted that the General Assembly is not limited by Article 11(2) except that it confirms the Assembly's lack of power to undertake coercive action on more than a recommendatory basis. The only other provision which purports to delimit the functions of the Council and the Assembly is Article 12. It has already been noted that Articles 10 and 14, as well as 11(2), are subject to the limitation contained in Article 12(1) which states that:

While the Security Council is exercising in respect of any dispute or situation the functions assigned to it in the present Charter, the General Assembly shall not make any recommendations with regard to that dispute or situation unless the Security Council so requests.

Article 12 is probably the most difficult provision, in constitutional terms, to reconcile with the practice of the General Assembly. As has been seen, the other provisions can be interpreted to enable the Assembly to pass resolutions on any matter concerning the maintenance of peace as long as they do not purport to be mandatory. However, as shall be illustrated when looking at the division of competence in practice, the Assembly often adopts resolutions on a matter at the same time at which the Security Council is considering the question.[17] Two arguments to escape Article 12 could be employed in this situation – that the Security Council, although considering the question and perhaps even adopting resolutions on it, is not actually performing the 'functions assigned to it in the Charter', or that the resolution adopted by the General Assembly is not actually a recommendation.[18]

It seems to have been accepted practice early in the life of the UN that when an item was placed on the Security Council's agenda it was deemed to be exercising its functions in accordance with Article 12(1). The theory behind the list of matters which the Secretary General submits to the General Assembly is that it tells the Assembly which issues it is not allowed to discuss because they are receiving attention in the Security Council.[19] In effect, this approach amounted to defining 'functions' in Article 12(1) with reference to Article 12(2) which states,

The Secretary General, with the consent of the Security Council, shall notify the General Assembly at each session of any matters relative to the maintenance of international peace and security which are being dealt with by the Security Council and shall similarly notify the General Assembly, or the Members of the United Nations if the General Assembly is not in session, immediately the Security Council ceases to deal with such matters.[20]

Professor Bowett subscribes to the view that Article 12(2) defines whether the Council is functioning or not. However, he recognises the artificiality of the process and concedes that, in practice, the Assembly is not limited by the list nor would it be reasonable to expect it to be. Even when the Council adopts a resolution the Assembly will sometimes adopt its own on the same question, the justification, according to this approach, being not one of legal interpretation 'but of necessity for the Assembly to promote the aims of the Charter when the Security Council cannot or will not do so'.[21]

The question of whether a recommendation adopted in the face of Article 12 with the requisite two-thirds majority with or without minority objections is *ultra vires* will be examined later. Suffice to say for the moment that the procedure in which the list of matters seized by the Security Council is also deemed to contain those matters in relation to which it is exercising the functions assigned to it may still be accepted at a very formal level, but in practice it has been disregarded.

Nevertheless, in the early years, this procedural rule was applied with some regularity. One of these cases was the Greek question (1947–48) which is worth examining in some detail because it is illustrative of how Western domination of the Organisation enabled it to manipulate the procedure to its own advantage.

The United States had committed itself by the Truman Doctrine to the economic and military support of Greece and Turkey. It was therefore interested in the prevention of a Communist takeover in Greece. In the Security Council it managed to establish a Commission to examine the situation.[22] In May 1947 the majority of the Commission reported that Yugoslavia, Bulgaria and Albania had supported guerrilla warfare in Greece.[23] The United States proposed that the Council endorse the Commission's recommendation to send a permanent body to Greece to observe her borders.[24] This was seen by the Communist countries as a Cold War move by a Council and a Commission dominated by Western countries. The proposal was vetoed by the Soviet Union.[25]

The United States simply waited for the regular session of the General Assembly in the autumn of 1947 to propose a similar resolution condemning Albania, Bulgaria and Yugoslavia and establishing a permanent Committee, the United Nations Sub-Commission on the Balkans (UNSCOB), to help observe the borders.[26] Thus the United States had successfully used its overwhelming support in the United Nations to pass resolutions to reinforce its sphere of influence in the Balkans and to prevent the encroachment of Communism.

Technically, however, the United States and its supporters managed to keep within the provisions of the Charter, in that after the Soviets had vetoed its last draft resolution in the Council, it proposed that the item be removed from the agenda to signify to the Assembly that it had ceased to deal with the matter allowing the Assembly to make recommendations thereon.[27] It was simply because the West dominated both organs that it could switch from Council to Assembly within the accepted constitutional procedure. It could easily win a procedural vote in the Council.

Whereas the Western States could use this method of transferring issues from the Council to the Assembly during the early Cold War period, the Non-Aligned group, once it became an established force in the 1960s, was not assured even with Socialist support, of winning a procedural vote in the Council and so in practice it tended to ignore procedural technicalities. In view of the importance of the United Nations to the Non-Aligned, it was not surprising that they took the attitude that their disregard of a technical procedure adopted during a period of Western domination was no more reprehensible than the cynical manipulation by the West of the same procedure during the earlier period. Indeed, the Assembly's approach breaks what in many ways was an artificial link between Article 12(2) and 12(1). The approach developed during the Cold War was that the Assembly would decide for itself whether the Council was functioning within the meaning of Article 12(1). This attitude to Article 12 seems set to continue despite the ending of the Cold War, although there is evidence that with the Security Council now 'functioning' more or less continuously and dealing positively with many issues brought before it, the Assembly has considerably less opportunity to assert its authority.

An examination of the meaning of the term 'recommendation' in Article 12 has important implications because the provisions granting powers to the General Assembly as regards international peace (Articles 10, 11 and 14) only envisage Assembly resolutions in the form of recommendations. The question remains whether the Assembly can pass resolutions which are not technically recommendations and so escape the limitation contained in Article 12. The International Court answered this question in the affirmative in the *Expenses* case.

Thus while it is the Security Council which, exclusively, may order coercive action, the functions and powers conferred on the General Assembly are not confined to discussion, consideration, the initiation of studies and the making of recommendations, they are not merely hortatory. Article 18 deals with 'decisions' of the General Assembly on 'important questions'. These 'decisions' do indeed include certain recommendations, but others have dispositive force and effect. Among these latter decisions, Article 18 includes suspension of rights and privileges of membership, expulsion of Members, 'and budgetary questions'.[28]

The Court's judgment confers recognition on non-recommendatory-type resolutions, which on a literal interpretation would not be subject to the limitation contained in Article 12. Chapter six which contains an examination of the concrete forms that General Assembly resolutions take will illustrate that the Assembly often condemns, decides (in a hortatory, non-mandatory sense), demands, or declares, thus leading to an argument that these types of resolution are not covered by Article 12.

Nevertheless, it is very difficult to maintain that all but a few General Assembly resolutions are compatible with this analysis. Often the resolution may 'demand' or 'decide' in one part and 'recommend' in another, particularly with the increased length of resolutions passed regularly on subjects such as the Middle East and South Africa. Also those resolutions which appear to confirm Security Council resolutions, and so could be said to be confirmatory rather than recommendatory, do often go beyond them and contain further recommendations than their Council counterparts.

The domestic jurisdiction limitation

Article 2(7) prohibits the *United Nations* from intervening 'essentially within the domestic jurisdiction of any State'.[29] This provision has already been examined in relation to the Security Council, when it was stated that domestic jurisdiction limitation is inapplicable not only in those cases requiring enforcement measures under Chapter VII, as catered for by Article 2(7) itself, but also in cases of a threat to the peace without such measures, or, indeed, in situations deemed to be of international concern requiring only pacification under Chapter VI.

The General Assembly, however, has not developed a similar jurisprudence, or, indeed, any discernable principles governing the applicability of Article 2(7).[30] It is submitted that an agreed interpretation is not possible because the equilibrium between national and international interests sought by the drafters of Article 2(7) is not constant.[31]

As will be shown below, the denial of the right to self-determination was originally within the domestic jurisdiction of a State and so outside the purview of the United Nations, but now it is of international concern and so subject to review. In the Security Council it only takes one permanent member to use Article 2(7) as a basis for its veto and so that body has a more substantial jurisprudence on the meaning of the domestic jurisdiction limitation. Nevertheless, it is possible to chart the involvement of the General Assembly in what might appear to be internal matters as developed in over fifty years of practice.

The first clear interference in domestic internal affairs involved the Assembly examining the regime of a State. In December 1946, the Assembly passed a resolution which recommended the banning of Spain from the United Nations and its specialised agencies and requested that all member States should recall their ambassadors from Spain. It also stated that if a democratic Spanish government was not established within a reasonable time, the Security Council should consider adequate measures to remedy the situation.[32]

The next area developed by General Assembly practice which effectively puts it outside the limitation contained in Article 2(7), concerned Non Self-Governing Territories. Rajan cites many cases which will be discussed elsewhere, Tunisia, Algeria, the Portuguese Territories, Namibia and Southern Rhodesia – to conclude that 'after all these actions … there is no shred of evidence to sustain the view that non self-governing territories fall under the domestic jurisdiction of their respective metropolitan powers',[33] despite objections by the colonial powers.[34] These objections are apt to be ephemeral, for example the United Kingdom initially relied on Article 2(7) to deny vehemently United Nations' jurisdiction as regards Southern Rhodesia,[35] but after UDI it was Britain which requested the Organisation's involvement.[36]

The Assembly's disregard of Article 2(7) on issues of human rights and fundamental freedoms can be traced back to the era of Western domination when that body was used to criticise the Eastern bloc. At its third annual session in 1949, the Assembly adopted a resolution expressing concern at the 'grave accusations made against the governments of Bulgaria and Hungary regarding the suppression of human rights and fundamental freedoms'.[37] At the same session the Assembly criticised the Soviet Union declaring that the measures preventing the wives of foreign nationals from leaving their own country to join their husbands were 'not in conformity with the Charter, and that if the wives were persons belonging to foreign diplomatic missions, such measures were contrary to diplomatic practice and likely to impair friendly relations between States'. The resolution therefore called on the Soviet Union to withdraw the measures.[38]

The use of Article 14 language in the latter case is illustrative of how that provision was used to empower the Assembly to discuss relatively trivial matters for the practice criticised was hardly likely to even remotely endanger peace. It is not surprising therefore, that with such a relatively minor matter escaping the provisions of Article 2(7), the Non-Aligned majority established since the 1950s has not paid much heed to its limitations.

The United Nations' involvement in the South African problem cannot be classified as a trivial concern, but it is a good illustration of how the Assembly has now elevated the denial of human rights and fundamental freedoms to one of international concern. Only the South African government has persistently based its objections on Article 2(7).[39] Although it was initially supported by some Western States,[40] it stood alone until the reform process led to free elections in 1994 and majority rule.[41]

A natural extension on the Assembly's concern for non self-governing territories and cases concerning human rights and fundamental freedoms, is that of cases concerning the denial of the right to self-determination, an issue also raised by the South African situation. It will be a constant theme throughout this Part that one of the Assembly's major purposes is the furtherance of the right to self-determination. It has virtually established that the denial of that right is a matter of international concern and so no longer within the sovereign domain of a State.[42] This trend has been reinforced in the post-Cold War era exemplified when the removal of the elected government in Haiti in 1991 by an internal military coup provoked a quick response from the General Assembly demanding, in a resolution supported by all members, 'the immediate restoration of the legitimate government' and 'the full observance of human rights in Haiti'.[43] Further evidence can be found in the Assembly's 1992 resolution which expressed support for the Central American Peace Process which had brought democracy to Nicaragua. It commended the factions in El Salvador for their efforts towards peaceful settlement and the restoration of democracy, as well as offering encouragement to the factions in Guatemala.[44]

The above instances all involve primary consideration of matters such as human rights and self-determination which may have consequences for international peace. It must be noted, however, that in cases primarily concerned with international peace and security, arguments based on domestic jurisdiction are used. Cases such as the Lebanon and Jordan (1958), Bangladesh (1971), Kampuchea (1979), and Afghanistan (1980), all involved arguments that the situation was internal and so covered by Article 2(7), but only usually by one party or power bloc involved in the dispute. Unlike the Security Council, however, these subjective arguments did not prevent the General Assembly from adopting resolutions. Indeed, the end of the Cold War and the withdrawal of superpower involvement from Afghanistan has not prevented the General Assembly from concerning itself with resolving the continuing conflict in that country.[45]

Arguments of *ultra vires*

States objecting to the General Assembly adopting resolutions sometimes argue that the resolution is *ultra vires*. The argument is normally founded on Article 12 or Article 2(7). The Assembly's consideration of the apartheid policies of the South African government over many years produced numerous objections based on Article 2(7). Until the reform process started in the 1990s culminating in elections in 1994, the South African ambassador had consistently asserted that his government must regard 'any resolution emanating from a discussion on or the consideration of the present item as *ultra vires* and, therefore, null and void'.[46] It is possible to find many examples of objections based on Article 2(7).[47] However, if the objectors are in the minority they do not appear to have any effect on the jurisdiction of the Assembly.[48] On these occasions, it sometimes appears, to the observer, that the Assembly's jurisdiction is determined by that body and not necessarily by the Charter.

An example of a resolution being introduced despite objections based on Article 12 is the Uniting for Peace Resolution of 1950 (reviewed more fully later in this chapter).[49] The resolution proposed to give competence to the Assembly, including the power to recommend enforcement measures, when the Security Council was paralysed by the veto. The Soviet Union and other Socialist States, being in the minority bloc at the time, objected to the resolution on the grounds, *inter alia*, that it was unconstitutional in that the 'functions' of the Security Council within the meaning of Article 12 included cases where the veto was used, since the veto was an integral part of the constitution of the Security Council. On this basis the Soviet representative thus asserted that the proposed procedure would amend the Charter without going through the amendment procedure envisaged in Article 109.[50] Nevertheless, the majority proceeded to adopt the resolution, the *procedure* of which has become established in Assembly practice, although the substantive powers embodied in the resolution have not. In other words, although the Uniting for Peace Resolution has been used to transfer a matter from the Council to the Assembly, it has not been used as a basis for recommendatory military action by the Assembly apart from peacekeeping operations.

From a legal point of view the Charter of the United Nations 'is the primary source of its jurisdiction'.[51] Admittedly, as far as the provisions conferring powers on the General Assembly are concerned, there is considerable confusion as to the limits of its jurisdiction. Nevertheless, Articles 12 and 2(7) represent relatively defined limitations on its competence, and it can be argued that clear breaches of these provisions are unconstitutional and therefore *ultra vires*. Even the doctrine of implied powers would not appear to save such resolutions. According to the World Court in the *Reparation* case, 'under international law, the Organisation must be deemed to have those powers which though not expressly provided in the Charter are conferred upon it by necessary implication as being essential to the performance of its duties'.[52] The Court does not allow the Organisation to imply powers which go against its Charter. Indeed, Ciobanu ties implied powers very securely to express provisions when he states that 'powers not expressed cannot freely be implied; implied powers flow from the grant of express powers, and are limited to those that are necessary to the exercise of powers expressly granted'.[53]

Even if a much more liberal approach is taken to implied or inherent powers than this there is little possibility of accommodating a clear breach of an express provision within their framework. Inherent powers have been defined very widely to allow international organisations to 'perform in principle every sovereign activity or take every action under international law, if they are really in a position to accomplish such purposes, provided their constitutions do not preclude such an activity'.[54] This approach to the question of powers seems to go beyond the *dictum* of the International Court in the *Reparation* case in that it gives the Assembly virtual *carte blanche* to determine its own competence as long as it does not do so in contradiction to the express terms.

However, there are many factors preventing what appears to be a clear breach of the Charter from being null and void. First there is a World Court judgment which, as part of a teleological approach to treaty interpretation, favoured a presumption against *ultra vires* where the action taken 'was appropriate for the fulfilment of one of the stated purposes of the United Nations'.[55] The presumption against *ultra vires* is a practical approach to the problem recognising that a resolution adopted according to the voting provisions of the Charter has to be presumed to be valid, otherwise the Assembly's resolutions would remain in a state of limbo until the unlikely event of their challenge before the International Court (an issue more fully examined in the context of the Security Council in chapter two). It is the lack of procedure for the challenge of resolutions that leads to this presumption. Judge Morelli made this clear in a separate judgment when he stated that 'the failure of an organ to conform to the rules concerning competence has no influence on the validity of the act, which amounts to saying that each organ of the United Nations is the judge of its own competence'.[56]

The same arguments apply to decisions of the Security Council except that in the Council the veto operates to varying degrees as a restraint on the abuse of power, although the end of the political limitations on the Council in the post-Cold War era has, as has been seen in chapter two, also resulted in the Council pushing its powers to the limit and perhaps beyond its constitution in the strict sense. However, given that the Council has a much greater competence in the field of international peace than the Assembly, it is the Assembly which is perhaps more likely to contravene the provisions of the Charter such as Article 12 which attempt to limit its competence and keep it as the subsidiary body.

The approach that recognises the theory of 'la compétence de la compétence', simply that the Council and Assembly act as judges of their own competence,[57] was not without recognition at San Francisco where the relevant Committee stated that 'it is inevitable that each organ will interpret such parts of the Charter as are applicable to its particular functions. This process is inherent in the functioning of any body which operates under an instrument defining its functions and powers'.[58] In addition to the legal recognition of the Assembly's (and Council's) ability to act as its own judge, it must not be forgotten that there is an inherent difficulty in making an *ultra vires* objection count, a problem made worse by the practice of the Assembly of not citing the source of its authority in its resolutions. If there is no clear basis as to the resolution it is indeed difficult to challenge it for the challenge itself must be based on an interpretation of the provision.

The principle of subsequent practice

A related question to that discussed in the above section is whether the Assembly has re-interpreted the Charter by its subsequent practice. The principle of subsequent practice as regards treaty interpretation is reasonably clear and accepted as affording legitimate evidence as to its correct interpretation.[59] A common, consistent practice by the vast majority of parties to a multilateral treaty such as the Charter of the United Nations 'must come near to being conclusive on how the treaty should be interpreted'. Indeed, this amounts to 'not so much the meaning of an existing text, as a revision of it, but a revision brought about by practice or conduct, rather than affected by and recorded in writing'. Further, 'conduct usually forms a more reliable guide to intention or purpose than anything to be found for instance in the preparatory work of the treaty simply because it has taken concrete and active, and not merely paper or verbal, form',[60] thus reflecting 'the parties' contemporary expectations'.[61]

So if the Assembly has consistently adopted resolutions on matters formally subject to Article 2(7) and Article 12 by a sufficiently large majority throughout its forty years of practice it might be possible to state that this amounts to a revision of those provisions. On the presumption that a consistent two-thirds majority, present and voting (which is required for important questions), is sufficient, it is submitted that such a revision has taken place. The revision amounts to a severe restriction on the domestic jurisdiction limitation contained in Article 2(7); a virtual disregard of the division of competence between the Assembly and the Council contained in Article 12; and, in effect, an interpretation of the vague powers contained in Articles 10, 11 and 14 to give the Assembly competence and powers with regard to any matter in international relations with the exception of the ability to take mandatory measures.

In this way the General Assembly has by subsequent practice extended its competence to the fullest extent as permitted by the doctrine of inherent powers, which permits the exercise of powers which fulfil the purposes of the UN, as long as they are not prohibited by the Charter. The exercise by the Assembly of mandatory powers in the field of peace and security is clearly prohibited by Article 11(2), and the Assembly has respected this limit on its powers. However, the contention that the Assembly has, by its practice, violated Article 2(7) and 12 is difficult to sustain given the opacity of both provisions, in particular the uncertainty as to the meaning of 'domestic jurisdiction' in Article 2(7) and 'functions' in Article 12. Thus it is impossible to argue that the Assembly has clearly breached these provisions by its subsequent practice.

The following section and chapter six will attempt to rationalise and categorise the practice of the Assembly first in the matter of competence, particularly as regards the Security Council, and, secondly, as regards the concrete forms the powers of the Assembly, derived from its competence, take.

The division of competence between the General Assembly and the Security Council in practice

Given that it has been established in this chapter that Article 11(2) only operated to prohibit the Assembly from taking mandatory, coercive action and that Article 12 had been revised by Assembly practice, it remains to be seen as to what form this revision has taken. A loose categorisation is made in the following section into situations in which the Assembly has acted in the following ways towards the Security Council: in a parallel manner; in a complementary way; in a manner which pre-empts or prejudices any potential decision or resolution of the Security Council; in a manner that concentrates on self-determination and human rights as opposed to security matters; and finally in a manner that amounts to performing the role of the Security Council.

Parallel resolutions

On a number of occasions the Assembly has acted in a parallel manner to the Security Council by simply repeating the resolutions of the Council. Good examples of this can be found in the Assembly's resolutions on the Gulf War between Iran and Iraq, on Cyprus after the Turkish invasion of 1974, and in the peace process in Cambodia in 1990–91.

During the Gulf War 1980–88, the General Assembly did little more than to parallel the Security Council. The Assembly adopted a resolution in 1982 on the conflict which was to all intents and purposes a reaffirmation of previous Council resolutions.[62] The only value of the resolution was that of repetition for it even recognised, when calling for a cease-fire, that 'the Security Council has already called for an immediate cease fire and end to all military operations'. It reflected the Council's jurisdictional findings when it deemed that the conflict endangered international peace and security. It did not seek to pre-judge the Council by determining that the conflict was a breach of the peace, although some members thought that the Assembly should have made such a determination.[63] It was not until 1987 that the Council finally reached such a conclusion.

Although the Iraq–Iran war was on the Council's agenda and was the subject of frequent resolutions calling for a cease-fire, the members of the Assembly apparently did not see the resolution as treading on the toes of the Council. The representative of Jamaica made it plain that nothing in the resolution 'proposes the removal of the issue from the purview' of the Council and was not 'an attempt to circumvent the fundamental role of the Security Council'.[64]

Sometimes, in the case of disputes which are never off the Security Council's agenda, it appears as if the General Assembly, in its annual session of 3–4 months, is taking part of the burden off the Council by adopting resolutions on the conflict. In some cases the Assembly seizes this opportunity either to complement the Council's resolutions or to pre-empt them. In the case of Cyprus, however, the Assembly has added little to the work of the Council except perhaps an increased weight of international opinion.

After the Greek backed coup against Makarios and the Turkish invasion of the northern part of Cyprus in 1974, the General Assembly virtually repeated earlier Council resolutions in its own resolution passed at its 29th session in 1974 which expressed grave concern 'about the continuation of the Cyprus crisis, which constitutes a threat to international peace and security', urged the withdrawal of foreign forces and the cessation of all 'foreign interference in its affairs'.[65]

By the time the Assembly passed this resolution the Turkish intervention had become a *fait accompli*. This partly explains why the Assembly and the Council share the responsibility of dealing with the Cyprus situation, for once the Council had acted promptly in accordance with Article 28(1) of the Charter during the initial crisis in 1974 and the situation had become ongoing, there was no practical reason why both organs should not share the burden even though the situation is primarily one of international peace and in theory Article 12 should apply.

Parallel resolutions by the General Assembly during the Cold War were less apparent than resolutions antagonistic towards the Security Council. The Gulf and Cyprus are examples of where neither superpower had the upper hand. As shall be seen, the Assembly tended to be the primary organ when it came to UN resolutions on superpower interventions, or situations in which one superpower was predominant. One of these instances followed the Vietnamese intervention in Kampuchea (Cambodia) in 1978, an action which was not condemned by the Security Council because of the Soviet veto, but which was consistently condemned by the General Assembly. However, since the end of the Cold War, the collapse of the Soviet Union, and the withdrawal of Vietnam from Cambodia, the warring factions in Cambodia have moved towards a peaceful settlement, guided by both the Security Council and the General Assembly with the latter acting more as the subsidiary body lending support to the Council by means of simple reiteration.

In addition, whereas the resolutions condemning the Vietnamese military intervention in Kampuchea were adopted by a majority, the resolutions supporting a Security Council backed peace plan were adopted without a vote. This added significantly to their weight. At its 45th and 46th sessions, the Assembly adopted resolutions supporting significant agreements between the warring factions, at Jakarta on 10 September 1990 and at Paris on 23 October 1991.[66] These agreements were effectively brokered by the permanent five of the Security Council and had received endorsement in that body. The General Assembly was simply adding its weight to the process and also to the mandate of the Secretary General who was responsible for the implementation of the peace plan under the Security Council's resolutions.

The end of the Cold War has seen an increase in parallel and complementary resolutions, although the overall impression is that the Assembly is simply silent on many matters with which the Council is dealing. The fact that no resolution is produced by the Assembly can disguise the fact that there are still major divisions in the plenary body. Having said that, occasionally, those divisions will surface and the Assembly will go beyond a simple parallel or complementary resolution. The failure of the Security Council to adopt anything other than a bland resolution dealing with the Israeli attack on the United Nations Interim Force in Lebanon (UNIFIL) base at Qana in Lebanon in April 1996,[67] provoked the Non-Aligned, at a resumed 50th session, to propose a much more condemnatory resolution which paralleled a draft heavily defeated in the Security Council.[68] This Cold War technique did succeed but only to a limited extent in that the resolution adopted, which was unequivocal in its condemnation of Israel and clear in its judgment that Israel should compensate Lebanon, secured only 64 votes in its favour with 2 against and 65 abstentions.[69] The view of the representative of the United States, who after referring to Article 12, stated that 'if the Assembly took action on a different resolution it would be a divided house, a United Nations speaking with two voices, and no clear direction',[70] did not prevent the adoption of the resolution, but reflects a continuance of Western objections to the competence of the Assembly based on Article 12.

Complementary resolutions

It can be strongly argued that when the Assembly acts in a parallel fashion, simply repeating the work of the Security Council, it is actually complementing the role of the primary organ by maintaining the focus of world attention on the dispute or situation. On other occasions the Assembly complements the Council in additional ways, without prejudice to the Council position.

As regards the Indonesian invasion of East Timor in 1975, although the General Assembly produced a resolution which was remarkably similar to its Council counterpart,[71] it could not be accused of merely repeating or paralleling the Council for it seized the issue and adopted its resolution *before* the Council. Indonesia had moved its troops into East Timor on 7 December, the General Assembly adopted its resolution on the 12th, whereas the Council could only virtually repeat the Assembly's call on the 22nd. The Assembly did not really pre-empt the Council for the resolution contained no findings under Article 39, but it did contain a request to the Council 'in conformity with' Article 11(3) to consider the situation.

The Assembly was not performing the Council's role, for the Council did act eventually except more slowly. It was a case of the Assembly aiding the Council, the machinery of which, on this occasion, lacked the necessary alacrity.

After the Security Council had failed to adopt a resolution which dealt more than temporarily with the Tunisian conflict,[72] the General Assembly held its Third Special Session in August 1961 under Article 20 of the Charter.

The representative of Tunisia stated that the General Assembly should act because of the inability of the Council to end French aggression and to secure the withdrawal of French troops who were in Tunisia 'against the will of the people'.[73] Nevertheless, the Assembly did not adopt a resolution condemning French aggression; instead it adopted one calling for negotiations and French withdrawal. The resolution classified the situation as a 'source of international friction' and a danger to international peace and security.[74]

Although the resolution did not favour the French, it built upon rather than detracted from the work of the Council. The Council was able to act with some immediacy and call for a cease-fire but as on so many occasions was unable to go that step further and recommend a basis for settlement. Instead, the Assembly performed this task making explicit what was implicit in the Council resolution, that the situation was of a kind that should be subject to pacific settlement. The Assembly did not upset the work of the Council by finding a 'breach of the peace' or 'act of aggression' which would not have induced any settlement.

In the post-Cold War period, there has been an increase in complementary resolutions. The Assembly's supportive resolutions on Iraq and Haiti in the 1990s have been dealt with in chapter four in which it was stated that these resolutions focused more on the human rights aspects of the conflict, while the Security Council dealt with the collective security issues. As shall be seen in the sections below there has been a similar development in longer running disputes and situations, primarily the Middle East and South Africa, which during the Cold War produced prejudicial rather than complementary resolutions.

Pre-emptive resolutions

With the change in composition of the Assembly during the 1960s, the new majority often found itself at loggerheads with the Security Council. The chief instance of this is when the Assembly pre-judged or pre-empted the work of the Council by making a determination of a threat to or breach of the peace within the meaning of Article 39. This was particularly so as regards colonial and neo-colonial situations.

As early as 1962 the General Assembly found 'that the policy and acts of the Portuguese Government with regard to the territories under its administration have constituted a serious threat to international peace and security'. This determination within the terms of Article 39 suggests that the situation required 'action' by the Security Council which should have had the question referred to it under Article 11(2). The resolution appeared to recognise this in that it requested the Security Council to take steps to 'secure the compliance of Portugal with its obligations as a Member State'.[75] Nevertheless, the Council did not enter into Chapter VII. Furthermore, it was not until 1972 that it found that the situation in the Portuguese territories was a 'danger' to international peace.[76]

In the case of Southern Rhodesia the Assembly found the situation constituted a threat to the peace in 1963 several years before the Security Council.[77] A finding of a threat to the peace is mainly a political decision and so a difference in the timing of such a finding in the two organs was to be expected. Nevertheless, once the situation came to a head with UDI in 1965 the Security Council might have been expected to take the lead. Not so, for the General Assembly was first to condemn UDI and referred the matter to the Security Council.[78] It even urged the Security Council to adopt enforcement measures under Chapter VII before the Council had even agreed to condemn UDI.[79]

The Assembly, throughout the problems in Southern Rhodesia, seemed to be pushing the Council, adopting resolutions which the Council often reluctantly followed, and above all acting as the conscience of the Security Council. There were objections. The Dutch representative pointed out that the Security Council had been seized of the problem since 1963 and so by virtue of Article 12 the Assembly could not make recommendations unless the Council so requested.[80] He also stated that the situation was not a threat to the peace with the consequence that no enforcement measures could be taken. His and other objections were ignored as the Council adopted mandatory economic measures against the minority Smith regime. Nevertheless, the Assembly did not stop pushing to have the embargo made more effective. It called on the Council to take the next logical and legal step within the meaning of Articles 2(5), 4 and 5 of the Charter of taking mandatory sanctions against the sanction breakers, principally South Africa and Portugal.[81] This call was repeated (but never followed) in 1973 in a resolution which contained an appeal to those vetoing permanent members (the United States, Britain and France) to stop preventing the Council from performing its duty.[82] It may have been stepping on the toes of the Council, but the Assembly took it upon itself to act as the conscience of the Council, particularly the permanent members.

During the early years of its consideration of the South African problem the Assembly was contented with finding that the continuance of the policies of the South African government 'seriously endangers international peace and security' while calling on the Security Council to consider the question under Article 11(3).[83]

However, four years later in 1965 the Socialist/Non-Aligned majority's patience ran out when it adopted a resolution which drew the Council's attention to the fact that the 'situation in South Africa constitutes a threat to international peace and security; that action under Chapter VII of the Charter is essential to solve the problem of apartheid and that universally applied economic sanctions are the only means of achieving a peaceful solution'.[84]

The General Assembly had pre-empted the Security Council's prerogative of making a determination under Article 39. The majority ignored the problem of division of powers. The representative of Norway, however, expressed the minority view that it was 'the Security Council and the Security Council alone, which has the authority to stipulate if a situation or crisis is of such a nature that sanctions should be imposed'. He stated that although the 'General Assembly can and should exert its influence on the Security Council', in his opinion, the resolution went too far in finding a threat to the peace.[85] Nevertheless, the Assembly maintained this attitude until its 46th session in 1991. Up until then it reiterated that the situation in South Africa constituted a threat to the peace,[86] and urged the imposition of mandatory economic sanctions by the Security Council under Chapter VII of the Charter.[87] However, the reforms started in the 1990s by the South African government resulted in a toning down of the Assembly's resolutions. Whereas the 1989 resolution reaffirmed that 'apartheid is a crime against humanity and a threat to international peace and security', the 1991 resolution simply reaffirmed the Assembly's 'support for the legitimate struggle of the South African people for the total eradication of apartheid through peaceful means'. It did not contain any call for the Security Council to impose mandatory sanctions.[88] Finally, in 1993 the Assembly and Security Council were in accord in supporting the peace process which led to free elections and majority rule in 1994.[89]

There appeared less Cold War antagonism between the Council and the Assembly over the illegal South Africa occupation of South West Africa/Namibia. In 1966 the General Assembly terminated South Africa's mandate over Namibia and called 'the attention of the Security Council to the present resolution'.[90] This represented quite a good example of the dovetailing of the Assembly and the Council; a fact recognised by the International Court in the *Namibia* case when it stated:

By resolution 2145 the General Assembly terminated the Mandate. However, lacking the necessary powers to ensure the withdrawal of South Africa from the Territory, it enlisted the help of the Security Council by calling the latter's attention to the resolution, thus acting in accordance with Article 11, paragraph 2 of the Charter.[91]

The Council went on to adopt resolutions for this purpose. However, this brief period of harmony was sandwiched between Assembly resolutions which went far beyond the rather tentative approach of the Council. The Assembly had first addressed the issue of South West Africa in 1946,[92] but it did not reach a jurisdictional finding until 1960 when it considered 'with grave concern that the present situation in South West Africa constitutes a serious threat to international peace and security'.[93] Nevertheless, it did not request, under Article 11(2) or (3), that the Security Council meet even though by finding a 'threat to the peace' it brought the situation within the ambit of the Council's primary responsibility.

After the termination of South Africa's mandate, the Assembly became increasingly exasperated with the Council's inability to end South Africa's presence in Namibia. For instance in 1981, the Assembly named France, the United States and the United Kingdom as being 'in collusion with the South African racists as manifested in their triple vetoes in the Security Council where the majority of the

world body demonstrated its determination to adopt concrete political and economic measures aimed at isolating terrorist South Africa in order to compel it to
vacate Namibia'.[94] It maintained this approach up until the independence of
Namibia in 1990, condemning the linkage of South African withdrawal from
Namibia with Cuban withdrawal from Angola contained in the 1988 peace plan
agreed between Angola, Cuba and South Africa.[95]

Western States objected to many of these resolutions, and used Articles 11(2)
and 12 as a legal basis.[96] However, the attitude of Western States was summed up
by the representative of Canada who in explaining his negative vote on a 1981 resolution stated that 'the authority of the General Assembly is recommendatory in
character; moreover, the General Assembly cannot arrogate to itself powers it
does not have by using language appropriate only to the Security Council. Nothing in this text, therefore, gives rise to a legal obligation'.[97] This is illustrative of
the Western States, realising that they could not stop the resolutions from being
adopted, simply refusing to accept that they imposed any obligation on members.
Since the resolutions were validly adopted according to the voting rules, arguments based on Articles 11 and 12 would have been futile, so the thrust of the
West's arguments, when it bothered to state one, was that the resolutions of the
Assembly were of paper value only, mere recommendations, the real power of
decision making lay with the Security Council. The Western States attempted to
confine the Assembly to a forum where the majority of members let off steam.

The Assembly's actions over Palestine also reflect upon the fact that in the early
years, when there was a Western majority in both organs, the Assembly acted as
a complement to the Council, whereas after the mid-1950s, with the increase in
newly independent, Non-Aligned countries, the Assembly's resolutions became
increasingly extreme and divorced from those of the Council.

After the failure of its partition plan for Palestine, reviewed in chapter six, the
Assembly set about complementing the Council in its efforts to restore peace and
stability to the region. For example it passed a resolution in 1948 which strongly
affirmed the General Assembly's 'support for the efforts of the Security Council
to secure a truce in Palestine'. To further the Council's efforts, the Assembly
appointed a mediator to 'promote a peaceful adjustment of the future situation in
Palestine' and to 'co-operate with the Truce Commission for Palestine appointed
by the Security Council on 23 April 1948'.[98]

From this relatively harmonious position the Assembly and Council became
increasingly divorced in their dealings with the Palestinian problem. Annual resolutions on the Palestine situation have been adopted since the mid-1970s, based
on the reports of the Committee on the Exercise of the Inalienable Rights of the
Palestinian people, a heavily biased Committee on which the West refuses to
serve.

In its resolutions on the Middle East question the Assembly showed the same
propensity for entering the Council's area of competence while isolating the generally pro-Israeli Western countries even though it often appeared as if the Assem-

bly was supporting the relevant Council resolution. For example, in 1971 the Assembly adopted a resolution which appeared to accord with the Council's actions in that it stated 'that the Security Council resolution 242 (1967) should be implemented in all its parts in order to achieve a just and lasting peace in the Middle East'. However, the resolution went further and found a 'threat to the peace' which the Council had not and suggested the Council take steps for the implementation of 242. The West's main objections, however, were with the alterations of the balance of the Council's resolution such as the Assembly's expression of grave concern at Israel's 'continued occupation' rather than with the introduction of the term 'threat to the peace' which in Assembly terms, unlike those of the Council, could not make the resolution mandatory.[99] The Dutch also felt that 'as a conscientious Member of the United Nations, that Article 12 of the Charter should be scrupulously observed'.[100]

Nevertheless, more than two-thirds of the Assembly were not so 'conscientious' and in 1975 it adopted a resolution which in addition to a finding of a threat to the peace provided an example of a comprehensive, pre-emptive request to the Council to take measures 'to ensure complete Israeli withdrawal from all the occupied Arab territories as well as a full recognition of the inalienable national rights of the Palestinian people and the attainment of those rights'.[101]

The resolutions became increasingly antagonistic; condemning the United States for aiding Israeli 'aggression' against the Palestinian people;[102] calling for voluntary measures against Israel and demanding that it comply with Article 25 as regards Council resolutions;[103] condemning Israel's links with South Africa; and criticising the United States for vetoing a draft resolution in the Security Council which prevented that body from taking Chapter VII action against Israel for its invasion of the Lebanon.[104] In effect, the Assembly arrogated to itself a virtually limitless competence as far as recommendatory resolutions were concerned.

Even with the superpower sponsored Middle East peace process starting after the Gulf Crisis with a Peace Conference in Madrid in October 1991, the General Assembly adopted a resolution two months later on Palestine at its 46th session, calling for a full International Peace Conference on the Middle East under the auspices of the United Nations. This was in effect a criticism of the peace process underway which was not under UN auspices. In addition, the resolution, while purporting to be furthering Security Council resolution 242 (1967), in effect went further by explicitly mentioning Jerusalem in the list of those territories from which Israel should withdraw, and stating that Israel should dismantle the settlements it has built in the Occupied Territories since 1967. Although the resolution attempted a balanced approach by stating that the guarantee of the security of all States in the area, in addition to freedom of access to holy places, were also principles for the achievement of a comprehensive peace, it effectively was an attempt to undermine a legitimate peace process by listing those principles on which the Assembly, not the parties, thought should form the basis for peace.[105]

With the South African situation finally resolved, the situation in the Middle East continues to divide the Assembly. The more pragmatic atmosphere in the General Assembly in the mid-1990s is reflected in the fact that it has adopted widely supported resolutions which now welcome the peace process based on Security Council resolution 242 started at Madrid and supplemented by the bilateral and multilateral process mainly involving the Palestinians and Israelis.[106] Libya, Lebanon, Syria and Iran voted against. It also adopted resolutions condemning Israel's approach to Jerusalem and the Golan Heights with Israel as the sole vote against,[107] while still insisting on supporting the more divisive recommendations of the Committee on the Exercise of the Inalienable Rights of the Palestinian People.[108] Although only Israel and the United States voted against the latter resolution, the far higher number of States abstaining undermined its value and also undermined the more widely supported resolutions encouraging the peace process.

Focus on self-determination and human rights

Many of the above instances can be seen as cases in which the General Assembly has acted within its own area of competence even though they also concern international peace and security. If a conflict is dominated by questions of fundamental human rights or the problem of self-determination then, arguably, the General Assembly has the primary role as the body responsible for the protection of those rights, even though the situation also involves the maintenance of international peace.

It has been suggested earlier in this chapter that the expansive jurisdiction of the General Assembly can be explained partly by its desire to further and protect the right of self-determination and human rights. These principles are enshrined in the Charter but no specific organ is entrusted with their protection. It is therefore natural that the Assembly, embodying the United Nations, should put itself forward as the defender of these principles. Often issues of self-determination and human rights involve questions of peace and security and thus frequently both the Security Council and the General Assembly are involved. Strictly, on this basis, the Assembly should only concentrate on the aspects of self-determination and human rights, without considering the security situation, but, as shall be illustrated below, this is often impossible in situations where the denial of self-determination is in itself seen as a threat to the peace.

The Assembly's resolutions on the Middle East and Southern Africa can be grouped together under this heading for they are illustrative of how, in long running situations, the Assembly has strayed from its true sphere of competence, particularly during the Cold War. This was usually due to a majority of members equating a denial of self-determination with a threat to the peace. The General Assembly then saw its function as trying to bring the Security Council into line with this finding and urging it to take the appropriate measures. These areas have been discussed above in the section on the pre-emption of the Council. This section is an alternative way of looking at the problem. The section on pre-judging can perhaps be seen as an example of how by ritualising the topics the Assembly loses sight of its purpose, namely the protection of fundamental human rights and the right of self-determination, and concentrates on the question of peace based on its finding of a threat, which, generally speaking, should be dealt with by the Security Council.

In the Southern Rhodesian situation the Assembly was primarily concerned with the implementation of the 1960 Declaration on the Granting of Independence to Colonial Countries and Peoples and not with problems of international peace and security as such.[109] However, this culminated in the merging of the two areas in 1963 when the Assembly decided that the failure to accord 'basic political rights' to the 'vast majority of the African population' and the 'entrenchment of the minority regime in power' created an 'explosive situation' which constituted a 'threat to international peace and security'.[110] The equation of a denial of human rights and self-determination with a threat to the peace shifted the emphasis towards the Council.[111] It could be argued that after the Council had made a similar finding in 1966 the Assembly should have left the situation to the Council. Nevertheless, the Assembly kept pre-judging the work of the Council until the settlement of the situation in 1980.

The situation on the Portuguese territories parallels that of Southern Rhodesia. For example in 1962, the Assembly found 'that the continued refusal of Portugal to recognise the legitimate aspirations of the Angolan people to self-determination' constituted a threat to international peace and security.[112]

The Socialist and Non-Aligned majority in the Assembly seemed to favour the view that a denial of self-determination constituted a threat to the peace.[113] Thus the Assembly was often in disagreement with the Council where the Western vetoes denied such findings. Thus with the Assembly and Council out of step, the Assembly found itself constantly urging the Council to align itself with the majority resulting in resolutions which pre-empt and pre-judge the work of the Council.

Again in the case of South Africa, the Assembly began by concentrating on the denial of self-determination and of human rights. In 1952 the Assembly established a Commission of Three to examine the question of race conflict in South Africa.[114] The Commission's report concluded that the racial policies of the government of South Africa were contrary to the Charter and the Universal Declaration of Human Rights and that the continuance of these policies would endanger friendly relations among States.[115] The Assembly established the basis of its examination of the South Africa problem in 1953 when it found that:

enduring peace will not be secured solely by collective arrangements against breaches of international peace, but that a genuine and lasting peace depends upon the observance of all the Purposes and Principles established in the Charter intended to achieve the maintenance of international peace and security, and especially upon respect for and observance of human rights and fundamental freedoms for all.[116]

This inevitably led the Assembly to find a threat to the peace and then to urge the Council to step in line. The problem, during the Cold War, was that with Western States believing that there was no question of finding a threat to the peace based solely on a denial of human rights, there was bound to be antagonism between the Council and the Assembly. The Western States believed that findings of a threat to the peace must be made by the Council alone which suggests that there must be something more than a denial of human rights.[117]

As long as the West took this view the two organs would not be in accord. The Assembly continued to attack an issue from the angle of a denial of human rights and self-determination, whereas a minority in the Council continued to look for some sign of a danger to international peace arising from something more than the internal situation. However, with the focus of self-determination moving away from decolonisation towards wider issues of democracy, as has been seen in chapter two, the Western States on the Council have now supported the equation of a denial of democracy and related denials of human rights with the concept of a threat to the peace in Haiti in 1993, bringing the Council's approach more in line with the Assembly's,[118] although technically the Council still insists on the internal situation having 'international repercussions'.

As has been seen, the General Assembly's consideration of the Palestinian problem has been expanded into a consideration of the whole Middle Eastern question which is essentially one of international peace. Nevertheless, the basis of the Assembly's involvement is centred around the self-determination of the Palestinian people. Its resolution of 1974 was a typical Cold War example containing an expression of deep concern 'that the problem of Palestine continues to endanger international peace and security'. Article 11(3) would tend to suggest that the Security Council should be called on to deal with the situation. However, the rest of the resolution is concerned with a reaffirmation of the Palestinians' right to self-determination, independence and sovereignty and recognises the 'right of the Palestinian people to regain its rights by all means in accordance with the purposes and principles of the Charter of the United Nations'.[119] For the Assembly the issues of self-determination and the maintenance of peace are inextricably linked. This was illustrated again in 1996, with the peace process between Israel and the Palestinians well underway, the Assembly produced a more considered resolution on Palestine at its 51st session when it expressed support for the process, 'noting with satisfaction the withdrawal of the Israeli army, which took place in the Gaza Strip and the Jericho area in accordance with the agreements reached by the parties, and the initiation of the Palestinian Authority in those areas, as well as the beginning of the redeployment of the Israeli army in the rest of the West Bank', as well as expressing its satisfaction at the holding of the first Palestinian general elections. While the resolution did recognise the right of all States in the region to live in peace and security, it affirmed the inadmissibility of acquisition of territory by war, the illegality of Israeli settlements in the occupied territories, and the right to self-determination of the Palestinian people, stating that the core of the

Arab–Israeli conflict was the issue of Palestine.[120] Although more conciliatory the resolution still contains most of the hallmarks of the Cold War approach to Palestine.

The difficulty is that since the resolutions are pro-Palestinian and thus anti-Israeli, Israel's supporters on the Security Council are unlikely to take up the Assembly's resolutions. This has led the majority of the Assembly to adopt resolutions which increasingly impinge on the area of competence of the Security Council. This trend has not discontinued with the end of the Cold War though it has become more focused on the current peace process.

The importance of the Assembly's competence in the areas of human rights and self-determination/democracy can be overshadowed by its resolutions on the Middle East. However, the end of the Cold War has perhaps seen the Assembly concentrating more on these issues. As has been stated in chapter four, it was the Assembly that led the way for the UN in dealing with the military coup in Haiti. This scenario has been repeated in the case of Burundi, when in November 1993, it condemned the assassination of the President of Burundi and the military coup there, and demanded the restoration of democracy.[121] It was not until August 1995, with the situation in Burundi having rapidly deteriorated with widespread violations of humanitarian law, that the Security Council became involved by establishing, *inter alia*, a commission of inquiry into the assassination of the President of Burundi in 1993.[122]

The General Assembly as primary organ

This section is concerned with instances when the Assembly has performed the functions of the Security Council. In other words it has taken over the role of the Council which has failed to fulfil its primary responsibility for the maintenance of international peace and security under Article 24.

There are three methods by which the General Assembly has attempted to become the primary organ as regards a situation concerning international peace: by means of the Interim Committee or Little Assembly, by the Uniting for Peace procedure in Emergency Special Session, or by Special Session under Article 20. Only the last of these is specifically authorised by the Charter. The former two methods were both created in the period of Western domination (1945–55) in an attempt to give the Assembly power when the Security Council was paralysed by the Soviet veto.

The first method the pro-Western majority employed in an attempt to give more primacy in affairs of peace and security to the Assembly concentrated on increasing the effective length of the Assembly's session beyond its four monthly regular session. The Assembly adopted a proposal by the United States creating a little Assembly consisting of all the members which could be convened all year round.[123] What was intended was to give the Assembly competence in the area of international peace when not in regular session, in other words an 'all year' Assembly.

Its responsibilities included the study of problems relating to international peace and to report to the Assembly at its regular session. Thus the power of recommendation still remained with the Assembly proper and so the Little Assembly did not represent a serious revision of the Charter to extend the Assembly's period of competence. In practice it represented even less of a threat to the Council's primacy for although it did submit reports to the General Assembly during the first decade, it was severely paralysed by a Soviet boycott and was eclipsed by another Western sponsored idea, the Uniting for Peace Resolution.

The creators of the Interim Committee saw it as a subsidiary organ of the General Assembly under Article 22. Prandler argues that it was created unconstitutionally, for theoretically its powers in the field of international peace undermined those of the Security Council and it is doubtful whether subsidiary bodies can have an independent scope of duties.[124] However, it can be contended that the Little Assembly's powers came under the Assembly's umbrella of powers, either Articles 10, 11 or 14, and so it had no duties independent of the Assembly, and only undermined the Security Council's competence in that it attempted to extend the Assembly's period of session.

The immediate reason for the adoption of the Uniting for Peace Resolution,[125] was the return, in August 1950, of the Soviet Union to the Security Council leading to the discontinuation of the Council as the body dealing with Korea. In fact the Assembly adopted a resolution on Korea after the Soviets had returned to the Security Council but before the Uniting for Peace Resolution was adopted.[126] However, the reasons for Uniting for Peace went beyond Korea, in that the Western influenced majority in the General Assembly was also of the view that the frequent use of the Soviet veto during the period 1946–50 was an abuse of that right and that the ideal of Great Power unanimity at San Francisco was no longer attainable. The Western States wanted an alternative form of collective security, based not on permanent member agreement in the Security Council, but on the basis of the will of the majority in the Assembly. Such a concept of collective security, whilst opening up the potential for economic and military actions against transgressors, also had the potential for allowing the General Assembly to authorise military action against one of the permanent members if the majority so wished, and if between them they had sufficient military might. It may be because this system of collective security was potentially dangerous that the resolution restricted the Assembly's power to recommend military measures to the most flagrant violations of international peace, namely breaches of the peace or acts of aggression, and did not expressly permit the Assembly to take such measures as a response to threats to the peace.

The method proposed by the United States, Canada, France, the Philippines, the United Kingdom, Turkey and Uruguay, by which paralysis of the Security Council would be circumvented was the Uniting for Peace Resolution, the salient part of which resolved:

[T]hat if the Security Council, because of lack of unanimity of the permanent members, fails to exercise its primary responsibility for the maintenance of international peace and security in any case where there appears to be a threat to the peace, breach of the peace, or act of aggression, the General Assembly shall consider the matter immediately with a view to making the appropriate recommendations to Members for collective measures, including in the case of a breach of the peace or act of aggression the use of armed force when necessary, to maintain or restore international peace and security. If not in session at the time, the General Assembly may meet in emergency special session within 24 hours of the request therefor. Such emergency special session shall be called if requested by the Security Council on a vote of any seven members [now presumably nine], or by a majority of the Members of the United Nations.[127]

The resolution was introduced at the height of the Cold War and predictably led to an East–West dichotomy in the discussions leading up to it. Since it was the time of Western domination, the Socialist countries argued against its adoption on the basis that Articles 10 to 14 of the Charter indicated that the Security Council and the General Assembly 'cannot be substituted for one another, they merely complement each other'.[128] The pro-Western States argued, *inter alia*, that the resolution was valid on a wide interpretation of Article 12, for when the Council was paralysed by the veto it was not 'functioning' in the sense of that provision.[129] To this the representative of the Soviet Union replied that the operation of the veto was an integral function of the Security Council. He also objected on the ground that the proposed resolution would only require a procedural vote to transfer the matter from the Security Council to the Assembly, whilst Special Sessions called for under Article 20 needed a substantive vote.[130] Finally the Soviet Union argued that the proposed resolution was unconstitutional because by Article 11(2) coercive action was within the sole ambit of the Council.[131]

In 1962, the World Court in the *Expenses* case stated that 'action' in Article 11(2) refers to coercive action but it failed to state whether this excluded the Assembly from recommending coercive measures. At some point the Court suggested that 'action' is restricted to mandatory, coercive action 'ordered' by the Security Council. In other words the Assembly may not be barred from recommending enforcement action as part of its significant responsibility for the maintenance of peace as recognised by the Court.[132] If this line of argument is accepted, and it is by no means settled, then the Assembly can recommend that members take economic and military measures when there is a breach of the peace or act of aggression. Furthermore, there appears to be no cogent objection to allowing the Assembly to recommend military measures to combat a threat to the peace.

It is this writer's opinion that the ambiguous statements of the Court, in addition to the presumption against *ultra vires*, signify that the Uniting for Peace Resolution is not unconstitutional. It represents an interpretation of Articles 11(2) and 12 that have been accepted and acted upon by the members of the United Nations, including the Soviet Union and other members originally opposed to the resolution,[133] although not to the extent of recommending military action. To cast doubts on the legal validity of the resolution would mean that any action taken under the resolution would be suspect until the World Court is asked to decide on the issue. This would jeopardise a not insignificant segment of Assembly practice.

However, when looking at the issue from the perspective of the ban on the use of armed force, a rule of *jus cogens* from which no derogation is allowed, contained in Article 2(4) of the Charter, doubts may be cast on the legality of the Uniting for Peace Resolution and the power of the Assembly to recommend military measures. The exceptions to Article 2(4) are explicitly stated in the UN Charter to include only action in self-defence under Article 51 of the UN Charter and military action by the Security Council within Article 42. To state that the General Assembly can authorise military action arguably creates a third exception which would be contrary to the *jus cogens* in Article 2(4). However, the Security Council is authorising military action on behalf of the *United Nations* and so a counterargument is that the exceptions to the ban on force are those undertaken in legitimate self-defence and those authorised by the *United Nations*. The question of which organ within the UN authorises them is an internal issue and does not affect the legitimacy of UN action *vis-à-vis* a transgressing State.[134] The internal issue can be resolved in favour of both organs having the ability to authorise military action given that the Assembly effectively has all those recommendatory powers the Council possesses. As has been seen in chapter three, the Council has developed the power to recommend military action, it follows that the Assembly also has such a power, although in practice it is the Council which invariably exercises the military option.

Despite the complex legal issues surrounding Uniting for Peace and the power it contains, in over forty years of practice there have been only nine emergency Special Sessions called using the procedure contained in the resolution for transferring a matter from the Council to the Assembly.[135] This cannot be regarded as making the procedure a major factor in the extension of the competence of the General Assembly. As has been pointed out, at the time of the resolution's adoption there was a significant link between both organs in that they were dominated by a Western majority. The West tried to strengthen the link in terms of the transfer of problems from one organ to the other by means of the Uniting for Peace Resolution. With the new majority in the Assembly the Uniting for Peace procedure has no such use, for the Security Council is not controlled by that majority but by the permanent members. Thus the procedure has become a vehicle, either for condemnation of aggressions not subject to Council disapproval because of the veto, or for the reinforcement of the Assembly's previous recommendations on a particular topic.

Before the adoption of the Uniting for Peace Resolution, President Truman spoke before the General Assembly and indicated that he envisaged the procedure being used in situations such as Korea.[136] In fact the Assembly had already made a substantial contribution to UN action in Korea by passing a resolution which allowed the UN force to continue its operations to establish 'a unified, independent and democratic government of Korea' after the Security Council had been deadlocked by the return of the Soviet representative.[137] This resolution implicitly authorised General MacArthur to cross the 38th parallel and so could be classified as authorising enforcement action. President Truman probably had this in mind when he and Secretary of State Acheson introduced the Uniting for Peace Resolution.

The early successes of the procedure lay in the development of peacekeeping function, namely the establishment of UNEF in the Middle East in 1956, and the facility to take over the running of ONUC in the Congo in 1960 when the Security Council was paralysed by the Soviet veto. However, the peacekeeping function has gradually gravitated towards the Security Council, evidenced by the failure of the General Assembly to produce any constructive resolution on the Middle East in its Fifth Emergency Special Session after the Six Day War in 1967. The resolution adopted merely passed the records of the session to the Security Council because after four weeks of discussion the Assembly itself could not agree on a compromise.[138]

Without a role in the peacekeeping function and with situations like Korea being unlikely to arise again it was becoming clear that the Uniting for Peace Resolution was not going to result in the primacy of the General Assembly in matters of international peace. Gradually its function was to evolve into one where the Assembly was used to condemn cases of direct superpower intervention which obviously resulted in a paralysed Security Council. The signs were there as early as the Second Emergency Special Session on Hungary in 1956 in which the Assembly adopted a resolution which virtually paralleled the draft resolution vetoed in the Security Council, in that it condemned the Soviet attack without classifying it as a breach of the peace or act of aggression as would seem to be required by the terms of the Uniting for Peace Resolution itself.[139] Again in 1958, when American and British troops were invited into Lebanon and Jordan respectively, the Assembly could merely adopt a non-descript resolution which called for non-interference in Arab countries.[140]

However, on rare occasions the General Assembly has managed to act in a manner which suggested that it was the primary organ. For example, during the Bangladesh crisis in 1971 the Security Council was hopelessly deadlocked and so sought the help of the Assembly which was in its 26th session at the time. The Council resolution cited the Uniting for Peace procedure although the Assembly did not meet in emergency special session.[141] The Assembly responded with commendable alacrity by adopting a resolution which found that the 'hostilities between India and Pakistan constitute an immediate threat to international peace and security' and called for a cease-fire and withdrawal.[142] Admittedly there was no recommendation of enforcement action (which was highly unlikely anyway); nevertheless, the Assembly made a finding of a threat and made the recommendations which the Council, at the minimum, should have made much earlier in the conflict. The Assembly was in fact performing the role of the Council, albeit at a relatively low level.

Since Bangladesh, the Uniting for Peace procedure has become indistinguish-able in its impact from Assembly actions taken in ordinary or special sessions. The Sixth Emergency Special Session on Afghanistan adopted a resolution which was a mirror image of the draft resolution defeated in the Security Council by the Soviet veto. It deplored the 'recent armed intervention' after expressing grave concern 'at the recent developments in Afghanistan and their implications for international peace and security'.[143] Its call for withdrawal was repeated annually until 1988. The Assembly's repeated condemnation may have contributed to the Soviet withdrawal in 1989 by adding to the weight of world opinion against its intervention, an argument that can be used to support most Assembly resolutions on a particular conflict. The advent of the Geneva Accords on Afghanistan in April 1988 led to the Assembly, at its 43rd session, supporting the implementation of the Accords but also urging a comprehensive internal settlement, a call repeated at subsequent sessions.[144]

As well as using the resolution as a means of expressing condemnation of mil-itary aggressions, Uniting for Peace has become an additional tool in the hands of the majority of the members, who, for example, in 1981 called the Eighth Emer-gency Special Session of the Assembly to discuss the Namibian situation. The res-olution produced added nothing to the plethora of Assembly resolutions passed at its annual sessions. It blamed the three Western permanent members for vetoing drafts aimed at introducing mandatory economic sanctions and called on the Council to respond to the 'overwhelming demand of the international community' to impose mandatory sanctions in the 'light of the serious threat to the peace'.[145]

In this respect emergency special sessions are little different from the special sessions which can be called by a majority of Members under Article 20 of the Charter which provides that 'the General Assembly shall meet in regular annual sessions and in such special session as occasion may require. Special sessions shall be convoked by the Secretary General at the request of the Security Council or of a majority of the Members of the United Nations'.

The procedure envisaged by the Charter for convoking a special session does not appear significantly different from that established under the Uniting for Peace Resolution, except for some confusion as to whether both are subject to simple procedural votes in the Council, or whether the Soviet argument was correct and the Uniting for Peace Resolution's introduction of a procedural vote was contrary to Article 20 which requires a substantive vote. The weight of opinion seems to be that they are both subject to a procedural vote.[146] In addition, the Uniting for Peace Resolution specifically grants the Assembly the power to recommend col-lective measures and establishes the machinery to enable it to carry out these measures. It has already been seen that Article 10 in itself grants the power to the Assembly to recommend voluntary measures, so that whether in normal or special session it has the same powers as those purportedly granted by the Uniting for Peace Resolution.[147] Subsequent practice also has shown that the

Assembly has the power to recommend voluntary measures, which means in effect that Article 20 and the Uniting for Peace Resolution are conterminous, their only impact is to extend the Assembly's powers of consideration and recommendation beyond the annual regular session. What seems to have confused the sponsors of the Uniting for Peace Resolution was doubts over whether the Assembly could recommend enforcement measures. They failed to take account of the perfectly valid argument in favour of the Assembly having this power, a power it had already utilised in the Korean situation. The Uniting for Peace Resolution thus remains an unnecessary monument to the era of Western domination of the Assembly.

There have been eighteen special sessions of the General Assembly, which, disarmament and economic matters apart, differed little from the Emergency Special Sessions of that body.[148] For example, the Eighth Emergency Special Session on Namibia discussed in the section above was a parallel of the Ninth Special Session which again produced nothing of difference from the annual Namibian debate.[149] Both procedures were used by the majority, particularly during the Cold War, in an attempt to assert the independence of the Assembly from the Security Council on matters relating to international peace.

Notes

1 H. Kelsen, *The Law of the United Nations*, 198 (1951).
2 See the *Yearbook of the United Nations* (1946–47), 51.
3 But see Article 35(1). B. Simma (ed.), *The Charter of the United Nations: A Commentary*, 282 (1994).
4 See for example GA Res. 721, 8 UN GAOR Supp. (No. 17) 6 (1953).
5 J. P. Cot and A. Pellet, *La Charte des Nations Unies*, 333–6, 2nd ed. (1991).
6 L. M. Goodrich, E. Hambro and P. S. Simons, *The Charter of the United Nations*, 143, 3rd ed. (1969).
7 8 UN GAOR Supp. (No. 16) para. 114.
8 *Repertory of the United Nations Practice*, Supp. (No. 1) 173 at para. 16. See also *Interpretation of Peace Treaties with Bulgaria, Hungary and Romania* case, I.C.J. Rep. 1950, 65 at 70; *Western Sahara* case, I.C.J. Rep. 1975, 4 at 31.
9 Simma (ed.), *The Charter*, 251.
10 See for example GA Res. 1663, 16 UN GAOR Supp. (No. 17) 10 (1961).
11 Cot and Pellet, *La Charte*, 283–5.
12 *Certain Expenses of the United Nations*, I.C.J. Rep. 1962, 151 at 164–5.
13 *Ibid.*, at 163. Emphasis added.
14 Simma (ed.), *The Charter*, 232–5; R .Y. Jennings, 'International Court of Justice Advisory Opinion of July 20, 1962', 11 *I.C.L.Q.* (1962), 1169 at 1173, 1181; J. Andrassy, 'Uniting for Peace', 50 *A.J.I.L.* (1956), 563 at 567–8, 571–2. But see J. F. Murphy, *The United Nations and the Maintenance of International Peace and Security*, 81–2 (1983).
15 J. F. Murphy, 'Force and Arms', in O. Schachter and C. Joyner (eds), *United Nations Legal Order: Volume 1*, 280 (1995).

16 Kelsen, *Law of the UN*, 205.
17 Simma (ed.), *The Charter*, 262.
18 See the opinions given by the UN Legal Counsel, *U.N. Juridical Yearbook* (1964) 228, (1968) 185.
19 For example UN doc. S/23370 (1992), which still lists the Palestine question first put on in 1947, the India–Pakistan question (1948), South Africa (1960), Western Sahara (1975). See further Simma (ed.), *The Charter*, 263.
20 See Simma (ed.), *The Charter*, 262.
21 D. W. Bowett, *The Law of International Institutions*, 48–9, 4th ed. (1982).
22 SC Res. 15, 1 UN SCOR Resolutions 6 (1946).
23 UN doc. S/360/Rev. 1 (1947).
24 UN doc. S/391 (1947).
25 SC 170 mtg, 2 UN SCOR (1947).
26 GA Res. 109, 2 UN GAOR Resolutions 12 (1947).
27 SC 170 mtg, 2 UN SCOR (1947).
28 I.C.J. *Rep.* 1962, 163.
29 See generally A. F. Perez, 'On the Way to the Forum: The Reconstruction of Article 2(7) and the Rise of Federalism under the United Nations Charter', 31 *Texas Journal of International Law* (1996), 353.
30 Cot and Pellet, *La Charte*, 159.
31 *Nationality Decrees in Tunis and Morocco* case, [1923] *P.C.I.J.* ser. B, No. 4 at 24.
32 GA Res. 39. 1 UN GAOR Resolutions 12 (1946).
33 M. S. Rajan, *The Expanding Jurisdiction of the United Nations*, 84 (1982).
34 For French objections see for example GA 996 plen. mtg, 3 UN GAOR SS (1961), re Tunisia; GA 956 plen. mtg, 15 UN GAOR (1960), re Algeria. For Portuguese objections see for example GA 1099 plen. mtg, 17 UN GAOR (1962).
35 GA 1163 plen. mtg, 17 UN GAOR 656 (1962).
36 SC 276 mtg, 21 UN SCOR 5 (1966).
37 GA Res. 272, 3 UN GAOR Resolutions 17 (1949).
38 GA Res. 285, 3 UN GAOR Resolutions 34 (1949).
39 GA 401 plen. mtg, 7 UN GAOR 332 (1952).
40 *Ibid.*, 334–5 (UK and France).
41 See GA Res. 48/159, 48 UN GAOR Supp. (No. 49) (1993); GA Res. 50/83, 50 UN GAOR Supp. (No. 49) (1995).
42 D. Ciobanu, *Preliminary Objections Related to the Jurisdiction of the United Nations Political Organs*, 40–2 (1975).
43 GA Res. 46/7, 46 UN GAOR Supp. (No. 49) 13 (1991). See also GA Res. 50/86, 50 UN GAOR Supp. (No. 49) 63 (1995).
44 GA Res. 47/118, 47 UN GAOR Supp. (No. 49) 38 (1992).
45 GA Res. 50/88, 50 UN GAOR Supp. (No. 49) 64 (1995).
46 GA 401 plen. mtg, 17 UN GAOR 336 (1962).
47 On Afghanistan see GA 1 plen. mtg, 6 UN GAOR ESS para. 112 (1980), Poland. On Kampuchea see GA 64 plen. mtg, 34 UN GAOR 60–1, 120 (1979), GDR, Bulgaria and Czechoslovakia.
48 But see Simma (ed.), *The Charter*, 154.
49 GA Res. 377, 5 UN GAOR Supp. (No. 20) 10 (1950).
50 GA 301 plen. mtg, 5 UN GAOR para. 138 (1950).

51 Ciobanu, *Preliminary Objections*, 67.
52 *Reparation for Injuries Suffered in the Service of the United Nations* case, I.C.J. Rep. 1949, 174 at 182.
53 Ciobanu, *Preliminary Objections*, 68.
54 A. Prandler, 'Competence of the Security Council and the General Assembly', *Questions of International Law* (1977), 153 at 167.
55 *Expenses* case, I.C.J. Rep. 1962 at 168.
56 *Ibid.*, 223–4.
57 Ciobanu, *Preliminary Objections*, 162–73.
58 UNCIO, vol. 13, 709.
59 Article 31(3)(d) Vienna Convention on the Law of Treaties, 1969, 1155 UNTS 331.
60 G. Fitzmaurice, 'The Law and Procedure of the International Court of Justice', 33 *B.Y.I.L.* (1957), 223–5. See also McNair, *Law of Treaties*, 424–31 (1961); G. Haraszti, *Some Fundamental Problems of the Law of Treaties*, 61–7, 138–45 (1973); I. M. Sinclair, *The Vienna Convention on the Law of Treaties*, 136–8, 2nd ed. (1984); V. D. Degan, *L'Interprétation des Accords en Droit International*, 18–24 (1963); S. Rosenne, *Developments in the Law of Treaties 1945–1986*, 224–45 (1989); C. F. Amerasinghe, *Principles of the Institutional Law of International Organizations*, 48–55, 418–21 (1996).
61 M. S. McDougal, H. D. Laswell and J. C. Miller, *The Interpretation of International Agreements and World Public Order*, 144 (1994).
62 GA Res. 37/3, 37 UN GAOR Supp. (No. 51) 14 (1982).
63 GA 41 plen. mtg, 37 UN GAOR (1982), Mexico and Bhutan.
64 *Ibid.*
65 GA Res. 3312, 29 UN GAOR Supp. (No. 31) 3 (1974).
66 GA Res. 45/3, 45 UN GAOR Supp. (No. 49) 12 (1990); GA Res. 46/18, 46 UN GAOR Supp. (No. 49) 19 (1991).
67 SC Res. 1052, 51 UN S/PV (1996).
68 UN doc. A/50/L.70 (1996).
69 GA 50/22C, 50 UN A/PV (1996), 25 April 1996. Since abstentions are not counted as votes the resolution was adopted by the necessary two-thirds majority – see F. L. Kirgis, *International Organizations and their Legal Setting*, 213, 2nd ed. (1993). See further the GA Resolution of 13 March 1997 calling on Israel to refrain from building a new settlement in East Jerusalem, adopted by 130 votes to 2 (Israel and the United States again) with two abstentions, after a similar text was vetoed by the US in the Council on 7 March 1997.
70 GA 113 plen. mtg, 50 UN A/PV (1996).
71 GA Res. 3485, 30 UN GAOR Supp. (No. 34) 118 (1975). Compare SC Res. 384, 30 UN SCOR Resolutions 10 (1975).
72 SC Res. 164, 16 UN SCOR Resolutions 9 (1961).
73 GA 966 plen. mtg, 3 UN GAOR SS 3 (1961).
74 GA Res. 1622, 3 UN GAOR SS Resolutions 2 (1961).
75 GA Res. 1807, 17 UN GAOR Supp. (No. 17) 39 (1962).
76 SC Res. 312, 27 UN SCOR Resolutions 10 (1972).
77 GA Res. 1889, 18 UN GAOR Supp. (No. 15) 46 (1963).
78 GA Res. 2024, 20 UN GAOR Supp. (No. 14) 55 (1965).
79 GA Res. 2151, 20 UN GAOR Supp. (No. 16) 68 (1966).

80 GA 1468 plen. mtg, 21 UN GAOR 4 (1966).

81 GA Res. 2652, 25 UN GAOR Supp. (No. 28) 89 (1970).

82 GA Res. 3116, 28 UN GAOR Supp. (No. 30) 99 (1973).

83 GA Res. 1663, 16 UN GAOR Supp. (No. 17) 10 (1961).

84 GA Res. 2054, 20 UN GAOR Supp. (No. 14) 52 (1965).

85 GA 1395 plen. mtg, 20 UN GAOR 12 (1965).

86 See the report of the Special Committee Against Apartheid, UN doc. A/34/22 (1979).

87 GA Res. 44/27, 44 UN GAOR (1989). Also GA Res. 45/176, 45 UN GAOR Supp. (No. 49) 42 (1990).

88 GA Res. 46/79, 46 UN GAOR Supp. (No. 49) 32 (1991).

89 GA Res. 48/159, 48 UN GAOR Supp. (No. 49) 45 (1993).

90 GA Res. 2145, 21 UN GAOR Supp. (No. 16) 2 (1966).

91 *Namibia* case, I.C.J. *Rep.* 1971, 16 at para. 106.

92 GA Res. 65, 1 UN GAOR Resolutions 123 (1946).

93 GA Res. 1568, 15 UN GAOR Supp. (No. 16) 33 (1960).

94 GA Res. 36/121, 36 UN GAOR Supp. (No. 51) 29 (1981).

95 GA Res. 43/26, 43 UN GAOR Supp. (No. 49) 29 (1988).

96 See for example GA 1671 plen. mtg, 22 UN GAOR 2 (1968), Netherlands.

97 GA 8 plen. mtg, 8 UN GAOR ESS 197 (1981).

98 GA Res. 186, 2 UN GAOR SS Resolutions 5 (1948).

99 GA 2016 plen. mtg, 26 UN GAOR 25 (1971), US.

100 GA 2009 plen. mtg, 26 UN GAOR 8 (1971).

101 GA Res. 3414, 30 UN GAOR Supp. (No. 34) 6 (1975).

102 GA Res. 36/226, 36 UN GAOR Supp. (No. 51) 47 (1981).

103 GA Res. 37/123, 37 UN GAOR Supp. (No. 51) 36 (1982).

104 GA Res. 40/168, 40 UN GAOR Supp. (No. 53) 57 (1985).

105 GA Res. 46/75, 46 UN GAOR Supp. (No. 49) 28 (1991).

106 See for example GA Res. 50/21, 50 UN GAOR Supp. (No. 49) 24 (1995).

107 GA Res. 50/22, 50 UN GAOR Supp. (No. 49) 25 (1995).

108 GA Res. 50/84, 50 UN GAOR Supp. (No. 49) 58 (1995). For Report see 50 UN GAOR Supp. (No. 35) (1995), para. 118.

109 See GA Res. 1747, 16 UN GAOR Supp. (No. 17A) 3 (1962).

110 GA Res. 1889, 18 UN GAOR Supp. (No. 15) 46 (1963).

111 See GA 1367 plen. mtg, 20 UN GAOR 11 (1965), where the Soviet Union makes this equation; contrast US and UK at 8 and 14.

112 GA Res. 1742, 16 UN GAOR Supp. (No. 17) 67 (1962).

113 GA 1099 plen. mtg, 16 UN GAOR 1304 (1962), Yugoslavia re Portuguese Territories.

114 GA Res. 616, 7 UN GAOR Supp. (No. 20) 8 (1952).

115 UN doc. A/2505 (1953).

116 GA Res. 721, 8 UN GAOR Supp. (No. 17) 6 (1953).

117 GA 98 plen. mtg, 35 UN GAOR 1716 (1980), UK.

118 GA Res. 48/27, 48 UN GAOR Supp. (No. 49) 29 (1993).

119 GA Res. 3236, 29 UN GAOR Supp. (No. 31) 4 (1974).

120 GA Res. 51/26, 51 UN A/PV (1996), adopted by 152 to 2 (US and Israel) and 4 abstentions.

121 GA Res. 48/17, 48 UN GAOR Supp. (No. 49) 21 (1993).

122 SC Res. 1012, 50 UN SCOR Resolutions (1995). See also SC Res. 1040, 1049, 1072,

51 UN S/PV (1996).

123 GA Res. 111, 2 UN GAOR Resolutions 15 (1947).

124 Prandler, *Questions of International Law* (1977), 154.

125 GA Res. 377, 5 UN GAOR Resolutions 10 (1950).

126 GA Res. 376, 5 UN GAOR Resolutions 9 (1950).

127 The resolution also established a Peace Observation Commission and a Collective Measures Committee.

128 GA 299 plen. mtg, 5 UN GAOR 305 (1950), Poland.

129 *Ibid.*, at 314, Bolivia.

130 GA 301 plen. mtg, 5 UN GAOR 332 (1950). But see Goodrich, Hambro and Simons, *The Charter*, 183; Andrassy, 50 *A.J.I.L.* (1956), 576.

131 GA 301 plen. mtg, 5 UN GAOR 332 (1950).

132 *Expenses* case, I.C.J. Rep. 1962, 162–5.

133 Blaine Sloane, *United Nations General Assembly Resolutions in Our Changing World*, 25 (1991).

134 *Expenses* case, I.C.J. *Rep.* 1962, 168.

135 1st 1956 UNEF; 2nd 1956 Hungary; 3rd 1958 Lebanon and Jordan; 4th 1960 Congo; 5th 1967 Middle East; 6th 1980 Afghanistan; 7th 1980 and 1982 Palestine; 8th 1981 Namibia; 9th 1982 Israeli Occupied Territories.

136 GA 295 plen. mtg, 5 UN GAOR (1950).

137 GA Res. 376, 5 UN GAOR Resolutions 9 (1950).

138 GA Res. 2256, 5 UN GAOR ESS Supp. (No. 1) 1 (1967).

139 GA Res. 1004, 2 UN GAOR ESS Supp. (No. 1) 2 (1956). Compare UN doc. S/3760/Rev. 1 (1956).

140 GA Res. 1237, 3 UN GAOR ESS Supp. (No. 1) 1 (1958).

141 SC Res. 303, 26 UN SCOR Resolutions 10 (1971).

142 GA Res. 2793, 26 UN GAOR Supp. (No. 29) 3 (1971).

143 GA Res. ES-6/2, 6 UN GAOR ESS Supp. (No. 1) 2 (1980). Compare UN doc. S/13729 (1980).

144 GA Res. 43/20, 43 UN GAOR Supp. (No. 49) (1988).

145 GA Res. ES-8/2, 8 UN GAOR ESS (1981).

146 Simma (ed.), *The Charter*, 346; Goodrich Hambro and Simons, *The Charter*, 183. But see S. D. Bailey, *The Procedure of the Security Council*, 199, 2nd ed. (1988).

147 Simma (ed.), *The Charter*, 235.

148 For example: 1st 1947 Palestine; 2nd 1948 Palestine; 3rd 1961 Tunisia; 5th 1967 S.W. Africa; 9th 1978 Namibia; 14th 1986 Namibia; 16th 1989 Apartheid; 17th 1990 drugs.

149 See GA Res. S-9/2, 9 UN GAOR SS Supp. (No. 2) 3 (1978).

CHAPTER SIX

The powers of the General Assembly in practice

Due to the poor drafting of Articles 10–14 of the UN Charter it has been possible to argue that these provisions can be interpreted to give the Assembly a wide range of recommendatory powers, equivalent to the Security Council's powers of recommendation within Chapters VI and VII. This chapter will contain an examination of how the practice of the Assembly has followed this path to such an extent that in certain areas of recommendation, for example on disarmament and on general principles of international peace, the General Assembly is undoubtedly the primary organ. Theoretically the Assembly's resolutions are non-mandatory, and in practice this remains so although in certain instances the language of the resolutions adopted during the Cold War reflected the Non-Aligned's desire to use the Assembly as a quasi-legislative body. There are indications that this trend has continued in the post-Cold War era, though there has been a substantial reduction in the quantity of resolutions adopted as well as a significant change in the subject matter covered in them.

Disarmament

Article 11(1) of the Charter states that:

The General Assembly may consider the general principles of co-operation in the maintenance of international peace and security, including the principles governing disarmament and the regulation of armaments, and may make recommendations with regard to such principles to the Members or to the Security Council or to both.

It is generally recognised that this is the basis of disarmament resolutions adopted by the General Assembly while resolutions concerning general principles, reviewed in the next section, come under Article 13(1)(a).[1] In fact the General Assembly has taken on the responsibilities of the United Nations as regards disarmament for the Security Council has abstained in general from exercising its general competence as regards disarmament given it under Article 26,[2] although it has made a recent specific exception for Iraq in the aftermath of the 1991 conflict.

In practice the Assembly has elevated disarmament from the relatively low-key treatment given to it under the Charter, to it being an important area of UN work. The work on disarmament is not only done in the regular and special sessions of the Assembly, but also by bodies set up or brought under the auspices of the United Nations, for example the Disarmament Commission and the Conference on Disarmament.

The Assembly has interpreted its powers under Article 11(1) widely to go beyond the recommendation of mere principles to resolutions establishing bodies to study the problem and to provide the machinery for the negotiation of disarmament. Indeed, it was remarkable that during the period of over forty years of superpower arms build-up in the Cold War, the discussions and agreements on disarmament, either inside or outside the United Nations, continued. To this extent the General Assembly proved an effective organ, not for achieving disarmament, but for maintaining a dialogue over levels and the regulation of armament. To this end, a major success was achieved during the period of *détente* in the 1970s, resulting in the adoption by consensus in 1978 of a resolution at the Tenth Special Session. The resolution embodied the goals, principles, objectives and priorities for disarmament and new machinery for putting them into effect.[3]

The Committee on Disarmament which has been meeting in Geneva since 1962, having a membership of 31 States under the co-chairmanship of the Soviet Union and the United States, was brought under UN auspices by the 1978 resolution. The resolution opened the Committee up to all nuclear weapon States and 32–35 others to be chosen in consultation with the President of the General Assembly, with a personal representative of the Secretary General serving as Secretary to the Committee. It was also agreed to establish a Disarmament Commission made up of the entire UN membership to follow up the work of the special session, make recommendations on various disarmament problems, and consider the elements of a comprehensive disarmament programme.

The resolution begins with a statement that 'States for a long time have sought to maintain their security through possession of arms yet the accumulation of weapons today constitutes much more a threat than a protection for the future of mankind'. 'The time has come', it says, 'to abandon the use of force in international relations and to seek security in disarmament through a gradual but effective process beginning with a reduction in the present level of armaments'. The document expands on these principles by emphasising the importance of refraining from threats against the sovereignty and territorial integrity of any State or against peoples under a colonial or foreign domination. Non-intervention in internal affairs, the inviolability of frontiers, and the peaceful settlement of disputes are also stressed. From these premises, the resolution states that all nations have the right to participate in disarmament negotiations, that disarmament measures should be equitable and balanced to ensure security to each State, and that they should be accompanied by adequate verification.

From general principles the resolution moves on to a more practical approach by establishing a programme of action which sets forth objectives and priorities, immediate and short-term measures to halt and reverse the arms race. Special importance is given to efforts to curb nuclear and other mass destruction weapons. Negotiations for the reduction of conventional arms and armed forces are also called for. Emphasising the need to work towards the complete elimination of nuclear weapons, the programme favours such measures as an agreement on a comprehensive nuclear test ban, further Soviet–United States negotiations on strategic arms limitations and reductions, nuclear weapon free zones, and expanded non-proliferation agreements. Suggested as especially desirable measures are steps by the Security Council to 'prevent the frustration' of the objective of a denuclearised Africa, and consideration of steps to give effect to the proposal for a nuclear weapon free zone in the Middle East. Other provisions call for an expert study of the relationship between disarmament and development, and continuation of a study of the inter-relationship between disarmament and international security.

The 1978 Special Session resolution has been analysed in some detail because it represents possibly the most important achievement of the United Nations as regards disarmament. Its adoption by consensus represented the crossing of ideological and political frontiers. It may appear, in some respects, naive, for example in expressing the hope that the Security Council would become involved in disarmament. However, it must be remembered that the period of *détente* had raised hopes of a Council less divided by East–West ideology. Undoubtedly, the resolution put the UN at the centre of the disarmament stage.

However, the next decade saw the return of the Cold War, which meant that disarmament talks, once again, were dominated by the spirit of confrontation.[4] The Twelfth and Fifteenth Special Sessions on disarmament in 1982 and 1988 produced no new concrete proposals or recommendations. Again there was revealed the schism in the Assembly which so often put the Western States in the minority, a trend that seems to have continued even with the end of the Cold War in the late 1980s, although the division is now more between those nuclear States unwilling to make concessions on the one hand, and those that say they are and the vast majority of non-nuclear States on the other. The Assembly has certainly expressed support for the several bilateral agreements between the superpowers for nuclear weapons reduction, for instance the Treaty on the Elimination of Intermediate Range and Shorter Range Missiles of 1987,[5] but it has continued a policy of confrontation with nuclear weapon States.[6]

Nevertheless, the States in isolation on disarmament matters are fewer than during the Cold War, and in some non-nuclear areas there has been consensus. Indeed, the number of rhetorical and confrontational resolutions coming from the First Committee has been reduced,[7] and the overall picture is of a future in which the General Assembly can become centre stage on disarmament matters if the member States voting for resolutions actually do carry out the content therein. The Assembly has recently made several encouraging, if small, initiatives in the area of disarmament. One small step was taken at the Assembly's 46th session in 1991 when it adopted a resolution without a vote on the issue of conventional arms. The resolution was inspired by the realisation that the end of the Cold War was not going to lead to a reduction in local or regional conflicts. The resolution invited member States to provide the Secretary General with annual reports from 1 January 1992, on their conventional arms inventories and the export or import of battle tanks, armoured combat vehicles, large calibre artillery systems, combat aircraft, attack helicopters, warships and missiles, as well as calling on steps to eradicate the illicit trade in all kinds of weapons.[8] The Secretary General's first report on the item of 'transparency of arms' showed that many States were willing to provide this data.[9] Such information is essential in order to prevent another arms race where secrecy over military expenditure and capability results in States arming themselves to a higher level than is necessary for defensive purposes simply because they have little idea of their potential enemy's level of armaments.

Further UN progress in disarmament was in evidence in 1992 when the Assembly welcomed the Convention on the Prohibition of the Development, Production, Stockpiling and Use of Chemical Weapons and on their Destruction, negotiated in the forum of the Disarmament Conference.[10] When the Convention comes into force it will establish an International Organisation for the Prohibition of Chemical Weapons, with powers to inspect State parties' compliance with the terms of the treaty, without giving much prior notice.[11]

From these recent developments, it can be seen that the Assembly, whilst not moving entirely away from rhetorical confrontation between non-nuclear and nuclear States in the area of nuclear weapons, is moving positively towards arms control in the area of conventional weapons,[12] although the voluntary register is only a small step; and is moving even further in the area of chemical weapons, not only by sponsoring a Convention, but also by insisting on enforcement mechanisms within a treaty system.[13]

General principles

Article 13(1)(a) of the Charter allows the Assembly to initiate studies and make recommendations for the purpose of 'promoting international cooperation in the political field and encouraging the progressive development of international law and its codification', while sub-paragraph (b) gives the same power, *inter alia*, 'in the realisation of human rights and fundamental freedoms'.

It is out of sub-paragraph (a) that the power to adopt resolutions enunciating general principles has developed. Nevertheless, sub-paragraph (b) is significant in that the general principles usually represent a compromise between those States supporting human rights, and those States who want to emphasise the (greater) importance of sovereignty and territorial integrity. This aspect will be concentrated on for it is illustrative of the influence of the various factions of the General Assembly, an influence which tends to result in an unsatisfactory compromise.

In 1949, a majority of States were still committed to the principle of the inviolability of the sovereignty of States which in 1945 was embodied in Article 2(7) of the Charter. The Draft Declaration on Rights and Duties of States was adopted unanimously in 1949 in accordance with Article 13.[14] It represented an affirmation and clarification of the sovereignty principle. It stated that every State had: complete jurisdiction in its own territory; the right of independence including freedom to choose its own government; the duty not to intervene in another State or to foment civil strife therein; and the duty to treat all persons under its jurisdiction with respect for their human rights and fundamental freedoms.

Although the balance of the resolution is clearly in favour of affirming the doctrine of absolute sovereignty, there are suggestions that perhaps this concept is subject to the principle of self-determination (right to choose a government) and respect for human rights. In 1949, it was the United States and its allies who supported these nascent principles, even advocating that all the contents of the draft resolution embodied international law, reflecting the Western majority's criticism of the form of government and abuse of human rights in Eastern Europe. The Eastern bloc doubted that the principles contained in the declaration embodied international law.[15]

However, by 1960 the tables had turned and it was the Soviet Union and the newly independent countries advocating firm anti-colonial and hence pro self-determination resolutions.[16] The Declaration on the Granting of Independence to Colonial Countries and Peoples recognised the 'increasingly powerful trend towards freedom' in dependent territories and emphasised that colonialism was not only a denial of self-determination but also of fundamental human rights and therefore was contrary to the Charter.[17] This represented a move away from the sovereignty principle at least in so far as metropolitan powers and their dominions were concerned.

The resolution was adopted by 89 votes to nil. However, nine Western and pro-Western States abstained, the United States abandoning its previous principled approach for more pragmatic reasoning. The all or nothing approach (no stage between a colony and an independent State) of the resolution was criticised by the representative of the United States because it would lead to the political fragmentation of some States and would 'fly in the face of political and economic realities in many areas of the world'.[18] During the Cold War, the United States' preference for an approach based on economic realities increasingly alienated it from the majority of Assembly members who preferred a more abstract, principled approach.

The impact of the decolonised majority became increasingly apparent in 1965 with the unanimous adoption of the Declaration on the Inadmissibility of Intervention in the Domestic Affairs of States.[19] Although compromise was necessary to achieve unanimity, the influence of the national liberation lobby eroded even further the Western support for non-intervention and sovereignty, and to this extent correlated with the decline in importance of Article 2(7).

The resolution declared that no State had the right to intervene in the affairs of another. This included indirect intervention which was defined as helping or financing subversive activities against a State. Thus far the Declaration entirely supported the Western view. However, the resolution proceeded to contradict itself. After reaffirming the principles of self-determination and respect for human rights and fundamental freedoms, it stated that 'all States shall contribute to the complete elimination of racial discrimination and colonialism'. This suggested that indirect intervention was permissible if it aided self-determination in colonial or racist situations. The Western States voted for the resolution on the under-standing that the word 'contribute' did not allow intervention in favour of self-determination.[20] Inevitably, the Soviets favoured the view that it did, and increased the Cold War rhetoric against the United States by accusing it of denying self-determination in Vietnam and the Dominican Republic,[21] whereas the United States accused the Soviet Union of intervention in violation of the sovereignty of Vietnam.[22]

Similarly in 1970, the Declaration on Principles Concerning Friendly Relations and Cooperation among States in accordance with the United Nations' Charter represented a compromise.[23] Indirect intervention was declared illegal but, at the same time, the declaration expressed the right of people to take 'forcible action in pursuit of their right to self-determination' and stated that they were 'entitled to seek and receive support in accordance with the purposes and principles of the Charter'. Support for forcible action suggested that the support could be forcible as well. However, the reference to the Charter tended to suggest that it was support short of the use or threat of force, which after all would be contrary to Article 2(4), and as the representative of Australia pointed out, a mere recom-mendatory Assembly resolution could not amend the Charter.[24] Most Western States explicitly granted their vote on the understanding that the Declaration did not diminish the principle of the non-use of force.[25] The Socialist and Non-Aligned nations did not express a view, probably in order not to provoke any neg-ative Western votes, but it is interesting that they saw the Declaration as a crystallisation of international law.[26]

The unhappy compromise between Western powers and the national liberation lobby was continued when, in 1974, the Assembly finally adopted by consensus the Definition of Aggression which has been discussed in chapter two. The Defi-nition purportedly outlawed indirect as well as direct aggression, but made this subject to the right of peoples striving to achieve self-determination 'to struggle to that end and to seek and receive support'. Indeed, despite the World Court's judgment in the *Nicaragua* case, which seized on those parts of the Definition which strengthened the principle of the non-use of force whilst ignoring those parts detrimental to it, the Assembly adopted a further resolution in 1987 which, while purporting to ban intervention and aggression, still declared that peoples, 'particularly those under colonial and racist regimes', had the right 'to achieve self-determination and have the right to seek and receive support'.[27]

Due to the inherent defect in each of the above resolutions it can be strongly argued that the power of the General Assembly to adopt resolutions on general principles has not led to 'the progressive development of international law' in the area of the non-use of force. Instead, the principle contained in Article 2(4) has been seriously weakened by these recommendations which suggest that the principle is subject to the use of allowable force in the pursuit of the right to self-determination or national liberation. This represents a serious undermining of the fundamental provision of the Charter.[28]

However, such a contention must be tempered in the light of the Court's judgment in the *Nicaragua* case when it relied on the 1965 Declaration on Non-Intervention, the 1970 Declaration on Friendly Relations, and the 1974 Definition of Aggression as evidence of *opinio juris* on the illegality of intervention in the form of funding of an armed opposition group within a State, arming and advising such a group, and virtually controlling such a group. It found that the United States' support for the Contra rebels in Nicaragua constituted an unlawful intervention and an unlawful use of force against Nicaragua. It also said that if clear evidence could be adduced to show that Nicaragua was supplying arms to the rebels in El Salvador this would be a breach of the principles of non-intervention and the non-use of force. The Court did not find sufficient evidence of this, but stated that even if there was adequate proof, the supply of arms did not constitute an intervention amounting to an 'armed attack' within the meaning of Article 51 of the UN Charter, which would justify the United States-sponsored operation as an exercise of the right of collective self-defence on behalf of El Salvador.[29]

The Court did not directly address the issue of self-determination since it was not raised in the case before it, although there were passages in the judgment which not only made clear that intervention to preserve or impose some form of ideology was unlawful, but also that human rights (and presumably self-determination) could not be enforced or protected by outside States by military means.[30] The judgment could be said to constitute a pro-Western interpretation of General Assembly resolutions, despite the fact that on the substantive issues the Court found against the major Western power involved. Furthermore, the judgment provided support for the fact that many aspects of the General Assembly's resolutions have passed into customary international law, whilst those parts which are too ambiguous to embody any legal obligation are effectively left behind as monuments to the Cold War.

With that confrontation now behind the Assembly it has the opportunity to produce resolutions that have greater clarity and so have a greater impact on customary international law. There is some evidence that such resolutions are emerging via the Sixth (Legal) Committee, and the Third (Social Humanitarian and Cultural) Committee of the Assembly, not only on enhancing the ban on the use of armed force within the meaning of Article 2(4),[31] but also on the provision of humanitarian assistance,[32] the prevention of terrorism,[33] on methods of making the UN machinery more effective,[34] the development of a new international humanitarian order,[35] the prevention of violent disintegration of States,[36] and the promotion of the rule of law within States.[37] Although some of these items reflect issues high on the Western agenda, the resolutions were adopted without dissent. However, there are still a number of purportedly normative resolutions which divide the Assembly in the post-Cold War era. For example the Assembly adopted a resolution during its 51st session in 1996 aimed at the elimination of coercive economic measures as a means of political and economic compulsion,[38] directed against certain Western States. In contrast, it now regularly adopts resolutions aimed at promoting genuine free and periodic elections and democratisation within States,[39] which fail to gain the support of about twenty, mainly developing, States.

Although not binding as such, General Assembly resolutions can eventually become so if they pass into customary international law as a result of States consistently referring to them as part of their legal arguments in disputes or in discussions in international settings.[40] The likelihood of this happening is increased if the resolution is adopted by consensus.

Cease-fire and withdrawal

Whereas Assembly recommendations on disarmament and those enunciating general principles on the use of force are directly adopted under Articles 11(1) and 13(1) respectively; resolutions which call for a cease-fire, withdrawal, or for voluntary measures or recommend a settlement cannot be attributed to any particular Charter provision, but, instead, are concrete manifestations of the general powers of Articles 10, 11(2) and 14. As has already been stated in chapter five, Article 10 can be interpreted to give the Assembly similar recommendatory powers to those granted to the Council in Chapters VI and VII. To a large extent the powers examined below are similar to those recommendatory powers employed by the Security Council.

The Assembly makes relatively few cease-fire and withdrawal calls. The Security Council usually responds first and makes the necessary call. However, if the General Assembly is in its regular session it may be able to make the call more quickly than the Council. The Assembly has made such calls in the case of the Indonesian invasion of East Timor in 1975,[41] and in the case of the Turkish invasion of Cyprus in 1974.[42]

During the Cold War, if the Council was deadlocked by a conflict of interests of the permanent members, the General Assembly sometimes took up the role of the organ making the preliminary call for a cease-fire and withdrawal. This was done either immediately, under the Uniting for Peace procedure, or by the Assembly waiting until its regular session. If done in emergency special session the call had greater immediacy than if the regular session was waited for. However, the Council was likely to be paralysed because of permanent member involvement and so any cease-fire call was seen largely as a gesture. In this respect it did not matter if the regular session was waited for.

In the case of the Soviet intervention in Hungary in 1956, the Assembly met in emergency special session and called for a cease-fire and a withdrawal of Soviet troops.[43] The call was seen as a gesture by some members or more optimistically as a warning or holding measure to prevent further Soviet interventions by others.[44] In the case of the Vietnamese intervention in Kampuchea (Cambodia) in 1978, the Assembly waited eleven months before calling for a cease-fire.[45] This wait could hardly justify some of the members hailing the resolution as a valiant effort to save the 'dying' Kampuchean people.[46] Often the Assembly passed a resolution in order to save the Organisation's face when the primary body was racked by arguments and vetoes. For example, the Assembly's resolution calling for a cease-fire in the Bangladesh situation was seen as essential in rescuing the UN from its 'darkest hour'.[47] In terms of effectiveness, therefore, the Assembly's calls did not directly bring about an immediate cease-fire or withdrawal, instead it added to the weight of opinion against belligerents which sometimes eventually led to a cease-fire and more importantly a withdrawal.

In terms of withdrawal calls, the Assembly's most important ones were in the cases of Hungary, Bangladesh, Cyprus, East Timor, Kampuchea, Afghanistan, Grenada and Panama.[48] In the cases of Bangladesh, Grenada, and Panama, withdrawal was achieved only after the intervening forces had achieved their objectives. However, in the case of Afghanistan, Soviet withdrawal in 1989 occurred without the political objectives behind the intervention being achieved. This was mainly due to the fact that the Soviet Union found that it could not achieve its goals after nearly a decade of fighting. However, it may be that the weight of world opinion represented by the Assembly in its annual resolutions was a factor influencing the decision to withdraw. Similarly, the withdrawal of Vietnamese troops from Cambodia in 1989 was due to a combination of factors, political and economic, including the consistent Assembly calls for Vietnamese withdrawal. Indeed, with withdrawal of foreign forces from the combat zones of Afghanistan and Cambodia, the Assembly, as part of the wider UN peace effort, called on the parties to the internal conflicts within those countries to cease hostilities so that the peace plans could succeed.[49] The Assembly acts to focus world attention and pressure on warring parties, and while its resolutions *per se* can only be said to have peripheral impact, they do serve to indicate the wider economic and political pressure that may be brought to bear on the conflict.

Whereas the number of Assembly calls on warring factions within States has increased in recent years, there have been very few such calls in inter-State situations, reflecting to a certain extent the nature of conflicts in the post-Cold War era, and also the presence of an active Security Council. The Assembly did call for the withdrawal of foreign (Russian) forces from the States of Latvia and Estonia in 1993.[50] Russian withdrawal was complete by the time of the Assembly's 44th session in 1994.[51]

Voluntary measures

The most radical interpretation of the Assembly's powers involves its use of voluntary measures. It has been seen in chapter three, in the case of the Security Council, that it can recommend military measures under Article 39 and has adopted the practice of suggesting economic measures under Article 41. Both these recommendatory powers used by the Security Council were not envisaged by the drafters of the Charter and so represent an extension by subsequent practice. It has been argued that the General Assembly has similar recommendatory powers to the Council, and by extension, it has the power to recommend military action and to recommend voluntary sanctions. The former power has been expressly granted by the Uniting for Peace Resolution, although it can be argued that the Assembly has had such powers from the time that the Security Council claimed similar powers, or simply that they are inherent in the Assembly's general recommendatory power.[52]

Nevertheless, the Assembly has very rarely used its power to recommend military action. The only clear instance, which occurred marginally before the Uniting for Peace Resolution was adopted, was in the case of Korea when the Assembly recommended a 'unified, independent and democratic' Korea be established and that UN forces remain in Korea for that purpose.[53] This implicitly authorised General MacArthur to cross the 38th parallel into North Korea. Paradoxically, although the Uniting for Peace Resolution was adopted only a few days later there has been no further clear instance of the Assembly recommending coercive measures in the form of military action.

Korea also involved one of the first instances of the Assembly recommending voluntary sanctions.[54] These were not only directed against North Korea, but also Communist China which had entered the war when General MacArthur's forces threatened the Chinese border, and involved an embargo on military supplies and equipment.[55] The Soviet Union declared these sanctions invalid on the grounds that they constituted 'action' within the meaning of Article 11(2).[56]

Since Korea, the Assembly has, in practice, firmly established the power to recommend voluntary sanctions. However, in contrast with the Korean precedent such sanctions have mainly been adopted on the instigation and affirmative votes of the Non-Aligned and Socialist majority. Voluntary sanctions have been called for in the cases of South Africa, the Portuguese territories, and Southern Rhodesia.[57] The Assembly's power to recommend voluntary measures has been confined, in practice, to colonial or racist situations (and then mainly in Africa), all of which have been terminated,[58] although by tying zionism to racism in 1975,[59] it was able to justify recommending voluntary measures against Israel.[60]

A US-instigated campaign in 1991 led to the repeal of the equation of zionism with racism at the Assembly's 46th session by a majority of 113 to 13 with 25 abstentions.[61] It is also interesting to note that at its 46th session, the Assembly did not explicitly repeat its call for voluntary measures in any of its numerous resolutions on the subject,[62] although as yet there has been no formal termination of the measures.

Although question marks must be raised against the effectiveness of voluntary measures themselves, the easing off of Assembly calls for sanctions in the past few years is indicative of the changed climate at the UN and the fact that of the established international pariahs only Israel remains, and it is negotiating with the Palestinians. Of the new international pariahs, Iraq, Libya and Yugoslavia (Serbia and Montenegro), Iraq and Libya have not been singled out by the Assembly yet. However, on 22 September 1992, the General Assembly, by a large majority of 127 votes to 6, denied the Federal Republic of Yugoslavia (Serbia and Montenegro) automatic membership of the General Assembly as successor State to the former, and much bigger, Socialist Federal Republic of Yugoslavia.[63]

Political settlement

Political settlement of a dispute or problem requires some degree of consent or a (greater) degree of coercion of the parties to the dispute. Whereas the Council has the option of using mandatory coercion, the Assembly only has the power of recommendation and therefore, in general (apart from the recommendation of measures), if it is to succeed it must try to attain some degree of cooperation from the parties. However, throughout its history the Assembly has shown a greater concern for voting victories than for concrete successes.

The partition of Palestine is a good example of a case where the Assembly sought to impose a solution on the area and the parties through the inadequate means of a non-binding recommendation. Palestine was the subject of the First Special Session of the Assembly in May 1947. The session was requested by the mandatory power, Britain, because it was dissatisfied with its position due to increasing antagonism between Jews and Arabs and the conflicting purposes of achieving a homeland for the Jews and independence for an Arab dominated Palestine. The session established a Special Committee on Palestine,[64] which submitted a report to the Second Annual Session of the Assembly. The report of the majority recommended partition of Palestine as a means of reconciling the above conflicting principles, whereas the minority believed a federated State could achieve this.[65]

The Assembly established an *ad hoc* committee consisting of every member to consider the report. The *ad hoc* committee did not use the report as a basis for negotiation between the parties, instead it supported the majority's proposals and recommended partition with economic union;[66] a proposal which favoured the Jews and which was supported by both the Soviet Union and the United States.[67] The solution recommended was an ideal one aimed at solving the problem of the mandate and the age old problem of a Jewish homeland all at one stroke. It was bound to fail because at no stage were the parties involved in the plan, a plan which was particularly unfavourable to one of the parties to the dispute, namely the Palestinians.

Only the representative of Columbia questioned the recommendation for partition in any great detail. First he criticised the theory behind the majority report stating that 'the legal competence of the General Assembly to set up two independent States in Palestine, without regard to the principle of self-determination has not been established to our satisfaction'.[68] He then proposed a resolution to improve the practical chances of the Assembly successfully helping to end the Palestinian problem,[69] by authorising the *ad hoc* committee to 'take all steps necessary to try to bring about an agreement between the representatives of the Arab and Jewish populations of Palestine as to the future government and political constitution of that country'.

Instead the majority continued on its course which was bound to alienate one of the parties and its supporters, namely the Arabs represented by the Arab Higher Committee. The United States proposed that two sub-committees be set up, one to examine the majority report of the Special Committee, and one to consider the minority report. States supporting the Jewish cause polarised around the first sub-committee while mainly Arab States were represented in the second sub-committee. The result was modified versions of both reports which were more extreme, for example the minority report abandoned the federated State ideal and recommended independence for Palestine based on self-determination.[70] The Assembly was, in effect, driving the two parties further apart. The *ad hoc* committee voted for the partition plan contained in the first sub-committee's report,[71] and finally the Assembly adopted the partition plan.[72] The resolution took the form of a recommendation but was obviously based on the premise that the Council would enforce it if it was ignored. This too was unrealistic, but at the time, the relative impotence of the Council was not clear.

Fighting between the two communities despite truce calls by the Council led to the Second Special Session of the Assembly in April and May 1948 one month before the end of the mandate. The idealistic approach of the First Session was replaced by disillusionment and the whole session was without effect. The Assembly failed to adopt a resolution on the state of its rapidly disintegrating partition plan. The United States reversed its support for partition and suggested UN trusteeship.[73] The Assembly did not take up this option. In effect, the Assembly abandoned Palestine to a military solution with the first Arab–Israeli war breaking out on 14 May as the mandate ended. The Assembly was guilty of attempting to decide the fate of Palestine by a majority of only vaguely interested States. It was concerned with voting victories rather than with any practical attempt at reconciliation and negotiation between the parties mainly concerned.

The modern Assembly is overwhelmingly pro-Palestinian in its approach to the Middle East crisis. Thus although its stance on the Middle East has altered, its basic approach has not changed. Its resolutions are pro-Arab and so are not conducive for encouraging Israel to negotiate.

Security Council resolution 242 adopted in 1967 and designed to induce all the parties to negotiate, is a good example of how the requirements of compromise necessary in the Council produce a more balanced approach. The Assembly, however, imposes the will of the majority and in so doing has undermined the Council's work which necessarily has to accommodate the views of the minority pro-Israeli members. The Assembly has consistently adopted resolutions which while purportedly supporting Council resolution 242, destroy its balance in a variety of ways. Although the post-Cold War Assembly has reduced its antagonism towards Israel, it still has not regained its neutrality in the dispute. For example a 1991 Assembly resolution purports to lay down the principles that would govern the negotiation of a solution to the problem at a proposed International Conference on the Middle East under UN auspices,[74] in effect undermining the Middle East peace process started at Madrid in October 1991 under United States and Soviet Union (now Russian) patronage outside the UN framework but operating within the terms of Council resolution 242.[75] The modern day Assembly still fails to adopt consensus resolutions on the question of Palestine and the situation in the Middle East, thereby alienating Israel and its supporters,[76] although it does appear to be more supportive of the peace process.[77]

The dispute over South West Africa (Namibia) was slightly different in that South Africa had breached international law by continuing to administer the territory. Thus the UN was in a difficult position, for it would have reflected badly on the Organisation's prestige to negotiate with an illegal occupier of a trusteeship territory. In effect, until the independence of Namibia in 1990, the United Nations was a party to a dispute with South Africa over Namibia. This is symptomatic of its attitude towards colonial, neo-colonial or racist situations in which the Assembly has a vision of itself as the representative of colonial or repressed peoples.[78]

In 1950 the International Court opined that South West Africa was still under a mandate which could only be modified by South Africa with the 'consent' of the United Nations.[79] The word 'consent' is important here for it is not only required of the UN to achieve a solution but also by South Africa. Without South Africa's consent, and in the absence of effective mandatory measures by the Council, the problem of Namibia was unlikely to be resolved by the UN. However, the Assembly ignored this fact and embarked on a unilateral approach to the problem by adopting resolutions on Namibia which although ideally and legally desirable were, nevertheless, unattainable. Although the Assembly's consistent pressure on South Africa may have contributed in a small way to the withdrawal from Namibia, it took an accord of 1988 negotiated outside the UN and sponsored by the superpowers to solve the problem. The accord, as shall be seen in chapter nine, linked South African withdrawal from Namibia with Cuban withdrawal from Angola. The Assembly had consistently rejected the notion of linkage,[80] and so was effectively undermining a legitimate peace process which resulted in an independent Namibia and the prosect of a peaceful Angola.

Ignoring for a moment the problem of self-determination, where the Assembly often loses its neutrality and objectivity, in other instances the Assembly does attempt to create a viable framework for the settlement of disputes. For example, in 1980, it passed a resolution on the Kampuchean problem,[81] which called for an International Conference on Kampuchea (Cambodia) and laid out the principles to be the basis of discussion: the negotiation of an agreement for Vietnamese withdrawal, observance of human rights, free elections, and non-interference. It did not purport to isolate Vietnam; its purpose was to give it a way out. Although the permanent five were involved in the Paris International Conference on Cambodia since it first met in July 1989, and it was the Security Council that converted an Australian peace proposal into a comprehensive peace plan in August 1990, it is the General Assembly that must take a great deal of credit for providing the initial framework for Vietnamese withdrawal and for the International Conference which finally, after a massive Security Council authorised peacekeeping operation, led to a relatively stable Cambodia. The Assembly encouraged and fully supported the International Conference on Cambodia and the agreements coming out of the conference in October 1991.[82]

In the same vein, the Assembly expressed its unanimous support for the Central American peace plan agreed upon in Guatemala on 7 August 1987.[83] This plan has, as shall be seen in Part Three, resulted in the end of civil wars in Nicaragua and El Salvador, and a peace process in Guatemala.[84] Although the details of the peace plans were negotiated by the Secretary General and finally authorised by the Security Council, the Security Council did not become fully involved until 1989. Similarly, it was the General Assembly's encouragement of the Secretary General in his 'good offices' role,[85] that eventually helped to produce the Geneva Accords of 1988 containing an agreement on Afghanistan, which while not settling the internal conflict, did lead to a Soviet withdrawal. It is the General Assembly, not the Security Council, which persists in trying to encourage a peaceful settlement in the Afghan conflict.[86] Cambodia, Central America and Afghanistan are good examples of the Assembly providing neutral modalities for belligerents to settle their differences in a diplomatic manner.

The peace processes in Cambodia, Nicaragua and El Salvador, each involved a Security Council authorised peacekeeping force to oversee a cease-fire but also to oversee peaceful elections there. The modern Assembly's concern for democracy has led it to support the election process within States. Indeed, it seems to have the primary role in this function, when the situation does not require a peacekeeping force, simply a team of election observers.

In October 1990, the General Assembly approved of the establishment of the UN Observer Group for the Verification of Elections in Haiti (ONUVEH).[87] This operation did not have any traditional peacekeeping or observation component and consisted entirely of civilian observers whose function was to report on the electoral process taking place in that strife torn country. Although peaceful elections took place on 16 December 1990, the elected government was ousted by a military coup in September 1991. It may be tentatively suggested that without the stabilising presence of a UN military component for at least one or two years, the chances of a stable government emerging from the electoral process in such a troubled country are much reduced. Further, the situation in Haiti was purely internal, unlike in Nicaragua, Namibia, El Salvador, Cambodia, and Western Sahara, which all had or continue to have international repercussions or implications in terms of outside States' involvement in the conflict.

It may be in recognition of these limitations that the General Assembly accepted a recommendation of its Third Committee on Social, Humanitarian and Cultural Affairs, when it adopted a resolution on 17 December 1991, on the issue of periodic and genuine elections. The Assembly affirmed 'that electoral verification by the United Nations should remain an exceptional activity of the Organisation to be undertaken in well-defined circumstances, *inter alia*, primarily in situations with a clear international character'. Despite this caveat the Assembly stressed its conviction that 'periodic and genuine elections are a necessary and indispensable element of sustained efforts to protect the rights and interests of the governed and that ... the rights of everyone to take part in the government of his or her country is a crucial factor in the effective enjoyment of all of a wide range of other human rights and fundamental freedoms, embracing political, economic, social and cultural rights', referring to the significance of the Universal Declaration on Human Rights and the International Covenant on Civil and Political Rights, 'which establish that the authority to govern shall be based on the will of the people, as expressed in periodic and genuine elections'.[88] After the UN sponsored Vienna Conference on Human Rights of June 1993,[89] the Assembly has moved away, despite the lack of support from about twenty States, from stressing the exceptional nature of UN election supervision, towards provision of assistance upon the request of any State subject to certain guidelines, while 'recognizing that the fundamental responsibility for ensuring free and fair elections lies with Governments'.[90]

Any requests for electoral assistance received by the Secretary General or the Electoral Assistance Division at the UN, established in April 1992, should be notified to the 'competent organ' of the UN, which presumably means either the General Assembly or the Security Council,[91] for approval or not as the case may be. Between April 1992 and April 1993, the Electoral Assistance Division provided electoral 'assistance' to 31 countries, although in the main this was simply advice usually in the form of sending a consultant to the requesting country.[92] Only in Angola, Cambodia, El Salvador, Eritrea and Mozambique, did the request result in an observer team whose purpose was to oversee the elections, although in other cases the UN consultants worked alongside observers from other countries or organisations. It appears that whilst General Assembly or Security Council consent has been sought for the establishment of observer teams, the Electoral Assistance Division, under the supervision of the Under Secretary General for Political Affairs, can provide advice and send consultants without specific authorisation from the Assembly or Council. The above cases all involved a peacekeeping force with election supervision functions, authorised by the Security Council, apart from Eritrea, where the civilian election supervision team was authorised by the Assembly.

The UN's Electoral Assistance Division was heavily involved in the referendum in the Ethiopian province of Eritrea in April 1993, which led to the secession of Eritrea from the rest of Ethiopia. The Mengistu regime in Ethiopia, which had held the country together by force, was finally overthrown by forces grouped under the Ethiopian People's Revolutionary Democratic Front, a close ally of the Eritrean People's Liberation Front (EPLF), in May 1991. The new provisional government of Ethiopia agreed that the EPLF could set up a separate interim administration in Eritrea which would mean that the province would be separately administered until a referendum on independence was held in April 1993. In May 1992, the Eritrean Referendum Commission requested that the United Nations undertake the verification of this referendum, along with other international observers, particularly from the Organisation of African Unity (OAU). In response to this the Secretary General, after receiving reports from the Electoral Assistance Division's consultants, requested that the General Assembly authorise the establishment of the UN Observer Mission to Verify the Referendum in Eritrea (UNOVER).[93] On 16 December 1992, the General Assembly acceded to this request.[94] A core team of 21 observers headed by the Secretary General's Special Representative arrived in January 1993, supplemented by an additional 86 observers in April.

In response to the question 'Do you wish Eritrea to be an independent country?', 99.8 per cent of the people that voted (98.2 per cent of those eligible) voted yes between 23 and 25 April 1993. UNOVER ensured the impartiality of the process by establishing a system of voter identification, observing the polling, making sure that the EPLF fighters remained in barracks during the polling, and making sure that those 300,000 of the 1.1 million registered voters who lived outside Eritrea were registered and could vote. The Secretary General's Special Representative stated that the vote was free and fair.[95] Eritrea made its formal declaration of independence on 24 May 1993, was recognised by Ethiopia as an independent country and was admitted to membership of the UN and OAU.

Although the examples of Haiti and Eritrea show that the Assembly has had mixed success in supporting free elections as part of a political settlement, it appears that this mechanism is now firmly entrenched in the modern-day Assembly's practice.

The Assembly's non-recommendatory powers

Articles 10–14 seem to create only recommendatory powers for the Assembly, but as has been seen in chapter four, theoretically the Assembly can adopt non-recommendatory resolutions. However, there is no power to enable the Assembly to adopt mandatory resolutions on security or human rights matters, so, although the resolutions may 'demand', 'decide' or 'declare', they are not mandatory decisions in the sense of Article 25 and Chapter VII. The Assembly uses its declaratory or condemnatory power to strongly emphasise the United Nations' position as regards a particular dispute. In effect it is acting in a quasi-judicial capacity similar to that of the Security Council. Although it does not possess mandatory powers either to oblige members to comply or to enforce its judgments in the case of non-compliance, it does possess the power to suggest voluntary measures, and if its judgment is based on international law, then it is binding in a more fundamental sense than that found in Article 25.

In 1956, the Assembly declared 'that by using its armed force against the Hungarian people, the government of [the Soviet Union was] violating the political independence of Hungary',[96] as a follow up to the emergency special session on Hungary calling for withdrawal. The resolution contained an 'objective', 'historical judgment' that the Soviet Union had breached Article 2(4).[97] In this respect the Assembly was acting like an international court in judging the Soviet Union guilty of a breach of the Charter. Although it has no power to make a binding judgment, the verdict is important if the principle contained in Article 2(4) is not to be destroyed by constant breach. In 1986, the Assembly condemned the United States' air raids on targets within Libya as 'a violation of the Charter and of International Law',[98] and in 1989 it deplored 'the intervention in Panama by the armed forces of the United States of America, which constitutes a flagrant violation of international law'.[99] More recently, in 1992, the Assembly condemned Serbia for violating the sovereignty of Bosnia.[100] Such resolutions, which are just a sample, offer evidence by way of State practice as to the status of Article 2(4) as a peremptory norm of international law, and in fact according to the World Court in the *Nicaragua* case they have helped to strengthen Article 2(4) despite its seemingly frequent breach.[101] In addition, the General Assembly has upheld international law in other areas – for example it has condemned breaches of international humanitarian law in the former Yugoslavia.[102]

Although the Assembly's declarations are often based on legal concepts it could be argued that they are unlikely to aid a peaceful settlement of the dispute simply because they put one of the parties in the wrong and therefore make it unlikely that it will comply. The Assembly's declarations on South Africa are a case in point. In 1952 the Assembly declared:

that in a multi-racial society harmony and respect for human rights and freedoms and the peaceful development of a unified community are best assured when patterns of legislation and practice are directed towards ensuring equality before the law of all persons regardless of race, creed, or colour, and when economic, social and cultural and political participation of all racial groups is on the basis of equality.[103]

Even a pre-eminent Non-Aligned State was compelled to abstain on the resolution because, 'it expressed general sentiments which are fine and with which we are in complete agreement, but it does not adequately provide a solution for the problem with which the world is faced today'.[104] However, there is a great deal to be said for the view that the Assembly should reflect the feelings of the international community and to leave the transgressing State, in this case apartheid South Africa, in 'no doubt' as to these sentiments.[105] Nevertheless, without effective enforcement action to reinforce its calls, the Assembly can ill afford to antagonise transgressing States when eventually they look for a method of escaping from their clearly untenable positions.

The Assembly clearly has developed a useful quasi-judicial capacity, in the sense that it passes numerous judgments on disputes, conflicts or situations. If these judgments are based on an objective determination of international law, as many are, they focus world attention on the problem and reinforce the provisions of international law. However, in certain cases, South Africa being a good example, the initial objective determinations give way to partisan determinations which add little to the judgment and in fact compromise the UN's neutrality. This abuse of its quasi-judicial power can be detected in its 1989 resolution which reaffirmed the Assembly's support for the African National Congress and other national liberation movements in South Africa 'which pursue their noble objective to eliminate apartheid through political, armed and other forms of struggle'.[106] After encouraging violence in the 1970s and 1980s the Assembly at its 46th session in 1991 called 'for an immediate end to violence' in South Africa and urged 'the South Africa authorities to take immediate further action to end the recurring violence and acts of terrorism',[107] as the reform process was underway, eventually leading to free elections and majority rule in 1994.

Notes

1 J. P. Cot and A. Pellet, *La Charte des Nations Unies*, 263, 2nd ed. (1991); L. M. Goodrich, E. Hambro and P .S. Simons, *The Charter of the United Nations*, 117, 3rd ed. (1969). The Assembly's powers regarding disarmament were recognised by the International Court in the *Legality of the Threat or Use of Nuclear Weapons* case, I.C.J. *Rep.* 1996, 1 at 8.

2 B. Simma (ed.), *The Charter of the United Nations: A Commentary*, 245 (1994).

3 GA Res. S-10/2, 10 UN GAOR SS Supp. (No. 4) 3 (1978).

4 Cot and Pellet, *La Charte*, 268.

5 *United Nations Disarmament Yearbook*, vol. 12, (1987), appendix VII.

6 GA Res. 50/64, 50 UN GAOR Supp. (No. 49) 84 (1995). But see GA Res. 50/65, 50 UN GAOR Supp. (No. 49) 84 (1995).

7 *UN Chronicle*, vol. 29, (1992), 76.

8 GA Res. 46/36 H,L, 46 UN GAOR Supp. (No. 49) 73 (1991).

9 UN doc. A/48/344 (1993). See further A/50/547 (1995); GA Res. 50/70 D, 50 UN GAOR Supp. (No. 49) 91 (1995).

10 GA Res. 47/39, 47 UN GAOR Supp. (No. 49) 54 (1992).

11 32 *I.L.M.* (1993), Article 8.

12 But see Simma (ed.), *The Charter*, 247.

13 Contrast the UN sponsored 1972 Convention on the Prohibition of the Development, Production and Stockpiling of Bacteriological (Biological) and Toxin Weapons and on their Destruction, 1015 UNTS 187.

14 GA Res. 375, 4 UN GAOR Resolutions 66 (1949).

15 4 UN GAOR Supp. (No. 2) Agenda Item 49 (1949).

16 GA 947 plen. mtg, 15 UN GAOR 1278–9 (1960).

17 GA Res. 1514, 15 UN GAOR Supp. (No. 16) 66 (1960).

18 GA 947 plen. mtg, 15 UN GAOR 1283 (1960).

19 GA Res. 2131, 20 UN GAOR Supp. (No. 14) 10 (1965).

20 GA 1st Committee 1406 mtg, 19 UN GAOR para. 17 (1965).

21 *Ibid.*, 1404 mtg, 306.

22 *Ibid.*, 1406 mtg, para. 17.

23 GA Res. 2625, 25 UN GAOR Supp. (No. 28) 121 (1970).

24 GA, 6th Committee 1178 mtg, 25 UN GAOR 9 (1970).

25 GA, 6th Committee 1181 mtg, 25 UN GAOR 21 (1970), New Zealand; 1182 mtg, 27, Portugal.

26 *Ibid.*, 1178 mtg, 7, Poland; 1180 mtg 17, Senegal.

27 Declaration on the Enhancement of the Effectiveness of the Principle of Refraining from the Threat or Use of Force in International Relations, GA Res. 42/22, 42 UN GAOR (1987).

28 J. Stone, *Conflict Through Consensus*, ch. 6 (1977).

29 *Case Concerning Military and Paramilitary Activities in and Against Nicaragua (Nicaragua v. United States of America)*, I.C.J. *Rep.* 1986, 14 at 97–117.

30 *Ibid.*, 130–5.

31 GA Res. 43/51, 43 UN GAOR Supp. (No. 49) 276 (1988).

32 GA Res.46/182, 46 UN GAOR Supp. (No. 49) 49 (1991).

33 GA Res. 44/29, 44 UN GAOR Supp. (No. 49) (1989). See also GA Res. 48/122, 48 UN GAOR Supp. (No. 49) 241 (1993); GA Res. 50/186, 50 UN GAOR Supp. (No. 49) 248 (1995).

34 GA Res. 46/59, 46 UN GAOR Supp. (No. 49) 290 (1991).

35 GA Res. 49/170, 49 UN GAOR Supp. (No. 49) 189 (1994).

36 GA Res. 51/55, 51 UN A/PV (1996).

37 GA Res. 48/132, 48 UN GAOR Supp. (No. 49) 250 (1993); GA Res. 49/194, 49 UN GAOR Supp. (No. 49) 212 (1994); GA Res. 50/179, 50 UN GAOR Supp. (No. 49) 240 (1995).

38 GA Res. 51/22, 51 UN A/PV (1996), adopted by 56 to 4 with 76 abstentions.

39 GA Res. 49/190, 49 UN GAOR Supp. (No. 49) 208 (1994); GA Res. 50/185, 50 UN GAOR Supp. (No. 49) 247 (1995).

40 See further R. Higgins, *The Development of International Law through the Political Organs of the United Nations*, 3 (1963); C. H. Schreuer, 'Recommendations and the Traditional Sources of International Law', 20 *German Yearbook of International Law* (1977), 103 at 118.

41 GA Res. 3485, 30 UN GAOR Supp. (No. 34) 118 (1975).

42 GA Res. 3212, 29 UN GAOR Supp. (No. 31) 3 (1974).

43 GA Res. 1004, 2 UN GAOR ESS Supp. (No. 1) 2 (1956).

44 GA 564 plen. mtg, 2 UN GAOR ESS para. 187, 209 (1956), UK and New Zealand.

45 GA Res. 34/22, 34 UN GAOR Supp. (No. 46) 16 (1979).

46 GA 67 plen. mtg, 34 UN GAOR para. 127 (1979), France.
47 GA Res. 2793, 26 UN GAOR Supp. (No. 29) 3 (1971). GA 2003 plen. mtg, 26 UN GAOR paras 37, 194, 245 (1971), Ceylon, Nicaragua and Tanzania.
48 GA Res. 1004 (1956); 2793 (1971); 3212 (1974); 3485 (1974); 34/22 (1979); GA Res. ES-6/2, 6 UN GAOR ESS Supp. (No. 1) 2 (1980); GA Res. 38/7, 38 UN GAOR Supp. (No. 47) 19 (1983); GA Res. 44/240, 44 UN GAOR Supp. (No. 49) (1989), respectively.
49 See for example, GA Res. 46/18, 46/23, 46 UN GAOR Supp. (No. 49) 19, 22 (1991).
50 GA Res 48/18, 48 UN GAOR Supp. (No. 49) 21 (1993).
51 UN doc. A/49/419 (1994).
52 Simma (ed.), *The Charter*, 235.
53 GA Res. 367, 5 UN GAOR Resolutions 9 (1950). See GA 293 plen. mtg, 5 UN GAOR paras 37, 70 (1950), France, USSR.
54 See also GA Res. 39, 1 UN GAOR Resolutions 63 (1946), re Spain.
55 GA Res. 500, 5 UN GAOR Supp. (No. 20A) 2 (1951).
56 GA 330 plen. mtg, 5 UN GAOR 739–40 (1951).
57 GA Res. 1663, 16 UN GAOR Supp. (No. 17) 10 (1961); GA Res. 2107, 20 UN GAOR Supp. (No. 14) 62 (1965); GA Res. 2151, 21 UN GAOR Supp. (No. 16) 68 (1966).
58 See GA Res. 48/1, 48 UN GAOR Supp. (No. 49) 12 (1993) re South Africa.
59 GA Res. 3379, 30 UN GAOR Supp. (No. 34) 83 (1975).
60 See for example GA Res. 39/146, 39 UN GAOR Supp. (No. 51) 50 (1984).
61 GA Res. 46/86, 46 UN GAOR Supp. (No. 49) 39 (1991).
62 GA Res. 46/74, 46/76, 46/82, 46/162, 46 UN GAOR Supp. (No. 49) 27, 29, 38, 126 (1991).
63 GA Res. 47/1, 47 UN GAOR Supp. (No. 49) 12 (1992).
64 GA Res. 106, 1 UN GAOR SS Resolutions 6 (1947).
65 2 UN GAOR Supp. (No. 11) (1947).
66 UN doc. A/364 (1947).
67 GA 124, 125 plen. mtgs, 2 UN GAOR 1324, 1359 (1947), US and USSR.
68 GA 127 plen. mtg, 2 UN GAOR 1398 (1947).
69 UN doc. A/518 (1947).
70 See GA 126 plen. mtg, 2 UN GAOR 1376 (1947).
71 See GA *Ad Hoc* Committee 32 mtg, 2 UN GAOR (1947).
72 GA Res. 181, 2 UN GAOR Resolutions 131 (1947).
73 UN doc. A/C.1/277–8 (1948).
74 GA Res. 46/75, 46 UN GAOR Supp. (No. 49) 28 (1991).
75 See UN doc. A/46/652 (1991). GA plen. mtg, 46 UN A/PV (1991).
76 GA Res. 50/22, 50/84, 50 UN GAOR Supp. (No. 49) 58 (1995).
77 GA Res. 50/21, 50 UN GAOR Supp. (No. 49) 25 (1995).
78 See further the Assembly's continued support for the process of self-determination in Western Sahara. GA Res. 50/36, 50 UN GAOR Supp. (No. 49) 132 (1995).
79 *International Status of South West Africa* case, I.C.J. Rep. 1950, 128.
80 GA Res. 43/26, 43 GAOR Supp. (No. 49) 29 (1988).
81 GA Res. 35/6, 35 UN GAOR Supp. (No. 48) 13 (1980).
82 GA Res. 46/18, 46 UN GAOR Supp. (No. 49) 19 (1991).
83 See GA Res. 42/1, 42 UN GAOR Supp. (No. 49) 14 (1987).
84 GA Res. 47/118, 47 UN GAOR Supp. (No. 49) 38 (1992).

85 GA Res. 42/15, 42 UN GAOR Supp. (No. 49) 38 (1987).
86 GA Res. 46/23, 46 UN GAOR Supp. (No. 49) 22 (1991). UN doc. A/46/577 (1991). GA Res. 50/88, 50 UN GAOR Supp. (No. 49) 62 (1995).
87 GA Res. 45/2, 45 UN GAOR Supp. (No. 49) 12 (1990).
88 GA Res. 46/137, 46 UN GAOR Supp. (No. 49) 209 (1991). See further E. Ebersole, 'The United Nations Response to Requests for Assistance in Electoral Matters', 33 *Virginia Journal of International Law* (1992), 91.
89 A/CONF.157/24.
90 GA Res. 49/190, 49 UN GAOR Supp. (No. 49) 208 (1994).
91 GA Res. 46/137, 46 UN GAOR Supp. (No. 49) 209 (1991).
92 UN Press Release GA/491, 16 April 1993.
93 UN doc. A/47/544 (1992).
94 GA Res. 47/114, 47 UN GAOR Supp. (No. 49) 195 (1992).
95 *UN Chronicle*, vol. 30(3) (1993), 39.
96 GA Res. 1131, 11 UN GAOR Supp. (No. 17) 64 (1956).
97 GA 618 plen. mtg, 11 UN GAOR para. 10 (1956), Peru.
98 GA Res. 41/38, 41 UN GAOR Supp. (No. 53) 34 (1986).
99 GA Res. 44/240, 44 UN GAOR Supp. (No. 49) (1989).
100 GA Res. 47/121, 47 UN GAOR Supp. (No. 49) 44 (1992).
101 *Nicaragua* case, I.C.J. *Rep.* 1986, 14 at 98.
102 GA Res. 48/88, 48/143, 48 UN GAOR Supp. (No. 49) 40 (1993).
103 GA Res. 616, 7 UN GAOR Supp. (No. 20) 8 (1952).
104 GA 401 plen. mtg, 7 UN GAOR para. 120 (1952), India.
105 GA 56 plen. mtg, 38 UN GAOR 8, 18, 23 (1983), Sierre Leone, India, China.
106 GA Res. 44/27, 44 UN GAOR Supp. (No. 49) (1989).
107 GA Res. 46/79, 46 UN GAOR Supp. (No. 49) 32 (1991).

PART THREE

Peacekeeping

CHAPTER SEVEN

Historical and political background

Introduction

A reasonably accurate definition of peacekeeping is to be found in the *Review of United Nations Peacekeeping*, published by the United Nations:

As the United Nations practice has evolved over the years, a peacekeeping operation has come to be defined as an operation involving military personnel, but without enforcement powers, undertaken by the United Nations to help maintain or restore international peace and security in areas of conflict. These operations are voluntary and are based on consent and cooperation. While they involve the use of military personnel, they achieve their objectives not by force of arms, thus contrasting them with the 'enforcement action' of the United Nations under Article 42.[1]

The development of a peacekeeping function is one of the most significant achievements of the United Nations in its attempt to maintain international peace and security. To the layman peacekeeping forces or the 'blue helmets' are concrete manifestations of the United Nations which offset the common view that the Organisation only produces rhetoric and ideologically motivated resolutions. To the political scientist peacekeeping probably represents the most concerted effort the international community makes in regulating conflict, with the exception of military enforcement action. Other peaceful mechanisms are generally unsuccessful as explained by Wiseman:

The tension and struggle between the forces for change and the forces for the maintenance of the *status quo* are constant and dynamic features of the international system. This struggle is manifested in the frequent occurrence of ferocious and intractable conflict. By contrast, but by no means as persistent and powerful as the systematic propensity to conflict, are the creation and utilisation of international structures, instruments, and procedures for the containment and resolution of these conflicts by political means. The attempts to superimpose peaceful regulatory systems upon the disordered world are extremely hazardous and difficult. The national political propensities to make war are far more powerful than the international processes to make peace. Nonetheless, the will, determination and imagination of peoples and States persist in the quest to make order out of chaos and prescribe peaceful measures for progressive social change.[2]

Peacekeeping is such a 'peaceful regulatory system'. Its success lies in the fact that it usually only has limited objectives, for example, in separating two protagonists, not by coercion as with military enforcement, but with their consent and hopefully with their cooperation. Other peaceful measures, such as resolving the conflict by negotiation, are not as successful for they involve far more ambitious objectives. The divisions between peacekeeping and peacemaking, and peacekeeping and enforcement will be examined in more detail in chapter eight.

To the international lawyer peacekeeping represents an intriguing puzzle, raising in particular such questions as the constitutional basis for such operations; whether nations hosting peacekeeping operations are surrendering their sovereignty; whether such forces can use force beyond that required for self-defence; and which political organ of the United Nations can authorise such forces? Consistent answers to such questions have proved difficult to arrive at given the *ad hoc* creation of such forces resulting in various mandates and sizes of forces.

In this respect peacekeeping reflects the crisis management approach of the Organisation's work concerning international peace and security. Despite the establishment, in 1965, by the General Assembly, of a Special Committee on Peacekeeping to try to formulate a more institutionalised basis for peacekeeping, forces are, in the main, only envisaged, created and assembled after a conflict has started, and then only if there is sufficient political consensus in the Security Council or the General Assembly. However, the 1990s has seen some hint of reform. At its 46th session the General Assembly welcomed the progress made by the Special Committee in 1990–91, 'in particular, the agreement reached on a number of conclusions and recommendations'.[3] Nevertheless, although the debate on the nature and role of peacekeeping in the post-Cold War era has intensified, with, for example, the Secretary General reporting on the command and control of peacekeeping operations,[4] the Security Council producing statements on improving the UN capacity for peacekeeping,[5] as well as the Special Committee's reports, the discussion appears, as yet, to be conducted at a very general level and is very much hampered by the requirements of political compromise. Although some members of the Committee have expressed a desire for an elaborate set of principles to govern UN peacekeeping operations, perhaps embodied in a General Assembly resolution, the Committee as a whole has generally only been able to re-state the importance of the established basic principles of peacekeeping, such as the need for consent, the neutrality of the force and the restriction on the use of force by peacekeepers.[6] Nevertheless, slow progress is being made, for instance in 1993, the Assembly urged implementation of a model agreement formulated by the Secretary General to govern relations between the UN and troop contributors.[7]

Furthermore, the Secretary General in a report entitled *Agenda for Peace*, prepared at the request of the Security Council following the summit meeting of Heads of State and Government of 31 January 1992, contained the following proposal to enhance preventive diplomacy:

United Nations operations in areas of crisis have generally been established after the conflict has occurred. The time has come to plan for circumstances warranting preventive deployment, which could take place in a variety of instances and ways. For example, in conditions of national crisis there could be preventive deployment at the request of the Government or all parties concerned, or with their consent; in inter-State disputes such deployment could take place when two countries feel that a United Nations presence on both sides of their border could discourage hostilities; furthermore, preventive deployment could take place when a country feels threatened and requests the deployment of an appropriate United Nations presence along its side of the border alone. In each situation, the mandate and composition of the United Nations presence would need to be carefully devised and clear to all.[8]

This proposal would enhance the Organisation's ability to prevent hostilities from breaking out but it must be made clear, as the Secretary General suggests, whether the particular force is a consensual, lightly armed peacekeeping force, or is of an enforcement type armed with both mandate and equipment to repel aggression. In his *Supplement to an Agenda for Peace* of 1995, the Secretary General made it clear, in the light of the UN's experiences in Bosnia and Somalia, that the line between peacekeeping and enforcement should not be blurred because of the danger of undermining the validity of consensual peacekeeping.[9] The importance of this distinction, and the problems of Bosnia and Somalia, will be returned to in the following two chapters.

Historical overview

The following peacekeeping and observer forces have been authorised by the United Nations:

UN Observers in Indonesia 1947–50.
UN Sub-Commission on the Balkans (UNSCOB) 1947–54.
UN Truce Supervision Organisation in Palestine (UNTSO) 1949–present.
UN Military Observer Group in India and Pakistan (UNMOGIP) 1949–present.
UN Emergency Force (UNEF I) 1956–67.
UN Observer Group in Lebanon (UNOGIL) 1958.
UN Operation in the Congo (ONUC) 1960–64.
UN Security Force in West Irian (UNSF) 1962–63.
UN Yemen Observation Mission (UNYOM) 1963–64.
UN Peacekeeping Force in Cyprus (UNFICYP) 1964–present.
UN India–Pakistan Observation Mission (UNIPOM) 1965–66.
UN Emergency Force (UNEF II) 1973–79.
UN Disengagement Observer Force (UNDOF) 1974–present.
UN Interim Force in Lebanon (UNIFIL) 1978–present.
UN Good Offices Mission in Afghanistan and Pakistan (UNGOMAP) 1988–90.

UN Iran–Iraq Military Observer Group (UNIIMOG) 1988–91.

UN Angola Verification Missions (UNAVEM I, II and III) 1989–present.

UN Transition Assistance Group (UNTAG), 1989–90.

UN Observer Group in Central America (ONUCA), 1989–92.

UN Iraq–Kuwait Observation Mission (UNIKOM), 1991–present.

UN Mission for the Referendum in Western Sahara (MINURSO), 1991–present.

UN Observer Mission in El Salvador (ONUSAL), 1991–95.

UN Transition Assistance Authority in Cambodia (UNTAC), 1991–93.

UN Protection Force in Yugoslavia (UNPROFOR), 1992–95.

UN Operations in Somalia (UNOSOM I and II), 1992–95.

UN Operation in Mozambique (ONUMOZ), 1992–94.

UN Observer Mission Uganda–Rwanda (UNOMUR), 1993–94.

UN Observer Mission in Georgia (UNOMIG), 1993–present.

UN Observer Mission in Liberia (UNOMIL), 1993–present.

UN Mission and Support Mission in Haiti (UNMIH and UNSMIH), 1993–present.

UN Assistance Mission for Rwanda (UNAMIR), 1993–96.

UN Aouzou Strip Observer Group (UNASOG), 1994.

UN Mission of Observers in Tajikistan (UNMOT), 1994–present.

UN Confidence Restoration Operation in Croatia (UNCRO), 1995–96.

UN Preventive Deployment Force in Macedonia (UNPREDEP), 1995–present.

UN Mission in Bosnia and Herzegovina (UNMIBH), 1995–present.

UN Transitional Administration for Eastern Slavonia, Baranja and Western Sir-muim (UNTAES), 1996–present.

UN Mission of Observers in Prevlaka (UNMOP), 1996–present.

UN Mission in Guatemala (MINUGUA), 1997–present.

Peacekeeping essentially emerged during the Cold War as an acceptable, non-aggressive, UN military presence. Enforcement action was not generally acceptable to the superpowers during the Cold War, and so less intrusive options were developed by the UN. This is explained by Professor Durch:

During the Cold War, the United Nations could not do the job for which it was created. Global collective security, the organising precept of its Charter, was impossible in a world divided into hostile blocs. But the UN did manage to carve out a more narrow security role. As a 'neutral' organisation, it could sometimes help to bring smaller conflicts to an end, keep them from flaring anew, and keep them from leading to a direct and potentially catastrophic clash of US and Soviet arms. Thus, the UN came to be associated over the years with more modest but, under the circumstances, more realistic objectives: the mediation of isolated and idiosyncratic conflicts, the monitoring of cease-fire arrangements and the separation of hostile armed forces. Novel kinds of field operations were developed to support this work, which can be grouped into two categories: Unarmed military observer missions … and armed peacekeeping missions … [T]he term 'peacekeeping' is used as a shorthand reference to both.[10]

Professor Wiseman has analysed United Nations' peacekeeping historically.[11] He labels the period 1946–56 as the 'nascent period' of peacekeeping with the creation of four observation teams, the so called 'generic antecedents' of full peacekeeping forces which emerged in 1956 with the creation of UNEF I. This represented the beginning of what Wiseman calls the 'assertive period' which ended in 1967 with the withdrawal of UNEF I. During this period eight peacekeeping (including observation) forces were created. The withdrawal of UNEF I in 1967 with the ensuing Six Day War called into question the effectiveness of United Nations' peacekeeping so that between 1967 and 1973 it went through a 'dormant period' when no forces were created. Paradoxically, it took another conflict in the Middle East, namely the Yom Kippur War of 1973, to spark off a 'resurgent period' in which three full peacekeeping forces were created. After the creation and emplacement of UNIFIL, and the authorisation without emplacement of UNTAG in 1978, the peacekeeping function of the United Nations was frozen for a decade due to a decline in East–West relations.

However, the *rapprochement* between the superpowers in the late 1980s, sparked off a revival, with four forces established between March 1988 and April 1989, culminating in the emplacement of UNTAG over ten years after it had initially been authorised. UNTAG was in many respects a novel development in that it combined peacekeeping, the separation of South African forces and SWAPO guerrillas, and peacemaking in the form of supervision and policing of elections that eventually led to the independence of Namibia in 1990. This trend has continued into the 1990s with similar combined forces in Central America, Western Sahara, Cambodia, Mozambique and Angola. This new integrated approach, which reflects the trend towards democracy in the 1990s after the collapse of Communism, has not replaced the traditional approach whereby peacekeeping is used to keep the parties apart whilst a separate political solution is sought, evidenced by the initial creation of forces in Yugoslavia and Somalia, though these were later either supplemented or replaced by military enforcement action.

The United Nations has currently seventeen forces on station around the globe with the prospect of many more being needed as the world is reshaped in the 1990s with the collapse of Communism and the re-surfacing of inter-ethnic rivalries. In this respect modern peacekeeping efforts follow a similar pattern to the earlier ones, such as UNTSO and the Middle East forces, needed when the State of Israel emerged after the Second World War, and forces such as ONUC in the Congo emplaced as a result of the decolonisation and independence of States. The latest resurgence of peacekeeping is not only a product of the loosening of political inhibitions in the Security Council but also a product of the numerous conflicts and situations that have rapidly broken out after the end of the Cold War.

The removal of the severest of political limitations in the Security Council has also led to a greater variety in the type and functions of the peacekeeping forces deployed by the UN. Essentially there are three types of peacekeeping operation being deployed by the Security Council: (i) the traditional 'buffer' type peacekeeping force derived from the UNEF I model; (ii) the integrated, multi-functional, force combining the traditional approach with peaceful solution (primarily the holding of elections); and (iii) quasi-enforcement operations in which the force is given a more aggressive mandate. The latter, being derived from the Operation in the Congo, while utilised in the early 1990s, have suffered a decline because of their ineffectiveness and their debilitating effect on the consensual type of operations, whether traditional or integrated.[12]

Political context

Professor Franck gives a relatively narrow definition of peacekeeping as 'the peaceful interpositioning of UN personnel, in response to an invitation of the disputants, to oversee an agreed cease-fire'.[13] Such a definition is applicable mainly to inter-State peacekeeping, where a force is placed between two formerly hostile States which have agreed a cease-fire; whereas the United Nations has also undertaken intra-state peacekeeping, for example in the Congo, where a force is placed within one factionalised State. Franck's definition also ignores the technique of observation from which inter and intra-State peacekeeping evolved. Observation has the limited function of reporting on the state of hostilities whereas peacekeeping has the more intrusive function of separating the parties to the cease-fire without the force generally having the power to enforce the peace. However, the divisions between observation, peacekeeping and enforcement action are unclear, there are grey areas in which one function merges into another since 'peacekeeping was developed from the roots of [both] collective security and peace observation'.[14] Nevertheless, these distinctions are important in order to understand the legal principles governing peacekeeping, examined in chapter eight, as well as the political factors examined next.

The main purpose of this section is to give a brief review of the creation of each force to try and analyse the historical and political circumstances under which they arose and to attempt to indicate in what circumstances peacekeeping forces are likely to be established in the future. It may be that the circumstances are different for observation teams compared to peacekeeping forces, although the distinction between the two has become increasingly difficult to make in the post-Cold War era.

Observation teams

The observation teams created in the nascent period (1946–56) all arose through the change that occurred in the international order following the Second World War. The first force to be created was the UN observation team in Indonesia in 1947 when a conflict arose involving the Dutch colonialists' attempt to maintain the old order against a rising tide of nationalism in Indonesia. The Security Council, with no direct permanent member involvement once the British withdrew their wartime forces, and with no member willing to stand in the way of decolonisation in this case, was able to authorise UN observers.

The need for such observers was apparent from the confused state of affairs in Indonesia with various cease-fire lines, sporadic fighting and changing areas under the control of each side. Observers were needed to report on the various stages achieved, with the help of quite vigorous Security Council resolutions, towards Indonesian independence.

Decolonisation was also the main cause of the conflict between the newly independent States of India and Pakistan over the disputed Indian state of Jammu and Kashmir which led to the Security Council establishing UNMOGIP in 1949. As with Indonesia, this again was a soft area of the world where none of the permanent members, particularly the superpowers, had sufficient interest in either side to protect them by the veto. As with all peacekeeping forces, UNMOGIP depended upon the cooperation of both parties. Thus such forces are not usually created and emplaced until the fighting has come to an end and the belligerents are willing to accept a cease-fire. However, observation teams are not meant as buffer forces, the smaller ones are often unarmed, they only observe the cease-fire and they are not usually large enough nor are they mandated to make the cease-fire effective as are peacekeeping forces proper. Thus UNMOGIP observed throughout the outbreak of hostilities in 1965 and was present to observe the new cease-fire. In 1965, the fighting between India and Pakistan was on a wider front than in 1947 necessitating the emplacement of another team, for a limited period, beyond UNMOGIP's patrol. UNIPOM was in place from 1965–66 again under a Security Council mandate, illustrating that this area of the world was not considered part of a power bloc. UNIPOM was removed after a limited period but UNMOGIP remains because its area of patrol, namely Kashmir, continues to constitute a potential flashpoint where the United Nations needs a constant monitoring presence.

Along with UNMOGIP another observation team, UNTSO, created under Security Council auspices in 1949, has lasted for nearly fifty years in an even more troubled area of the world. Unlike UNEF which was emplaced between Israel and Egypt for eleven years from 1956–67 and for a further six years from 1973–79, UNTSO has observed various cease-fires, truces and armistices between belligerents in the Middle East. The peculiar fact is that there is no Security Council resolution directly authorising UNTSO, nor, as with UNMOGIP, is there any periodic renewal of its mandate. It has a loose mandate which is best described as observing and reporting to the United Nations on the situation in the Middle East. Its longevity is probably a testimony to the fact that the Security Council, particularly the permanent members, needs to keep in constant touch with the situation in an area where they have interests, but in which neither is paramount, and UNTSO provides them with valuable, neutral information. UNTSO thus acts to some extent as an effective brake on the possibility of escalation based on a hasty, one-sided account of a conflict. In many respects it is similar to fact finding bodies authorised by the Security Council under Article 34, although it consists of military observers as opposed to civilian personnel. During the period of UNEF's interpositioning, UNTSO observers worked alongside the peacekeeping force; however, unlike UNEF, UNTSO observers were used after the Six Day War, as it was a political necessity for the United Nations to maintain some presence in the area.

Observation is sufficiently flexible to be used equally successfully in intra-State conflicts such as Indonesia as well as in inter-State conflicts as in the Gulf War between Iran and Iraq, which after nearly a decade of fighting, stagnated sufficiently to allow a UN observer force (UNIIMOG) into the area in August 1988. It can also be of value where there is a combination of the two situations evidenced by UNOGIL in the Lebanon in 1958 and by UNYOM in the Yemen in 1963. In both cases there arose the problem of outside military interference in a civil war. The countries involved, either directly or indirectly, were again situated in the intermediate areas of the world beyond the direct hemispheric influences of the superpowers, and of any of the other permanent members, thus allowing the Security Council to mandate both forces. Nevertheless, the fact that the Middle East was subject to superpower claims was evidenced by the United States' intervention in Lebanon despite UNOGIL's report that the country was not being undermined by the United Arab Republic.

However, during the Cold War, when the conflict in question was nearer both politically and geographically to the superpowers to amount to an East–West power struggle, there was less likelihood of an observation team being sent to the area by the Security Council. After the Second World War the world order changed dramatically to an East–West divide based on ideology. Nowhere was this best evidenced than in the Balkans where the pro-Western Greek government alleged military support for the Communist insurgents from the surrounding Communist countries of Bulgaria, Albania and Yugoslavia. Although the Security Council was able to create a Commission of Investigation, it was left to the General Assembly, in 1947, to create a Sub-Committee which had observation functions. The Soviet Union objected to this. The Cold War motivations behind UNSCOB limited its effectiveness, as evidenced by the refusal of the Socialist States to allow it on their territory.

Sometimes the United Nations has found it necessary to create a force which combines observation with other duties due to the circumstances of the situation. Although the main Indonesian question had been settled earlier, there were still disputes over several islands in the Indonesian archipelago. One such island was Irian where guerrilla warfare was being carried out by Indonesians parachuted into the jungle and Dutch armed forces in the western part of the island. The Netherlands and Indonesia came to an agreement on 15 August 1962 which provided for the administration of West Irian to be transferred by the Netherlands to a United Nations Temporary Executive Authority (UNTEA) pending a transfer of the territory to Indonesia. A United Nations Security Force (UNSF) was to observe the cease-fire which was to take place before authority was transferred to UNTEA, and then to police the island until the transfer of sovereignty to Indonesia.[15]

Thus the force was really created by the parties although it required the approval of the General Assembly, as the body responsible for questions of self-determination, rather than the Security Council. Surprisingly, taking into account the large role given to the Secretary General in the control of UNTEA and UNSF, the Soviet Union voted for the creation of these bodies. At the time the continuing Congo question had provoked Soviet objections as regards the amount of control the Secretary General had over ONUC and of the ability of the General Assembly to mandate such a force in the absence of Security Council consensus. Nevertheless, the Soviet Union was willing to vote in the Assembly for the creation of a force and an authority whose control amounted to virtual temporary sovereignty over the island.

The reasons for the Soviet Union's support were twofold. Again the crisis was relatively minor and did not involve questions of superpower influence, except to the extent of the Soviet Union's uneasy courtship with the Non-Aligned of which Indonesia was a member. Also, the Soviet assent was due to the agreement of the parties which led to the creation of the United Nations' force.

Indeed, all observer teams and peacekeeping forces depend on the cooperation of the parties; some arise directly from an agreement between the parties which the Security Council (or more rarely the Assembly, if the agreement calls for it) has the option of approving. Under the armistice agreement of 1949 between Israel on the one hand and Egypt, Syria, Jordan and Lebanon on the other UNTSO was given specific duties;[16] UNYOM directly arose out of an agreement between Yemen, Saudi Arabia and the United Arab Republic negotiated by Secretary General U Thant;[17] UNMOGIP was a direct creation of the Karachi Agreement between India and Pakistan,[18] with which the Security Council had very little involvement; the Agreement on Disengagement between Syria and Israel called for the establishment of UNDOF.[19] Other forces are either requested by the States involved such as ONUC or UNFICYP, or are consented to by the parties on the initiative of the United Nations, for example UNEF. However, to say that only in the latter situation does the initiative for the creation of a force come from the United Nations would be an exaggeration ignoring the often significant contribution of the Secretary General in the negotiation process.

Furthermore, the observer forces in Afghanistan and Angola coming towards the end of the Cold War, were the result of express or tacit agreements between the superpowers to allow observer forces into areas of global as well as regional confrontation. UNGOMAP, in Afghanistan to oversee Soviet troops withdrawal, was a product of 1988 superpower accord as well as an agreement between the regional States involved, Pakistan and Afghanistan.[20] UNAVEM, in Angola was a product of regional agreements of 1988 involving Cuba, Angola and South Africa, but was also backed by the Soviet Union and the United States.[21] Both were primarily a result of the Soviet Union withdrawing from its zones of influence as a prelude to the collapse of the Eastern bloc and ultimately of the Soviet Union in 1991. The collapse of that country, the emergence of new States, and resulting intra-State conflicts has necessitated the creation of observer forces in Georgia in 1993 (UNOMIG) and Tajikistan in 1994 (UNMOT).[22]

Furthermore, in the period of the late 1980s when there was a distinct warming in superpower relations, UN observer teams were allowed into what were formerly 'no-go' areas including those areas dominated by the eventual winner of the Cold War, the United States. In particular, the long-standing internationalised civil wars in Nicaragua and El Salvador have been brought to an end by an ongoing Central American peace process started by the States in the region with the Guatemala Accords of 1987.[23] After many years of keeping the United Nations out of its hemisphere, the United States consented to the creation of ONUCA in Nicaragua and ONUSAL in El Salvador.

Indeed, the current trend in peacekeeping and observation is to combine peacekeeping and peacemaking, in that the parties to the conflict not only agree to a peacekeeping or observer force to keep the parties apart or to monitor a cease-fire, they also agree to a specific method of settling the dispute. The dominant method chosen in intra-State conflicts has been the choice of a democratic government through free and fair elections reflecting the trend towards democracy in the post-Cold War era. Such forces are not too dissimilar from that involved in West Irian in 1962–63, in that they have a separate peacekeeping or observation component and then an additional component established to supervise the chosen method of pacific settlement. In 1989 the Security Council established the United Nations Mission to Verify the Electoral Process in Nicaragua (ONUVEN) at the request of the parties. A similar request by the opposing factions in Angola in 1991 resulted in the establishment of a second UNAVEM team to observe the cease-fire between the factions and to supervise elections, although the failure of UNITA to observe the election results of September 1992 led to the re-igniting of the conflict, which the Security Council has attempted to deal with by the creation of a larger force (UNAVEM III) in 1995.

The integrated method is sufficiently flexible to allow for variations. In El Salvador the initial agreement was for observation by ONUSAL of the human rights accord reached by the parties in July 1990 (the San José Agreement)[24] while the parties continued negotiation on a cease-fire and on a peaceful solution, which eventually resulted in peaceful elections in March 1994. In the long running dispute over Western Sahara, the initial agreement of 1988 between Morocco and the Popular Front for the Liberation of the Sanguia el-Harura and the Rio de Oro (POLISARIO) brokered by the Secretary General and the OAU, eventually took the form of an acceptable plan in 1990.[25] Under this plan the UN force, MINURSO, would supervise a cease-fire between the parties and conduct a referendum in which the Western Saharan people would choose between integration with Morocco and independence. However, the referendum has been delayed on numerous occasions mainly due to disagreements on those entitled to vote. This illustrates, along with the problems in Angola, the high risk factor in combining traditional peacekeeping with peaceful settlement through 'win-or-lose' elections or referenda.

The new observer teams are in the main needed because of the instability caused by the collapse in the bipolar world. One product of this instability is the greater willingness of the United Nations to use force. It did so against Iraq in 1990–91. When the Iraqis accepted the cease-fire in April 1991, the Security Council established UNIKOM to oversee it on the Iraq–Kuwait border. This was the first time the UN had placed a peacekeeping force between two parties, one of which was in reality the UN authorised Coalition. As well as showing the Security Council's increasingly flexible approach to its powers, it reveals the different conceptions States have of enforcement and peacekeeping. Iraq, while fighting against the Coalition in February and March 1991, accepted the peacekeeping force without much argument, although in reality it had little choice.

The Gulf Crisis also saw the expansion in the use of UN military personnel in an essentially observatory capacity in the provision of humanitarian aid to the Kurdish population in the north. The end of the Coalition campaign against Iraq saw the Iraqi regime still powerful enough to brutally suppress Kurd and Shia revolts against it starting in March 1991. The Kurdish repression in particular saw a flood of refugees flee across the borders into Iran and Turkey. Western States initially responded by airlifts of food and clothing and eventually by limited military intervention in the north to protect the Kurds and to encourage them to return to Iraq. On 20 May 1991, Iraq consented to the presence of 500 UN guards to replace the 15,000 Western troops in the north of Iraq.[26]

Such a humanitarian function has been undertaken by UN military personnel before, for instance by UNIFIL in Lebanon when the force was powerless to perform its other functions, but such a trend seems set to continue if the increasing number of inter-ethnic wars produces huge waves of refugees attempting to flee from the combat zones. The observer forces placed in the troubled Great Lakes region of Central Africa in 1993, UNOMUR on the Ugandan/Rwandan border and UNAMIR in Rwanda, are testimony to the international community's greater, though still limited, concern for inter-ethnic conflicts in Africa. However, these efforts were supplemented by a Security Council authorised French military operation in Rwanda in 1994, and a largely aborted multinational force authorised by the Security Council for eastern Zaire in 1996. The overall sparseness of the UN response to African conflicts is further indicated by the limited UN presence in Liberia since 1993 (UNOMIL), where the burden of the peacekeeping effort has been undertaken by the Economic Community of West African States Monitoring Group (ECOMOG), created by a regional organisation, ECOWAS.

Peacekeeping forces

Observation, supervision, and enforcement are the three possible stages of United

Nations' military involvement in a conflict. The first two are peacekeeping functions, observation has already been discussed, but it must be remembered that
there is often a thin line between observation and full peacekeeping as evidenced
by the mandate and functions of UNSF in West Irian and many of the recent forces
with integrated or combined mandates performing several functions. Similarly,
there is a grey area between peacekeeping and enforcement action highlighted by
the actions of ONUC in the Congo, and UNOSOM II in Somalia.

For the purposes of this section peacekeeping involves not only observation of
the cease-fire but also supervision, which in most instances of inter-State conflict
entails the creation of a buffer zone between the former belligerents, a function
too large, and requiring a different mandate than that granted to observation
teams. Peacekeeping evolved from observation so as to give the United Nations a
more active role after the cessation of hostilities. UNEF I was the first 'dramatically innovative venture' into peacekeeping proper.[27] It was created in 1956 by the
General Assembly after a joint Anglo/French/Israeli plan to prevent Egyptian
nationalisation of the Suez Canal. Permanent member involvement prevented the
creation of such a force in the Security Council, so the question passed to the General Assembly where UNEF I was created with the substantial assistance of the
Secretary General.

It might be argued that the above procedure could have been successfully
utilised in other instances of permanent member involvement so as to create
peacekeeping forces in the Assembly when such efforts have been vetoed in the
Security Council. There are two factors which prevent such a course being
chosen more often. First, even though the United Kingdom and France vetoed any
attempts to pacify the situation in the Council they only abstained (along with the
Soviet bloc) on the Assembly resolution creating UNEF I, and, in fact, they eventually consented to the placement of the force. Although the Assembly could,
theoretically, create peacekeeping forces in cases of permanent member intervention, when the Council is blocked by the veto, political reality prevents such a
course without the consent of all the parties concerned. In the Suez case, the two
permanent members involved had reached a stage where to continue would have
brought them under unbearable international pressure, while to withdraw would
have been too costly politically; the peacekeeping force was consented to because
it maintained the *status quo* achieved so far. To this end it also met the requirements of the other two parties; Egypt because it was being heavily defeated, and
Israel because it had gained a considerable amount of territory. The circumstances
were ripe for a UN peacekeeping force to fill the vacuum.

A second factor which prevented the creation of further forces by the Assembly instead of the Council is the attitude among the permanent members that such
forces should only be created by the Security Council. Originally, the French and
the Soviet Union took this line in relation to UNEF I and ONUC leading to their
challenge of being assessed for financial contributions in the *Expenses* case of
1962. The evidence is that the United States and the United Kingdom adopted this

line from 1960 onwards. Evan Luard has accurately summarised the reasons for this.

First, the outright opposition of the Soviet Union and France to the use previously made of the Assembly, their refusal to contribute to the costs of peacekeeping operations the Assembly had authorised, and the prolonged financial crisis which resulted from this constitutional difference in view, all served to induce some caution among other major powers in mobilising the Assembly. Secondly, the increasing size of the Assembly, as well as the change in its composition (in which Afro-Asian Members came to hold more than two-thirds of the votes) meant that it came to be thought a less suitable instrument for use in such situations, by the US as much as by the Soviet Union. Thirdly, the far less use of the Soviet veto in the Council reduced the need for an alternative agency. Finally, the desire of the other permanent members to retain the special influence which they held in the Security Council also encouraged the restoration of the Council's supremacy in security questions.[28]

Communist China has sometimes objected in the past to peacekeeping on the grounds that it was a creation of the superpowers, at other times it supports the emplacement of a force by the Security Council depending on the circumstances of the case. Recently China has shown a more positive attitude to peacekeeping, illustrated by the fact that it joined the Assembly's Special Committee on Peacekeeping in 1988, and has generally supported the Council's post-Cold War peacekeeping efforts.[29]

The Middle East has been the area in which peacekeeping, whether by the United Nations or by other agencies, has been most utilised. UNEF I was withdrawn in 1967. UNEF II, authorised by the Security Council, was emplaced between Egypt and Israel following the Yom Kippur War of 1973. The danger of superpower intervention as well as the consent of the combatants were direct factors leading to its creation. UNEF II was not only a buffer between the two parties, it was also an indirect buffer between the superpowers backing Israel and Egypt. When Egypt changed its allegiance to become more pro-Western, the United States was able to sponsor negotiations between the Israelis and the Egyptians leading to the Camp David Accords. Although the peace agreement between Israel and Egypt provided for a continued United Nations' peacekeeping presence, the Egyptian defection had practically destroyed the superpower accord behind UNEF II, and so the force was discontinued in 1979 to be replaced by a United States-sponsored multinational force. However, superpower agreement still continued as regards UNDOF created in 1974 as a buffer on the Israeli–Syrian front, as each party remained fairly firmly placed in the Western and Eastern camps. Even with the demise of the Soviet Union, Syria remains Israel's most dangerous enemy necessitating a continued peacekeeping presence.

Middle Eastern peacekeeping forces have the regional function of separating two or more belligerents but they have had wider functions than the maintenance of stable Arab–Israeli relations, they were placed so as to add an extra check on the possibility of escalation in an area where although both superpowers had clients neither had regional dominance. Similarly, UNIFIL was created in 1978 not only to secure Israeli withdrawal from Lebanon, but also to perform the unstated, global function of separating American-backed Israel and Soviet-supported Syria from engaging in conflict using Lebanon as a battleground, which might have sucked in one or both superpowers. When creating such a force the Security Council only lists the local functions of the force as regards the two belligerents, nevertheless, peacekeeping has played and continues to play a much more global function in the Middle East. The global function has continued with the end of the Cold War, which while producing new opportunities for peaceful settlement of old problems, has led to instability in many areas of the globe where previously superpower pressure resulted in a precarious *status quo*. The Middle Eastern peacekeeping forces, UNIFIL, UNDOF and UNTSO are needed to maintain this stability while the peace process, which started in 1991, is given a chance to succeed.

ONUC, in the Congo, was created in an atmosphere of potential superpower intervention after the Belgians withdrew in 1960. Indeed, it was the Soviet Union's charge that ONUC was leaning towards the pro-Western factions in the Congo which led to the Soviet veto of any continuing Security Council control over the force, which in turn led to the General Assembly having control of the operation for a while. However, ONUC managed to tread the neutral tightrope sufficiently to preclude any overt superpower intervention. The members of the Security Council, particularly the superpowers, probably originally authorised the operation because the Congo represented an area in which both superpowers would have liked to have a base, but neither was willing to disturb the global *status quo* by intervening. Thus to concretise this mutual non-intervention, and to assuage each superpower's fear of the other intervening, the United Nations was called to fill the vacuum.

ONUC's operation, and more recently UNOSOM II's activities in Somalia, probably represent the only attempts by the United Nations to fully modify peacekeeping to suit a case of intra-State conflict. One could argue that UNIFIL in Lebanon, UNFICYP in Cyprus, UNTAG in Namibia, and UNPROFOR in Yugoslavia, are further examples of United Nations' peacekeeping operations being authorised in intra-State conflicts. However, it is perhaps more realistic to view these three forces as a hybrid between intra and inter-State peacekeeping forces. UNIFIL was created after Israel intervened in 1978 and has acted to a certain extent as a buffer between two factions, pro-Israeli and anti-Israeli, as well as between Israel and Syria. Nevertheless each faction is in itself so fragmented that the situation has become one of civil war. Nevertheless, UNIFIL's main function still remains to supervise Israeli withdrawal, rather than to prevent a civil war which was one of ONUC's main tasks, or to disarm the factions in a civil war, which became one of UNOSOM II's main functions.

UNFICYP was created in 1964 after fighting had broken out between the Greek and Turkish Cypriot communities on the island. It was thus a civil war situation akin to that in the Congo, except with fewer parties. Indeed, the fact that there were only two parties enabled UNFICYP to function similarly to an inter-State peacekeeping force, by separating the two communities. This function became particularly evident after the Turkish invasion and occupation of the northern third of Cyprus in 1974. UNFICYP evolved into a true buffer force between two belligerents after this date.

In the case of UNTAG, both the Soviet Union and the United States consented, along with the regional powers, to a large UN presence in an economically rich and strategically important area of the world. Although created on paper in 1978, UNTAG was not emplaced until April 1989 as a result of an interim period in which global attitudes between the superpowers and regional attitudes between Angola and South Africa, hardened. The new *realpolitik* of the late 1980s meant that the Soviet Union and its allies no longer objected to the linkage of Cuban withdrawal from Angola with South African withdrawal from Namibia.

UNTAG, like UNSF before it, was given a mixture of peacekeeping, observer and police functions, relating to the cessation of hostilities, withdrawal of forces and keeping the peace during a peaceful transition to independence. Such a mixed or integrated approach to peacekeeping has been continued in areas of the world where the end of the Cold War has seen the local factions, in what were internationalised civil wars, so exhausted that political settlement is the only viable option remaining to them. The wars in Central America have already been mentioned, but by far the most ambitious project in this respect was the huge peacekeeping force, UNTAC, sent to Cambodia pursuant to the Paris Peace Accords which were signed by the four factions in the conflict in October 1991.[30]

However, whilst in Namibia and Cambodia the parties to the conflicts which had lasted for many years, were ready to negotiate, the end of the Cold War has set loose new conflicts which require what could be described as old fashioned peacekeeping simply to keep the parties apart, with any attempts at peaceful solution being a separate and daunting enterprise. The UN operation in Yugoslavia, UNPROFOR, was like ONUC in the Congo in some respects, given that Yugoslavia was a single State until its rapid disintegration started with the civil war in Slovenia and Croatia in June 1991. However, unlike ONUC, whose aim was to keep the Congo intact, UNPROFOR was present to oversee the break-up of Yugoslavia into several nations, with its principal task being a buffer force between Croatia and the remains of Yugoslavia (Serbia and Montenegro), while a peaceful solution to the problem of an international frontier and the Serbian enclaves in Croatia was negotiated. However, as in the Lebanon, the emerging States, particularly Bosnia, broke down into several factions themselves, leaving UNPROFOR in a vulnerable position, and forcing the peacekeepers to concentrate on the provision of humanitarian assistance to the suffering civilians in Bosnia. Although, as shall be seen in chapter nine, there were attempts by the Security Council to modify UNPROFOR's mandate to enable it to act more effectively in Bosnia, these were at best described as half-hearted, and it was left to the

Croats and Muslims to force the issue by military action in Bosnia and in the Serbian enclaves in Croatia, combined with widespread NATO airstrikes under Security Council authority. These actions led to the Dayton Peace Accords of November 1995,[31] and the replacement of UNPROFOR with the more coercive, NATO-led, Implementation Force (IFOR).

As has been noted in the discussion of observer forces, the provision of humanitarian aid has become an increasing feature in many of the most recent UN forces, as the massive displacement of refugees from internecine conflicts shocks the world's conscience. The initial force sent to Somalia in 1992, UNOSOM I, was a response primarily to the starvation resulting from the increasingly anarchic situation in that country following the overthrow of President Barre in January 1991. Its functions were to oversee an agreed cease-fire and to provide urgent humanitarian assistance. Its failure to do so and its replacement in 1993, initially by the US-led enforcement action (UNITAF), and then by UNOSOM II, a much more aggressive force, illustrates the weakness of traditional peacekeeping where there is no effective cease-fire leading to the temptation to supplement by enforcement action. The crisis caused by the Congo operation, and the ignominious withdrawal of UNOSOM II from Somalia in March 1995, illustrate that this temptation must be resisted, least of all because it undermines the neutrality and consensual basis of peacekeeping.[32]

The collapse of the bipolar world has led to the UN being sucked into the vacuum. In many instances the end of the Cold War has also allowed peaceful initiatives in the old conflicts where the factions, no longer propped up by outside States, are ready to settle. Angola, El Salvador, Western Sahara, Cambodia and Mozambique are the newest examples of an approach to peacekeeping that integrates it with a peaceful solution. However, in the conflicts that have emerged out, or escalated as a result, of the Cold War, peace initiatives are separate and usually less successful. In this respect they are like many of the older forces, some of which are still in place, such as UNFICYP in Cyprus. Indeed, there is plenty of evidence to suggest that whereas such forces are essential to maintain the regional and sometimes the global *status quo*, they can hinder a peaceful solution because the parties are happier with that situation than any of the alternatives. Forces such as those emplaced in Cambodia and Western Sahara, clearly have an advantage, but since they still depend on consent for their success, such forces cannot always be authorised. It appears there will always be a need for traditional peacekeeping forces.

Notes

1 *The Blue Helmets: A Review of United Nations Peacekeeping*, 4, 2nd ed. (1991). See further 3–9, 3rd ed. (1996). See also A. B. Fetherston, 'Putting the Peace back into Peacekeeping: Theory must Inform Practice', 1 *International Peacekeeping* (1994), 3 at 4.

2 H. Wiseman, *Peacekeeping: Appraisals and Proposals*, 1 (1983).
3 GA Res. 46/48, 46 UN GAOR Supp. (No. 49) (1991). UN doc. A/46/254 (1991).
4 UN doc. A/49/681 (1994).
5 S/PRST/1994/22.
6 UN doc. A/50/230 (1995). But see B. Simma (ed.), *The Charter of the United Nations: A Commentary*, 574 (1994).
7 GA Res. 48/42, 48 UN GAOR Supp. (No. 49) (1993). UN doc. A/46/185 (1993).
8 Boutros Boutros-Ghali, *Agenda for Peace*, 16–17 (1992). 31 *I.L.M.* (1992), 953 at 962.
9 UN docs S/1995/1; A/50/60, para. 35.
10 W. J. Durch (ed.), *The Evolution of UN Peacekeeping*, 1 (1993).
11 Wiseman, *Peacekeeping*, ch. 2. See further R. S. Lee, 'UN Peacekeeping: Development and Prospects', 28 *Cornell International Law Journal* (1995), 619; R. Wedgewood, 'The Evolution of UN Peacekeeping', 28 *Cornell International Law Journal* (1995), 631.
12 R. Higgins, 'Second Generation Peacekeeping', 89 *Proceedings of the American Society of International Law* (1995), 275 at 279. United Nations, *The Blue Helmets: A Review of United Nations Peace-Keeping*, 7, 3rd ed. (1996).
13 T. M. Franck, *Nation against Nation*, 168 (1985).
14 P. F. Diehl, *International Peacekeeping*, 5 (1994).
15 274 UNTS 6311.
16 42 UNTS 252, 42 UNTS 304, 42 UNTS 327, 42 UNTS 288 respectively.
17 UN docs S/5298, S/5321 (1963).
18 UN doc. S/1430/Add 1 (1949).
19 UN doc. S/11302/Add 1 & 2 (1974).
20 Geneva Accords, 27 *I.L.M.* (1988), 577.
21 UN docs S/20345, S/20346 (1988).
22 See generally R. Allison, *Peacekeeping in the Soviet Successor States* (1994).
23 26 *I.L.M.* (1987), 1164.
24 UN doc. S/21541 (1990).
25 UN doc. S/21360 (1990).
26 UN doc. S/22513 (1991).
27 Wiseman, *Peacekeeping*, 19. F. L. Fabian, *Soldiers without Enemies*, 3 (1971).
28 E. Luard, *The United Nations*, 46–7 (1979).
29 But see the Chinese veto of 10 January 1997 of the proposed creation of a military component for MINUGUA in Guatemala, on the basis of Guatemala's support for Taiwan – SC 3730 mtg, 52 UN S/PV (1997). It reversed its opposition on 20 January 1997 when it voted for SC Res. 1094, 52 UN S/PV (1997) creating the force, after the Non-Aligned members threatened to pass the matter to the Assembly under the Uniting for Peace Resolution.
30 UN doc. S/23179 (1991).
31 35 *I.L.M.* (1996), 75.
32 Higgins, 89 *Proceedings of the American Society of International Law* (1995), 279; Diehl, *International Peacekeeping*, 188. This fact was recognised by the Secretary General in *Supplement to An Agenda for Peace* of 1995 (UN doc. S/1995/1 para. 35), after advocating a more flexible approach in his 1992 *An Agenda for Peace*, 31 *I.L.M.* (1992), 953.

CHAPTER EIGHT

The legal parameters of peacekeeping

United Nations peacekeeping has grown with the Organisation, but was not envisaged by the founders. It became a useful, arguably necessary, element of the restricted Cold War collective security function of the UN.[1] Its constitutionality has not really been in doubt since the World Court's decision in the *Expenses* case in the early 1960s, although debates have continued as to the exact constitutional basis of the power. Such issues will be considered in this chapter, but it will be seen that the desire to find an express Charter base for the power is unnecessary in the light of the doctrines of implied, or perhaps more accurately, inherent, powers. For external purposes there appears to be no doubt that the UN can create peacekeeping forces, the internal question of which organ is empowered to create and control the force is less clear, with both the Security Council, the General Assembly and the Secretary General involved in the area. The final constitutional issue raised in this chapter is the trend towards the UN 'sub-contracting'[2] peacekeeping operations to other organisations/bodies, as well as the undertaking of such operations by outside bodies with no express UN approval or authorisation.

The chapter will then consider the legal principles which govern a peacekeeping force's emplacement, operation and withdrawal, drawing out some of the problems that have arisen with the recent expansion of peacekeeping to include pacific settlement and, occasionally, enforcement.

Constitutional issues

In chapter three, the World Court's opinion in the *Expenses* case was discussed, and it was concluded that the Court viewed peacekeeping as justifiable either under a liberal approach to the implied powers of the UN or, perhaps more accurately, as an inherent power of the UN. Peacekeeping fulfils the purposes of the UN in its task of maintaining international peace and security, albeit in a minimal way, and it does not breach any of the express provisions of the Charter. To look at it a slightly different way, since it can be seen that the greatest extent of the UN powers is the power to take coercive military action, while at the other end of the scale the UN can simply encourage pacific settlement, then the development of a non-coercive military presence which is aimed at facilitating the end of conflicts, and encouraging peaceful settlement, cannot be challenged as unconstitutional. Indeed, the International Court in the *Expenses* case was at pains to point out that peacekeeping was conceptually and constitutionally different from enforcement, when it quoted the following section of the Secretary General's report on the setting up of UNEF I in 1956.

the functions of the United Nations Force would be, when a cease-fire is being established, to enter Egyptian territory with the consent of the Egyptian Government, in order to help maintain quiet during and after the withdrawal of non-Egyptian troops, and to secure compliance with the other terms established in the [General Assembly] resolution of 2 November 1956. The Force obviously should have no rights other than those necessary for the execution of its functions, in co-operation with local authorities. It would be more than an observers' corps, but in no way a military force temporarily controlling the territory in which it is stationed; nor, moreover, should the Force have military functions exceeding those necessary to secure peaceful conditions on the assumption that the parties to the conflict take all necessary steps for compliance with the recommendations of the General Assembly.[3]

The Court made it clear that the verb 'secure' did not imply enforcement action so as to allow the Force to secure a cease-fire or to halt military movements without the cooperation of the parties.[4] UNEF would only secure such interim measures by cooperation and consent, and, if necessary, by negotiation.

The competence of the General Assembly

The *Expenses* case also made it clear that the authorisation of such consensual, non-enforcement, military activities is within the powers of the General Assembly as well as the Security Council which, as the World Court explained, has 'primary' but not exclusive competence under Article 24(1) of the UN Charter to maintain or restore international peace and security.[5] Indeed, the first full-scale peacekeeping force, UNEF I, was authorised by the General Assembly after the vetoes of the United Kingdom and France had paralysed the Security Council. Politically, the peacekeeping function of the UN is now firmly in the control of the Security Council, though a great deal of delegation of the organisational and logistical side is given to the Secretary General, legally the General Assembly possesses the power as well.

The World Court in the *Expenses* case clearly stated that the UN General Assembly had the power to create peacekeeping forces but it did not feel the need to recognise any particular Charter provision, an approach which itself supports the doctrine of inherent powers. However, it is relatively simple to point to Charter provisions which give the Assembly a significant secondary competence in the field of collective security, sufficient enough for it to mandate peacekeeping forces. Article 10 of the Charter allows the Assembly to make recommendations on any matter 'within the scope of the present Charter'. If Article 10 is insufficient to grant the Assembly the full range of recommendatory powers, Article 14 re-emphasises its potentially wide jurisdiction with specific reference to international security by providing that 'the General Assembly may recommend measures for the peaceful adjustment of any situation, regardless of origin, which it deems likely to impair the general welfare or friendly relations among nations'.

However, to prevent any clash between the work of the Security Council, the primary organ, and the General Assembly, Article 14, as well as Article 10, is subject to the limitation contained in Article 12 which provides that the General Assembly cannot adopt recommendations on a conflict while the Council is exercising the functions assigned to it by the Charter. As has been seen in chapter five, Article 12 is probably the most difficult provision, in constitutional terms, to reconcile with the practice of the General Assembly. The Assembly often adopts resolutions on a matter at the same time at which the Security Council is considering the question. Although disregarded in general, it will be seen that in the area of peacekeeping the Assembly, when it has created forces, has not infringed the requirements of Article 12, in that it has created forces only when the Council has desisted from dealing with the matter or has not touched the matter in a deliberate effort to enable the Assembly to deal with it.

Furthermore, the creation or mandating of peacekeeping forces does not infringe the requirements of Article 11(2) which provides that 'any ... question on which action is necessary shall be referred to the Security Council by the General Assembly either before or after discussion'. As has been seen in chapter five, the World Court's judgment in the *Expenses* case can be interpreted as stating that Article 11(2) only forbids the Assembly from *ordering* member States to adopt coercive measures, whether military or economic. This certainly does not prohibit the Assembly from creating a consensual peacekeeping force, nor, although this is more contentious, does it prevent the Assembly from recommending enforcement action. Such a power appears to be *intra vires*, which with the recent expansion of peacekeeping by the Security Council into the area of quasi-enforcement, signifies that the Assembly could also, if the political circumstances so permit, recommend a quasi-enforcement peacekeeping force along the lines of that sent to Somalia by the Security Council in 1993.

Paradoxically, the Uniting for Peace Resolution of 1950 which expressly recognised this power (but only in relation to breaches of the peace and acts of aggression), whilst being accepted in practice as a procedure of moving items from the Security Council's agenda to the General Assembly's (meeting in Emergency Special Session), has failed to make the intended impact in the realm of collective security in its proper sense. No UN enforcement action has been authorised by it, although it was used to authorise the first UN peacekeeping force, UNEF I in the Sinai, in 1956.[6]

Beyond the creation of UNEF I, the General Assembly has rarely exercised its inherent power to create a significant peacekeeping force. It did approve in 1962 of the creation of a UNTEA and a UNSF in West Irian as requested by the Netherlands and Indonesia as part of their agreement to end the conflict over the territory.[7] Furthermore, it did take over the control of ONUC in the Congo in September 1960, at a time when the Security Council, having placed ONUC in an impossible position, then ceased to deal with the conflict due to deadlock between the superpowers. In the Security Council the United States proposed that the matter be transferred to the General Assembly under the auspices of the Uniting for Peace Resolution.[8] The Assembly's contribution to ONUC was a resolution which recommended 'vigorous action' to restore law and order and to preserve the unity, integrity and political independence of the Congo.[9] Although the World Court in the *Expenses* case thought that the actions of ONUC in the Congo did not constitute enforcement action,[10] the Assembly certainly, by recommending 'vigorous action', seemed to be taking a quasi-enforcement approach to peacekeeping, which although controversial, seems to be within the powers of the Assembly.

Although the Assembly's practice in the field of peacekeeping is limited, its contributions have had much wider significance. First, it created the paradigm inter-State peacekeeping force in the form of UNEF I; second, it contributed to the concept of peace enforcement by peacekeeping forces in civil wars when it took over the mandating of ONUC; and finally, its creation of UNTEA and UNSF was the forerunner of the combination of peacekeeping and peaceful settlement, successfully used by the Security Council after the Cold War. In many ways, the Assembly, which was not constrained by the veto, gave birth to several aspects of peacekeeping, which were nurtured by the Security Council as it reasserted supremacy in peacekeeping matters.

The competence of the Security Council

The competence of the Security Council in the area of peacekeeping is much less controversial. Although there is no express power granted in the UN Charter allowing for the creation of peacekeeping forces, the arguments for recognising that the Council has power to create a peacekeeping force are much clearer than those put forward for the Assembly. First of all, according to Article 24(1), 'in order to ensure prompt and effective action by the United Nations, its members confer on the Security Council primary responsibility for the maintenance of international peace and security'. Given that the main aim of the UN is to achieve international peace and security it is recognised that Article 24(1) confers upon the Council general powers to achieve these purposes. This is implicitly recognised in Article 24(2) which states that 'in discharging these duties the Security Council shall act in accordance with the Purposes and Principles of the United Nations'.

An examination of the specific powers of the Security Council indicates that peacekeeping falls somewhere between Chapter VI and Chapter VII. Peacekeeping constitutes a concrete military presence and therefore does not simply consist of mere recommendations for settlement as found in Chapter VI. However, peacekeeping is not pure military enforcement action as envisaged under Chapter VII.

Sometimes peacekeeping is closer to or linked to pacific settlement and therefore can be seen as a power linked to Article 36(1) of Chapter VI which provides that 'the Security Council may, at any stage of a dispute ... recommend appropriate procedures or methods of adjustment'.

On other occasions peacekeeping is solely concerned with overseeing provisional measures (cease-fires, withdrawals) in which case the nexus is Article 40 which contains the power to call for provisional measures. Generally peacekeeping forces are created to facilitate the observance of such measures, when they have been accepted by the parties to the conflict. Furthermore, the nature of traditional peacekeeping based on the UNEF I model remains consensual and non-offensive whether or not the call for provisional measures is mandatory.[11]

However, the Security Council has occasionally used peacekeeping forces to enforce provisional measures – a practice which dates back to the Congo in 1960. This is still reconcilable with Article 40 in that the provision goes on to say that 'the Security Council shall duly take account of failure to comply with provisional measures'. In these instances then, although it is arguable that the peacekeeping force is not taking enforcement action in the full blown sense of Article 42, it is taking action which is closer to Chapter VII action, in that it is enforcing provisional measures. This type of action has been taken much more readily in the post-Cold War era, in Somalia, and to a lesser extent in Bosnia.[12]

In many ways the enforcement of provisional measures is similar to enforcement action under Article 42, particularly when the provisional or interim measures are so widely drawn as to include the maintenance of the integrity of a nation as in the Congo or, perhaps less obviously, 'to use all necessary means to establish as soon as possible a secure environment for humanitarian relief in Somalia'.[13] This has led Professor Bowett to describe ONUC's constitutional base as being somewhat wider than Article 40, seeing it as a force 'for the purpose of supervising and enforcing compliance with the provisional measures ordered under Article 40 and for other purposes which were consistent with the general powers of the Council under Article 39'.[14] This involves recognising that ONUC had gone beyond Article 40, but not as far as Article 42, by suggesting that the general powers of Article 39 were utilised. It must be pointed out, however, that the provisions of Article 39 have been used as authority for the recommendation of enforcement action in the Korean War.[15]

It would be best to summarise ONUC's actions having as their constitutional base the enforcement of provisional measures under Article 40, but since these measures were increasingly widely drawn so as to cope with an ever-deteriorating crisis, they, despite the judgment of the World Court in the *Expenses* case, amounted to at least *de facto* enforcement action. It could be argued that ONUC was acting in defence of its purposes. However, this is a wide interpretation of self-defence, going far beyond that authorised for other peacekeeping operations, which are only allowed to use self-defence when fired on. Allowing a force to take positive action in defence of its purposes is little different from allowing it to enforce them. A similar argument can be made as regards the mandate and activities of UNOSOM II in Somalia in 1993 where the actions taken against General Aideed's faction in particular constituted an offensive, not defensive, operation.[16]

The near disaster of the peacekeeping operation in the Congo in the 1960s led to a return to consensual, non-offensive peacekeeping operations, tightly controlled by the Security Council. The end of the Cold War has seen a continuation of close control, or 'micro-management',[17] of consensual peacekeeping operations by the Security Council. However, a contrast can be drawn between non-offensive peacekeeping operations which are kept on a short rein, and the enforcement operations authorised by the Security Council in Haiti, Rwanda and Zaire which have arisen with the end of the Cold War. The constitutional link between the Security Council and these type of operations is normally less strong, despite the fact that these operations represent a much greater use of force with potential to embroil the United Nations in a continuing, and possibly escalating, conflict. Those States contributing to the more aggressive enforcement operation are unwilling to submit their actions to continuous, and potentially debilitating UN review. In particular, the United States, although willing to seek UN authorisation for its military actions, is not willing to have them placed under the command and control of the UN.[18] Political realities have meant that the greater the level of UN sanctioned military involvement the less control the UN has over it.

The lack of control over such military actions is an inevitable consequence of the decentralisation of enforcement action under Chapter VII of the Charter. Nevertheless, in the case of quasi-enforcement peacekeeping operations, the constitutional bridge is stronger than in the case of full enforcement actions, where the reporting obligation is on the contributing States alone. Indeed, in the case of Somalia, although UNITAF was given a relatively free rein,[19] UNOSOM II was subjected to much closer political control and review by the Security Council and the Secretary General,[20] although the United States supplied, *inter alia*, a 'Quick Reaction Force that could intervene in support of UNOSOM II but would not be part of the operation'.[21]

The role of the Secretary General

From the relatively narrow provisions of the UN Charter concerning the office of Secretary General, the various holders of this post have developed an impressive set of powers to be used in the peaceful settlement of disputes and situations. Article 97 states that the Secretary General 'shall be the chief administrative officer of the Organization'. However, unlike the Secretary General of the League of Nations, who was simply a civil servant, the Secretary General is granted somewhat wider powers in the Charter. Article 98 provides that the Secretary General 'shall perform such other functions as are entrusted to him' by the Security Council, General Assembly, Economic and Social Council and the Trusteeship Council. Under this provision the Secretary General carries out the mandates granted to him by the Security Council or the General Assembly. This may range from sending a fact finding mission, to offering his good offices, to the organisation and emplacement of a peacekeeping force.

The only autonomous power granted to him in the Charter is contained in Article 99 which provides that '[t]he Secretary General may bring to the attention of the Security Council any matter which in his opinion may threaten international peace and security'. Given the importance of the concept of a 'threat to the peace' in the workings of the Security Council, particularly as regards internal conflicts, this is potentially a very important provision. However, it has been little used by the office holders, although one notable exception was when Secretary General Hammarskjöld brought the deteriorating situation in the Congo to the attention of the Security Council in 1960 explicitly relying on Article 99.[22]

Nevertheless, despite the fact that the Charter explicitly only grants the Secretary General the autonomous power to bring to the attention of the Security Council threats to international peace, over the years the office holder has developed an impressive set of implied and inherent powers, such as good offices, mediation, even arbitration and fact finding. These powers have developed either with the acquiescence of the Security Council and General Assembly, or sometimes with their active encouragement in the sense that it has been recognised that the Secretary General has powers not dependent on a specific mandate from one of the other principal organs of the United Nations.[23]

The Secretary General's powers seem to have stretched as far as to allow the office holder, on his own authority, to send a fact finding mission to a conflict, they have not formally extended as far as the authorisation of an observer force or peacekeeping force, they still have to be mandated by the Security Council.[24] However, greater activity by the United Nations in the late 1980s as the Cold War came to an end did see the possible extension of the Secretary General's powers to at least the negotiation and emplacement of an observer force in exceptional circumstances as in the initial deployment of UNGOMAP to Afghanistan following the Geneva Accords of 1988, retrospectively endorsed by the Security Council.[25] Normally, however, although the Secretary General may be heavily involved in the negotiations about a possible peacekeeping force, Security Council, or exceptionally General Assembly, authorisation must be forthcoming before the force is emplaced.[26]

The Secretary General's powers in the field of peacekeeping have expanded over the years from the holder of the office simply being the administrator of forces to becoming the instigator and executive commander of the forces within the overall framework of the Security Council's mandate.[27] It must be noted that this only applies to peacekeeping forces. In the enforcement operations in Haiti, Rwanda, Somalia (UNITAF) and IFOR in Bosnia, the Secretary General does not have any political control over the forces. In general, they are commanded, both politically and militarily, by a State or a group of States, operating under a loose Security Council mandate, although generally, as with consensual peacekeeping forces, the Secretary General is required by the Council to provide regular reports on the progress of the force.

The UN and regional peacekeeping

A genuinely consensual peacekeeping operation undertaken by an organisation outside the UN does not require the permission of the UN before it is undertaken. As has been seen in chapter one, the constitutional link between the UN and other organisations is to be found in Chapter VIII of the UN Charter. Article 52 actually encourages regional organisations or arrangements to 'make every effort to achieve peaceful settlement of local disputes ... before referring them to the Security Council', as long as their activities in this field are consistent with the Purposes and Principles of the United Nations. Consensual, neutral peacekeeping conforms with the UN Charter and is a mechanism developed to facilitate the settlement of disputes.

However, when the activities or mandate of the force include enforcement, then the constitutional position is changed, for Article 53(1) of the UN Charter provides that Security Council authorisation is required for any enforcement action taken by regional arrangements or agencies. This provision is effective in asserting the constitutional superiority of the UN over regional bodies in the field of enforcement action because of the near universal membership of the UN and because regional organisations, in their constituent documents, themselves do not claim superiority, or indeed sometimes recognise UN superiority in this matter.[28]

Nevertheless, there are several instances where the relevant regional organisation has, in practice undertaken enforcement action under the guise of a peacekeeping mandate, without authorisation from the Security Council. The Arab League's Syrian dominated Arab Deterrent Force (ADF) first positioned in October 1976 in response to the civil war in Lebanon is such an example.[29] On another occasion the Security Council has retrospectively endorsed a regional organisation's quasi-enforcement peacekeeping operation. This was the case in Liberia, where the overtly aggressive, Nigerian dominated ECOWAS Monitoring Group (ECOMOG), which had operated in the country since August 1990, mainly against the National Patriotic Front of Liberia (NPFL) faction, was endorsed by the Security Council in 1992.[30] Furthermore, the Cotonou peace agreement of July 1993, contained provisions for the involvement of UN observers in the disarmament and elections process. UNOMIL's presence in Liberia has not led to a peaceful solution, indeed in September 1994 the Security Council requested that ECOMOG protect UNOMIL personnel.[31]

During its long involvement in Liberia, ECOMOG has overstepped the boundary between neutral peacekeeping and military enforcement action. The UN Security Council has apparently retrospectively endorsed the action as coming with the provisions of Chapter VIII of the UN Charter, illustrating a dangerously relaxed approach to the constitutional requirement that such actions must be prospectively endorsed. The danger in allowing greater unauthorised regional enforcement action, as opposed to consensual peacekeeping, is that, as these two examples clearly show, they are likely to be abused by the regional superpower.

Nevertheless, practice is not settled and in other instances, the Security

Council has, in accordance with Article 53, prospectively authorised organisations to undertake enforcement action alongside a UN peacekeeping operation.
This has been seen in the conflict in Bosnia, reviewed in chapter three, where the
members of NATO were authorised to take enforcement action alongside the UN
peacekeeping force (UNPROFOR), and with the advent of the Dayton Accords of
November 1995 to supply the 'muscular' force (IFOR/SFOR) to replace UNPRO-
FOR and oversee the implementation of the peace agreement.

However, despite having brought the NATO-led operation under the umbrella
of the UN Security Council by resolution 1031 of December 1995, it is clear that
IFOR/SFOR is under the command and control of NATO leaders not the UN. As
with enforcement actions by *ad hoc* military coalitions, the centralisation of coercion in the hands of the Security Council is purely formal. In practical terms the
operation is outside the control of the United Nations.[32]

The legal principles governing peacekeeping operations

In the above section various constitutional issues concerning the Charter basis,
mandating and control of peacekeeping forces were examined. Fundamental differences were seen as regards consensual peacekeeping forces and the more
aggressive enforcement operations. In essence that section was concerned with
the establishment of military operations. In this section, attention is focused on the
legal principles which operate to regulate the competence of the operation once it
is on the ground.

Consent

Traditional peacekeeping follows from the parties to the conflict accepting a
cease-fire or a withdrawal, and then agreeing to the presence of a force on their
soil. Normally consent is obtained from the legitimate governments concerned,
which is relatively straightforward when dealing with an inter-State conflict as in
the case of the establishment of UNIIMOG, following the Iranian and Iraqi governments' acceptance in August 1988[33] of the cease-fire called for by the Security
Council.

However, when dealing with an intra-State conflict, for example, the conflict
between the Greek and Turkish communities in Cyprus between 1964 and 1974,
it could be argued that the consent of all factions should be obtained, although this
is not always possible, and so consent is only obtained from the government, as
was the case in Cyprus in 1964.[34] This has led to problems in intra-State peacekeeping operations such as UNIFIL in southern Lebanon, where the initial
emplacement of the force in 1978 was gained at the request of the very weak
Lebanese government,[35] without the consent or cooperation of the numerous factions that actually controlled southern Lebanon. This has led to UNIFIL being
rendered largely ineffective except for the basic provision of humanitarian assistance to the affected population of southern Lebanon.

In its more recent peacekeeping attempts, the UN has tried to gain the consent of all the factions in a civil war, whether governmental or not. This was the approach in Yugoslavia and in Cambodia for instance, but it still appeared that the forces in these countries were under severe pressure with some of the factions breaking their agreements to submit to UN supervision. The lack of accountability of these factions on the international plane may account for their less than cooperative approach.

What is clear is that if the consent of the government concerned is not given or is withdrawn, then the peacekeeping operation cannot remain on that State's territory, unless the UN is prepared to change its mandate to one of enforcement. Such a change of mandate is theoretically possible, as was stated by the Secretary General in his initial report on UNEF I in 1956:

While the General Assembly is enabled to establish the Force with the consent of those parties which contribute units to the Force, it could not request the Force to be stationed or operate on the territory of a given country without the consent of the Government of that country. This does not exclude the possibility that the Security Council could use such a Force within the wider margins provided under Chapter VII of the United Nations Charter. I would not for the present consider it necessary to elaborate this point further, since no use of the Force under Chapter VII ... has been envisaged.[36]

Despite the possibility of a force initially emplaced as a consensual, non-offensive peacekeeping operation, being converted into an enforcement action under Articles 39 and 42 of the Charter, the likelihood is slim. First of all, States contributing to a peacekeeping force do so on a voluntary basis, they would have to give permission for their troops to be used in an entirely different fashion, thus making drastic changes of mandates unlikely. Secondly, peacekeeping forces would have to be rearmed and more than likely would have to be considerably expanded if they were to become effective enforcement units. Finally, such a conversion in mandate would make it less likely that States would willingly accept peacekeeping forces in the future, in other words drastic changes of mandate would jeopardise the neutrality of peacekeeping.

However, the change from peacekeeping to enforcement, not by the rearming and re-mandating of an existing force, but its replacement by an enforcement action, has become a reality in the post-Cold War era, exemplified by the action in Somalia, described in chapter three, where the original UNOSOM, emplaced with the agreement of the Somali factions in April 1992 primarily to observe a cease-fire,[37] was replaced by a much more belligerent enforcement operation, UNITAF, under the command and control of the United States, but operating under a Security Council mandate adopted under Chapter VII 'to use all necessary means to establish as soon as possible a secure environment for humanitarian relief operations in Somalia'.[38] When UNITAF was itself replaced by UNOSOM II in May 1993, its mandate was akin to the coercive mandate of UNITAF rather than the consensual mandate of its predecessor.[39]

Non-consensual operations such as UNITAF and UNOSOM II by their very nature infringe the sovereignty of their host State, and the only limitations on their presence on the host State's soil are practical ones. In the case of Somalia, the failure to achieve any sort of settlement in the country led to the ignominious withdrawal of UNOSOM II in March 1995.[40] However, the need for consent in traditional peacekeeping operations was graphically illustrated in 1967, when Secretary General U Thant ordered the withdrawal of UNEF I, after President Nasser of Egypt made it clear that Egypt's consent had been withdrawn. Although it may be argued that the General Assembly, as the author of UNEF's mandate, was responsible for its status and therefore it, not the Secretary General, had the power to withdraw the force, U Thant's decision *vis-à-vis* Egypt was essentially correct.[41] Indeed, it is highly likely that at least some contributing States would have withdrawn their troops if U Thant had not withdrawn UNEF I.[42] Nevertheless, the withdrawal of UNEF I and the ensuing Six Day War illustrated the limitations of peacekeeping.

Similar limitations were shown as regards the position of UNPROFOR in Croatia in March 1995, when the Croatian government informed the Secretary General that it was terminating the peacekeeping force's mandate as it had failed to make any progress in the Serb occupied UN Protected Areas of Croatia,[43] which had been put under UN control in the cease-fire agreement between Serbia and Croatia of February 1992 – the agreement which had also consented to the establishment of UNPROFOR.[44] In reality this was Croatia's attempt to force the UN into making progress on the eventual incorporation of the Serb enclaves into Croatia, and so as an interim measure the Croatian government was happy to accept the creation of a new, smaller UN peacekeeping force – UNCRO – in March 1995,[45] with a mandate mainly limited to the monitoring of the borders between Serbia and Croatia.[46] The Security Council expressly recognised that UNCRO was 'an interim arrangement to create the conditions that will facilitate a negotiated settlement consistent with the territorial integrity of the Republic of Croatia'. The territorial integrity of Croatia was almost completely restored in September 1995 by a Croatian military offensive which ignored the presence of UNCRO.

Such inherent limitations in consensual peacekeeping are not fully recognised in the status-of-force agreements arrived at between host State and the UN.[47] The true nature and extent of the consent element is not really dealt with to the extent that the rights of the host State to terminate the mandate are not mentioned, though the presumption must be that in the absence of clear words to limit the host State's sovereignty, the sovereign right to withdraw consent unilaterally must remain. Status-of-force agreements skirt round this fundamental issue to the extent that even when a peacekeeping force has crossed the threshold from consensual operation to enforcement operation, as with ONUC in the Congo, the agreement still generally follows the same ambiguous model.[48]

The model agreement prepared by the Secretary General in 1990 deals in reasonable detail with logistics, facilities and privileges and immunities, and attempts to 'strike a balance between the sovereign rights of a host State and the peacekeeping interests of the international community'.[49] It does not, however, deal with the fundamental basis of peacekeeping, namely the consent of the host State, containing instead ambiguous undertakings to reflect the 'exclusively international nature of the United Nations peacekeeping operation'.[50] From these vague undertakings it appears that the host State's agreement to allow the force on its territory does not restrict its sovereignty in any way and that it has the sovereign right to revoke its agreement whenever it wishes to remove the force from its territory.

Nevertheless, the model agreement does give a number of rights to the peacekeeping force while it has the consent of the host State, including freedom of movement throughout the country'.[51] However, this freedom can be in practice very limited, particularly when the UN force does not have agreements with every faction in an internal strife. In such cases, the force's freedom of movement is heavily restricted and is dependent on the cooperation and consent of any armed group who wishes to stop UN supplies or personnel from moving. Much of UNPROFOR's tasks in Bosnia in the period 1992–95, before the signing of the Dayton Agreements in November 1995, were subject to the consent and cooperation of the various factions in the Bosnian conflict, even though there was a status-of-forces agreement, but only with the Bosnian government, guaranteeing UNPROFOR freedom of movement.[52]

Neutrality

Not only is the consent of the host State necessary, its continued cooperation with the peacekeeping force throughout the length of its stay is essential. The Israeli occupation of the Golan Heights since 1967 has been a major obstacle to permanent peace between Israel and Syria, but despite the fact that they have been sworn enemies since the creation of Israel, both manage to cooperate with UNDOF, established by the Security Council, pursuant to the Agreement on Disengagement between Israel and Syria of 31 May 1974,[53] which followed the 1973 Yom Kippur War. This buffer force of over 1,000 lightly armed peacekeepers has been highly successful in maintaining calm on the Israeli/Syrian front despite the fact that Israel has invaded Lebanon on several occasions, acts which, bearing in mind Syrian involvement in Lebanon, could have started a new conflict between the two States. The high level of cooperation with UNDOF is illustrated by the fortnightly inspections of designated demilitarised areas by UNDOF members accompanied by liaison officers from Syria and Israel.

One of the reasons for UNDOF's success is the fact that it is impartial or neutral in the conflict. Neutrality is another of the essential features of peacekeeping deriving from the non-prejudicial nature of provisional measures as embodied in Article 40 of the UN Charter. Neutrality distinguishes peacekeeping from collective security in the shape of enforcement action 'which is designed to provide a military advantage ... to either side'.[54] In many ways the modern consensual approach to peacekeeping builds on the fundamental principles of consent and neutrality. This is the modern type of peacekeeping operation which is emplaced particularly in intra-State conflicts in which the UN not only provides a peace-keeping force at the request of the parties to oversee a cease-fire between the war-ring factions, it also supervises the agreed mode of peaceful settlement, usually in the form of a referendum or free and fair elections. However, in these operations, as shown by the difficulties faced in particular by peacekeepers in Angola and Western Sahara, the principle of neutrality is much more readily compromised, so endangering the status of the force in the country in question, and consequently causing concern about the success of these more ambitious types of operations.

Nevertheless, it can be readily seen that UNTAC, which successfully oversaw elections in Cambodia in 1993, was in many respects the culmination of UN peacekeeping in that its mandate covered every aspect of traditional peacekeep-ing (cease-fire and withdrawal), as well as containing the features of the new forces with integrated mandates (administration, policing and election supervi-sion). Furthermore, this new approach is firmly based on the principles of consent, neutrality and cooperation forged by traditional peacekeeping forces during the Cold War. This was reflected in the words of the UN Secretary General at the sign-ing of the Final Act at the Paris Peace Conference in October 1991 when he said that the aim of the operation 'is to encourage the establishment of a neutral polit-ical environment in which the Cambodian people can freely determine their future'.[55] Despite the fact that the 'Khmer Rouge accused the peacekeepers of sup-porting the interests of the Vietnamese-backed party of the extant government and of failing to ensure that all Vietnamese troops were withdrawn from the country',[56] UNTAC achieved its tasks of supervising a cease-fire and overseeing elections in a neutral and impartial way. Nevertheless, the inherent defect in the 'winner take all' approach of democratic elections, has meant that the Khmer Rouge have taken up arms again, thus jeopardising the precarious peace in the country.

Although the new integrated approach to peacekeeping preserves the impar-tiality of the UN, the trend towards quasi-enforcement in other situations under-mines it. This is clearly illustrated by the third phase of the UN's operation in Somalia, when UNOSOM II replaced UNITAF. Resolution 814 of 26 March 1993 authorised UNOSOM II under Chapter VII of the Charter and clearly envisaged it operating with an enforcement mandate where necessary unlike UNOSOM I, whose neutral and consensual mandate to deliver humanitarian aid was totally ineffective in the civil war situation. Although UNOSOM II was more effective in securing the delivery of aid, it lost its neutrality when it intervened in the civil war against one of the factions – the Somali National Alliance (SNA).[57]

The sobering experience of Somalia has led to a reappraisal of the value of the quasi-enforcement approach to peacekeeping. In the Secretary General's final report to the Security Council on UNOSOM II, of 28 March 1995, he made it clear that it must not be forgotten that the UN operation (along with substantial assis-tance from other organisations), helped to save over a quarter of a million lives in

Somalia. Nevertheless the report shows that there has been something of a re-evaluation of peacekeeping in civil wars after Somalia. While recognising the necessity of providing humanitarian aid the Secretary General almost appeared to be advocating a return to traditional values in peacekeeping:

The experience of UNOSOM II has thus confirmed the validity of the point … that the responsibility for political compromise and national reconciliation must be borne by the leaders of the people concerned. It is they who bear the main responsibility for creating the political and security conditions in which peacemaking and peace-keeping can be effective. The international community can only facilitate, prod, encourage and assist. It can neither impose peace not coerce unwilling parties into accepting it.

There are also important lessons to be learnt about the theory and practice of multifunctional peace-keeping operations in conditions of civil war and chaos and especially about the line that needs to be drawn between peace-keeping and enforcement action. The world has changed and so has the nature of the conflict situations which the United Nations is asked to deal with. There is a need for careful and creative rethinking about peacemaking, peace-keeping and peacebuilding in the context of the Somali operation.[58]

The Secretary General developed this point in his *Supplement to an Agenda for Peace* of 1995, when again he seemed to advocate a re-establishment of a clear divide between peacekeeping and enforcement, when after referring to the UN's involvement in Bosnia and Somalia, he wrote:

In both cases, existing peace-keeping operations were given additional mandates which required the use of force and therefore could not be combined with existing mandates requiring the consent of the parties, impartiality and the non-use of force. It was also not possible for them to be executed without much stronger military capabilities than had been made available, as in the case of the former Yugoslavia. In reality, nothing is more dangerous for a peace-keeping operation than to ask it to use force when its existing composition, armament, logistics and deployment deny it the capability to do so. The logic of peace-keeping flows from the political and military premises that are quite distinct from those of enforcement, and the dynamics of the latter are incompatible with the political process that peace-keeping is intended to facilitate. To blur the distinction between the two can undermine the validity of the peacekeeping operation and endanger its personnel.[59]

Although ambiguous about the future role of enforcement operations in internal conflicts, the Secretary General is much more cautious in 1995 after the sobering experiences of Bosnia and Somalia about undermining the traditional values of peacekeeping than he was in his *Agenda for Peace* of 1992.[60]

Composition and financing

The essential impartiality of consensual peacekeeping is reflected not only in the forces' mandates but also in their functions (reviewed in chapter nine) and their composition. Professor Diehl makes the point well.

The concept of neutrality goes beyond the purpose of the force to the composition and activities of the troops. Most U.N. peacekeeping forces are composed of military personnel from nonaligned states; typically Canada, Fiji, and Sweden have been among the most generous contributors of troops. Soldiers from the major powers, or those from states with a vested interest in the conflict in hand (such as Saudi Arabia in Middle East operations), are explicitly not used. One could hardly imagine an effective collective security operation without the effective contributions of the major military powers, yet a similar contribution to peacekeeping jeopardizes its neutral character and perhaps its chances of success.[61]

UNEF II for instance, in place between Egypt and Israel between 1973 and 1979, was composed of troops from Australia, Austria, Canada, Finland, Ghana, Indonesia, Ireland, Nepal, Panama, Peru, Poland, Senegal and Sweden. The permanent members are generally not involved in peacekeeping directly though they do help extensively with airlifts in particular. One of the rare exceptions to this is · the large British component of UNFICYP, in place in Cyprus since 1964, despite previous British rule in that country.[62]

There are further indications that the principle that contributing States should in the main be non-aligned to reflect the impartial nature of peacekeeping has been relaxed recently. For example there was a significant deployment of 800 Russian troops to reinforce UNPROFOR's supervision of the cease-fire around Sarajevo in February 1994. The Russian presence was meant to have a reassuring effect on the Bosnian Serbs who were worried that UNPROFOR with its large Western contingent (Britain and France) lacked the necessary neutrality. Further permanent member involvement in the former Yugoslav peacekeeping operations can be seen in the former Yugoslav Republic of Macedonia. In this situation the traditional reluctance of the United States to allow its troops to be under UN command, as opposed to US command, has been less pronounced. The United States has contributed significantly to UNPREDEP in the former Yugoslav Republic of Macedonia, which was originally an element of UNPROFOR allocated to Macedonia in December 1992, because of the Security Council concern 'about possible developments which could undermine confidence and stability in … Macedonia or threaten its territory'.[63]

At the time it was formally separated from UNPROFOR at the request of the government of Macedonia in March 1995,[64] UNPREDEP consisted of about 1,100 troops, half of which came from the United States.[65] The mandate of the force remained preventive, namely to help stop the conflict in Bosnia spreading to the former republic of Macedonia.[66] In January 1996, the Secretary General reported that although the mandates of UNCRO in Croatia and UNPROFOR in Bosnia had expired, there was a need for UNPREDEP to continue as a fully independent mission, as requested by the government of Macedonia. In concluding his report the Secretary General applauded UNPREDEP as a new type of preventive operation, as originally advocated by him in his *An Agenda for Peace* of 1992,[67] stating that the 'force has demonstrated that preventive deployment can work where there is political will, a clear mandate and purpose, and the necessary commitments on part of all the parties concerned'.[68]

Is it still true, however, that normally permanent member troops operate outside the peacekeeping umbrella, which is under UN command and control. However, in the case of enforcement operations, which, as has been seen in chapter three, are only subject to UN authorisation rather than command and control, the permanent members, in particular France (in the case of Rwanda), and the United States (in the cases of Somalia – UNITAF, and Haiti), are willing volunteers. Furthermore, when UNOSOM II took over from the US-led UNITAF in 1993, the core 'peacekeeping' force which was under UN command and control was supplemented by three different US-led elements which in differing ways were not within the UN chain of command.[69] As well as adding to the confusion characteristic of the UN involvement in Somalia, this again illustrates how as soon as the operation approaches the level of enforcement, there is less centralisation and collectivity than in the less intrusive and consensual peacekeeping operations. It is arguable that only a few countries are capable, by themselves, of mounting an enforcement action in any significant sense, and therefore any action must involve them solely or at least centrally. This is certainly reflected in the above actions.[70]

Problems of lack of collectivity in enforcement actions would be overcome to a certain extent if the agreements envisaged under Article 43 for the creation of a UN army were actually finalised. Prospects of this still seem to be remote, although there are greater moves towards having troops available for UN operations in the area of consensual peacekeeping where the Secretary General has made significant advances in the area of stand-by arrangements. 'The purpose of stand-by arrangements is to have a precise understanding of the forces and other capabilities a Member State will have available at an agreed state of readiness, should it agree to contribute to a peacekeeping operation'. However, there is no obligation on those States who have agreed to ear-mark and have ready peacekeeping troops. 'When the need arises, they will be requested by the Secretary General and, provided the Member State agrees, they will be rapidly deployed to set up a new peace-keeping operation or to reinforce an existing one'. The stand-by system preserves the voluntary nature of troop contributions to peacekeeping operations. Although this can be seen as continuing its *ad hoc* nature, and a continuing flaw in the proper centralisation of peacekeeping, the stand-by arrangements have 'the potential of providing the United Nations with the capacity to deploy needed resources rapidly'.[71] Indeed, it could be argued that the 50 or so States, who have pledged over 50,000 'fully operational' troops,[72] seem to have committed themselves to future peacekeeping operations when requested by the Secretary General, subject to them opting out. A system of opting out, as opposed to opting in as traditionally operated both for peacekeeping and enforcement operations, is a small step towards greater centralisation in the peacekeeping system. If this process is successful and the Security Council and Secretary General not only command and control a peacekeeping force, but can call on States to provide already earmarked troops as well, then the gap in terms of centralisation, between peacekeeping and enforcement, has, in effect become wider.

This division is made even clearer when the financing of peacekeeping operations is considered. Traditional peacekeeping operations, though not normally financed out of the regular budget of the UN, are financed out of special peacekeeping accounts set up by the UN to which member States are obliged to contribute as these are considered as expenses of the Organisation to be borne by the members under Article17(2) of the UN Charter.[73] Although the scale of assessment is different from the regular budget, with more contributions required from the permanent members and developed member States in particular, peacekeeping forces are certainly collectively funded to a greater extent than enforcement operations which are usually funded by those States contributing troops.[74] Following the financial crisis caused by the refusal to pay contributions to UNEF and ONUC by France and the Soviet Union which led to the *Expenses* case, an attempt was made to move over to voluntary financial contributions in the case of UNFICYP in Cyprus. Inevitably this led to the burden of financing, as well as troop provision, falling on the contributing States. The situation proved so unsatisfactory that it was decided in 1993 that the costs of UNFICYP not covered by voluntary contributions should be treated as expenses of the Organisation within the meaning of Article 17(2).[75]

Restrictions on the use of force

Another important aspect of peacekeeping, which distinguishes it clearly from enforcement, is that the forces are only authorised to use force in self-defence. This limitation is more akin to a personal right of self-defence by individual soldiers if shot at, rather than the much wider right of a State to self-defence.[76] Given that peacekeeping does not infringe the sovereignty of any State, it cannot be imbued with rights, such as the right to self-defence contained in Article 51 of the UN Charter, which belong to States. A description of how this limitation fits into the ideology of peacekeeping (as well as how the restriction is much greater in the case of observation) is given by Professor Diehl.

Peacekeeping forces also have the distinguishing feature of being only lightly armed. A typical peacekeeping soldier is equipped only with a rifle, and peacekeeping units only have access to vehicles for transportation purposes ... and not to those that might be used for attack ...

Peacekeeping troops are only lightly armed because their mission is not a traditional one, and they are designed to use arms in self-defense; peacekeeping troops have neither an offensive military mission nor the capability to carry one out. Peacekeeping troops are not designed to alter the prevailing distribution of power in the area of deployment, nor do they wish to appear threatening to the disputants or the local population.

This characteristic contrasts with collective security forces, whose only equipment restrictions are dictated by weapons availability and strategy. Furthermore, this differs from observation forces, who usually carry no weapons at all. Unlike observers, peacekeeping troops must protect themselves and retain the means to exercise their right of self-defense ... Peacekeeping must also provide a visible deterrent, with the threat of defensive military actions, in patrolling buffer and other demilitarized zones; small, unarmed observer forces are generally considered inadequate for the task.[77]

This severe limitation on the use of force by peacekeepers does not unduly hinder the work of inter-State peacekeeping forces when both States have consented to the force, but it does present problems in the intra-State situation when only the host government has given consent, or if the leaders of the factions in the conflict agree to the force but are unable or unwilling to control their forces.

The problem is particularly acute in the case of UNIFIL established at the request of the Lebanese government in March 1978, following the partial withdrawal of Israel from Lebanon. The Secretary General made it clear that the force would only use force in strict self-defence of troops and units, and would not undertake any of the responsibilities of the Lebanese government.[78] Unfortunately, UNIFIL is in a difficult situation in that for most of its life it has operated in a hostile environment, in an area of Lebanon containing various armed factions and not controlled to any degree by the Lebanese government, although in 1991 that government began to assert some authority in the south. Between 1978 and 1990, UNIFIL lost 130 soldiers from hostile acts. This has meant that UNIFIL has been unable as yet to fulfil either aspect of its mandate, first of ensuring the effective restoration of Lebanese sovereignty in the south, and secondly of supervising Israeli withdrawal from Lebanon given Israel's continued maintenance of a security zone in the area south of the Litani river.[79]

In a report of January 1996, in which a further extension of UNIFIL's mandate was recommended, the Secretary General notes that hostilities were still continuing in southern Lebanon, and that UNIFIL was being regularly fired on. He concludes that 'although there has been no progress towards the implementation of the mandate of UNIFIL, the Force's contribution to stability in the area and the protection it is able to afford the inhabitants remain important'.[80] This must be contrasted with the following assessment: 'UNIFIL can be judged on two levels, as a peacekeeping force and as a humanitarian organization. On the first level, its record is dismal'.[81] Although there have been suggestions that UNIFIL be given a tougher mandate in the form of enforcement powers,[82] the United Nations has decided not to endanger the force further, and possibly escalate the conflict as well, by making UNIFIL the enemy of one or more factions.

The same dilemma – whether to remain neutral and non-coercive, or whether to tackle the faction which appears to be preventing a peaceful solution to the conflict emerging – has faced the UN in a number of intra-State conflicts. The problem was perhaps even more acute in the case of UNPROFOR, emplaced in the disintegrating State of Yugoslavia. Initially, in February 1992, the force was agreed to by Croatia and Serbia since its main task was to oversee a cease-fire between those two former Republics.[83] In this it did carry out the task of a traditional UN peacekeeping force. However, having its headquarters initially in Sarajevo, the capital of Bosnia, another former Yugoslav Republic and nascent State,

inevitably meant that it would be sucked into the internecine conflict between the
Serbs, Muslims and Croats in Bosnia. Initially this took the form of Security
Council authorisation in May 1992 of a limited force to attempt to secure the air-
port for the arrival of humanitarian aid.[84] This was dependent on the factions
agreeing to a cease-fire, which they apparently did on 5 June 1992. This cease-fire
was breached on numerous occasions, putting the lives of the UN force at risk, and
often leading to the suspension of aid flights to the beleaguered city.

The deteriorating situation in Sarajevo and in the rest of Bosnia led the Security Council to cross the threshold from peacekeeping to enforcement actions in
resolution 770 of 13 August 1992, when it authorised States to 'take all measures
necessary' to facilitate the delivery of aid to the city and the rest of Bosnia. However, as has been seen, UNPROFOR in the main limited its use of force very
strictly, preferring to negotiate the transportation of food, rather than force a way
through, or indeed to take any significant action in self-defence. Furthermore,
UNPROFOR was totally inadequate to protect Muslim enclaves in Bosnian Serb
territory – the so-called 'safe areas', despite authorisation to respond to attacks
against those areas in self-defence.[85] UNPROFOR's humiliation was complete
when the Bosnian Serbs swept a contingent of UNPROFOR aside in July 1995
when taking the safe area of Srebrenica.[86] This led to greater authorisation of
NATO action in the form of airstrikes and to the creation of a rapid reaction force
with enforcement capability.[87] These offensive actions, combined with a Muslim
and Croat offensive in the west, led to the Serbs negotiating peace at Dayton in
November 1995.

Although on paper at least, UNPROFOR was authorised to use enforcement
action or at least to use significant amounts of self-defence, in practice coercive
action was left to NATO, culminating in the replacement of UNPROFOR with a
NATO-led force – IFOR, with licence to take enforcement action if the Dayton
Agreement is broken. In giving out the message that UNPROFOR was mandated
to act against the Bosnian Serbs, and adding to this the coordination between
UNPROFOR and UN authorised airstrikes by NATO, the UN had removed the
essential neutrality of the force, making it a target of Serb aggression, as shown
by the taking hostage of over 300 UNPROFOR personnel in May 1995.

The situation of UNPROFOR in Bosnia also shows that once a peacekeeping
mission uses force beyond that required for personal self-defence, the line
between defensive and offensive action becomes very unclear. As has already
been stated in this chapter, the widely drawn mandates of UNITAF and UNOSOM
II in Somalia in 1993, meant that it was possible to argue that the forces were acting in defence of their purposes, but this is a long way from acting in strict self-
defence. There is the danger that once a peacekeeping force is allowed to use force
in defence of its purposes instead of simply in defence of its personnel, the action
becomes an enforcement action.[88]

The continual widening of a peacekeeping force's mandate when combined
with a parallel widening of the right of self-defence, was to be seen for the first

time in the UN's operation in the Congo. Initially the ONUC was sent as a consensual, non-offensive, operation, at the request of the government of the Congo in July 1960, to provide assistance to that government until the Congolese security forces could fulfil their tasks following the breakdown of order on Belgian decolonisation.[89] By the time ONUC arrived it was in a precarious position, with fighting continuing in the Congo, rival governments being established, and the attempted secession of the Katanga region of the country with the active assistance of Belgian troops and mercenaries. A simple UNEF-type mandate based on consent and with strict limitations on the use of force was clearly insufficient to prevent the collapse of the Congo altogether, although initially Secretary General Hammarskjöld seemed to take the opposite view.[90]

The increasing internationalisation of the civil war led to the General Assembly, and then the Security Council, adopting resolutions which seemed to authorise the use of force by the almost 20,000 strong UN force. In resolution 161 of 27 February 1961, the Council found that the situation in the Congo was a 'threat to international peace and security' and urged that ONUC 'take immediately all appropriate measures to prevent the occurrence of a civil war in the Congo, including arrangements for cease-fires, the halting of all military operations, the prevention of clashes, and the use of force, if necessary, in the last resort'. In resolution 169 of 24 November 1961, the Council went further by widening ONUC's mandate. The force was directed to maintain the territorial integrity and political independence of the Congo, to assist the central government to restore order, and to 'secure the immediate withdrawal and evacuation from the Congo of all foreign military … personnel not under United Nations' command, and mercenaries'. In addition, it welcomed the restoration of the central government in August 1961, and rejected the Katangese claims to secession. To further these ends it authorised the use of force to expel foreign troops and mercenaries 'if necessary'.

Although ONUC, in the main, tried to keep within the principles of peacekeeping, particularly in the period before the adoption of resolution 161, namely by negotiating cease-fires and by not overtly siding with any one of the factions, it eventually had to use force to subdue the Katangese rebellion in April 1961, again in December 1961, and between December 1962 and January 1963.[91] It is very difficult to see ONUC as a true peacekeeping operation, in that it was authorised to use force beyond that necessary for strict self-defence, it was not impartial in the conflict, it received little cooperation, and although it did have the formal consent of the central government, the fact was that for a period until August 1961 there was no real government in the Congo. On the other hand, ONUC was not clearly an enforcement action as undertaken by the UN force in Korea for instance, a view reinforced by the International Court in the *Expenses* case.[92]

In reality the Congo was the first example of a quasi-enforcement action, which bridges the divide between peacekeeping and enforcement, and although such an operation can be successful in the situation in hand, as the Congo illustrates, it does undermine the institution of peacekeeping in a more general way. States are going to be much more circumspect in inviting peacekeeping forces into conflict zones, if there is an implied threat that the operation may take on board greater enforcement. Nevertheless, it is arguable that in intra-State conflicts, unless the parties are willing to consent to settlement, then the choice is between an ineffective force such as UNIFIL, or a potentially effective force such as ONUC, or no force at all. Furthermore, circumstances sometimes dictate that there is really little choice but to use force beyond the narrowly defensive. In such cases the UN force should have clear (limited) goals, be fully equipped to carry out enforcement action, and should have the support of the international community. Some or all of these requirements were lacking in the UN operations in the Congo, Bosnia, and Somalia. Nevertheless, the success of the UN force in the Congo, and the effectiveness of the UN authorised force in Bosnia after Dayton, show that such an approach, though dangerous, can successfully bring to an end apparently intractable conflicts. The UN must only authorise force beyond the defensive when all other avenues have been exhausted, and it is necessary to control or bring to an end a situation of extreme danger or suffering.

Notes

1 See also A. James, 'United Nations Peacekeeping and Non Alignment', in M. S. Rajan *et al.*, *The Non Aligned and the United Nations*, 93–9 (1987).
2 Also described as 'franchising'. See T. M. Franck, 'The United Nations as Guarantor of International Peace and Security: Past, Present and Future', in C. Tomuschat (ed.), *The United Nations at Age Fifty: A Legal Perspective*, 25 at 31–3 (1995).
3 *Certain Expenses of the United Nations* case, I.C.J. Rep. 1962, 151 at 171.
4 *Ibid.*, 170.
5 *Ibid.*, 162.
6 SC Res. 119, 11 UN SCOR Resolutions 9 (1956).
7 GA Res. 1752, 17 UN GAOR Supp. (No. 17) 70 (1962).
8 SC Res. 157, 15 UN SCOR Resolutions 8 (1960).
9 GA Res. 1474, 2 UN GAOR ESS Supp. (No. 1) 1 (1960).
10 I.C.J. *Rep.* 1962, 151 at 166, 177.
11 See further D. W. Bowett, *United Nations Forces*, 274–312 (1964).
12 E. Clemons, 'No Peace to Keep: Six and Three Quarters Peacekeepers', 26 *New York University Journal of International Law and Politics* (1993), 107.
13 SC Res. 794, 47 UN SCOR Resolutions (1992).
14 Bowett, *United Nations Forces*, 180.
15 Sir Gladwyn Jebb (UK), SC 477 mtg, 5 UN SCOR (1950).
16 P. F. Diehl, *International Peacekeeping*, 188 (1994).
17 Secretary General in *Supplement to An Agenda for Peace*, UN doc. A/50/60, S/1995/1, para. 39.
18 T. Stein, 'Decentralized Law Enforcement: The Changing Role of the State as Law Enforcement Agent', in J. Delbrück (ed.), *Allocation of Law Enforcement Authority in the International System*, 125 (1995).

19 United Nations Blue Book Series, *The United Nations and Somalia 1992–1996*, 33 (1996).
20 SC Res. 814, 48 UN SCOR Resolutions (1993). See further Secretary General, *Supplement*, para. 80.
21 UN Blue Book Series, *Somalia*, 43.
22 SC 873 mtg, 15 UN SCOR (1960).
23 See the General Assembly's Declaration on the Prevention and Removal of Disputes and Situations which may Threaten International Peace and Security and the Role of the United Nations in this Field, GA Res. 43/51, 43 UN GAOR Supp. (No. 49) (1988).
24 See R. Lavalle, 'The "Inherent" Powers of the UN Secretary General in the Political Sphere: A Legal Analysis', 37 *N.I.L.R.* (1990), 22.
25 SC Res. 622, 43 UN SCOR Resolutions (1988).
26 Simma (ed.), *The Charter*, 592.
27 Secretary General, *Supplement*, para. 38. Command in the field is in the hands of the chief of mission.
28 See H. G. Schermers and N. M. Blokker, *International Institutional Law* 1068–70, 3rd ed. (1995). See also Article 103 of the UN Charter.
29 See I. Pogany, *The Arab League and Peacekeeping in the Lebanon* (1987).
30 SC Res. 788, 47 UN SCOR Resolutions 99 (1992).
31 S/PRST/1994/53; UN doc. S/1994/1167.
32 See also the 'franchising' of Commonwealth of Independent States' and Russian 'peacekeeping' forces in Georgia and Tajikistan. Franck in Tomuschat (ed.), *The United Nations*, 32–3.
33 SC 2823 mtg, 43 UN SCOR (1988); UN doc. S/20093 (1988).
34 SC 1095 mtg, 19 UN SCOR (1964).
35 UN doc. S/12611 (1978).
36 UN doc. A/3289 (1956).
37 UN doc. S/24480 (1992).
38 SC Res. 792, 47 UN SCOR Resolutions 44 (1992).
39 SC Res. 814, 48 UN SCOR Resolutions (1993).
40 See Security Council Presidential Statement, S/PRST/1995/15, which pledged continued UN support in the form of humanitarian assistance and facilities for negotiation.
41 UN doc. A/6370 (1967). See further A. Di Blase, 'The Role of Host State Consent with Regard to Non-Coercive Actions by the United Nations', in A. Cassese (ed.), *United Nations Peacekeeping: Legal Essays*, 55 (1978).
42 R. Higgins, *United Nations Peacekeeping: Documents and Commentary, vol. 1: Middle East 1946–1967*, 339 (1969).
43 UN doc. S/1995/206.
44 SC Res. 743, 47 UN SCOR Resolutions 8 (1992).
45 SC Res. 981, 50 UN SCOR Resolutions (1995).
46 UN doc. S/1995/222 para. 84.
47 See F. L. Kirgis, *International Organizations in their Legal Setting*, 722–3, 2nd ed. (1992).
48 UN doc. S/5004 (1961), replacing the more general agreement in UN doc. S/4839 Add.5 (1960).
49 Kirgis, *International Organizations*, 730.
50 UN doc. A/45/594 (1990), paras 6 and 7.

51 *Ibid.*, para. 12.
52 UN docs S/24075, S/24540 (1992). Contrast with IFOR, Article 6, Annex 1A of the Dayton Accords 1995, 35 *I.L.M.* (1995), 75.
53 UN doc. S/11302 (1974).
54 Diehl, *International Peacekeeping*, 7–8.
55 UN Press Release, 23 October 1991; SC 3057 mtg, 47 UN SCOR (1992).
56 Diehl, *International Peacekeeping*, 197.
57 *Ibid.*, 188.
58 UN doc. S/1995/231, paras 64–5.
59 UN docs S/1995/1, A/50/60, para. 35.
60 31 *I.L.M.* (1992), 953 at 966.
61 Diehl, *International Peacekeeping*, 8.
62 For reasons see R. Higgins, *United Nations Peacekeeping: Document and Commentary, Volume IV, Europe 1946–1979*, 161 (1981).
63 SC Res. 795, 47 UN SCOR Resolutions 37 (1992).
64 SC Res. 983, 50 UN SCOR Resolutions (1995).
65 UN doc. S/1995/222/Corr. 1.
66 UN doc. S/1992/222 paras 84–5.
67 UN doc. A/47/277, S/24111 (1992), paras 28–32.
68 UN doc. S/1996/65.
69 UN Blue Book Series, *Somalia*, 44–5.
70 See for example J. Morris, 'Force and Democracy: UN/US Intervention in Haiti', 2 *International Peacekeeping* (1995), 391 at 397.
71 Report of the Secretary General on stand-by arrangements for peacekeeping, UN doc. S/1994/777.
72 UN doc. S/1995/943.
73 *Expenses* case, I.C.J. *Rep.* 1962, 151 at 180.
74 SC Res. 940, 49 UN SCOR Resolutions (1994), para. 4 (Haiti); SC Res. 929, 49 UN SCOR Resolutions (1994), para. 3 (Rwanda); SC Res. 794, 47 UN SCOR Resolutions (1992) para. 11 (Somalia – UNITAF). But see SC Res. 814, 48 UN SCOR Resolutions (1993), para. 15 (Somalia – UNOSOM II).
75 SC Res. 831, 47 UN SCOR Resolutions (1993). GA Res. 47/236 47 UN GAOR Supp. (No. 49, vol. II) 36 (1992).
76 M. von Grunigen, 'Neutrality and Peacekeeping', in Cassese (ed.), *United Nations Peacekeeping*, 137–8.
77 Diehl, *International Peacekeeping*, 7.
78 UN doc. S/12611 (1978).
79 SC Res. 425, 33 UN SCOR Resolutions 5 (1978).
80 UN doc. S/1996/45. Approved in SC Res. 1039, 51 UN SCOR Resolutions (1996).
81 M. Ghali, 'United Nations Interim Force in Lebanon', in W. J. Durch (ed.), *The Evolution of UN peacekeeping*, 152 at 197 (1994).
82 *Ibid.*, 201.
83 SC Res. 743, 47 UN SCOR Resolutions 8 (1992).
84 SC Res. 758, 47 UN SCOR Resolutions 17 (1992).
85 Safe areas under UNPROFOR protection were designated in SC Res. 819, 824, 836, 844, 48 UN SCOR Resolutions (1993), all adopted under Chapter VII of the UN Charter. Resolution 836 authorised UNPROFOR in carrying out its mandate in the safe

areas 'acting in self-defence, to take the necessary measures, including the use of force, to reply to bombardments against the safe areas by any of the parties ...'.
86 UN doc. S/1995/775.
87 SC Res. 998, 50 UN SCOR Resolutions (1995).
88 Diehl, *International Peacekeeping*, 188.
89 SC Res. 143, 15 UN SCOR Resolutions (1960).
90 UN doc. S/4389 (1960).
91 UN doc. S/5240 (1963).
92 I.C.J. *Rep.* 1962, 177.

CHAPTER NINE

Peacekeeping in practice

This chapter will contain an examination of the different types of job performed by the blue helmets from simple supervision of a cease-fire to the provision of humanitarian assistance, together with an evaluation of the effectiveness of the different tasks performed by such forces. The chapter will be practice-based ranging from the tasks performed by small observer forces in Kashmir and Afghanistan to the larger inter-State forces as found in the Middle East, to the intra-State forces in the Congo, Bosnia and Somalia. A number of forces will be examined in detail, sometimes in the form of case studies, others which have been examined in some detail in chapters seven and eight, will simply be referred to.

Generally speaking the general functions that are characteristic of a peace-keeping force follow from the legal principles that govern it and have already been detailed in chapter eight. The consensual, voluntary, and essentially pacific nature of peacekeeping means that the traditional force is restricted to observation and supervision of provisional measures accepted by the parties. More specifically the functions of a particular force depend on its mandate which is usually located in the enabling resolutions of the Security Council or General Assembly, and in the reports of the Secretary General, who is delegated the task of setting up the force. Usually the same model, derived from the principles governing UNEF I, is used with variations for the particular situation in question. Increasingly a marked difference can be seen between the mandates governing inter-State peacekeeping forces and those governing intra-State forces. In the latter case, if the force is con-sensual, then its functions can extend to consensual disarmament, election super-vision and perhaps human rights monitoring. If the agreement of the parties to the peacekeeping force breaks down then sometimes the peacekeeping force is given coercive functions such as compulsory disarmament or the forceful delivery of humanitarian assistance to needy populations.

Observation and fact finding

Military observers, generally unarmed, are regularly dispatched to trouble spots with the consent of the parties, to report on the status of the conflict. This usually occurs after a cease-fire has been agreed, indeed, the presence of the observers may have been negotiated as an integral part of the cease-fire.

The necessity of having international observation of a cease-fire was recognised by the UN Security Council in the Indonesian crisis which erupted in 1947. The Security Council's call to the parties to cease hostilities forthwith[1] was followed by varying cease-fires and demarcation lines being established on the islands. Military observers were established 'to observe any possible violations of the cease-fire; to investigate, where possible, allegations of violations of cease-fire orders; and to gather any other data that might be of value to the Commission and to the Security Council'.[2] These functions remained basically the same with the creation of the Good Offices Committee which became the United Nations' Commission on Indonesia,[3] although instead of observation of temporary cease-fire lines, the team was given the task of observing the demilitarised zone created under the Renville Agreement. The observers, through fulfilling their mandate of reporting on each stage achieved towards Indonesian independence, contributed to the eventual success in achieving these objectives.[4]

Although the Indonesian situation was settled with the help of the UN and its observers, such overall political successes are relatively rare. However, this does not undermine the success of the observer team in the much narrower terms of fulfilling its mandate. As has already been explained in chapter seven, UNTSO's longevity arises out of the political necessity for the United Nations to have a constant presence in the most volatile area of the world. Its duties have ranged from observation of the 1949 truce and subsequent armistice agreements,[5] to general observation in the whole Middle Eastern theatre, with specific roles being granted to it after the 1956, 1967 and 1973 conflicts. In addition, a body of UNTSO observers was sent to Beirut in 1982, to observe on the activities of the multinational force, Israeli withdrawal and the situation in the refugee camps.[6]

The continuing functions of UNTSO are those of observation and reporting. Its success should be measured by the fulfilment of these functions which it has done admirably since the 1949 armistice. UNTSO, like all peacekeeping operations, was not designed to stop wars and so its effectiveness should not be measured by the frequency with which conflicts occur in the Middle East. Indeed, it is precisely because of that frequency that UNTSO is so important. This was amply illustrated by the outbreak of the Yom Kippur War in 1973. The Secretary General reported to the Council that Egypt had struck first. Egypt had asserted the opposite,[7] but so accurate was the Secretary General's report that the Egyptian government abandoned its version.[8] At a time of heightened international tension with the danger of hostilities escalating, the correct ascertainment of the facts was essential.

A similar low-key, but essential function, has been performed by UNMOGIP since 1949,[9] of monitoring the cease-fire line between India and Pakistan in Kashmir. Although its presence may well have helped to restrain the parties, the cease-fire line was breached in 1965 and 1971 during conflicts on a wider front than that patrolled by UNMOGIP.[10] Nevertheless, the 1965 hostilities and, in particular the 1971 conflict, were not disputes directly over the status of Kashmir[11] and so it appears to be a reasonable assumption that without UNMOGIP there may well have been more wars over the disputed area.

Paradoxically, although UNMOGIP may have contributed effectively to preventing either side from resorting to force to settle their dispute, it has effectively helped to cement the *status quo* during which the dispute is unlikely to be resolved. The cease-fire line patrolled by UNMOGIP is seen by both sides as preferable to either of them giving concessions following diplomatic negotiations. Peacekeeping has had the effect of making provisional measures permanent by hindering the peacemaking process. On the other hand, it has helped to prevent the occurrence of more conflicts.

A modern example of how the basic observation function is still used by the UN is shown by the conflict that has erupted in the former Soviet Republic of Tajikistan. In his initial report of 30 November 1994, the Secretary General gave a stark picture of the task facing the UN in an essentially lawless country, even at the very basic level of observation.[12] Despite this pessimism, and the further complication of the situation by the presence of Russian and CIS 'peacekeeping' forces on the borders and within Tajikistan, the Secretary General, under his own powers as with UNGOMAP in Afghanistan, had despatched UN officials and a small team of 15 military observers drawn from existing peacekeeping forces in response to the agreement arrived at by the Tajik parties in Tehran on 17 September 1994, concerning a temporary cease-fire both within the country and on the Tajik–Afghan border during the talks between the government and the opposition.[13]

In asking for a formally mandated force of 40 military observers, the Secretary General noted that the force's tasks would be to observe on the implementation of the agreement, which not only provided for a cease-fire, but also the cessation of terrorism, sabotage, hostage taking, murder of civilians; the prevention of blockades; and the non-use of the mass media or religion for hostile purposes. The small number of observers is explained by the fact that the UN would be there simply to observe, and the responsibility of settling the conflict must be on the parties,[14] reflecting the more cautious approach towards peacekeeping since Somalia. The Security Council, in formally authorising the force in December 1994,[15] refined this point even further by 'emphasizing that the primary responsibility rests with the Tajik parties themselves in resolving their differences, and that the international assistance provided by this resolution must be linked to the process of national reconciliation, including *inter alia* free and fair elections and other confidence building measures by the parties'.

UNMOT was thus created, mandated to monitor the implementation of the cease-fire agreement and to provide its good offices, for an initial period of six months as long as the cease-fire held. A year later in reporting on the activities of UNMOT and requesting a further renewal of its mandate, the Secretary General reported on the numerous violations of the Tehran Agreement by both sides, observed and investigated by UNMOT – such as cease-fire violations, attacks on civilians and border incidents. Although maintaining relations with the parties, as well as the Russian and CIS forces, had proved difficult, lines of communication were still open. This, along with a fresh agreement in August 1995 between the government and the opposition outlining the fundamental principles for establishing peace and a national accord,[16] led the Secretary General to request an extension of the mandate despite the deteriorating situation on the ground.[17] The Security Council renewed the mandate of UNMOT on the condition that the Tehran Agreement did remain in force and the parties remained committed to democracy.[18]

Observation need not be directed at a cease-fire, but can also be directed at a withdrawal of troops as well. UNGOMAP as regards the Soviet presence in Afghanistan,[19] UNAVEM I as regards Cuban presence in Angola, as well as more recently UNASOG, which oversaw withdrawal of Libyan troops from the Aouzou Strip area of Chad in 1994,[20] were solely concerned with observation and reporting of foreign troop withdrawal. UNAVEM I was established after Cuba and Angola signed a bilateral accord on 22 December 1988,[21] providing for the withdrawal of Cuban troops from Angola, which was linked to the tripartite accord between Angola, Cuba and South Africa concerning the withdrawal of South African troops from, combined with the eventual independence of, Namibia, signed the same day.[22]

The bilateral accord provided that the 50,000 Cuban troops present in Angola, 'in accordance with Article 51 of the UN Charter', were to be withdrawn by 1 July 1991, after phased withdrawal within Angola to the 15th and 13th parallels, providing that no flagrant violations of the tripartite agreement occurred. Angola and Cuba then requested that the Security Council verify 'the redeployment and the phased and total withdrawal of Cuban troops' from Angola. In anticipation of this agreement, on 20 December 1988, the Security Council decided to establish UNAVEM for a period of 31 months, to carry out the mandate provided for in the agreement between Angola and Cuba.[23] In fact Cuban troop withdrawal was completed ahead of schedule by the beginning of June 1991.[24]

UNAVEM I was successful in carrying out the traditional limited mandate of an observer force – namely observation of compliance with an agreement to withdraw. The supervision of peaceful elections, a much more ambitious mandate, though successfully carried out by UNAVEM II, did not result in a peaceful solution to the conflict, leading to the continuation of the civil war and the creation of another UN force – UNAVEM III in February 1995.

Other UN operations with a simple observer function include UNSCOB, created by the Assembly in 1947 on a Western initiative,[25] to undertake 'continuous observation of the general circumstances prevailing in the frontier areas' of Greece,[26] and to report on any support from Albania, Yugoslavia and Bulgaria for the Greek guerrillas, a mandate it was only partially able to fulfil because it could not deploy in the Communist countries because of lack of consent.[27] UNYOM was

created in 1963 by the Security Council,[28] following an agreement between
Yemen, Saudi Arabia and the United Arab Republic on disengagement from the
Yemen civil war,[29] although its ability to fulfil this function was limited by its
small size and the continuation of the conflict.[30] UNIIMOG was created by the
Security Council in 1988,[31] to observe the cease-fire agreed to by Iran and Iraq, a
task it successfully performed,[32] though a more permanent settlement of the dispute was only arrived at when Iraq agreed on 15 August 1990 to Iranian terms to
enable it to concentrate its forces in and around Kuwait.[33] UNOMIG was created
in 1993 by the Security Council primarily to observe the precarious cease-fire in
Georgia between secessionists in Abkhazia and government troops,[34] and
although the UN presence is deemed necessary,[35] it has had limited influence on
the deteriorating situation.

Observer forces with more ambitious mandates built around the core function
of observing a cease-fire include UNOMIL in Liberia. This force, emplaced in
1993, was dependent on the effective supervision and implementation of the 1993
Cotonou Agreement between the parties to the civil war by ECOMOG.[36]
UNOMIL's job was essentially one of observation of the Agreement, and presumably of ECOMOG. Although the situation deteriorated with UNOMIL's
arrival, some progress has since been made and UNOMIL's mandate has been
widened to include human rights monitoring and election supervision,[37] with elections scheduled for May 1997, illustrating how the mandates of observation teams
are flexible and can be multi-functional.

Observation teams are often involved in fact finding when fulfilling their mandate to observe and report on the status of the conflict. For instance it is often
necessary for them to try to establish which side, if any, breached a cease-fire. This
has certainly been one of the tasks undertaken by UNMOT in Tajikistan. Other
forces are mainly concerned with fact finding. In 1958 the Security Council
decided to despatch 'an observation group to proceed to Lebanon so as to ensure
that there is no illegal infiltration of personnel or supply of arms or other matériel
across the Lebanese borders' from the United Arab Republic.[38] The use of 'ensure'
in paragraph 1 of the enabling resolution suggests that UNOGIL was being
directed to forcibly prevent infiltration. Practically, such a mandate would be
impossible for an observation team, numbering 100, to perform. Indeed, the Secretary General's interpretation of UNOGIL's mandate, which was not contested in
the Council, emphasised that its role was strictly limited to observing whether illegal infiltration occurred, and that it was there with the consent of the Lebanese
government.[39]

Even after the United States had intervened in mid-July, UNOGIL's functions
probably remained investigatory and observational as envisaged by Article 34 of
the UN Charter. It was essentially different from most other types of peacekeeping forces which are usually created to perform some role in relation to provisional measures called for by the Assembly or the Council; UNOGIL's mandate
was to ascertain the facts before the United Nations could adopt any further

measures. Although UNOGIL consisted of a team of military observers and therefore is included in this chapter, it could easily be classified with non-military investigatory teams established by the Council.

UNOGIL observed and reported that there was no significant infiltration of Lebanon from the United Arab Republic and to that extent it had fulfilled the terms of its mandate.[40] However, on a wider view, its reports did not prevent military intervention by the United States, although its continued presence along with the American marines, in addition to the establishment of a new government under General Chehab, probably had the effect of stabilising the situation.

Supervision

Whereas observation involves a limited, often unarmed, military presence of less than 100 troops, supervision involves the emplacement of a much larger, lightly armed military presence of several thousand soldiers. While the former involves the function of observation and reporting, the latter involves the securing of a cease-fire and, if necessary and agreed upon, withdrawal of troops usually to the positions occupied by the parties before the cease-fire was adopted. The model for this type of operation was UNEF I established between Egypt and Israel in 1956. The Secretary General described the basic nature and role of UNEF as follows:

The Force has no rights other than those necessary for the execution of the functions assigned to it by the General Assembly and agreed to by the country or countries concerned. The force is paramilitary in character and much more so than an observer corps, but it is in no sense a military force, exercising through force of arms, even temporary control over the territory in which it is stationed; nor does it have any military objectives, or even military functions exceeding those necessary to secure peaceful conditions on the assumption that the parties to the conflict will take all the necessary steps for compliance with the recommendations of the General Assembly …[41]

Clearly the force, by its size and the fact that it carried arms, had some military presence, though nothing like the coercive capacity of ONUC in the Congo, or UNOSOM II in Somalia, or IFOR in Bosnia.[42] UNEF I was allowed to use force but only within narrowly defined limits as outlined in chapter eight. In the case of UNEF I the principle applied was that, according to the Secretary General, 'men engaged in the operation may never take the initiative in the use of armed force, but are entitled to respond with force to an attack with arms, including attempts to use force to make them withdraw from positions which they occupy under orders …'. Thus in the case of UNEF, it could protect its positions and personnel from attack, allowing it to use some force to maintain its position between the opposing sides, although if faced with overwhelming fire-power it would have no choice but to withdraw. It was not allowed, nor had it the capacity, to take any wider forceful action. A wider definition of self-defence would probably have blurred the distinction between peacekeeping and enforcement.[43]

UNEF I's mandate had four aspects: to secure the cease-fire which was rapidly achieved with the cooperation of the parties to the conflict; to supervise the withdrawal of foreign troops which was achieved relatively slowly due to the reticence of Britain and France;[44] and to patrol the armistice lines. As regards the latter, UNEF took over most of UNTSO's patrols and was reasonably efficient taking into account Israel's repudiation of the Israeli–Egyptian Armistice in 1956 and its consequent withdrawal from the Mixed Armistice Commission.[45] Israel's withdrawal from the Commission had a potential influence on the fourth aspect of UNEF's mandate, namely the observation of the armistice agreement.

Nevertheless, although no longer recognising the Agreement *de jure*, Israel continued to recognise it *de facto*, which contributed to UNEF's success in reducing the number of fedayeen raids from the Gaza Strip and in keeping the number of border incidents to a minimum level during the force's stay.

UNEF I 'ranked among the most effective of United Nations' peacekeeping operations' in that it not only fulfilled its mandate, but also helped to secure over a decade of relative peace in the Middle East.[46] On the other hand, it could be said that UNEF I did not contribute a great deal towards a peaceful solution of even part of the Middle Eastern question. One could perhaps go further and argue that the parties, particularly Egypt, used the decade in which UNEF was *in situ* as a breathing space in which they rearmed in preparation for the next conflict, using UNEF's buffer to hide behind. Certainly UNEF's contribution to peace was severely questioned when President Nasser withdrew Egypt's consent to the presence of UNEF which led to its removal in 1967; an action which, in itself, suggested that Egypt no longer wanted peace and therefore no longer required UNEF. Despite arguments to the effect that Egypt had no right to withdraw consent, it is doubtful whether a peacekeeping force could remain on a State's territory without that State's consent.

UNEF I, as well as UNEF II which operated in a similar fashion between 1973 and 1979,[47] and UNDOF on the Golan Heights from 1974,[48] illustrate, within the limits of consensual operations, the relative effectiveness of peacekeeping forces in supervising cessation of hostilities in inter-State conflicts. In intra-State conflicts the UN has had some success in peacekeeping, primarily in the Congo and Cyprus, though they both illustrate the problems of peacekeeping, whether quasi-enforcement or consensual, in intra-State conflicts. Both forces will be analysed in some detail.

UN Operation in the Congo

The Republic of the Congo achieved independence from Belgium on 30 June 1960. As with many colonies, the Congo was something of an artificial construction consisting of many tribal areas. The Belgian authorities had done little to unify the colony before independence and so within a few days of its achievement disruptions between the various factions occurred resulting in Belgian intervention which was characterised as humanitarian by the Belgian government.

President Kasavubu and Prime Minister Lumumba sent a cable to the Secretary General requesting United Nations' military assistance to protect the Congo 'against the present external aggression which is a threat to international peace'.[49] The Secretary General, utilising Article 99 of the Charter, asked that the President of the Council convene that body.[50] The resultant resolution was the work of Dag Hammarskjöld, as were the two subsequent Council resolutions.

On 14 July 1960 the Council adopted resolution 143, which made no jurisdictional finding but called upon Belgium to withdraw and decided to authorise the Secretary General to take the necessary steps to provide military assistance, 'in consultation with the Government of the Congo' until the Congolese security forces could fully meet their tasks. To all intents and purposes this appears to be another case of the United Nations filling the vacuum created by the breakdown in security, but the simplicity of this belies the complexity of the civil war situation facing the United Nations. ONUC was to assist the government in restoring law and order 'but which government? that of Lumumba? Kasavubu? Ilea? Mobutu?'.[51]

Despite the creation of ONUC, the situation deteriorated and on 11 July 1960 Tshombe, President of the Katangese provincial government, declared Katanga's secession. Belgian troops remained despite resolution 143. Again on the Secretary General's initiative the Security Council adopted resolution 145 on 22 July 1960. The resolution recognised the unity of the Congo, again called on the Belgians to withdraw while authorising the Secretary General 'to take all necessary action to this effect'. It also requested that all States refrain from interference which might undermine the territorial integrity and political independence of the Congo.

Belgium refused to withdraw from Katanga with the consequence that ONUC could not enter the province without using force, an event which the previous resolutions had not catered for. Under these circumstances the Council adopted resolution 146 on 9 August 1960. The resolution called on the government of Belgium to withdraw its troops from Katanga; declared that ONUC should enter Katanga; reaffirmed that ONUC 'will not be a party to or in any way influence the outcome of any internal conflict, constitutional or otherwise'; and called upon members 'to accept and carry out the decisions of the Security Council' in accordance with Articles 25 and 49.

By September 1960 the Congo was in a state of constitutional as well as military upheaval with Kasavubu and Lumumba dismissing each other from office followed by the coup by the army chief of staff General Mobutu on 14 September. This combined with the continuing attempt to secede by Katanga and the problem of how much force was to be used to enable ONUC to carry out its mandate divided the Council. The Soviet Union was particularly critical of the Secretary General who had so far masterminded the operation.[52] This resulted in the Soviet veto of another Hammarskjöld-proposed resolution.[53] The deadlock in the Council was a reflection of the increasing internationalisation of the civil war, with the

Soviets supporting Lumumba, the Americans supporting Kasavubu, whilst the French, British and Belgians showed support for Tshombe.

The United States proposed that the matter be transferred to the General Assembly under the auspices of the Uniting for Peace Resolution. This proposal was adopted by procedural vote,[54] despite the negative votes of the Soviet Union and Poland who stated that the Uniting for Peace Resolution was unconstitutional. Besides, they argued, the Assembly was about to start its regular annual session anyway.

Although opposed by the Eastern bloc the Assembly adopted a resolution on 20 September 1960. This resolution stated, *inter alia*, that to safeguard international peace it was 'essential for the United Nations to continue to assist the Central Government of the Congo' and to this end requested the Secretary General to take 'vigorous action' to restore law and order and to preserve the unity, integrity and political independence of the Congo. It also requested all States to refrain from intervening and reminded members of Articles 25 and 49.[55] However, the Assembly then split into factions none of which could form the necessary majority to adopt a significant resolution.

The death of Lumumba and the deterioration of the situation into civil war finally united the Council sufficiently to enable it to adopt resolution 161 on 27 February 1961 which contained two parts. Part A categorised the crisis as a 'threat to international peace and security' and a 'serious civil war situation'. It urged that 'the United Nations take immediately all appropriate measures to prevent the occurrence of a civil war in the Congo, including arrangements for cease-fires, the halting of all military operations, the prevention of clashes, and the use of force, if necessary, in the last resort'. It also urged the withdrawal of all Belgian troops and advisers as well as mercenaries; and decided to investigate the death of Lumumba. Part B also found a 'threat to international peace and security'. It also noted the violation of human rights and fundamental freedoms in the Congo and urged self-determination through free and fair elections without outside interference.

On 24 November 1961 the Security Council adopted resolution 169 which reaffirmed the mandate of ONUC as being far more than the simple supervision of provisional measures.

(a) To maintain the territorial integrity and political independence of the Republic of the Congo;
(b) To assist the Central Government of the Congo in the restoration and maintenance of law and order;
(c) To prevent the occurrence of civil war in the Congo;
(d) To secure the immediate withdrawal and evacuation from the Congo of all foreign military, paramilitary and advisory personnel not under United Nations' command, and mercenaries; and
(e) To render technical assistance.

It welcomed the restoration of a Central Government on 2 August 1961 in accordance with the *Loi Fondamentale*, and deplored armed action against the government specifically by the secessionists in Katanga aided by external resources and mercenaries. It completely rejected the claim that Katanga was a 'sovereign independent nation'. To this end the resolution authorised the Secretary General to take 'vigorous action', including the requisite measure of force 'if necessary' for the expulsion of foreign military personnel not under United Nations' command.

The Council resolutions establishing and mandating ONUC (143, 145, 146) were essentially the work of Secretary General Hammarskjöld. It is important, therefore, to ascertain his views as to their basis. His use of Article 99 to start the Council in motion gives the first indication as to the possible constitutional base of the action for he believed that his use of Article 99 necessarily implied a finding by himself of a situation falling within Article 39 of the Charter.[56] However, he did not want to categorise the Belgian intervention as aggression in order to obtain the support of the Western powers on the Council. On the other hand, a characterisation of the situation as a mere breakdown in internal law and order would have indirectly justified Belgian intervention and would not have been acceptable to either the Socialist or Afro-Asian members of the Council. The Secretary General found a path through this minefield by proposing to create such conditions as to facilitate Belgian withdrawal with a United Nations force filling the vacuum.[57]

It must be noted that the first three enabling resolutions made no finding under Article 39 despite the Secretary General's belief that Article 99 necessarily implied a 'threat to the peace'. The Secretary General was intent on obtaining a mandate for the force, hence the resolutions had to be constitutionally ambiguous in order to obtain sufficient consensus. However, they do contain inferences as to where they could be placed under the Charter. Resolutions 143 and 146 contained provisions indicating that the force was to comply with Article 2(7), in that ONUC was to provide military assistance in consultation with the Congolese government and would not intervene or influence the outcome of any internal conflict. Indeed, the Secretary General initially seemed to view ONUC as similar to interpositional, consensual peacekeeping as being undertaken at the time by UNEF I.[58] This would seem to suggest that ONUC was either created under the recommendatory powers of Chapter VI or under the doctrine of implied powers since Chapter VI does not contain any specific provision under which a peacekeeping force could be established.

However, the last of Hammarskjöld's inspired resolutions, 146, contained references to Article 25 suggesting that the resolutions were 'decisions' not recommendations and so were mandatory without containing an express or implied finding under Article 39. As the situation deteriorated so the Council began to cross the threshold into Chapter VII. References to non-intervention in resolution 146 probably signified that the authorisation to ONUC to enter Katanga was, theoretically, not seen as enforcement action under Article 42 but as a provisional measure under Article 40.[59] This certainly accords with the Secretary General's revised view.[60] Without a determination within the terms of Article 39, which necessarily internationalises the situation, provisional measures under Article 40, although made mandatory by reference to Article 25, cannot escape the limitation in Article 2(7), because they are not enforcement measures.

Assuming, after resolution 146, that ONUC was operating under Article 40, could the General Assembly then take over the operation of the force when the Security Council became paralysed by the veto? The day-to-day operation of the force did not require supervision by the Security Council or by the General Assembly; the only action required by either organ was when the mandate of the force needed adjusting. Thus if the mandate provided by the Security Council was sufficient for the force to continue day-to-day operations, there would be no legal need for the General Assembly to adopt a resolution. However, there was a political need to show that a majority of members supported the action.

The problem is whether the General Assembly, acting under the Uniting for Peace Resolution, altered the mandate in its resolution 1474. There are suggestions that it did for it requested that the Secretary General take 'vigorous action' to restore the unity and independence of the Congo. By itself, this request could, at the most, be classified as a recommendation of enforcement action, which would have been within the Assembly's powers, but would have constituted an alteration of the mandate. The Security Council had only called for mandatory provisional measures under Article 40. The General Assembly could be seen as recommending enforcement action similar to the power exercised by both the Security Council and the General Assembly during the United Nations' action in Korea. This would put ONUC beyond the pale of a peacekeeping force and would have made it an enforcement action.

However, there are suggestions in Assembly resolution 1474 that all that body intended was a reaffirmation of the Security Council's resolutions; in other words, it did not intend to alter the mandate. References in the resolution to Articles 25 and 49 indicate a confirmation of Council resolution 146 for such Articles do not apply to Assembly recommendations. If the Assembly was trying to take mandatory enforcement action that would have been unconstitutional. This was affirmed in the *Expenses* case in which the World Court opined that the Assembly had not taken enforcement action as regards its handling of ONUC.[61] Although its reasoning is not clear, the Court's judgment also suggests that the Assembly's contribution to ONUC's mandate was not recommendation of enforcement action, but simply a reaffirmation or possibly a reinterpretation of the mandate created by the Security Council.

The following Council resolution, 161, made arguments relating to the legality of the Assembly's contribution somewhat academic, for it comprehensively reinterpreted ONUC's mandate in terms which went beyond those in the Assembly's resolution. The Council found a threat to the peace. Such an implied finding within the terms of Article 39 placed the whole operation under Chapter VII. So even if the operation remained under Article 40, there was the possibility of making it into enforcement action at a later stage. Also, it is arguable that such a finding renders the limitation contained in Article 2(7) redundant.

There appears to be two alternatives: either resolution 161 went beyond provisional measures, or the finding of a threat to the peace was merely a sign of a deteriorating situation rather than a method by which the mandate could be changed. It appeared to go further than previous Council resolutions in that the emphasis was no longer on helping the Congolese government which appeared to have disintegrated, instead it was reduced to maintaining the Congo's integrity, to prevent its break-up by factionalisation and secession, a Congo in which a new government could be elected. To this end it authorised the use of force in the last resort. The International Court was of the opinion that this did not amount to enforcement action. Nevertheless, for one thing, Article 2(7) no longer seemed important to the Council, to the extent of involving the consent of the Congolese government, for one did not exist at the time. For another, resolution 161 authorised the use of force by ONUC 'in the last resort', in other words the use of force was not limited to merely self-defence. This last factor seems to push ONUC beyond a force overseeing the implementation of provisional measures to a force authorised to use enforcement measures. However, such a mandate can be reconciled with Article 40. The authorisation to use force in the last resort came at the end of a list of provisional measures, 'cease-fires', 'halting of all military operations', and 'the prevention of clashes', and so can be seen as coming within an authorisation merely to enforce provisional measures as provided by the last sentence of Article 40 which reads, 'the Security Council shall duly take account of a failure to comply with such provisional measures'. What is clear is that the mandate was for the enforcement of provisional measures and not the simple supervision of them as with the dominant UNEF I model.

Security Council resolution 169 contained a comprehensive restatement of ONUC's mandate. It was able to contain a reassertion that ONUC was assisting the Congolese government because the central government had been restored. The force therefore returned, to some extent, to the consensual type of peacekeeping force exemplified by UNEF. However, the mandate also referred to the prevention of civil war as one of the force's purposes. This must be read in conjunction with the mandate's requirement (d) of ensuring the withdrawal of foreign military personnel and mercenaries, for it was the internationalisation of the civil war that constituted the threat to the peace.

The mandate contained in resolution 169 was in the nature of a series of widely drawn provisional measures. It was meant to enable ONUC to preserve the Congo intact to enable a peaceful settlement between all the factions to occur. It was not an authorisation for ONUC to enforce a political solution. Efforts to prevent secession may have appeared as if ONUC was being used by the central government to enforce its will on the secessionists. However, the basis of ONUC's action towards secession was that it arose because of foreign intervention and foreign engineering of a revolt, which was not in accord with the widest interpretation of ONUC's mandate, namely the protection of the territorial integrity and independence of the Congo.

The Congo was to remain as a whole, but if the secession was wholly or mainly indigenous, ONUC's action would have been an enforcement of that aim. However, the Council resolutions made it clear that that organ believed that the secession was being caused from outside the country. This was evidenced by resolution 169 which authorised the use of force solely for the expulsion of foreign military elements. Whether there would have been a Katangese secession anyway remains conjecture; the fact remains that foreign military involvement provided the situation with the necessary international element to have allowed ONUC to operate without it technically becoming an enforcement action under Article 42, in that its use of force was confined to the enforcement of the provisional measures outlined in the mandate.

The effectiveness of ONUC can be determined by its fulfilment of the purposes listed in Council resolution 169.[62] As regards the directive to ONUC to maintain the territorial integrity and political independence of the Congo, the Secretary General states that the most serious threat to this was from the Katangese secessionists. Although integrity was restored in a symbolic sense in August 1960 with Tshombe's consent to ONUC's entry into Katanga, further secessionist activities meant that the full integration of the province was only achieved when a public renunciation of secession was announced by Tshombe combined with the complete freedom of movement achieved by ONUC throughout Katanga, the neutralisation and disarming of the Katangese gendarmerie, the elimination of Katanga's airforce and the flight of the mercenaries.

In relation to assisting the Congolese government in the restoration and maintenance of law and order, the Secretary General noted that until the formation of a recognisable central government in August 1961, ONUC was unsuccessful in this part of its mandate. After that date, particularly with the termination of Katanga's secession, ONUC restored law and order to the whole of the Congo by 1963. The formation of a central government acceptable to all the parties, including, eventually, Katanga, also helped ONUC to carry out successfully the third part of its mandate, namely the prevention of civil war in the Congo. The ending of the Katangese provincial government's secession necessarily entailed ONUC effectively carrying out the fourth part of its mandate, namely, the removal of foreign military and paramilitary personnel and mercenaries.

It can be seen from the above that ONUC's success depended heavily on it ending the Katangese secession and as has been seen, ONUC's operation to carry this out came perilously close to being enforcement action. It is submitted that ONUC was successful because it overstepped basic peacekeeping principles. Its mandate was so widely drawn that its fulfilment entailed going beyond the maintenance of the *status quo*, which is the normal purpose of peacekeeping forces, to providing a solution to the conflict.

From the once disintegrating Congo there arose a relatively stable African State, Zaire, a fact that must, in part, be due to the United Nations' Operation in the Congo. Despite its operational difficulties, in terms of its contribution to the settlement of a crisis and to international peace, ONUC must be judged one of the most successful peacekeeping operations undertaken by the United Nations.[63] However, by blurring the distinction between peacekeeping and enforcement, ONUC's wider impact on the peacekeeping function must call into question the value of this type of peacekeeping. Indeed, the failure of the quasi-enforcement method in Somalia in particular shows how precarious and dangerous such a method is, when the UN is faced with a more intractable enemy. Simply because the UN succeeded in the Congo did not mean that it could repeat its success elsewhere.

UN Peacekeeping Force in Cyprus

Violence broke out between the Greek and Turkish Cypriot communities after the President of Cyprus, Archbishop Makarios, had proposed constitutional amendments on 30 November 1963. The threat of Turkish intervention arose.[64] This led to proposals for a joint British/Turkish/Greek 'peacemaking' force to be interposed between the two communities.[65] The Soviet Union characterised this proposal as enforcement by NATO and stated that only the Security Council could take any practical measures.[66] Furthermore, the Cypriot government wanted a United Nations', not a guaranteeing powers', presence.[67]

The non-permanent members of the Council, excluding Czechoslovakia, sponsored resolution 186 which was adopted by the Council on 4 March 1964. The resolution noted that the situation 'with regard to Cyprus is likely to threaten international peace and security'; called on members 'to refrain from any action or threat of action likely to worsen the situation in Cyprus, or to endanger international peace'; asked the government of Cyprus which had 'the responsibility for the maintenance of law and order' to take measures to stop the violence; recommended the creation 'with the consent of the government of Cyprus' of UNFICYP; and recommended that the 'function of the force should be, in the interests of preserving international peace and security, to use its best efforts to prevent a recurrence of the fighting, to contribute to the maintenance and restoration of law and order and a return to normal conditions'.

The Secretary General's interpretation of UNFICYP's mandate made it clear that what was contemplated was a consensual-type peacekeeping operation based on UNEF I, avoiding any action 'designed to influence the political situation in Cyprus except through creating an improved climate in which political solutions may be sought'.[68] This neutralist policy was meant to allay fears of enforcement. Nevertheless, ONUC's actions under a neutralist stance came perilously close to enforcement, and the Secretary General's interpretation of the use of force by UNFICYP had a similar potential, envisaging the possible use of force by UNFICYP to carry out its mandate.[69] As with ONUC, UNFICYP's mandate, outlined in resolution 186, contained a series of widely drawn provisional measures. However, unlike in the Congo situation where the Council was faced with a threat to the peace, here the Council did not make a crucial Article 39 finding. Thus UNFI-CYP was created following non-mandatory provisional measures and so could not undertake enforcement action without a finding in the terms of Article 39.

Between 1964 and 1974, UNFICYP did not act as a buffer force between the two communities, but rather as a police force since there were not, as such, definable cease-fire lines. This situation changed in 1974. A Greek-backed coup against Makarios and the imminent invasion by Turkey led the Council to meet on 16 July 1974 at the request of Secretary General Waldheim and the Cypriot representative.[70] In the Council's first meeting some of the members stated that there was a threat to international peace.[71] Indeed, resolution 353, adopted on 20 July 1974, the day Turkey invaded, stated that there was a 'serious threat to international peace and security', and demanded 'an end to foreign military intervention' in Cyprus. This implied finding under Article 39 combined with the peremptory language and a call for a cease-fire suggested mandatory provisional measures under Article 40.

Nonetheless, UNFICYP's original constitutional basis, founded on non-mandatory provisional measures, was not changed and brought within Chapter VII, although its functions were to change from it being an intra-State to, factually speaking, an inter-State peacekeeping force. The Secretary General reported on the measures proposed by the foreign ministers of Greece, Britain and Turkey (but not Cyprus), that UNFICYP should create a security zone between the Turkish forces in the north of the island and the Greek Cypriot forces in the south. The Security Council requested that he implement his report.[72]

Although the Cypriot government had consented to the original emplacement of UNFICYP in 1964, it objected somewhat to the new deployment saying that it appeared to perpetuate foreign military intervention.[73] It did not go as far as to withdraw its consent but its cooperation seemed to become unimportant with all the negotiations about the security zone taking place between Greece, Britain, Turkey and the Secretary General. However, although there was no effective government for the whole island, there was a need to involve the two Cypriot factions as well as the guaranteeing powers to obtain a lasting cease-fire and to allow UNFICYP to perform its new functions.[74]

If we turn now to the effectiveness of UNFICYP, in the period 1964 to 1974, UNFICYP, after initial difficulties, succeeded in securing a virtual end to the fighting on the island, although its attempts at creating a return to normal conditions on Cyprus were a limited success.[75] As early as 1967, the Secretary General warned that excessive confidence in the presence of UNFICYP had reduced the parties' willingness to negotiate a settlement.[76]

In the period before the Turkish invasion, UNFICYP's major preoccupation was to try to maintain the *status quo* on the island. This remained its position towards the new *status quo* imposed on the island following the Turkish invasion and occupation of the northern part of the island in 1974. UNFICYP was power-less to prevent the invasion, instead its functions were changed to that of a buffer force. In carrying out its revised mandate successfully, UNFICYP has helped to entrench the post-1974 position on the island, with the cease-fire line becoming 'more and more an international frontier'.[77]

The Security Council has encouraged peacemaking through the Secretary Gen-eral's good offices and has called upon all States not to recognise any Cypriot State other than the Republic of Cyprus.[78] A parallel can be drawn with the Congo situation where the Council was also concerned to keep the nation intact. How-ever, in that case the Council took positive action through its peacekeeping force to maintain the integrity of the Congo, whereas UNFICYP is used to supervise a division of the island State whilst any progress towards reintegration must come about via separate peacemaking attempts by the Secretary General.

More recent forces have, as with UNFICYP, the basic core function of a buffer force, supervising an established cease-fire between the parties. UNIKOM was established by the Security Council in 1991, following the conflict against Iraq, to monitor the demilitarised zone between Iraq and Kuwait and to deter violations of the boundary by its presence.[79] Although originally not authorised to take any mil-itary action to prevent Iraqi entry into the demilitarised zone,[80] and subsequently the demarcated boundary between the two States, violations of the zone by Iraq led the Security Council in 1993 to increase its strength and authorised it to take physical action to prevent small scale violations of the zone/boundary.[81] Thus UNIKOM is not simply authorised to supervise, it can take limited enforcement action.

Although UNPROFOR struggled and ultimately failed to achieve its mandate in the intra-State conflict in Bosnia, it did also act as an inter-State buffer force between Croatia and Serbia from 1992.[82] In turn this force was replaced by UNCRO in 1995,[83] which itself was replaced in the remaining problem areas after the peace agreements of 1995.[84] In January 1996 UNCRO was replaced by a very limited observation team – UNMOP – in the Prevlaka peninsula region of Croa-tia.[85] In the same month a more elaborate force, UNTAES, was established in the eastern Slavonian region to supervise the peaceful integration of the region into Croatia, involving the temporary administration of the region,[86] though its com-ponent of nearly 5,000 troops acts as a buffer between Croatia and Serbia.

Disarmament/demobilisation

Whereas the supervision of a cease-fire and often withdrawal of troops to prior positions is a relatively normal function of peacekeeping – in effect a supervision of the return to the *status quo ante*, the supervision by a peacekeeping force of a process of disarmament and even further the disbandment or demobilisation of one or more of the armed forces involved in the conflict is a much rarer event in that it signifies a willingness to alter the local balance of power. Nevertheless, the recent peacekeeping operations which combine consensual peacekeeping with the supervision of a peaceful settlement, have included disarmament, a necessary part of the peace process, within the mandate of the force. The purpose of this section will not be to review all the UN forces which have been involved in such a task. It will be simply to give one or two examples and contrast them with the alternative, and more dangerous approach, of enforced disarmament.

Whereas ONUVEN, the Observer Mission to supervise the elections in Nicaragua, was emplaced in August 1990, the military component of the peace effort was not authorised by the Security Council until 7 November 1989, with a mandate to verify compliance with the undertakings in the Guatemala Agreements of 1987 on the cessation of aid to irregular forces and the non-use of territory of one State for attacks on other States.[87] An advanced party of ONUCA arrived in December 1989. ONUCA, a team of about 260 military observers, successfully carried out this initial aspect of its mandate, enabling peaceful elections, supervised by ONUVEN, to take place in Nicaragua on 25 February 1990. However, unusually in this type of operation, no real attempt had been made to reduce the danger of the Contra resistance in Nicaragua taking up arms again. This seemed a real possibility if the elections returned the left-wing Sandinista government.

However, in something of a surprise result, the right-wing opposition secured victory. This led, in part, to the Contras agreeing to voluntary demobilisation in March 1990. The Secretary General reported that agreement had been achieved on the modalities of demobilisation, under ONUCA (reinforced by armed personnel) supervision, involving the disbandment of Contra rebels in their camps in Honduras and at ONUCA-secured temporary assembly points inside Nicaragua. It was agreed that as part of this process ONUCA would be responsible 'for the taking delivery of weapons, matériel and military equipment, including military uniforms of the Nicaraguan resistance'.[88]

The process proved difficult, requiring a renegotiation of the modalities for demobilisation in Nicaragua including a clear agreement on the separation of forces resulting in the withdrawal of government forces from around the security zones and surrounding areas designated for Contra demobilisation,[89] and a commitment by the Nicaraguan government to resettle former Contras in specially created development areas, to give them economic aid and to permit them to join the police forces in those areas.[90] With these concessions made, the demobilisation of nearly 22,000 members of the Contras was achieved by the end of June 1990. While noting that the numbers of arms, particularly heavy weapons, handed in and destroyed by ONUCA, was not always as high as expected, the Commander of ONUCA and the Secretary General expressed satisfaction with the demobilisation and disarmament process.[91]

It must be stressed that ONUCA supervised a process of voluntary disarmament and demobilisation, and that the normal timetable in such a situation is first of all to diffuse the situation by overseeing disarmament and demobilisation and then to supervise the chosen method of peaceful settlement. However, this proved difficult to achieve in the attempted settlement of the Cambodian conflict.

The military component of UNTAC was to verify withdrawal of all foreign forces and to monitor the cessation of outside military assistance; and to supervise the cease-fire and related measures such as the cantonment of the various armed bands and their subsequent disarmament and demobilisation.

As with the initial demobilisation of SWAPO forces in Namibia,[92] UNTAC ran into serious problems concerning the cantonment of the Khmer Rouge.[93] The process envisaged the emplacement of the peacekeeping force to be followed by the demobilisation and disarmament of the four factions involved in the conflict, beginning on 13 June 1992. This would entail the collection of the arms of what was estimated to be 200,000 troops from the various factions gathering in 95 UN controlled regroupment areas. The Secretary General reported on 21 July 1992 to the Security Council that less than 5 per cent of this figure had been cantoned.[94] In addition, the Khmer Rouge had stepped up its cease-fire violations.[95]

The Council attempted once more to obtain Khmer Rouge compliance with the peace process when it adopted resolution 783 on 13 October 1992, but with no evidence that its demands were being heeded it changed tack on 30 November 1992, when it asked the Secretary General to consider the implications for the elections of the non-compliance of the Khmer Rouge, determining that the elections would proceed in May 1993 in all areas of Cambodia to which UNTAC had access. In addition, it suggested various types of embargoes that should be emplaced against Khmer Rouge held areas. The emphasis was no longer on encouraging the Khmer Rouge to participate in the election process, but shifted to trying to proceed without them despite the fact that only about 25 per cent of the troops of the four factions had by that time entered the cantonment sites so creating the potential for conflict in an atmosphere of distrust and non-cooperation on the part of the Khmer Rouge.[96] In these less than satisfactory conditions UN supervised elections were held in May 1993, and the results were welcomed by the Security Council.[97] Nevertheless, the presence of a significantly armed rebel faction, the Khmer Rouge, has prevented a real peace from emerging in Cambodia.[98]

UNTAC certainly did not have the mandate to enforce the disarmament of the factions. To have attempted to do so would have led to the UN becoming a faction in a civil war. Unfortunately it did not follow the consensual path in its operation in Somalia.[99] It has already been noted in chapter eight that the decisions to attempt to disarm the factions in Somalia, put UNITAF and then UNOSOM II beyond the pale of traditional peacekeeping, and set an almost impossible task in the increasingly hostile environment. Resolution 794 of December 1992, which authorised UNITAF, did not specifically authorise forceful disarmament. However, as the *UN Chronicle* reports the Secretary General in his report on the establishment of UNITAF 'discussed his vision of future activities ... which he had outlined in a letter to the United States' President. At least the heavy weapons of the organised factions would have to be neutralised and brought under international control and irregular forces and gangs had to be disarmed'. Further UNITAF 'should try to induce individuals to hand in small arms and weapons and begin the task of clearing mines'.[100]

UNITAF was emplaced on 9 December 1992 and took a fairly aggressive approach towards disarming the various factions in the country and in opening up humanitarian aid routes.[101] It used substantial offensive force. Nevertheless, the US-led and dominated force did not attempt to directly impose a peaceful settlement on the Somali factions by the use of military force. Instead it attempted to create more peaceful conditions in which negotiations for peace could be undertaken. Furthermore, the United States appeared anxious to withdraw and be replaced by a new UN force. The United States had begun to reduce its troop commitment in February 1993, even before the Security Council approved the Secretary General's proposal[102] for a 28,000 strong UN force (UNOSOM II) under Chapter VII of the Charter on 26 March 1993. Resolution 814 authorised UNOSOM II to use armed force if necessary to ensure the delivery of humanitarian assistance, but also stressed the need to restore peace, to disarm factions, and to protect relief workers, explicitly encouraging the wider use of force by UNOSOM II. In addition, the force was responsible for returning hundreds of thousands of refugees, clearing land mines, setting up a police force, and helping to rebuild the economy.

UNITAF handed over responsibility for the policing of Somalia on 4 May 1993. Conflict between UNOSOM II and the SNA was a direct result of attempts to disarm the faction. Although the Secretary General and the Security Council continued up until November 1993 to affirm the need to forcefully disarm the faction, the Security Council then requested a fundamental review of the operation following the US statement that it intended to withdraw its contribution to UNOSOM II.[103]

In February 1994, with the withdrawal of US marines underway, the Security Council restricted UNOSOM II's mandate to consensual peacekeeping, including the encouragement of the factions' 'cooperative efforts to achieve disarmament'. The new mandate made it clear that coercive methods of disarming the factions or carrying out other aspects of the mandate were not to be used, despite the fact that the resolution was adopted under Chapter VII.[104] Despite this move aimed at restoring the UN neutrality, its force was still subjected to attack and the evidence was that the factions were rearming during the final year of its stay,[105] until its withdrawal in March 1995.[106]

The basic principles of peacekeeping, reviewed in chapter eight, reveal that to depart from consensual peacekeeping is to undermine the whole basis of this limited form of military action. The above examples also tend to show that on a case-by-case analysis the consensual path is at least as successful, if not more successful, than the enforcement approach in achieving, in this instance, disarmament. Thus the consensual approach to disarmament not only preserves the integrity of UN peacekeeping it also is more effective in promoting peaceful settlement.

Human rights monitoring

The UN Operation in Cambodia, and later multi-functional UN operations, have, when necessary, contained a human rights monitoring function.[107] The origins of this particular peacekeeping function are to be found in the UN peacekeeping Operation in El Salvador,[108] which will be reviewed here.

It was the continuation of the Central American peace process from Nicaragua into El Salvador which necessitated a further development of the integrated peacekeeping and peacemaking (in the form of pacific settlement) approach. Whereas the Nicaraguan operation required the supervision of a cease-fire and elections, ONUSAL was initially set up to verify that the parties to the long running civil war, namely the US backed government and the left-wing Farabundo Marti National Liberation Front (FMLN) comply with the human rights accord they signed at San José in July 1990.[109] Although not the normal sort of provisional measure that the UN had been requested to oversee in the past, it can be seen that the observance of human rights by both parties to a particularly dirty civil war is an interim measure or a first step towards a lasting political settlement.

In May 1991, the Security Council, in establishing ONUSAL and outlining its initial mandate, restricted ONUSAL to a Human Rights Division verifying compliance with the San José Agreement.[110] However, the Council urged the parties to agree on a cease-fire and on a final pacific solution to the conflict, and stated that upon these agreements ONUSAL would then become an integrated peacekeeping operation, verifying provisional measures as well as overseeing a peaceful solution.

Such an approach illustrates the highly flexible and dynamic nature of peacekeeping in the post-Cold War era. The major element of ONUSAL was formed from the disbanding of ONUCA illustrating how UN peacekeeping has been tied into the Central American peace process. The parties formally ended the civil war by agreements made on 31 December 1991 and on 16 January 1992, and the peaceful solution was detailed in the latter agreement and in negotiations lasting until June 1992.[111] The agreement contained a cease-fire commencing on 1 February 1992, continuing for nine months until the FMLN's military structure was dismantled with its members being integrated into the civil and political life of the country, including its institutions. Later negotiations revealed the extent of the government's concessions which included the establishment of a new police force, a reformed electoral code to legalise the FMLN as a political party, as well as government purchase of land for peasants. The aim of the agreements was to address the social inequalities that led to the civil war, to create a 'revolution by negotiation' according to the Secretary General.[112] In order to service these agreements the Security Council expanded ONUSAL's mandate by dividing the force into two with a military division to verify cease-fire arrangements and a police division to monitor public order pending the formation of a new national police force.[113]

The formal ending of the civil war on 15 December 1992 was followed by a request by the government of El Salvador in January 1993 that the UN verify elections scheduled for March 1994.[114] However, the Security Council made it clear in a Presidential statement on 9 February 1993 that neither the government nor the FMLN had fully complied with the accords, in particular the government's obligations regarding its armed forces and the FMLN's duty to destroy its weapons under ONUSAL supervision. Despite these difficulties, the Security Council enlarged ONUSAL's mandate to include an electoral component to monitor and verify the elections in resolution 832 of 27 May 1993.[115] Elections were successfully held on 20 March 1994.

The initial component of ONUSAL, the Human Rights Division, was emplaced before a cease-fire, in July 1991, its task to 'investigate acts committed or situations existing as of the date of its establishment' relating to violations of human rights of civilians, specifically 'rights to life, to integrity and security of the person and to personal liberty', but not generally breaches of humanitarian law governing combatants.[116] Further details of the Missions' Mandate can be found in the San José Agreement which requests UN supervision, namely to verify observance of human rights, to receive and investigate communications received from individuals, to visit and interview individuals, to collect information, and to make recommendations to the parties.

In its initial reports in 1991 ONUSAL's Human Rights Division expressed concern that the continuing armed conflict was clearly adversely affecting the human rights of the civilian population. The Secretary General made it clear in this early period that ONUSAL was not concerned with directly observing or becoming involved in the civil war – its job was to report on compliance with the San José Agreement.[117] This fundamental problem for the protection of human rights was removed with the cease-fire agreement of February 1992. The Director of the Human Rights Division was happy to report that this constituted a radical transformation in the situation in which ONUSAL was operating. Further he expressed his hope 'that a whole series of acts and situations which violate human rights and are related to the armed conflict will now rapidly disappear'.[118] A few months after the cease-fire ONUSAL's reports began to reveal that there had been a rapid decrease in human rights violations,[119] although there were still a significant number of 'instances of unwarranted use of force and threats of violence and intimidation'.

At this stage (August 1992), the Human Rights Division began to stress the importance of the State in protecting human rights.[120] In furtherance of this the Human Rights Division began, after the formal ending of hostilities in December 1992, to make recommendations with a view to institutionalising human rights in El Salvador. It recommended, *inter alia*, ratification of international human rights conventions including the Optional Protocol of the International Covenant on

Civil and Political Rights giving individuals the right of complaint to the Human Rights Committee, and recognition of the compulsory jurisdiction of the Inter-American Court of Human Rights. Furthermore, it recommended wholesale reform of the judiciary within El Salvador, and an improvement in the criminal investigation capability of the police, as well as a compensation fund for the victims of serious human rights abuses.[121] By April 1994 ONUSAL was able to report continuing improvement in human rights observance and progress in the implementation of its recommendations.[122] The success of the peace process, not only in the supervision of elections, but in the dramatic decrease in human rights abuses is testimony to ONUSAL's successful fulfilment of its mandate.[123]

Referendum/election monitoring

As has been stated in chapter seven, the end of the Cold War has removed the barriers that had prevented peacekeeping developing from its traditional base, although traditional peacekeeping forces are still being authorised. The natural successor to the traditional peacekeeping force – the integrated multi-faceted force which combines traditional peacekeeping functions with the overseeing of a peaceful solution, normally in the form of elections or a referendum – is the subject of this section. Although normally assisting in a peace process agreed to by the parties, the UN has occasionally, in the cases of West Irian and Cambodia, assumed temporary sovereignty over a country by administering it during the transitional period.

The origins of this approach can be traced back to the Cold War period, when the Netherlands and Indonesia sought and were granted General Assembly approval for the creation of a UNTEA and a UNSF on West Irian in 1962, to supervise a cease-fire between the belligerents, and then to assume temporary authority over the island pending the transference of sovereignty to Indonesia.[124] UNTEA and UNSF carried out these functions successfully and were withdrawn in 1963. However, the final aspect of the peaceful solution agreed to by the Netherlands and Indonesia[125] was not carried out when Indonesia refused to hold a plebiscite before 1970 as stipulated.

This type of operation was resurrected towards the end of the Cold War with the UN operation in Namibia.

UN Transition Assistance Group in Namibia
During the period of *détente* in the late 1970s, there arose the false hope that a solution to the Namibian problem was at hand. In 1976, the Security Council declared that the Namibian people should be 'enabled freely to determine their own future' by the means of free elections under UN supervision.[126] Indeed, optimism was so high despite South African non-committal, that Canada, West Germany, France, Britain and the United States made a proposal for the settlement of the Namibian situation detailing the electoral process.[127] This led in 1978 to the

appointment of a Special Representative and a decision by the Security Council to establish UNTAG in accordance with a report by the Secretary General 'to ensure the early independence of Namibia through free elections under the supervision and control of the United Nations'.[128]

The Secretary General's report of 1978 recognised the 'unique character' of the proposed operation, in that it entailed not only a peacekeeping operation in the true sense to supervise a cease-fire between SWAPO and South African forces, but also supervision of free and fair elections leading to an independent State. This resulted in the Secretary General recommending a large military force of some 7,500 with a component of several hundred police and civilian administrators. The mandate of the military component was interpreted to include: the monitoring of the cessation of hostile acts; the restriction of South African and SWAPO forces to base; the phased withdrawal of all except a specified number of South African forces; the prevention of infiltration; and the monitoring of the demobilisation of civilian police forces.

The mandate of UNTAG appeared widely drawn in 1978. Despite its division into military and police components, the overall mandate was for UNTAG to keep and enforce the peace in Namibia during the independence process. As with ONUC, there existed the possibility of a peacekeeping force crossing the threshold and becoming an enforcement action. Nevertheless, the internal nature of the conflict necessitated such a widely drawn mandate.

As with all peacekeeping forces, before UNTAG could be emplaced it needed the consent of all the parties to the conflict. SWAPO had consistently accepted resolution 435, while South African consent was not forthcoming until 22 December 1988 when it signed, along with Cuba and Angola, a tripartite agreement consenting to the UN plan.[129] The plan was acceptable to the South Africans because the accord linked Cuban withdrawal from Angola with South African withdrawal from Namibia. The agreement was also the result of pressure by the United States on South Africa and the Soviet Union on Cuba and Angola. The agreement envisaged the independence process commencing on 1 April 1989.

The Security Council welcomed the agreement while stating that UNTAG's mandate was the same as that envisaged in 1978 following a further report by the Secretary General.[130] SWAPO and South Africa agreed to a cease-fire to commence on 1 April so preparing the ground for UNTAG.

UNTAG's constitutional base remained in the Security Council resolution of 1978 and the accompanying report by the Secretary General. The military component's task was to oversee the implementation of provisional measures necessary for the success of the independence process to be monitored by the civilian component. As has been stated, UNTAG's mandate contained the possibility of it being able to enforce the peace, but it did not do this when faced with a breakdown in the cease-fire. Indeed, the agreements between South Africa and the United Nations on the status of UNTAG foresaw it having a neutral and impartial function.[131]

Although the Security Council decided to implement its plan for Namibian independence in its original and definitive form, it eventually decided to reduce the size of UNTAG to 4,500, following intense pressure from the five permanent members, who thought that the improved climate in southern Africa in addition to financial constraints meant that a smaller peacekeeping force was sufficient for the tasks.[132] The wrangling over the size of the force combined perhaps with some complacency as to the anticipated success of the peace process, may have resulted in the inauspicious start to the UN plan, when on 1 April 1989, the cease-fire was breached. Several hundred SWAPO guerrillas infiltrating from Angola, were met with force by South African troops purportedly acting under UNTAG authority due to the fact that the UN had only 1000 troops in Namibia with very few in the border area.[133] There was no doubt that the South African forces enforced the peace in a way that the peacekeeping force was not mandated to. On the other hand, SWAPO appeared to be in breach of the tripartite accord which confined the guerrillas to bases inside Angola. However, although SWAPO consented to the UN plan as laid down in 1978, it was not a party to the agreement which finalised the details. The peace process seemed to have ignored the fact that all the parties to the dispute should have fully consented to all aspects of the peace agreement before the peacekeeping force was emplaced.

During the fighting between SWAPO and the South African forces, the United Nations appeared helpless. It required a new agreement on 8 April between the original signatories to the tripartite accord and this time consented to by SWAPO before a new cease-fire could be made effective. The fresh agreement between South Africa, Angola and Cuba with the United States and the Soviet Union overseeing it, provided for a cease-fire and a withdrawal of SWAPO fighters to north of the 16th parallel under UN supervision. This agreement was reported to the Security Council by the Secretary General.[134]

The shaky start to the UN plan gave rise to fears that the elections, scheduled for 1 November 1989 might be delayed. However, the Joint Monitoring Commission of Angola, South Africa and Cuba, agreed on 14 May 1989 that the situation was normalised sufficiently for the plan to proceed on schedule.[135] UNTAG then successfully ensured a free and fair election on 11 November 1989 at which 97 per cent of the electorate voted. Full independence was achieved on 21 March 1990.[136]

This technique, though successful in Namibia, is quite a high risk strategy. It has not yet brought an end to the conflict between POLISARIO guerrillas and Moroccan troops, which had started in 1976 when Spain withdrew from its former colony of Western Sahara. The plan was for the UN to supervise a referendum in Western Sahara in which the people would determine its future status – either as an independent State or as part of Morocco. The referendum was originally scheduled for January 1992, but has been postponed because of cease-fire violations and disagreements on the composition of the electorate in Western Sahara, with MIN-

URSO, established in 1991,[137] having tremendous difficulty due to its limited numbers (about 350), and due to the fact that the UN is accused by POLISARIO of favouring Morocco in the drawing up of the census list of those entitled to vote in the referendum. In these circumstances, with two of the basic principles of peacekeeping in jeopardy, namely unconditional acceptance of the provisional measures by the parties, and neutrality, not in this case in the UN's supervision of the cease-fire, but in the administration of the peace process, serious doubts have been raised against the prospect of obtaining a successful outcome to this long running dispute.[138]

The idea of having a referendum as a means of finalising the status of a disputed territory is the proposed method of settling the dispute and conflict over Western Sahara, and has so far proved as unsuccessful as the West Irian experiment. One of the problems with this method of settlement as the parties jostle for a better position in the pre-election period is that the UN's neutrality is more easily, and more readily, called into question. In addition, the loser in the electoral contest may well feel that it has little option but to take up arms again. These problems have been illustrated by the UN's difficulties in Angola.

UN Angola Verification Missions

After UNAVEM I had successfully supervised the withdrawal of Cuban troops from Angola in June 1991, UNAVEM II was created following the Lisbon Agreement of 31 May 1991 detailing a cease-fire and the holding of elections by 30 November 1992. The parties requested UN supervision of the cease-fire and of the elections, leading to a revised mandate for the UN force.[139] UNAVEM was to become an integral component in the second stage of peacekeeping, the implementation of an agreed peaceful solution, involving not only traditional peacekeeping functions, the overseeing of the cease-fire to be carried out by the military component of the force, but also the supervision of the Angolan police force, and of the elections, to be carried out by police and civilian elements.[140] To this end the size of the force was increased from 70 military observers, to 350 military observers, 90 police observers, and 71 civilian election observers.

The elections were held on 29 and 30 September 1992 under UNAVEM II's supervision and were declared generally free and fair by the Secretary General's Special Representative.[141] The governing party, the MPLA, won the largest share of the vote with the result that UNITA challenged the validity of the elections. At a meeting of the Security Council on 6 October 1992, an Ad Hoc Commission was sent to Angola to support the implementation of the Peace Accords. The four member Commission met with the leaders of the two factions and was satisfied with assurances that they would take every step possible to prevent violence in the country. The Council appeared satisfied with this when on 19 October 1992 it made a statement welcoming the Commission's contribution to reducing tension and to finding a solution to the difficulties that had arisen since the elections. It called upon all the parties to abide by the commitments entered into by them, in particular with regard to the demobilisation of their troops and the formation of the Unified Armed Forces, and to refrain from any action that would increase tension.

Nevertheless, in a later report the Secretary General recognised that immediately after the election results were announced on 17 October 1992, UNITA launched a nationwide operation to occupy municipalities in Angola by force, and by 23 November 1992 it had control over two-thirds of the 164 municipalities in the country.[142] The fighting continued despite a demand for a cessation of hostilities by the Security Council on 30 October 1992 which was specifically directed at UNITA, effectively labelling it as the responsible party.[143] UNITA charges that UNAVEM II was guilty of colluding with the governing MPLA faction were rejected as 'baseless' by the Security Council in a prior statement of 27 October 1992. Despite an apparent agreement by UNITA to accept the election results, and a recommitment to the Peace Accords by both parties on 19 and 26 November, coupled with a further call for a cease-fire by the Council on 30 November, the fighting continued. Evidence that the Council's patience was wearing thin was to be found in the Presidential statement of 22 December 1992 which called on the parties to agree on a 'realistic plan' for the implementation of the Accords. It also urged the parties to 'produce early evidence of their willingness and ability' to work together to implement the Accords 'so that the international community would feel encouraged to continue committing its scarce resources to the continuation of the United Nations operation in Angola on its present scale'.

Pressure on the parties led to the signing of the Lusaka Protocol in November 1994,[144] leading to the creation of a larger peacekeeping force (UNAVEM III) in February 1995,[145] with the multi-functional mandate, *inter alia*, of providing good offices, to monitor the extension of State administration throughout the country, to supervise the disengagement and cease-fire of the warring parties, to help the demobilisation and disarmament of UNITA (and the return to barracks of the government forces), supervision of the Angolan police force and the verification of a second round of Presidential elections. Delays in the implementation of the Protocol have not prevented the Security Council scheduling a withdrawal of the force early in 1997.[146]

Despite difficulties for peacekeepers in Angola and Western Sahara, the relative successes of the operations in Nicaragua, El Salvador, Namibia and Cambodia, have ensured the development of this precarious, but potentially rewarding method of settlement. Nevertheless, the strain on the UN's budget, the uncertainties about the success of election supervision, and the extent to which the world community sees election supervision as part of a wider acceptance of some sort of right to democracy, call into question whether the UN's combined approach to peacekeeping and election supervision will continue, although the current signs are that it will, as illustrated by the UN's commitment to elections in Haiti.

In October 1990, the General Assembly approved the establishment of the

ONUVEH.[147] This operation did not have any military peacekeeping or observation component and consisted entirely of civilian observers whose function was to report on the electoral process taking place in that strife-torn country. Although peaceful elections took place on 16 December 1990, the elected government was ousted by a military coup in September 1991. The dictatorship was only removed following the Security Council's threat of a US-led military action in July 1994,[148] followed by the temporary occupation of the island by the US-led Multinational Force in Haiti (between September 1994 and March 1995). Only after this military enforcement action was taken could the UNMIH carry out its tasks of helping to restore democracy and supervise further elections in the country. Reporting seven months after UNMIH took over from the multinational force, in November 1995, the Secretary General stated that UNMIH's 'robust presence' of 6,000 troops and nearly 1,000 police from the United Nations Civilian Police (UNCIVPOL)[149] was helping to secure democracy by, *inter alia*, frequent patrols, the escorting of humanitarian relief, logistical and security support for elections, support and training for the Haitian police, and the successful supervision of elections.[150] In June 1996, with its major tasks complete, but with the potential of the destabilisation of the democracy still present, the Security Council scaled down its presence in Haiti, by replacing UNMIH with UNSMIH to help secure the stability of the country through the presence of 500 troops, and to supervise the local police force through the presence of 300 civilian police.[151]

UN Operation in Mozambique

A further success, which perhaps illustrates the increasing confidence and ability of the UN in this type of operation, was in Mozambique. The Secretary General assessed the success of the Mozambique operation in the following terms:

Over a three day period from 27 to 29 October 1994, Mozambique conducted the first free and fair multi-party elections in the country's history. The elections brought together in an open democratic contest the ruling Frente da Libetaçao de Moçambique (FRELIMO) and the Resistência National Moçambicana (RENAMO), the country's two major political parties and former foes, after a long running conflict which had claimed the lives of hundreds of thousands of people, driven millions from their homes and destroyed much of Mozambique's economic and social infrastructure. Against this tragic background, the elections symbolised a new spirit of reconciliation among the people of Mozambique. The elections were also a culmination of a major success story in United Nations peacemaking, peacekeeping, and humanitarian and election assistance. Through a complex, multifaceted and highly innovative strategy which broke new ground in how the United Nations dealt with parties in a conflict situation, a formerly socialist Government, committed to a one-party State, negotiated with an armed, rebellious group to create peace for their country.[152]

In outline the 'mandate of ONUMOZ was to verify and monitor the implementation of the General Peace Agreement for Mozambique signed by the Government of Mozambique and RENAMO in Rome on 4 October 1992. The peace accords required the United Nations to supervise the cease-fire between the two parties, provide security for key transport corridors, monitor a comprehensive disarmament and demobilisation programme, coordinate and monitor humanitarian assistance operations throughout the country and provide assistance and verification for national elections'.[153]

UN election supervision was essentially the last stage in the process of settlement after the others had been successfully supervised and encouraged by ONU-MOZ's military component. After considerable obstacles were surpassed, and with UN encouragement, the parties finally approved of a National Elections Commission in January 1994, and a system of elections by proportional representation in December 1993.[154] The Commission laid down the election timetable and was responsible for the 'conduct, preparation and organisation of the elections'.[155] The Electoral Division of ONUMOZ 'established its own network of monitoring activities, with 148 officers stationed throughout the provinces to cover voter registration, civic education, political campaigns and party political access to, as well as impartiality of, the media, polling, vote counting and vote tabulation at the provincial counting centres. Complaints of alleged irregularities in the electoral process were to be transmitted to the [Elections Commission], while ONUMOZ was mandated to carry out separate investigations'.[156] In the end there were 2,300 observers from the UN, EU and Non-Governmental Organisations (NGOs) as well as provision for up to 35,000 monitors from the different parties[157] – again illustrating the greater emphasis being put in recent peacekeeping operations on the parties to undertake settlement. This contrasts, for example, with the earlier UNTAC, where a considerably larger force was deployed and the emphasis was on the UN to push through the settlement of the conflict. The electoral process in Mozambique was essentially peaceful, and despite a last minute boycott of the first day of the three day voting period, the UN declared the elections free and fair.[158]

The success of ONUMOZ is explained by the Secretary General as being due to 'the deep desire of the Mozambican people – and of the principal parties involved in the process – for peace'.[159] The involvement of the parties in the institutions and mechanisms of the whole process from cease-fire to elections is essential if the UN is to succeed with a smaller force. A lack of commitment by the parties to the peace process can lead to the unravelling of the process set up by a small force as in the case of Angola. Where there is such uncertainty a much larger force is needed, as evidenced by the change from UNAVEM II to UNAVEM III and by the significant presence of UNTAC in Cambodia.

Humanitarian assistance

The efforts of UNPROFOR in Bosnia, reviewed in chapter eight, reflect a recent trend in peacekeeping towards the provision of humanitarian assistance. This, as with the actions of UNPROFOR, is usually based on the cooperation and consent of the parties wherever necessary. It is not solely a recent development with UNIFIL being directed in 1982 to assist the people of southern Lebanon when it could not carry out the remainder of its mandate because of the Israeli invasion.[160] The provision of humanitarian assistance is a function given to peacekeeping forces when wider, more ambitious aims, have not been achieved. Nevertheless, although in some ways a sign of a failed peacekeeping enterprise, there is no doubt that despite the adverse publicity these limited operations attract they save thousands of lives, whether the force is of the usual consensual peacekeeping type or of an enforcement nature as in the case of UNITAF and UNOSOM II[161] in Somalia reviewed above and in chapter eight. Recent internecine conflicts have led to an increase in these activities as evidenced by the presence of the UN guards in northern Iraq from May 1991 to protect the humanitarian assistance being given to the Kurds.[162]

UN Assistance Mission for Rwanda

The increasing linkage of humanitarian assistance with peacekeeping is shown by the UN's failures in Rwanda. The UN's involvement in the situation started with the deployment of UNOMUR in August 1993[163] on the Ugandan side of the border to observe whether there were any military supplies reaching the Rwandese Patriotic Front (RPF) who were fighting Rwandan government forces in the north of the country. In parallel to the agreement to deploy border observers, the RPF and the government had reached agreement on a comprehensive settlement process involving the establishment of a transitional government until elections, the repatriation of refugees and the integration of the armed forces of the two sides. The Arusha Accords of August 1993 also called for the development of a neutral international force to help implement the agreement. Following a report by the Secretary General,[164] the Security Council established UNAMIR, a force of about 1,500, with the mandate of: contributing to the security of the capital – Kigali, monitoring observance of the cease-fire and the security situation, assisting with mine clearance, reporting on violations of the Arusha Accords' provisions on the integration of the armed forces, monitoring the process of repatriation of refugees, investigating and reporting on the activities of the police, and assisting 'in the coordination of humanitarian activities in conjunction with relief operations'.[165]

UNAMIR was originally consented to as a multi-faceted peacekeeping operation. However, the failure to establish the transitional institutions as required by the Arusha Accords led to a stalling of the peace process and an increase in violence in January 1994. Nevertheless, in this period UN humanitarian aid programmes assisted by UNAMIR had been well established on the ground. This, combined with the prospect of the agreement being reactivated persuaded the Security Council to renew UNAMIR's mandate in April 1994.[166] This immediately preceded the deaths of the Presidents of Rwanda and Burundi in a plane crash on 6 April 1994 which sparked off a civil war in Rwanda involving mass killings on both sides. In these conditions UNAMIR's mandate in practice was much reduced – rescuing civilians and providing humanitarian assistance while trying to persuade the warring factions to agree to a cease-fire. In these circumstances, the Secretary General outlined three options to the Security Council: the reinforcing and re-mandating of UNAMIR to allow it to coerce the parties into a cease-fire, the reduction of UNAMIR to a small group to act as an intermediary, or the complete withdrawal of UNAMIR.[167] On 21 April the Security Council adopted the second alternative and UNAMIR was reduced to 270 with the tasks of acting as an intermediary between the factions as well as assisting in the resumption of humanitarian assistance.[168]

The revised mandate meant that the UN was incapable of action in the face of killings of such ferocity that it was estimated that 200,000 people died in the first three weeks of fighting in April. In response, on 17 May, the Security Council authorised a new force of 5,500 troops (UNAMIR II) with a restricted mandate 'to contribute to the security and protection of displaced persons, refugees and civilians at risk in Rwanda, including ... the establishment and maintenance of secure humanitarian areas', and 'to provide security and support for the distribution of relief supplies and humanitarian relief operations'. Although not granting enforcement powers to UNAMIR II, the Security Council did explicitly recognise that it 'may be required to take action in self-defence against persons or groups which threaten protected sites and populations ... or the means of delivery and distribution of humanitarian relief'.[169]

However, the poor response of the international community meant that the deployment of UNAMIR could only be achieved in July at the latest. The Secretary General suggested to the Security Council that it may wish to take up the offer made by the French government to deploy an enforcement operation for a limited period of two months while UNAMIR was brought up to strength.[170] On 22 June 1994, the Council authorised the French government under Chapter VII of the UN Charter to use 'all necessary means' to 'contribute to the security and protection of displaced persons, refugees and civilians at risk in Rwanda'.[171] The French military operation (Operation Turquoise) established a humanitarian protection zone in south-west Rwanda covering one-fifth of the territory. With the French commencing their withdrawal by 31 July and the deployment of UNAMIR still awaited, the military situation was stabilised only when the RPF achieved military control over the country in August 1994. This however caused massive flows of refugees adding to the humanitarian crisis. In these circumstances an under-resourced UNAMIR was deployed to provide stability and to provide support for humanitarian assistance operations. Given the horror of the previous weeks in which it was estimated that half a million people died, 3 million were displaced internally and 2 million fled to neighbouring countries (out of a population of 7 million), the situation was stabilised and humanitarian aid was getting through. However, the situation in the refugee camps was made worse by the continuing outbreak of inter-ethnic violence.[172]

In these circumstances the Secretary General again outlined three options to improve security in the camps: a UN peacekeeping force established under normal principles, a UN force under Chapter VII to enforce security, or a multinational force under Chapter VII but not under UN command to enforce security.[173] After some prevarication the Security Council, on 30 November 1994, implicitly took the first option by reiterating that UNAMIR was responsible for contributing to the security of refugees. No mention was made of Chapter VII in that resolution.[174] However, States contributing to UNAMIR were unwilling to deploy observers in Zaire and Tanzania, leading the Secretary General to conclude that securing these camps through a peacekeeping operation was not a viable alternative.[175] In fact rudimentary security was provided by Tanzanian and Zairian troops.

The problem of refugees outside of Rwanda remains the most serious obstacle to peace and despite the fact that even in the face of intense efforts from the countries concerned, the UN High Commissioner for Refugees (UNHCR) and other organisations, 1.5 million refugees remained in camps in neighbouring countries by February 1996. Incredibly, in the face of this, the newly installed Rwanda government withdrew its consent for a UN presence necessitating the withdrawal of UNAMIR in March 1996,[176] despite the fact that UNAMIR had been reduced to 1800 and its mandate had been similarly stripped down to essentially humanitarian tasks while only providing its good offices for the achievement of the original Arusha Accords (which it must be remembered provided for elections). With the UN's military presence withdrawn, further serious humanitarian and inter-ethnic problems with the refugee camps necessitated the authorisation under Chapter VII, though not the emplacement, of a multinational force in eastern Zaire in November 1996 'for humanitarian purposes', namely the repatriation of refugees and the provision of humanitarian assistance.[177]

In one of his last reports on UNAMIR the Secretary General pointed to the obvious need for its continued presence particularly in areas where the refugees were expected to return to ensure their safety. However, even with this major concern in mind the Secretary General managed a very optimistic conclusion:

When Rwanda emerged from civil war and genocide with the establishment of the Government of National Unity on 19 July 1994, conditions in the country were nothing short of disastrous. There was no administration, no functioning economy, no judicial or education system, no water or electricity supply and no transport; the population, moreover, was still in a state of profound shock.

Today, conditions in Rwanda are returning to normal, though a significant portion of the population are still refugees or displaced persons. This progress has been achieved essentially through the efforts of the people of Rwanda. But UNAMIR, other United Nations and international agencies and non-governmental organisations have worked with the Government to restore basic infrastructures and to rehabilitate vital sectors of the economy. UNAMIR engineers have participated in the construction of transit camps for returning refugees. Its Civilian Police Unit has assisted in the establishment and training of a new gendarmerie and communal police. Its specialised units have helped clear mines. In cooperation with United Nations agencies and non-governmental organisations, UNAMIR has assisted orphans, moved to reopen schools and contributed to the rehabilitation of health care and sanitation facilities. It has also provided humanitarian assistance and helped to ease the appalling prison situation. UNAMIR by its presence has provided a sense of security and confidence to the representatives of United Nations agencies, intergovernmental institutions and non-governmental organisations who, throughout the country and sometimes under very difficult circumstances, have worked for the recovery of Rwanda.[178]

While not supervising elections as originally intended, UNAMIR successfully, if belatedly, performed many tasks. However, the one function that helped to maintain the UN's presence, and to a lesser extent its credibility, was its continued support for humanitarian aid and assistance programmes. In such an internal situation, it appears that the performance of such a limited, though essential, task by the UN is still feasible because it is impartially done – and therefore represents the essence of peacekeeping. Other more grandiose schemes such as the supervision of elections, and even the supervision of a cease-fire, are much more vulnerable because they will usually favour one side over the other.

Furthermore, it must be noted that it was in the periods in which a UN peacekeeping force was absent, that the Security Council authorised enforcement actions, first by the French in 1994, and then by Western States (Canada, US, UK and France) in 1996, essentially to perform humanitarian tasks. This had the benefit of not compromising the neutrality of UN peacekeeping, but it was deficient in that the enforcement actions were too late and generally insufficient to prevent or stop the genocide in 1994 or to halt the suffering of the refugees in 1996–7. The UN's failure was not so much in performing the task of peacekeeping but was due to the lack of effective enforcement action, a natural consequence of the decentralised system of military measures which has been developed by the Security Council (reviewed in chapter three), and which very much depends on the willingness of the militarily powerful States to intervene in an effective and not just a token fashion.

Notes

1 SC Res. 27, 2 UN SCOR Resolutions 6 (1947).
2 UN doc. S/586 (1947).
3 SC Res. 31, 2 UN SCOR Resolutions 8 (1947); SC Res. 67, 4 UN SCOR Resolutions 2 (1949).
4 R. Higgins, *United Nations Peacekeeping: Documents and Commentary, Vol. II, Asia 1946–1967*, 61–86 (1970).
5 SC Res. 48, 54, 3 UN SCOR Resolutions 17, 22 (1948); UN doc. S/928 (1948); SC Res. 72, 4 UN SCOR Resolutions 7 (1949).
6 SC Res. 516, 37 UN SCOR Resolutions 8 (1982).
7 SC 1743 mtg, 28 UN SCOR 15, 4 (1973).
8 SC 1745 mtg, 28 UN SCOR 2 (1973).
9 SC Res. 39, 3 UN SCOR Resolutions 2 (1948). Observers were emplaced after the Karachi Agreement between India and Pakistan, UN doc. S/1430/Add. 1, Ann. 26

(1949).

10 On the 1965 breach see UN doc. S/6710 (1965). On the 1971 breach see UN doc. S/10412 (1971).

11 The wider 1965 conflict led to the creation of another observer force – UNIPOM – to oversee the cease-fire and withdrawal of troops following the conflict. SC Res. 211, 20 UN SCOR Resolutions 13 (1965). This task was successfully undertaken by UNIPOM, see UN doc. S/6719 (1965), and it was withdrawn, leaving UNMOGIP to patrol the continuing flashpoint of Kashmir.

12 UN doc. S/1994/1363, para. 12.

13 UN doc. S/1994/1102 and annex 1.

14 UN doc. S/1994/1363.

15 SC Res. 968, 49 UN SCOR Resolutions (1994).

16 UN doc. S/1995/720, annex.

17 UN doc. S/1995/1024.

18 SC Res. 1030, 50 UN SCOR Resolutions (1995). For further renewal see SC Res. 1089, 51 UN S/PV (1996).

19 UN docs S/19834 (1988); S/19835 (1988); SC Res. 622, 43 UN SCOR Resolutions 14 (1988); UN doc. S/20465 (1989).

20 SC Res. 915, 926 49 UN SCOR Resolutions (1994).

21 UN doc. S/20345 (1988).

22 UN doc. S/20346 (1988).

23 SC Res. 626, 43 UN SCOR Resolutions 19 (1988).

24 UN doc. S/22644 (1991).

25 GA Res. 109, 2 UN GAOR Resolutions 12 (1947).

26 UN doc. A/521 (1948).

27 For examples of its reports see UN docs A/374 (1948); A/1857 (1951).

28 SC Res. 179, 18 UN SCOR Resolutions 2 (1963).

29 UN doc. S/5298 (1963).

30 UN docs S/5927, 5142 (1964).

31 SC Res. 619, 43 UN SCOR Resolutions 11 (1988).

32 UN doc. S/20442 (1988).

33 UN doc. S/22263 (1992).

34 SC Res. 858, 48 UN SCOR Resolutions (1993).

35 UN doc. S/26259 (1993).

36 SC Res. 856, 48 UN SCOR Resolutions (1993).

37 SC Res. 1020, 50 UN SCOR Resolutions (1995). But see SC Res. 1083, 51 UN S/PV (1996).

38 SC Res. 128, 13 UN SCOR Resolutions (1958).

39 UN doc. S/4029 (1958).

40 UN doc. S/4040 (1958).

41 UN doc. A/3943 (1958).

42 See Dayton Accords 1995, 35 *ILM* (1996) 75, Annex 1A, Article IV.

43 UN doc. A/3943 (1958).

44 UN doc. A/3568 (1957).

45 UN docs S/3659 (1956), A/3694 (1957).

46 R. Higgins, *United Nations Peacekeeping: Documents and Commentary, Vol. 1: Middle East 1946–1967*, 481 (1969).

47 UN doc. S/11052/Rev. 1 (1973); SC Res. 370, 28 UN SCOR Resolutions (1973). On the fulfilment of its mandate see W. J. Durch (ed.), *The Evolution of UN Peacekeeping*, 131 (1994).
48 UN doc. S/11302 (1974); SC Res. 350, 29 UN SCOR Resolutions (1974). On its success see Durch (ed.), *UN Peacekeeping*, 152.
49 UN doc. S/4382 (1960).
50 SC 873 mtg, 15 UN SCOR para. 18 (1960).
51 T. M. Franck, *Nation against Nation*, 176 (1985).
52 SC 901 mtg, 15 UN SCOR paras 20–85 (1960).
53 UN doc. S/4523 (1960).
54 SC Res. 157, 15 UN SCOR Resolutions 8 (1960).
55 GA Res. 1474, 4 UN GAOR ESS Supp. (No. 1) 1 (1960).
56 J. Lash, 'Dag Hammarskjöld's Conception of his Office', 16 *International Organisation* (1962) 551.
57 G. Abi-Saab, *The UN Operation in the Congo*, 13 (1978).
58 UN doc. S/4389 (1960); SC 873 mtg, 15 UN SCOR paras 18–29 (1960).
59 R. Higgins, *United Nations Peacekeeping: Documents and Commentary, Vol. 3: Africa 1946–1967*, 54 (1980); D. W. Bowett, *United Nations Forces*, 176 (1964); Abi-Saab, *The UN Operation in the Congo*, 105.
60 SC 920 mtg, 15 UN SCOR para. 75 (1960).
61 I.C.J. Rep. 1962, 151.
62 UN doc. S/5240 (1963).
63 E. W. Lefever, *Crisis in the Congo*, 181 (1965).
64 UN doc. S/5488 (1963).
65 UN doc. S/5508 (1964).
66 UN doc. S/5526 (1964).
67 SC 1095 mtg, 19 UN SCOR paras 124–7 (1964).
68 UN doc. S/5653 (1964).
69 UN doc. S/5671 Annex 1 (1964).
70 UN docs S/11334, S/11335 (1974).
71 See for example SC 1779 mtg, 29 UN SCOR 5 (1974), USSR.
72 SC Res. 355, 29 UN SCOR Resolutions 8 (1974).
73 SC 1789 mtg, 29 UN SCOR 11 (1974).
74 UN doc. S/11473 (1974).
75 UN docs S/6102 (1964), S/8141 (1967).
76 UN doc. S/7969 (1967).
77 L. Mates, 'The United Nations and the Maintenance of International Peace and Security' in Rajan (ed.), *The Non Aligned and the United Nations*, 90 (1987).
78 SC Res. 550, 39 UN SCOR Resolutions 12 (1984).
79 UN doc. S/22454 (1991).
80 SC Res. 689, 46 UN SCOR Resolutions 15 (1991).
81 SC Res. 806, 48 UN SCOR Resolutions (1993).
82 SC Res. 843, 47 UN SCOR Resolutions (1993).
83 See chapter eight for an analysis of UNCRO's limited achievements.
84 The Security Council also authorised a UN police force for Bosnia (UNMIBH). SC Res. 1035, 50 UN SCOR Resolutions (1995).
85 SC Res. 1038, 51 UN SCOR Resolutions (1996).

86 SC Res. 1037, 51 UN SCOR Resolutions (1996).

87 SC Res. 644, 44 UN SCOR Resolutions (1989).

88 UN doc. S/21194 (1990), approved in SC Res. 650, 45 UN SCOR Resolutions 14 (1990).

89 UN doc. S/21259 (1990), approved by SC Res. 653 45 UN SCOR Resolutions 15 (1990).

90 UN doc. S/21341 (1990).

91 *Ibid.* 27(3) *UN Chronicle* (1990), 4–8.

92 *Keesing's* (1989), 36576.

93 See The United Nations Blue Book Series, *The United Nations and Cambodia 1991–1995*, 16–19 (1995).

94 UN doc. S/24286 (1992).

95 See the condemnation in SC Res 766, 47 UN SCOR Resolutions 41 (1992).

96 UN doc. S/24800 (1992).

97 SC Res. 840, 48 UN SCOR Resolutions (1993).

98 P. F. Diehl, *International Peacekeeping*, 199 (1994).

99 See also the disarmament/demobilisation aspects of the Dayton Accords and IFOR's mandate to enforce them if necessary; 35 *I.L.M.* (1996), 75, Annex 1A, Article IV.

100 30(1) *UN Chronicle* (1993), 16.

101 But see The United Nations Blue Book Series, *The United Nations and Somalia 1992–1996*, 41 (1996).

102 UN doc. S/25168 (1993).

103 SC Res. 885, 48 UN SCOR Resolutions (1993).

104 SC Res. 897, 44 UN SCOR Resolutions (1994). Clarified by Secretary General's report UN doc. S/1994/12.

105 31(3) *UN Chronicle* (1994), 22.

106 SC Res. 954, 49 UN SCOR Resolutions (1994).

107 UN Blue Book Series, *Cambodia*, 12.

108 See generally, T. F. Acuna, *The United Nations Mission in El Salvador: A Humanitarian Law Perspective* (1995).

109 UN doc. S/21541 (1990).

110 SC Res. 693, 46 UN SCOR Resolutions 33 (1991).

111 UN doc. S/23999 (1992).

112 29(2) *UN Chronicle* (1992), 30.

113 SC Res. 729, 47 UN SCOR Resolutions 1 (1992).

114 UN doc. S/25241 (1993).

115 See also SC Res. 888, 48 UN SCOR Resolutions (1993). See further GA Res. 47/118, 47 UN GAOR Supp. (No. 49) 38 (1992), which not only expressed support for the peace process in El Salvador but also welcomed the agreement between the government of Guatemala and the rebel faction reached in Mexico City in April 1991 as a first step in ending the civil conflict in that country.

116 UN doc. S/23037 (1991).

117 UN doc. S/23222 (1991).

118 UN doc. S/23580 (1992).

119 UN doc. S/24066 (1992).

120 UN doc. S/24375 (1992).

121 UN doc. S/25521 (1993).

122 UN doc. S/1994/385 (1994).
123 UN doc. S/1994/1220.
124 GA Res. 1752, 17 UN GAOR Supp. (No. 17) 70 (1962).
125 274 UNTS 6311.
126 SC Res. 385, 31 UN SCOR Resolutions 8 (1976).
127 UN doc. S/12636 (1978).
128 UN doc. S/12827 (1978); SC Res. 435, 33 UN SCOR Resolutions 13 (1978).
129 UN doc. S/20346 (1988).
130 SC Res. 628, 629, 632, 44 UN SCOR Resolutions (1989). UN doc. S/20412 (1989).
131 UN doc. S/20412/Add 1 (1989).
132 UN doc. S/20412 (1989).
133 *Keesing's* (1989), 36576.
134 United Nations, *The Blue Helmets: A Review of United Nations Peacekeeping*, 218, 3rd ed. (1996).
135 *Ibid.*, 219.
136 UN doc. S/20967 (1990).
137 SC Res. 690, 46 UN SCOR Resolutions 35 (1991).
138 On efforts to break the deadlock over the identification process see UN docs S/1995/924, S/1996/43, S/1996/913. MINURSO's mandate was renewed by SC Res. 1086, 51 UN S/PV (1996).
139 SC Res. 696, 46 UN SCOR Resolutions 37 (1991).
140 UN doc. S/22627 Add 1 (1991).
141 29(4) UN Chronicle (1992), 9.
142 UN doc. S/24858 (1992).
143 SC Res. 785, 47 UN SCOR Resolutions 89 (1992).
144 UN doc. S/1994/1441.
145 SC Res. 976, 50 UN SCOR Resolutions (1995).
146 SC Res. 1087, 51 UN S/PV (1996).
147 GA Res. 45/2, 45 UN GAOR (1990).
148 SC Res. 940, 49 UN SCOR Resolutions (1994).
149 See further E.G. Primosch, 'The Role of the United Nations Civilian Police (UNCIVPOL) within United Nations Peace-Keeping Operations', 43 *I.C.L.Q.* (1994), 425.
150 UN doc. S/1995/922.
151 SC Res. 1063, 1086, 51 UN S/PV (1996).
152 United Nations Blue Book Series, *The United Nations and Mozambique 1992–1995* 3 (1995).
153 *Ibid.*, 4. On Rome Agreement see UN doc. S/24635 (1992). On mandate see SC Res. 797, 47 UN SCOR Resolutions 108 (1992).
154 UN doc. S/1994/89.
155 UN Blue Book Series, *Mozambique*, 56.
156 *Ibid.*, 57.
157 UN doc. S/1994/1196.
158 UN doc. S/1994/1282.
159 UN Blue Book Series, *Mozambique*, 67.
160 SC Res. 511, 37 UN SCOR Resolutions 6 (1982).
161 UN Blue Book Series, *Somalia*, 5.

162 UN doc. S/22513 (1991).
163 SC Res. 846, 48 UN SCOR Resolutions (1993).
164 UN doc. S/26488 (1993).
165 SC Res. 872, 48 UN SCOR Resolutions (1993).
166 SC Res. 909, 49 UN SCOR Resolutions (1994).
167 UN doc. S/1994/470.
168 SC Res. 912, 49 UN SCOR Resolutions (1994).
169 SC Res. 918, 49 UN SCOR Resolutions (1994). The resolution imposed a mandatory
     arms embargo against Rwanda under Chapter VII of the Charter.
170 UN doc. S/1994/728.
171 SC Res. 929, 49 UN SCOR Resolutions (1994).
172 S/PRST/1994/59.
173 UN doc. S/1994/1308. See also UN doc. S/1994/1344.
174 SC Res. 965, 49 UN SCOR Resolutions (1994). See also SC Res. 997, 50 UN SCOR
     Resolutions (1995).
175 UN doc. S/1995/65.
176 UN doc. S/1995/1002. SC Res. 1029 51 UN S/PV (1996).
177 SC Res. 1080, 51 UN S/PV (1996).
178 UN doc. S/1996/149.

Index